The One Year® Devotions for Active Boys

THE ONE YEAR® DEVOTIONS FOR ACTIVE BOYS

Tyndale House Publishers, Inc.
Carol Stream, Illinois

Jesse Florea
Karen Whiting

Visit www.cool2read.com.

TYNDALE, Tyndale's quill logo, The One Year, and One Year are registered trademarks of Tyndale House Publishers, Inc. The One Year logo is a trademark of Tyndale House Publishers, Inc.

The One Year Devotions for Active Boys

Designed by Ron Kaufmann

Edited by Sarah Rubio

For manufacturing information regarding this product, please call 1-800-323-9400.

ISBN 978-1-4143-9404-6

Printed in the United States of America

20 19 18 17 16 15 14
7   6   5   4   3   2   1

Dedicated to my grandsons, Joseph Pena, Ethan Whiting, and Thomas Pena. May the Lord bless you and help you grow in your faith and love. Have fun as you serve the Lord.

—KAREN

To every boy who's growing into a man after God's own heart. Real men never stop seeking after the Lord! And to my brothers: Alex, Seth, Taylor, and Lane. You represent what manhood is all about. It's been awesome watching you mature from boys to men.

—JESSE

JANUARY

NOT OF THIS WORLD

YOU'RE AN ALIEN. Not a spaceship-flying, green-goo–spewing, mind-meld–controlling alien with cat eyes and glowing fingers that you might see in movies and on TV. But if you follow Jesus Christ, Earth is not your home. That means you're an alien.

You may live in this world now, but as a Christian, your forever home is heaven. In 1 Peter 2:11 (NIV84), the apostle Peter calls you "aliens and strangers in the world" and encourages you as one of Christ's followers to stay away from sinful desires. That's not easy. You may be an alien, but you're also a human. And as a human, you naturally want to sin.

What tempts you most? Is it saying mean things, talking back to your parents, watching movies with your friends that your parents wouldn't approve of, or looking at inappropriate websites? Whatever it is, God can help you overcome that temptation because of two facts:

Fact one: You're a Christian, so the Holy Spirit lives inside you.
Fact two: "The Spirit who lives in you is greater than the spirit who lives in the world." (1 John 4:4)

With God in your life, you have the power to resist temptation and be a good alien.

EXPERIMENT: GO UFO!
Aliens need transportation. Make a UFO and see how far it can fly.

Stuff You Need
- ☞ Paper or Styrofoam plate
- ☞ Pencil
- ☞ Balloon
- ☞ Clear tape
- ☞ Scissors (optional)

Try It
1. Poke a hole through the middle of the plate.
2. Gently push one end of the balloon through the hole.
3. Wrap tape around this end of the balloon, so it won't fall through the hole.
4. Blow up the balloon.
5. Hold your UFO over your head, and let go of the balloon. Watch it zoom around the room. Experiment by trying different sizes of balloons and plates, putting the balloon at different spots on the plate, creating wings, or cutting and folding flaps.

✝ PRAY
Ask God to help you avoid temptations that come your way.

Life's Guidebook Says
Dear friends, I urge you, as aliens and strangers in the world, to abstain from sinful desires, which war against your soul. 1 PETER 2:11, NIV84

GOD'S CHOSEN ARMY

A STRIKE FORCE is a special team of well-trained warriors. In the Old Testament, God chose a special strike force to help the Israelites defeat some bullies. And God put Gideon in command.

Gideon had gathered a large army of 32,000 men. God said, "That's too many! Israel will boast that it won the battle through its own strength. Send home anyone who trembles with fear." *Whoosh*—22,000 men ran home. That left 10,000 fighting men.

God spoke again. "Take them to the water to drink. Keep only those who lapped the water like a dog. I will save you from the enemy with these 300 men."

Gulp! Gideon was nervous, but he trusted God. The enemy had more men and camels than you could count—probably over 130,000 warriors. Yet God knew the 300 men he had chosen could win, because he was on their side. God had mighty plans for his strike force. He has mighty plans for you, too, and can help you overcome any foe.

PUZZLE IT OUT: FINDING GOD'S CHOICES

Answer each of the questions about Gideon by circling the correct choice. Place each letter in order in the spaces below to find the answer to the question. (Hint: You can find all the answers by reading Judges 6–8.)

1. Gideon was from the _____ family.
   R. smartest   **S.** weakest   **T.** silliest

2. What animals did the Midianites have?
   Z. horses   **A.** camels   **B.** dogs

3. What did the enemy's army look like?
   I. a swarm of locusts   **J.** a swarm of bees   **K.** a school of fish

4. What men did God choose?
   C. men who shook with fear   **D.** men who drank like dogs   **F.** men who kneeled

5. How could so few men win the battle?
   X. They had better weapons.   **Y.** God was with them.   **Z.** They knew more tricks.

6. How many men did God choose in total?
   C. 200   **D.** 300   **E.** 301

7. Gideon was a _____.
   Q. king   **R.** prophet   **S.** judge

What made Gideon special?
He ___ ___ ___ ___   ___ ___ ___.

✝ PRAY

Ask God to help you overcome an obstacle that is facing you today.

Life's Guidebook Says

When Gideon took his warriors down to the water, the Lord told him, "Divide the men into two groups. In one group put all those who cup water in their hands and lap it up with their tongues like dogs. In the other group put all those who kneel down and drink with their mouths in the stream." JUDGES 7:5

Answers: 1. S; 2. A; 3. I; 4. D; 5. Y; 6. E (300 + Gideon); 7. S

GOD CHOSE THE SMALLEST SON

WHEN TEAMS GET PICKED for a game, who gets picked first? You might say it's normally the biggest or most popular kids who go first. But if you want to make the best team, you may want to choose differently. You can't always judge by looks.

God doesn't judge by physical appearance. When he sent Samuel to find a new king for Israel, he told the prophet not to choose based on the man's looks. Samuel went where God sent him, to a man named Jesse and his eight sons. God didn't choose the oldest, strongest, or best-looking son. Instead he had Samuel wait until Jesse's youngest son returned from watching the sheep. That son played his harp, wrote songs, and helped the family as a shepherd. Not much in the way of hero material. God told Samuel to choose the shepherd boy, named David. And David became a mighty warrior and the king of Israel.

EXPERIMENT: OPTICAL ILLUSIONS

God knows that our eyes can trick us and keep us from knowing the truth. Try some optical illusions as reminders that your eyes can be fooled.

1. Pencil-in-Water Trick

Place a pencil in a glass that is half filled with water. Look at it from the side. The pencil looks broken.

2. Invisible Sticker

Place a sticker under an empty glass. You can see it from the side. Fill the glass with water and watch the sticker disappear.

✝ PRAY

Ask God to help you see below the surface of people and find the truth.

Life's Guidebook Says

The LORD said to Samuel, "Don't judge by his appearance or height, for I have rejected him. The LORD doesn't see things the way you see them. People judge by outward appearance, but the LORD looks at the heart." 1 SAMUEL 16:7

QUIET HERO

No one even looked at the man as he sat by the gate. The man listened. He paced back and forth. He wrote letters. No sword, no shouting, no horseback riding. Doesn't sound like a hero, but God used this man, whose name was Mordecai, to help save thousands of people.

Mordecai overheard a plot to kill the king and sent a letter to his cousin, Queen Esther. Mordecai's tip saved the king's life. But the king forgot Mordecai because he was such a quiet man. One night the king reviewed his journal and remembered Mordecai—*Oops!* He decided to honor him. The king told Haman, a man who hated Mordecai, to parade Mordecai through the streets and cheer for him. That made Haman so angry that he plotted to kill Mordecai and all his people, the Jews.

Mordecai sent another letter to the queen asking for her help. She felt afraid, but Mordecai showed his great faith by saying that it was possible that God had allowed her to become queen she could save her people. His faith inspired Esther to action, and together they saved their people.

Listening is a great skill that everyone, especially a leader, needs.

QUIZ: DID YOU LISTEN?

Test yourself to see if you have really listened lately. Answer yes or no in the blanks below.

____ Do you know the last thing your mom asked you to do, and did you do it?
____ Do you know if your best friend sounded happy, sad, bored, or excited today?
____ Do you remember the lesson from Sunday school or what your pastor said at church this past Sunday?
____ Do you remember the lessons you learned in school today?
____ Did you hear God through the Bible or an answered prayer today?
____ Did you hear someone say something good to you today ("Thanks," "I love you," "Good job")?
____ Did you hear your own voice today? Did you say good things or complain?
____ Did you hear any inappropriate language from your mouth today?

✝ PRAY

Ask God to help you listen well and follow only the best advice for your life.

Life's Guidebook Says
[Mordecai said,] "If you keep quiet at a time like this, deliverance and relief for the Jews will arise from some other place, but you and your relatives will die. Who knows if perhaps you were made queen for just such a time as this?"
ESTHER 4:14

GOD SENT JESUS

GO OUTSIDE AND LISTEN. What do you hear? Maybe birds, cars, thunder, or airplanes. At the baptism of Jesus, people heard God's voice coming from heaven. *Amazing!* The voice said, "You are my Son. . . . I am very pleased with you" (Mark 1:11, NIrV). God wanted people to know that Jesus is special. He is the only Son of God.

People also saw God's Spirit, in the form of a dove, flap its wings and fly down to rest on Jesus. This was a rare time when people actually heard and saw God as Father, Son, and Holy Spirit together.

Amazingly, in Isaiah 42:1 God told the people that he would put his Spirit on his Son and be very pleased with him. God had this plan centuries before it happened!

God sent Jesus, but the Jews were expecting a different kind of hero. They wanted an earthly king who would rule the world. They wanted a mighty warrior. Jesus preached love, peace, and obedience to God's commands. He didn't care about earthly power and wealth. He had created everything, so he already owned it. God sent a hero who can give us real joy and freedom in heaven forever.

WEIRD FACTS: WHAT'S THAT SOUND?

- ☞ A whip cracks because the tip moves so fast that it breaks the sound barrier. It's actually a sonic boom.
- ☞ If it's too noisy to hear someone talk, then it is too loud for your ears and could cause hearing loss.
- ☞ God spoke in a gentle whisper to Elijah (1 Kings 19:12-13).
- ☞ Sound travels through water three times faster than it travels through air.
- ☞ Nehemiah said God put a plan in his heart (Nehemiah 2:12) and that he put an idea in his mind (Nehemiah 7:5). God can speak in different ways.
- ☞ Radio waves travel faster than sound, so a broadcast on radio can be heard sooner 10,000 miles away than it is heard in the back of the room where it is said.

Jesus told people that his followers know his voice (John 10:27). Listen carefully to know when he is talking to you.

✝ PRAY

Thank God for sending Jesus and speaking to you in the Bible.

Life's Guidebook Says

A voice spoke to [Jesus] from heaven. It said, "You are my Son, and I love you. I am very pleased with you." MARK 1:11, NIrV

7

WORK FOR GOD

"MY PLEASURE."

If you've eaten at a Chick-fil-A, you've heard those words. When you say, "Thank you," workers at this restaurant chain don't say, "You're welcome," "No problem," or "No, thank you." They say, "My pleasure." Chick-fil-A restaurants are run differently. They're closed on Sundays, so the workers can go to church if they want to.

When you go to church and hear the pastor, he's working for God. But you don't have to be a pastor to do God's work. Dan Cathy, the president of Chick-fil-A, also teaches Sunday school and tells people about Jesus. And he's not the only businessman who follows God.

One day when Jesus walked along the shore, he saw Simon Peter with his brother Andrew and called, "Come, follow me." They left their nets to become Jesus' disciples. But at times they returned to their boats and fished. Fishing was their business.

The apostle Paul made tents, and Luke was a doctor. They worked to pay their bills, but the most important thing in these men's lives was doing what Jesus wanted them to do.

Right now you're a student learning skills and gaining knowledge. But what do you want to do when you grow up? No matter what it is, you can use your skills and talents to serve God.

PUZZLE IT OUT: DIAL UP A SECRET MESSAGE

Look at a phone to decode this message. The first digit in each number tells you what number to find on the phone. The second number tells you what position to count to in order to find the letter in the code. So *94* equals *Z*.

What did Jesus tell the men he chose?

— ———— ———— ——— ———————— —— ———.
43 91 43 53 53 61 21 52 32 93 63 82 33 43 74 42 32 73 74 63 33 61 32 62

✝ **PRAY**

Ask God to help you choose to follow him.

Life's Guidebook Says

One day as Jesus was walking along the shore of the Sea of Galilee, he saw Simon and his brother Andrew throwing a net into the water, for they fished for a living. Jesus called out to them, "Come, follow me, and I will show you how to fish for people!" MARK 1:16-17

Answer: I will make you fishers of men.

GOD ZAPPED SAUL

SAUL WAS A BULLY! He hated Christians and hurt them whenever he could find them. He had them thrown into jail and even killed. He convinced his religious leaders to let him get rid of followers of Jesus Christ. Saul believed he was helping God, because he thought Christians were a bunch of liars who wanted to destroy his faith.

Zap! A light from heaven struck Saul on his way to hunt down more Christians. Saul had authority, a letter from the Jewish high priest putting him in charge of wiping out Christians. The bright light zapped his eyesight and left him blind.

He heard a voice from heaven that asked, "Why are you opposing me?"

Saul had no clue what the voice meant, so he asked, "Who are you, Lord?"

The voice replied, "I am Jesus, the one you are opposing."

Whoa! Hold on! What did this mean? Jesus really existed and had really risen! Hurting any of his followers hurt Jesus. For three days Saul sat without eating or drinking. The zapping and voice from heaven gave him a lot to think about. He had really messed up trying to do things his own way. God would make sure he'd be a useless wimp! Served him right.

Then a man came, anointed Saul, and restored his sight. God changed Saul's name to Paul, and from that day on, Paul worked for Jesus with all his heart and never tried to hurt anyone again, even his enemies.

PLEXER

Word puzzles called plexers are groups of letters arranged to give a coded meaning. For example, the one below means "I understand."

See if you can solve this plexer to find out where God first spoke to Saul.

PRAY

Ask God to show you what he wants you to do today.

Life's Guidebook Says

As [Saul] was approaching Damascus on this mission, a light from heaven suddenly shone down around him. He fell to the ground and heard a voice saying to him, "Saul! Saul! Why are you persecuting me?" ACTS 9:3-4

Answer: On the highway

GOD CHOSE YOU

YOU MAKE IMPORTANT CHOICES every day. When will you do your homework? Will you play a game on the computer? Will you eat healthy foods? Will you be kind or mean to people you see? God lets you choose.

But God wants you to choose to work for him. *Wow!* God wants to use you and the talents he gave you. He desires that you put the knowledge you have learned from studying the Bible to good use.

God used what Paul already knew. Paul had studied under one of the most admired Jewish teachers. That helped Paul understand the Scriptures and become a great preacher.

God prepared Peter as he fished, and Peter already understood what made wiggly fish swim into the nets. Peter used what he knew to fish for men.

God will use your talents and what you have learned. You can share the Scriptures you know and tell others how God's Word has helped you. You can use your strength to help around your home. You can even use simple talents, like smiling, to brighten people's days. The choice is up to you!

LIFTOFF LIST

I know God wants me to choose to follow him because . . .

___ he made me.
___ I believe God the Father sent Jesus to die for me.
___ when I read God's Word, I see ways I can live it.
___ I know God listens when I pray and he'll answer me.

Choices I can make today:

___ Smile at everyone I meet
___ Complete my homework
___ Help make dinner
___ Compliment a friend, brother, or sister
___ Stand beside someone when I see a bully try to bother him or her
___ Share with a friend how God helped me this week

What will you choose to do today to work for God?

_____

_____

✝ PRAY

Ask God to help you use your talents to help others.

Life's Guidebook Says

You are God's chosen people. You are holy and dearly loved. So put on tender mercy and kindness as if they were your clothes. Don't be proud. Be gentle and patient. COLOSSIANS 3:12, NIrV

MONKEY BEHAVIOR

SQUAWK! EEK! BABY MONKEYS scream when they see snakes, even harmless ones. When a harmless snake slithers by the mother monkey, she stays still or holds her baby by the tail to keep it from panicking. If the snake is poisonous, the mother monkey grabs her baby and runs away. The baby watches its mother and remembers what she does. Soon the baby learns to tell the poisonous snakes from harmless ones. Monkeys learn fast and remember what they learn, so experts can train them to be helpful to people.

Capuchin monkeys can help disabled people. They brush people's hair, open doors, fetch things, and even serve food. They also chatter a lot and make the people they help laugh with their funny actions.

You learn by observing and imitating too. That's how you learned to talk. You figure out the difference between good and evil from your parents, pastors, and God's Word. It's not a skill you're born with—you have to train to learn the difference between right and wrong (see today's verse). Practicing soccer or guitar trains you to be good at those activities. But it's up to you to make good choices and to use your skills to serve other people and God.

LIFTOFF LIST

Check off what you have done to help others and what you do to learn to make good decisions.

___ I made and served a snack.

___ I carried in groceries.

___ I helped a neighbor with yard work.

___ I read the Bible and prayed over a decision.

___ I discussed what happened when I did something wrong that caused problems.

___ I obeyed my parents about a safety issue.

___ I listened to the sermon and tried to apply it this week.

___ I scheduled enough time for doing my schoolwork and sleeping.

___ I took care of a pet.

✝ PRAY

Ask God to help you learn from Scripture to make good decisions.

Life's Guidebook Says

Solid food is for those who are mature, who through training have the skill to recognize the difference between right and wrong. HEBREWS 5:14

JUMPING KANGAROOS

WHO DO YOU THINK would win in a boxing match between a man and a kangaroo? If it was between a baby human and a baby kangaroo, it wouldn't even be close. The human baby would win every time.

The average human baby weighs about 7 pounds and is about 20 inches long. Baby kangaroos are the size of a jelly bean. They can't walk or jump for months after they're born.

Newborn kangaroos, called joeys, are tiny, pink, hairless, and blind. Joeys don't look like kangaroos. After being born, the joey smells the milk inside its mother's pouch and crawls toward it. The baby grasps its mother's fur and pulls itself up into the pouch.

At about 5 months, a joey peeks out of the pouch for the first time. It has short fur and big floppy ears, but it still can't walk or jump. At 6 months, the joey jumps out of the pouch and starts leaping. At four-and-a-half pounds, the little kangaroo grows fast. It hops in and out of the pouch for 10 months. At 16 months, the kangaroo leaps out forever.

A man in the Bible took way longer than six months to make his first jump. Paul met a man who was crippled since birth. Seeing that the man listened to him and had faith, Paul said, "Stand up!" The man felt so joyful that he jumped up and started walking! Make sure to live in a way that shows God how joyful you are for his saving and healing you. Maybe you could jump around like a kangaroo.

EXPERIMENT: JUMPING PUFFS OF CEREAL
Try using static electricity to make cereal jump.

Stuff You Need
- ☞ Puffed cereal
- ☞ Plate
- ☞ Piece of wool (or a wool sock)
- ☞ Comb

Try It
1. Place a few pieces of puffed cereal on a plate.
2. Rub wool over the comb for twenty seconds.
3. Pass the comb over the cereal, and watch the pieces jump.

✝ PRAY
Jump high and yell praises to God with each leap.

Life's Guidebook Says
Paul called to him in a loud voice, "Stand up!" And the man jumped to his feet and started walking. ACTS 14:10

WATERFALL–CLIMBING FISH

YOU MAY HAVE SEEN salmon swimming upriver, even up waterfalls. That's an amazing feat. But you've probably never seen the Nopoli goby fish in Hawaii climb 300 feet—that's as high as a football field is long—straight up a slippery rock wall in the middle of a waterfall. While it may sound impossible, the goby inches its way up using the same muscles it uses for eating. The jaw muscles that the goby uses to suck up food can also be used to suction itself to a slippery wall. The goby also has a sucker on its belly that helps it hold on as it climbs. Water flows down as the fish climbs up, making the fish's accomplishment even more amazing.

The goby has an amazing mouth. In Matthew 17:14-27, Jesus used the ability of another fish with an interesting mouth to prove a point to his disciples. When he needed to pay a tax, he told Peter to toss a fishing line into the Sea of Galilee. God's Son didn't want Peter to sell the fish; he said the first fish Peter caught would have a coin in its mouth. Sure enough, when Peter pulled out his catch, the fish's mouth contained a large silver coin.

God provided the coin to pay taxes for Jesus and Peter. Do you think Jesus smiled or laughed at the look on Peter's face when he found the coin? God made fish and has the power to use them—or anything else in his creation—for his purpose. He knows your needs and can meet them in a multitude of ways. Be on the lookout for how God is working in your life . . . and look for money-carrying fish.

PLEXER

Word puzzles called plexers are groups of letters arranged to give a coded meaning. For example, the plexer below means "I understand."

> stand
> I

Can you figure out this one?

✝ PRAY

Tell God you'll trust him to provide all your needs.

Life's Guidebook Says
This same God who takes care of me will supply all your needs from his glorious riches, which have been given to us in Christ Jesus. PHILIPPIANS 4:19

Answer: Fish going up waterfall

WHAT'S THE BIG IDEA?

DONKEYS CAN HELP YOU carry a heavy load or give you a ride up steep canyon trails. But in the Old Testament, Balaam discovered that a donkey could save his life.

No *hee-haw* or braying for Balaam's donkey. It shocked its master by opening its mouth and speaking just like a human!

Balaam was on his way to see some officials. God had specific plans for Balaam, which Balaam wasn't following. God was angry, so he sent an angel to kill Balaam. Balaam couldn't see the sword-wielding angel. But the donkey could, so it stopped. *Whack!* Balaam struck the donkey for stopping. The donkey tried to squeeze by the angel. *Crunch!* Balaam's foot got smashed between the donkey and the wall. *Whack!* He struck the donkey again.

The donkey stopped moving, and Balaam struck it a third time. Finally, the donkey turned around and God allowed it to speak. "Why did you hit me those three times?" it scolded. The donkey also asked, "Have I ever done anything like this to you before?" Balaam said, "No." The donkey had always been faithful to Balaam.

When God opened Balaam's eyes, he saw the angel waving a sword, ready to slay him. The angel explained that he would have killed Balaam if the donkey had not turned away.

Balaam fell on the ground and said, "I have sinned."

God used an angel and a donkey to open a man's eyes, mind, and heart. Balaam liked money more than God or the people he served. But with his donkey's help, Balaam followed God's instructions. Don't wait for a talking donkey to save you (it probably won't happen). Decide for yourself to open your eyes, mind, and heart to God's instructions.

PUZZLE IT OUT: THE BIG IDEA

Fill in the blank with the missing letter to complete each word. Then unscramble those letters to find a word that describes how God wants you to act every day. (Hint: The words are in today's story.)

sco __ded
__it
__nstructions
__ngel
__inally
__hree
__ollowing
mo __th

— — — — — — —

✝ PRAY

Ask God to help you follow him faithfully.

Life's Guidebook Says

The LORD opened the donkey's mouth. It said to Balaam, "What have I done to you? Why did you hit me those three times?" NUMBERS 22:28, NIrV

Answer: Faithful

LION-FLAVORED HONEY

WHAT DO MEAT-EATING BEES have to do with the Bible? Good question! For thousands of years, some people doubted the biblical account of what happened to Samson. You probably remember that Samson was one of the strongest men who ever lived. He killed 1,000 men with the jawbone of a donkey (Judges 15:15). He even tore a lion apart with his bare hands (Judges 14:6). Later, Samson walked past the dead animal. He stopped when he saw something strange. *Buzz!* A group of bees had been busy making honey in the lion's body. Samson scooped out the honey and ate it. He even gave his parents some, but he didn't say he got the honey from a lion's carcass, which is pretty gross.

Samson used his honey of a discovery to make a riddle about the lion that he told to a group of people called the Philistines. The Philistines got angry because they couldn't figure it out. They threatened Samson's wife to get the answer to the riddle. God had chosen Samson to rescue his people from the Philistines, but Samson made many wrong choices. Samson's wife tricked him into revealing the answer to the riddle, and he had to pay the Philistines with money and clothes.

For years, many people didn't believe bees would make honey in a dead lion. Then a scientist in Panama discovered that some bees use protein from dead animals to make honey. These bees don't have hair on their legs to collect pollen, so they make honey in a different way. When you read something in the Bible, you can trust it's true. It may take science a while to figure out how something happened, but God's Word never lies.

WACKY LAUGHS

Q. Why did the bees fly away from the hive and go to church?
A. They were bee-leavers.

Q. What did God say to the bee?
A. "You are my bee-loved insect."

Q. What did the bees think of Samson's riddle?
A. They thought it was a humdinger.

✝ PRAY

Thank God for giving you his Word, which can make you more powerful than Samson.

Life's Guidebook Says

Work hard so you can present yourself to God and receive his approval. Be a good worker, one who does not need to be ashamed and who correctly explains the word of truth. 2 TIMOTHY 2:15

CLOSEMOUTHED

HOW WOULD YOU FEEL if you were surrounded by lions? Scared? Nervous? Like a snack? Daniel didn't feel that way at all. He was confident, because he always followed God. So when King Darius threw Daniel into a lions' den for praying to God, he wasn't surprised to find their mouths clamped shut. The lions' mouths would not open an inch. Daniel walked among hungry lions that never touched him. Daniel knew God had sent an angel, who shut the mouths of the lions.

Many Scriptures mention lions. In Proverbs, the lion is called stately and mighty among beasts (30:30). Lions are powerful, wild animals that can weigh 500 pounds and grow eight feet long. Jesus is called the Lion of the tribe of Judah (Revelation 5:5). And the prophet Isaiah says that lions and calves will live side by side in peace (Isaiah 11:6).

At one point, the Bible even compares Satan to a lion prowling for its prey (1 Peter 5:8). Lions often prefer to attack old and weak animals. Satan also looks to bully and attack people when they are weak from fear or temptation.

But neither Satan nor the roar of a lion should scare you, because God is on your side. He can defeat both with his mighty power.

WEIRD FACTS: ROARING LIONS

- ☞ A lion's roar can be heard five miles away in all directions.
- ☞ The tassel at the end of a lion's tail is used for communicating. It can signal directions or invite another lion to come close.
- ☞ Lions eat only every third or fourth day.
- ☞ Talk about a big gulp—a lion can drink for twenty minutes after eating.
- ☞ Lions see five times better than people, so don't play hide-and-seek with one.
- ☞ The Swahili word for *lion* is *simba* and means "king," "strong," and "aggressive."
- ☞ A lion killed a bad prophet but did not eat him. (1 Kings 13:26)

✟ PRAY

Ask God to help you trust him in dangerous situations and help you not be afraid.

Life's Guidebook Says

[Daniel said,] "My God sent his angel to shut the lions' mouths so that they would not hurt me, for I have been found innocent in his sight. And I have not wronged you, Your Majesty." DANIEL 6:22

HOG WILD

PIGS CAN REALLY GO hog wild and create big problems. They dig up fields, kill other animals, and spread disease. In 2013, two dozen wild pigs raced across a 2,000-acre ranch in Okeechobee, Florida (hey, that's fun to say. Try saying "O-kee-cho-bee" 10 times really fast). They plowed up fields and ruined crops as they pushed their snouts into the ground and turned over the soil in their hunt for food. They flattened the land in minutes. Wild pigs run up to 30 miles an hour, swim well, and have supersharp tusks.

Farmers compare having wild pigs in their fields to having large rats in their houses. These pigs have lots of babies and are really hard to get rid of. About 25 years ago, only two million pigs roamed wild in the United States. Now there are six to eight million wild pigs wreaking havoc in 47 states.

Obviously, pigs can be a problem. Even the Bible doesn't speak too kindly about these swine. The apostle Peter compared pigs to people who know the right things to do but choose to sin instead. In 2 Peter 2:21-22, he says, "It would be better if they had never known the way to righteousness than to know it and then reject the command they were given to live a holy life. They prove the truth of this proverb: 'A dog returns to its vomit.' And another says, 'A washed pig returns to the mud.'"

Those are two pretty gross examples—vomit and filth. It's nearly impossible for a pig to stay clean. And the Bible is clear: Don't act like a pig.

PUZZLE IT OUT: SWINE TIME
Answer true or false.

1. Pigs eat only food from plants.   **T or F**
2. Pigs can't sweat.   **T or F**
3. Pigs roll in mud to cool off.   **T or F**
4. Pigs have three toes.   **T or F**
5. Pigs have a great sense of smell.   **T or F**
6. Pigs are cannibals.   **T or F**
7. Like a person's hair, a pig's tail can be straight, curly, or kinky.   **T or F**
8. Pigs can see sideways.   **T or F**

✝ PRAY
Ask the Lord to help you stay clean and not act like a pig by returning to your old, dirty habits.

Life's Guidebook Says
Remember, it is sin to know what you ought to do and then not do it.
JAMES 4:17

Answers: 1. False; 2. True; 3. True; 4. False (they have 4 toes); 5. True; 6. True; 7. True; 8. True

SOARING WITH EAGLES

HAVE YOU EVER WANTED to stay in bed and not get up for the day? Young eaglets feel that way. They'd rather stay in a soft nest than venture into the world. They might never try to fly if not for their wise mothers. A mother eagle stirs up the nest by pulling out everything soft. She tosses out feathers, animal skin, and anything else that is cozy. Soon the eaglets wiggle around looking for a soft place to rest, but the sticks and thorns in the nest hurt and make them uncomfortable. The mother eagle then spreads her wings wider than the nest, and one of the eaglets gingerly steps on a wing. The mother flutters her wings and the baby tightens its claws to cling to her feathers. The mother soars into the air, carrying the eaglet high above the earth. Then she lurches and the eaglet topples off her wing. The little eaglet flops, tumbles, and rolls. It beats its wings in the air. About halfway back to earth, the mother bird swoops down and collects the eaglet back onto her wing. She soars upward again and repeats the process until the little bird learns to fly.

Sometimes God is like a mother eagle. He urges us to trust him and move out of our comfort zones. Maybe he pushes us to try something new. And when we are afraid, he carries us. Even if it feels as if we are tumbling and failing, God will always catch us. He never stops caring for us as he teaches us to soar with him.

EXPERIMENT: SOARING HIGH

Exercises that involve jumping are called plyometrics. They strengthen muscles that help you jump high in the air. Try to do 20 or 30 of these exercises each day for a week.

- ☞ Deep knee-bend jumps. Crouch until you can almost touch the floor. Then explode upward in a huge jump.
- ☞ Toe raises. Rise onto your toes and then lower to let your heels touch the floor.
- ☞ Jumping rope. This will help you gain rhythm and coordination in jumping.

✝ PRAY

Ask God to give you the courage to follow him and the ability to trust him in any situation.

Life's Guidebook Says

[The Lord] was like an eagle that stirs up its nest. It hovers over its little ones. It spreads out its wings to catch them. It carries them on its feathers.
DEUTERONOMY 32:11, NIrV

CHECK YOUR HEADING

POOF! AN ANGEL APPEARED. Philip had just walked 30 miles north from Jerusalem to Samaria, where he told the people about Jesus' love and power.

The angel said, "Get up! Go south to Gaza." *Whoa!* Last time Philip checked, south was the opposite of north.

But when an angel tells you to do something, you do it! Philip spun around and jogged south. *Crunch!* Philip heard wheels spinning up dust from the dirt road. He spotted an Ethiopian man in a chariot. The Holy Spirit told Philip to run to the man. Philip sprinted over and listened as the man read from Isaiah, words Philip knew better than a road map.

Philip asked, "Do you understand what you are reading?"

"How can I unless someone explains it to me?" the Ethiopian said. "Who was slaughtered like a lamb?"

Philip hopped in the chariot. As they rode, Philip explained that the prophet Isaiah was writing about Jesus. Philip told the Ethiopian that Jesus died so he could be forgiven for his sins. The Ethiopian wanted to become a Christian immediately. He saw some water, jumped out of the chariot, and *splash!* Philip baptized him! As soon as the two men walked out of the water—*whoosh!*—Philip disappeared. Faster than a rocket, he reappeared at Azotus, many miles to the north. The Lord had more work for him to do.

LIFTOFF LIST

Philip followed God's leading by listening to the angel and following the Holy Spirit. Check off different ways that you've seen God guide you.

___ I know the one road to heaven that takes me to the real Leader! (John 14:6)

___ When I'm stuck, I check with God's Word. (Psalm 119:105)

___ God moves my sins to another galaxy, far, far away. (Psalm 103:12)

___ Today, I did some cool things for someone. (1 Corinthians 13:4)

___ God's better than a compass. He can direct my heart. (2 Thessalonians 3:5)

___ It's okay to make plans, but I need to let God direct my path. (Proverbs 16:9)

✝ PRAY

Ask God to lead you and direct your decisions.

Life's Guidebook Says

An angel of the Lord said to [Philip], "Go south down the desert road that runs from Jerusalem to Gaza." ACTS 8:26

BULLIES WITH CHARIOTS

PHARAOH WAS A BIG BULLY. As the leader of Egypt, he forced God's people to work for him as slaves for many years. When God sent Moses to ask Pharaoh to let his people go, Pharaoh said, "No!" Then he made the people work even harder.

God changed Pharaoh's mind after sending lots of problems on the Egyptians. Pharaoh was no match for God's power—not to mention all the flies; gnats; and dead camels, donkeys, and cows God used to show his might to Pharaoh. At last, Moses led the people out of captivity and toward the Promised Land.

Oops! Instead of really letting God's people go, Pharaoh decided to bully them one more time. The Israelites had to walk, but Pharaoh had chariots and weapons. He led his army against the Israelites.

Pharaoh thought his chariots and army were mightier than Israel's God. *Wrong!* God performed a few miracles at just the right time. God parted the Red Sea to let his people walk across and escape. Pharaoh's army galloped after them. *Splash! Crash!* God closed the sea. Water flowed and covered the entire army. God destroyed Pharaoh's army and kept his people safe.

The Israelites celebrated their freedom from the bully. They sang, danced, and ate. But mostly, they praised God for saving them.

WACKY LAUGHS
Try these jokes with friends, and then share the chariot stories you've learned.

Knock, knock.
Who's there?
Wheel.
Wheel who?
Wheel have a great time traveling with God.

Q. Why did the bully go to the barber shop?
A. He wanted to tease hair.

Q. How did the barber stop the bully?
A. He cut him off.

✝ PRAY
Praise God for his power to keep you safe from bullies.

Life's Guidebook Says
When Pharaoh's horses, chariots, and charioteers rushed into the sea, the LORD brought the water crashing down on them. But the people of Israel had walked through the middle of the sea on dry ground! EXODUS 15:19

THE GREATEST FLIGHT

ELISHA SAW HORSES and a fiery chariot swoop down and take his best friend, Elijah, to heaven. Just imagine if that happened today and a detective investigated Elijah's disappearance.

Detective: You were the last person to see Elijah. What happened?

Elisha: God sent down a chariot of fire from heaven. Elijah stepped in. *Swoosh!* He blasted off in a whirlwind into the sky.

Detective: Can anyone confirm your story?

Elisha: Earlier, the prophets in Bethel and Jericho said, "Do you know that the Lord will take your master away from you today?"

Detective: *Hmm . . .* Did anyone else witness this UFO?

Elisha: Fifty men stood at a distance. They may have seen it.

Detective: What were Elijah's last words?

Elisha: He asked, "What can I do for you before I'm taken away from you?" I said I wanted a double portion of his spirit.

Detective: What's that?

Elisha: The first son inherits a double portion. I wanted to be the new prophet.

Detective: Sounds like motive for murder.

Elisha: No! I loved him. I want to work for God like Elijah.

Detective: How did Elijah respond?

Elisha: He said if I saw him taken, it would happen. I did! I'm the new prophet!

Detective: Sounds like things worked out for you . . . and Elijah.

EXPERIMENT: UP IN A WHIRLWIND!

Create a whirlwind that will lift a marble off the ground. The next time you watch a rocket blast off on TV, think about how God's powerful fiery chariot took Elijah to heaven.

Stuff You Need
- ☞ Marble
- ☞ Flat surface, like a table or hard floor
- ☞ A jar with a little lip at the opening and a neck that is not thinner than the rest of the jar (a jelly jar works well).

Try It
1. Place the jar upside down over the marble.
2. Move your hand in a circular motion until the marble is zooming around the lip of the jar.
3. Lift the jar while continuing to spin it and watch the marble rise off the table or floor!

✝ PRAY
Ask God to give you the power to stand up for his truth.

Life's Guidebook Says
As [Elisha and Elijah] were walking along and talking, suddenly a chariot of fire appeared, drawn by horses of fire. It drove between the two men, separating them, and Elijah was carried by a whirlwind into heaven. 2 KINGS 2:11

THE NEW BICYCLE

JAMES STOOD BACK and admired his new green bicycle. It had looked shiny and big in the store, but it looked even better in the garage. He hopped on and timed himself as he sped around the bike trail behind his home. He knew that he owned the fastest bike in the neighborhood. The next day, he rode his bike to school and locked it at the bike rack. When school ended, James dashed to the bike rack to ride home.

What? No bicycle. Someone had sawed off the lock. He looked everywhere but couldn't spot his green bike. He walked home with tears rolling down his cheeks.

His parents reported the theft to the police and asked friends to pray. Two days later friends gave James a used bicycle. It wasn't new, shiny, or even green. But it had twenty-four speeds and a basket to carry his books. His dad suggested James time how fast he could ride. James rode faster than he had on his green bicycle. He smiled a little and realized the bicycle he was riding didn't make him fast—it was the powerful legs that God had given him. Having a new bike was nice, but knowing God and understanding his power was even better. He decorated his bike and put a cross sticker on his helmet to remind himself that God would never let him down.

AWESOME ACTIVITY: JAZZ UP YOUR CHARIOT

☞ Add some style to your bicycle with colored waterproof tape, decals, or paint. Tape can be wrapped around the handlebars or other parts of the bicycle.

☞ Use decals to create a pattern on your helmet, and use a permanent marker to add a design, such as your initials.

☞ Cut thin plastic straws (coffee stirrers work) into short pieces and slice them open to make spoke covers to slip on your bicycle's wheels.

✝ PRAY

Thank God for providing what you need, even if it is not new or shiny. Thank him for giving you muscles and brains to power you through life.

Life's Guidebook Says

Some nations boast of their chariots and horses, but we boast in the name of the LORD our God. PSALM 20:7

INVISIBLE CHARIOTS

YOU CAN'T FIGHT GOD. That's what the king of Aram discovered. Whenever he wanted to attack Israel, he made secret plans to mobilize his army. But there are no secrets with God. God knew the king's plans and told them to his prophet Elisha. Then Elisha informed the king of Israel, and Aram's plans were foiled.

Finally, the king of Aram got upset. He decided to capture Elisha so he couldn't ruin Aram's plans. The Arameans had a huge army with many horses and chariots. They surrounded the city of Dothan. Elisha's friend was worried. But the man of God could see things that others couldn't. Elisha asked God to open the other man's eyes. Suddenly, he saw the hillside covered with horses and chariots of fire. It was God's army.

The Aramean army decided to attack. They couldn't see God's warriors. *Zap!* Now they couldn't see anything at all. God struck the enemy blind.

Elisha led the blind army into Samaria, Israel's capital city, where God restored their sight. "Let's kill them," the king of Israel said. But Elisha told the king to feed the enemy and send them home. The king followed his instructions, and the gangs of Arameans stopped bullying Israel.

God always wins. He has legions of angels that he can send to help you. You may not be able to see God or his angels, but God sees you. When you pray, God can show you his answer and give you the help you need.

PLEXER

Try this plexer to discover what kind of trip this book will help you take. (If you don't remember what a plexer is, see p. 9.)

> BjolurBnLeyE

✝ PRAY

Ask God to let you see what he sees.

Life's Guidebook Says

Elisha prayed, "O LORD, open his eyes and let him see!" The LORD opened the young man's eyes, and when he looked up, he saw that the hillside around Elisha was filled with horses and chariots of fire.   2 KINGS 6:17

Answer: Journey through the Bible

NOISES THAT SCARED AN ARMY

WOULD YOU EAT A DONKEY'S HEAD or bird poop? Probably not—unless you were *really* hungry. The Israelites *were* really hungry after Ben-hadad, king of Aram, and his men had surrounded Samaria and not let any food in. The people were starving. They were paying big bucks to eat bird poop. The king of Israel was about to give up. But the prophet Elisha told him to have hope and trust the Lord.

That night the Aramean army heard bumps in the night, sort of like thunder or an avalanche of big boulders tumbling down a mountain. They became scared, thinking they were being attacked. Second Kings 7:6 says that the soldiers thought "it sounded like chariots and horses and a huge army. So the soldiers spoke to one another. They said, 'Listen! The king of Israel has hired the Hittite and Egyptian kings. He has paid them to attack us!'" (NIrv). But it wasn't an army that made the noise—it was God.

The Arameans panicked, running like scared kittens into the night. They left their tents, their horses, their donkeys . . . and their food!

Four starving lepers crept into the Aramean camp that night and discovered mountains of food. *Hoorah!* God's people held a big party to celebrate that they were saved.

WEIRD FACTS: CHARIOTS

☞ The original Olympics included chariot races.

☞ Roman chariots with two horses were called *bigas*. A *triga* was a chariot with three horses.

☞ Four-horse chariots were called *quadrigas*. The strongest two horses pulled from the center. The other two horses were tied to the center horses with ropes and rode beside the center ones.

☞ Teams of horses move faster than one horse. Jesus sent his disciples out in teams too. How do you think it helps to do God's work as part of a team? If one person feels discouraged, the other can cheer him up. Have you ever worked for God as part of a team?

☦ PRAY

Ask God to calm you when you hear a scary noise. Trust him to always protect and provide for you.

Life's Guidebook Says

Don't be afraid, for I am with you. Don't be discouraged, for I am your God. I will strengthen you and help you. I will hold you up with my victorious right hand. ISAIAH 41:10

PATHWAY TO TREASURE

How GOOD ARE YOU at following clues? If you're a good detective, try letterboxing. Letterboxing began more than 150 years ago in England, when a man named James Perrott hid a bottle in Dartmoor National Park and left clues for others to find it. Today, more than 20,000 letterboxes are hidden all over North America.

If you want to begin letterboxing, all you need are a compass, a pad of paper, a pencil, a rubber stamp, and an ink pad. Then search the Internet (letterboxing.org is a good website) to print off clues to a letterbox hidden near you. Once you find a box, put your personal stamp in the hidden book and write your "trail name" (a name you make up, such as "Sherlock Searcher" or "Better than Bilbo"). Then stamp your pad of paper with the special stamp that's in the box.

Following directions while letterboxing can lead to tons of fun. God also wants us to follow his directions. He speaks to us through his Word. Sometimes he guides us through wise people in our lives, like our parents or a pastor. Other times he speaks through dreams and visions. God has a plan, and that includes directing his servants. Through prayer and with the Holy Spirit, we can understand what God wants us to do.

PUZZLE IT OUT: FIND YOUR HEADING

Follow the directions to get to your destination. Look up the Bible verses and go in the direction mentioned. Use each space as a block. Start at the school and see where you arrive.

Pet Store	Paul's House	Playground	Timothy's House
Fire Station	School	Hospital	Ball Field
Grocery Store	Andrew's House	Police Station	Mary's House
Peter's House	Toy Store	Church	Park

1. After school, walk two blocks ___ (Matthew 2:9) then two blocks ___ (Exodus 40:24).
2. When you leave this spot, walk two blocks ___ (Exodus 10:19).
3. Leave here and go three blocks ___ (Deuteronomy 2:3), then one block ___ (Luke 12:54). Go inside and visit a friend.
4. Then go three blocks ___ (Genesis 4:16), and you will arrive at your destination.

Where did you end up? _____

List the places you went: _____, _____, _____

✝ PRAY

Ask God to guide you and send you where he needs you.

Life's Guidebook Says

The LORD says, "I will guide you along the best pathway for your life. I will advise you and watch over you." PSALM 32:8

Answers: You are at Timothy's house. You went to the park, a toy store, and the pet store.

STONY CHOICES

WHACK! THUMP! STONES WHIZZED through the air and hit Stephen. He could make the people stop, if he would stop talking about Jesus. No way! Stephen would never do that. He believed that angels had rolled away the huge stone from in front of the grave and that Jesus had risen from the dead. He believed Jesus was the Son of God. He believed these things so strongly that he was willing to die for his beliefs.

Stephen preached to the people about how God had shown his power throughout history. He pointed out a fact: the people were stubborn. That made them angry. They didn't want to believe the truth about Jesus, even though all the evidence was there—his body was gone; he had appeared to his disciples; he had even done miracles. As Stephen spoke, God opened up the heavens to him. He actually saw Jesus standing at God's right hand (Acts 7:56)! The people didn't want to hear it. They put their hands over their ears and dragged Stephen out of the city.

Instead of begging for mercy, Stephen begged God to forgive the people who were killing him. Can you think of anybody else who did the same thing?

When Jesus was on the cross, he said, "Father, forgive them, for they don't know what they are doing" (Luke 23:34). Stephen followed Christ so closely that he echoed his Savior's words even as he was being persecuted for his faith.

Have you ever been made fun of or injured because you follow Christ? How did you respond? Follow the example of Jesus and Stephen, and remember to pray for people who don't understand the truth.

EXPERIMENT: ROCK-HARD STOMACH

Some animals, like crocodiles, swallow stones to help with digestion. Scientists have even found stones in stomachs of dinosaur skeletons. Make your own leaf-crushing stomach.

Stuff You Need
- ☞ Stones
- ☞ Large plastic bag that seals tight
- ☞ Green leaves

Try It
1. Place leaves and stones in bag.
2. Seal bag.
3. Shake the bag about one minute.
4. Rub the bag hard for about one minute.
5. Continue shaking and rubbing the bag until you see the leaves become crushed pieces.

✝ PRAY

Ask God to help you forgive those who make fun of you or hurt you.

Life's Guidebook Says
[Stephen] fell to his knees, shouting, "Lord, don't charge them with this sin!" And with that, he died. ACTS 7:60

ROCKY REMINDER

WIND AND RAIN WHIP across rocks for centuries, acting like sculptors. Erosion changes the shapes of boulders. When you stare at rocks, sometimes you start to see shapes. At the Garden of the Gods in Colorado Springs, Colorado, people stop their cars to stare at the "kissing camels" on top of the natural sandstone formations. In other places in the world, people have carved huge rocks to sculpt shapes. At Stonehenge in Wiltshire, England, huge stones have been set up like dominoes. On Easter Island in the Pacific Ocean, ginormous heads have been carved from stone and placed all over the island. Archaeologists study many stone shapes that were carved long ago to learn more about history.

God created rocks and used them as special reminders for his people. When God's people finally made it to the Promised Land, God performed a miracle by holding back the waters of the Jordan River. As the twelve tribes of Israel passed through on dry ground, God told a member of each tribe to pick up a rock. They carried the stones into the Promised Land and piled them up as a reminder of God's power.

WEIRD FACTS: STONES AND ROCKS

☞ Rocks are formed in different ways:
- Sedimentary rocks form from sand and soft earth being pressed together over time.
- Igneous rocks form as hot lava cools after a volcanic eruption.
- Metamorphic rocks form from great heat and pressure under the earth's surface.

☞ Geodes are dull-looking rocks on the outside. But the inside contains beautiful crystal formations and colors.

☞ Archaeologists have found stones with eyes or hands carved on them.

☞ Abraham and Jacob built stone altars to show where God spoke to them.

✟ PRAY

Ask Jesus, the Rock, to help you remember the powerful ways that he's worked in your life.

Life's Guidebook Says

[God said to Joshua,] "You can tell [the people], '[The stones] remind us that the Jordan River stopped flowing when the Ark of the LORD's Covenant went across." These stones will stand as a memorial among the people of Israel forever.
JOSHUA 4:7

THE REAL ROCK

CLIMBING TO THE TOP of a mountain takes strong leg muscles, plus balance and endurance. So can you imagine climbing to the highest elevation in all 50 states with only one leg? Sure, Nebraska might be easy. But Mount McKinley in Alaska stands at more than 20,000 feet tall!

Todd Huston doesn't have to imagine accomplishing this feat, because he did it in world-record time. At 14, Todd's legs got caught in the propeller of a boat. After many surgeries, doctors were able to save one of his legs, but his right one had to be amputated. Todd didn't stop being active. He learned to use his artificial leg as well as he used his real one. Then he set a goal for himself to climb the highest peak in all 50 states in the least amount of time. He did it in less than 67 days—beating the old record by 35 days. (Although eventually his record was broken again.)

Todd talks about his journey and shares his faith with people all over the world. He knows that God can help people face any problem they encounter. He has stood on the top of the Rocky Mountains, but he knows we need to stand on the real Rock—Jesus Christ.

Rocks are solid and last a long time. Jesus is called the Rock, because he is strong and lasts forever. We can lean on him and trust him to be there for us.

LIFTOFF LIST

Find a smooth stone. Write your name on it with a permanent marker. Place it on your desk or a shelf as a reminder to stand solid for God. Check off the ways you already are a rock-solid stone.

_____I gave my heart to Jesus.

_____I obey God.

_____I believe Jesus died for my sins.

_____When I disobey, I am sorry and ask to be forgiven.

_____Each day I find one way to help without being asked.

_____I read my Bible.

_____I pray every day.

_____I thank people who help me.

_____I go to church every Sunday.

_____I go to Sunday school.

_____I help at church.

✝ PRAY

Praise God for being the Rock you can lean on anytime.

Life's Guidebook Says
The LORD is my rock, my fortress, and my savior; my God is my rock, in whom I find protection. PSALM 18:2

TALKING ROCKS

WHAT DID THE PIECE of granite say to the piece of quartz?

"You rock!"

What did the quartz say back?

"No, *you* rock!"

Okay, rocks and stones don't really talk, but they do tell some interesting and important stories. In the study of archaeology, scientists use rocks to help date the time period where they're digging. And when they're digging in the Holy Land, old ruins, carvings in stone, and remains from the past help show that the Bible is true.

Last century, archaeologists made some amazing discoveries. While digging in the city of Dan, a team found a rock with an inscription that talked about an ancient military victory. It mentioned "the king of Israel" and "the House of David."

You might think that everybody knows David was the king of Israel. But this was one of the first discoveries from the time of David that used his name and title. Until this point, some historians thought that David was a myth. Now there was evidence that he lived and was a king—just like the Bible says!

The names of numerous other biblical people have been discovered etched in rocks that are thousands of years old. And each time an ancient writing is found, it just confirms that the stories in the Bible are true.

When Jesus walked the earth, some religious leaders complained to him, asking him to tell his followers to stop praising him and calling him King. Jesus replied that if the people became silent, the stones would cry out.

The stones are crying out today to confirm the truth of the Bible and that Jesus is the King of kings.

WACKY LAUGHS

Q. Why was David able to kill Goliath with a sling?

A. Because he was only a stone's throw away.

Q. A shark chased three sea creatures: a flounder, an angelfish, and an eel. They came upon some rocks and tried to throw them at the shark. The angelfish tossed a rock and missed. The flounder threw a rock and flat missed. The eel threw a rock and hit the shark. *Smack!* The shark swam away. So what does this prove?

A. Let he who has no fin cast the first stone.

✝ PRAY

Pray for people who do not believe Jesus lived, died, and came back to life. Pray that God's Spirit would help them see the rock-solid truth.

Life's Guidebook Says

[Jesus] replied, "If they kept quiet, the stones along the road would burst into cheers!" LUKE 19:40

ROCKS ON FIRE!

IF YOU WANT TO START a wood fire, you probably don't want to dump a ton of water on the wood. Water makes it hard to light a fire. But that's exactly what God's prophet Elijah did, and he did it to prove a point about God's power.

Back in Elijah's day, he came face-to-face with some strange dudes. These men believed an idol named Baal was a god. *That's bad.* They worshiped Baal and did not believe in the one true God. They cut themselves and burned their children as sacrifices to Baal. That's *really* bad! God loves us and never wants us to harm a child or ourselves.

Elijah dared people to put God and Baal to a test. On one side stood Elijah—God's lone prophet. On the other side stood 450 prophets of Baal. Elijah told them to stack up wood and an animal sacrifice. He'd do the same. Then each side would call to their god to send down fire. The god who sent down fire would be the one true God. All the people thought that was a good idea. The prophets of Baal prayed for a fire to burn the wood. Nothing happened. They cried out all day and cut themselves until their blood gushed out. But not one spark flew.

In the evening Elijah made an altar of twelve stones to represent the tribes of Israel. He stacked his wood and laid an ox on top. Then he poured water over the wood three times. Elijah said one loud prayer asking God to start a blazing fire. *Whoosh! Sizzle!* Fire came from heaven. God's fire burned up the wood, the stones, and even the water around the altar. Those rocks were literally on fire for God!

A fire in your heart for God is way better than burning rocks. Pray for that kind of fiery passion for God! It will rock your world.

PLEXER

Solve this plexer to find out where Elijah faced off against the prophets of Baal. (If you don't remember what a plexer is, see p. 9.)

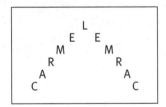

✝ PRAY

Ask God to set your heart on fire for him.

Life's Guidebook Says
Immediately the fire of the LORD flashed down from heaven and burned up the young bull, the wood, the stones, and the dust. It even licked up all the water in the trench! 1 KINGS 18:38

Answer: Mount Carmel

DOWN BUT NOT OUT

WHAT GOES AROUND comes around.

Maybe that's what Paul was thinking while the people of Lystra threw stones at his head. Paul had been there when the people of Jerusalem stoned Stephen to death. Now he was the target of people's anger after telling them about the good news of Jesus Christ.

Stones pulverized Paul's body. The people believed if rocks broke Paul's bones, then he'd stop preaching about Jesus. They left Paul for dead. But nothing got Paul down. With God's power, he stood up and walked back to town.

Paul traveled everywhere he could, telling people about Jesus. He didn't care how mad unbelievers got or how they bullied him. And they did a lot of mean things to him. Men beat him, whipped him, and threw him in jail. God didn't always protect Paul from danger. He was shipwrecked, left hungry and cold, and dragged out of cities.

Paul's troubles made him tough and showed people that he trusted God no matter what. He loved God and would do anything for him. When you have problems, remember Paul and trust God to get you through the worst days you can imagine.

PUZZLE IT OUT: MAKING THE RIGHT CHOICES

Decide if each activity is a good or bad choice. Circle the letter or number under the column you choose.

	Good	Bad
Cleaning your room	P	N
Letting a friend copy your homework	U	S
Throwing stones at a neighbor's car	M	A
Reading the Bible	L	B
Helping your mother cook dinner	M	E
Lying	2	1
Cheating in a game	3	1
Going to church	9	5

Now fill in the blanks with the letters or numbers you circled to find verses about wise choices.

___ ___ ___ ___ ____   ____ ____ ____:9-11

What do these verses tell you about making good choices?

_____

✝ PRAY

Ask God to help you trust him in tough times and tell others about Jesus without fear.

Life's Guidebook Says

Some Jews arrived from Antioch and Iconium and won the crowds to their side. They stoned Paul and dragged him out of town, thinking he was dead. But as the believers gathered around him, he got up and went back into the town.
ACTS 14:19-20

Answer: Psalm 119

31

CAST NO STONES

"HEY, SCRAWNY," one boy yelled at Chip. "You're so weak that you couldn't lift a toothpick with both arms!"

A lot of the boys laughed. Chip didn't. He felt smaller than he already was. It wasn't his fault that his team lost the kickball game. Sure, he had dropped the last ball. But a lot of players had made mistakes during the game.

The biggest boy stepped forward and pushed Chip. "Loser."

Suddenly, Dave, the most popular boy in school, walked into the circle. Everyone stopped what they were doing. Dave held out his hand and helped Chip up. He turned and stared at the boys who were being mean to Chip. "Bullying is not cool," Dave said. Everyone went back into the school, leaving the bullies alone.

In Jesus' day, a group of religious leaders, called Pharisees, sometimes bullied the people. Once when Jesus visited the Temple, a group of Pharisees dragged a woman before him. They told Jesus that she deserved to be stoned to death because of her actions. It was the law! A crowd surrounded Jesus and the woman. Jesus knew they were trying to trick him. He bent down and wrote something in the dust with his finger. Then he stood and said, "All right, but let the one who has never sinned throw the first stone!" (John 8:7).

No stones whizzed by. The crowd knew they'd all made mistakes. Jesus told the woman to go home and stop sinning. Just like God forgave the woman, he forgives us of all the mistakes we make and wants us to make better choices in the future.

EXPERIMENT: FIZZLE STONES
Stuff You Need
☞ Baking soda
☞ Coin or small toy
☞ Vinegar

Try It
1. Mix 2 tablespoons baking soda with 2 tablespoons water to make a dough.
2. Squish the dough around a coin or small toy to form a rock. Let dry.
3. To uncover the treasure, drop the rock into a bowl of vinegar (enough vinegar to cover the rock). Watch the rock fizzle and bubble until it disappears to reveal the hidden treasure. Remember that God makes your sins disappear and also knows the treasures inside of you!

✝ PRAY
Thank God for forgiving your sins, and ask him to help you stand with someone who is being bullied.

Life's Guidebook Says
[The Pharisees] kept demanding an answer, so [Jesus] stood up again and said, "All right, but let the one who has never sinned throw the first stone!" JOHN 8:7

FEAR OF MISSING OUT

WHAT ARE YOU AFRAID OF? Some kids are afraid of the dark or loud noises or getting sick or losing their parents. But researchers have discovered a new fear that's sweeping the world—the fear of missing out (called FOMO).

FOMO causes us to act in strange ways. We check our smartphones all the time. We answer a call when we're talking face-to-face with a friend. And we constantly think about the fun we *could* be having instead of what we're currently doing. If you're afraid that you're missing out, you probably are. You're missing out on real-world, real-time relationships—including your relationship with God.

God doesn't want a part of your attention as you daydream about doing some other fun activity. He wants your whole attention. And the Bible is clear that God doesn't want you to fear anything . . . except him. Job 28:28 says, "The fear of the Lord is true wisdom." That doesn't mean we should be afraid of God, but we should respect his power and position in our lives.

If anybody in the Bible had a reason to be afraid, it was Job. His children were killed. His money was taken away. And he became so sick that he nearly died. But instead of getting mad at God, Job continued to trust and fear the Lord.

Job never suffered from FOMO, because he understood that everything comes from God, including true happiness.

PUZZLE IT OUT

Answer the questions and read the shaded boxes to discover the missing word from this famous quote from Job.

1. A group of wolves is called a _____.
2. The color of dirt.
3. You hit a baseball with a _____.
4. Opposite of big.
5. If you have a question, you _____ your hand.
6. You dye these at Easter.

"The LORD gave me what I had, and the LORD has taken it away. _____ the name of the LORD!"—Job 1:21

✝ PRAY

Ask God to give you a healthy fear of him.

Life's Guidebook Says

This is what [God] says to all humanity: "The fear of the Lord is true wisdom; to forsake evil is real understanding." JOB 28:28

Answers: 1. Pack; 2. Brown; 3. Bat; 4. Little; 5. Raise; 6. Eggs. Missing word: Praise

FEBRUARY

EXTRA SALTY

DID YOU KNOW there's a huge sea where it's impossible to sink to the bottom? Being safe around the water is superimportant. But even if you don't know how to swim, you can float safely in the Dead Sea. That's because the Dead Sea is nearly 10 times saltier than the ocean. All of that salt makes you float like a log. You can't sink! But so much salt isn't all good. If you have any cuts or scrapes, the Dead Sea makes them sting like crazy. And you definitely don't want to get any of this salty water in your eyes.

The Dead Sea is the lowest place on earth. Bordering Israel and Jordan in the Middle East, it sits at 1,360 feet *below* sea level.

When you think about low places in the Bible, it's hard to get lower than Sodom and Gomorrah. In the book of Genesis, it says the people in those cities were so evil that God sent angels to destroy them. But before God wiped these places off the planet, he saved Lot and his family. They were the only good people in town. As they fled, the angels told them not to look back. Lot's wife didn't obey. She looked back and immediately turned into a pillar of salt. Now that's extra salty!

The Bible tells us these evil cities were located near the Salt Sea—now called the Dead Sea (Genesis 14:8). Archaeologists have been searching for the remains of these cities, but so far they haven't been able to find them. As the Dead Sea evaporates and grows smaller, experts hope to find the buried cities. But they probably won't find Lot's wife.

WACKY LAUGHS

Q. What Bible character was most interested in buying property?
A. Lot

Q. What did the math book say to the science book?
A. "I've got a lot of problems."

Q. How did the centipede get its name in the *Guinness Book of World Records*?
A. It had a lot of feats.

✝ PRAY

Ask God to help you to always follow his commands.

> *Life's Guidebook Says*
> *Lot's wife looked back as she was following behind him, and she turned into a pillar of salt.* GENESIS 19:26

GOD BLESS YOU!

The tickle starts inside you
    And itches to get out.
Your face begins to wiggle,
    You feel it in your snout.
You try to fight the feeling
    Of swarms of angry bees.
There's just no way to stop it—
    The power of a sneeze!

ACHOO! A SNEEZE LEAVES your lips going about 100 miles per hour. That's faster than a cheetah. Doctors say sneezing is your body's way of getting rid of nasty germs. A single sneeze can send 100,000 germs into the air. (Maybe that's why your mom always says to cover your mouth.) Some people say it's impossible to keep your eyes open when you sneeze. Next time you feel a sneeze coming on, try to keep them open. Just don't try to stop the sneeze. Sneezing is good for you—it can even save your life.

Don't believe it? In the Old Testament, the prophet Elisha traveled around telling people about God. In the city of Shunem, a woman invited him to stay with her family anytime he was in the area. She even had a special room for him. One day, the woman's son was working in the fields when he complained that his head hurt. He went home and suddenly died. The woman put her dead son in Elisha's room and then went out to find the prophet. When Elisha heard what happened, he rushed back to Shunem. Second Kings 4:32 tells us, "When Elisha arrived, the child was indeed dead, lying there on the prophet's bed." Elisha prayed to God and laid his body over the child's. Slowly, the child's body grew warmer. *Achoo! Achoo! Achoo! Achoo! Achoo! Achoo! Achoo!* Seven sneezes later, the boy was alive again!

WEIRD FACTS: *GESUNDHEIT!*
- ☞ A woman in England sneezed for 978 straight days. That's a record nobody wants to break!
- ☞ Iguanas sneeze more often than any other animal. Scientists say these lizards sneeze to get rid of certain salts that are a normal by-product of their digestive processes.

✝ PRAY
Thank God for his healing powers and for how he designed your body to protect itself with a sneeze.

Life's Guidebook Says
Elisha got up, walked back and forth across the room once, and then stretched himself out again on the child. This time the boy sneezed seven times and opened his eyes! 2 KINGS 4:35

THE HAND OF GOD

THINK FAST: NAME SOMETHING that God wrote with his hand.

Did you think about the Ten Commandments? In Exodus 24:12, the Lord says to Moses, "I will give you the tablets of stone on which I have inscribed." It's kind of cool to think about what God's handwriting looks like. But in another story in the Bible, people shook in fear as God wrote something.

The book of Daniel tells how King Belshazzar threw a huge party. The guests were drinking from gold and silver cups that had been taken from God's Temple in Jerusalem. They were praising the idols they'd made from gold, silver, bronze, iron, wood, and stone. Suddenly, what looked like the fingers of a human hand appeared out of nowhere and started to write on the wall (Daniel 5:4-5). The king trembled in terror and called his wisest men to read the message. Nobody could read it but Daniel. The prophet told the king that because he hadn't humbled himself before God, the Lord would bring the king's reign to an end and divide his kingdom. That same night the king died.

A floating hand may seem scary, but there's nothing scarier than worshiping an idol. *No problem,* you might think. *I don't have any golden calves in my bedroom.*

While you might not worship the false idols of the Old Testament, anything that takes God's place in your heart is an idol.

LIFTOFF LIST

What idols are trying to take over first place in your heart? It's easy for a good thing to become a god thing if you're not careful. Check anything on this list that could become an idol for you, and then make sure it doesn't.

___ Being popular
___ Being the best at sports
___ Beating the latest video game
___ Having the newest smartphone
___ Earning the best grades
___ Wearing the coolest clothes

✝ PRAY

Tell God that you want to serve him with all your heart, mind, soul, and strength. Ask him to always be number one in your life.

Life's Guidebook Says

"You must not make for yourself an idol of any kind or an image of anything in the heavens or on the earth or in the sea. . . . I, the LORD your God, am a jealous God who will not tolerate your affection for any other gods." EXODUS 20:4-5

A CRAZY KING

HOW DOES A PERSON go from being one of the most powerful leaders in the world to eating grass like a cow? Well, have you heard the saying "The bigger they are, the harder they fall"? That was certainly true for Goliath. But the same thing could be said for King Nebuchadnezzar of Babylon.

This king, mentioned in the Old Testament, is best known for how his fiery furnace backfired when Shadrach, Meshach, and Abednego were shoved inside. But the history books remember him as one of the best builders of all time. Nebuchadnezzar's grand palace was known throughout the land as the "Marvel of Mankind." And his Hanging Gardens of Babylon were recognized as one of the Seven Wonders of the Ancient World. So maybe it's no wonder that Nebuchadnezzar looked out on his kingdom and said, "Look at this great city of Babylon! By my own mighty power, I have built this beautiful city as my royal residence to display my majestic splendor" (Daniel 4:30).

Just one problem: God doesn't like pride.

As those words left the king's mouth, he heard a voice from heaven saying that he'd no longer rule the kingdom and would live like an animal until he learned "that the Most High rules over the kingdoms of the world and gives them to anyone he chooses" (Daniel 4:32). The Bible says Nebuchadnezzar lived that way until his hair was as long as eagles' feathers and his fingernails looked like bird claws. *Gross!* After seven years of living like a wild animal, Nebuchadnezzar looked to heaven and regained his sanity. He worshiped the Most High and understood that even the mightiest people on earth are nothing compared to God.

AWESOME ACTIVITY: ANIMAL ANTICS

Pretend to be your favorite animal. Act like that animal for your parents or your brother or sister. See if they can guess what animal you're pretending to be. Then think about what it'd be like to actually live like that animal.

☞ What would be the best part?

_____

☞ What would be the worst part?

_____

✝ PRAY

Praise God that he humbles the exalted and exalts the humble. Ask him to help you stay humble.

Life's Guidebook Says

"Now I, Nebuchadnezzar, praise and glorify and honor the King of heaven. All his acts are just and true, and he is able to humble the proud." DANIEL 4:37

HAIR—PULLING ADVENTURE

NOBODY LIKES to get his hair pulled. Don't believe it? Go pull your sister's hair. Wait, that'd be a bad idea. Instead, just imagine what would happen if you pulled your sister's hair. Not pretty, huh?

Now imagine what it'd be like for God to pull your hair. *Ouch!* But that's exactly what happened to Ezekiel. During the time that Ezekiel was a prophet, God's people were ruled by good kings, bad kings, and superevil kings. And from reading the Old Testament, it's obvious most of the kings were bad. King Jehoiachin fell into that category. God allowed him to be captured and imprisoned by Judah's enemies for 37 years. During the sixth year of Jehoiachin's captivity, Ezekiel had a vision of a figure that looked like a man . . . except there were some differences. Okay, a lot of differences.

For one thing, from the waist down the figure looked like a burning flame. From the waist up, he looked like gleaming amber. Before Ezekiel could run in fright, this figure reached out his hand, grabbed Ezekiel by the hair, and transported him to Jerusalem (Ezekiel 8:3). Suddenly, Ezekiel stood in the Temple and looked at an idol that was built to a false god. God wasn't happy. His house was being ruined by evil idols and sinful actions.

Many times in church we hear about God's kindness and love. That's all very true. Love oozes from God. When we believe in Jesus as our Savior, we're called children of God. But God is also perfectly holy. He won't tolerate continuous sinful behavior. God gave Ezekiel a warning: because the people thumbed their nose at his power, he was going to do a lot worse to them than hair pulling. *Double ouch!*

PLEXER

See if you can solve this plexer. (If you don't remember what a plexer is, see p. 9.)

hairhairhairhairhair

✟ PRAY

Thank God that he won't stand for sin. He understands that you make mistakes, but ask him to help you learn from the bad things you do.

Life's Guidebook Says

[God said,] "Is it nothing to the people of Judah that they commit these detestable sins, leading the whole nation into violence, thumbing their noses at me, and provoking my anger? Therefore, I will respond in fury. I will neither pity nor spare them." EZEKIEL 8:17-18

Answer: Shrinking hairline

PIGGING OUT

HAVE YOU EVER SEEN a pig fly? Jesus did.

Pigs aren't known for their athletic ability. They're more famous for their bacon (or is that bakin'?) than for running a 100-yard dash. Pigs can run about 11 miles per hour. A hippo, which is much bigger, can sprint three times as fast. The Bible doesn't talk a lot about pigs, except in the Old Testament when God tells his people *not* to eat them.

But as Jesus walked the earth, he ran into a herd of pigs after he crossed the Sea of Galilee. God's Son didn't mind the swine, but the two men possessed by demons who walked out of the graveyard did bother him (Matthew 8:28). When the men saw him, they shouted, "Why are you interfering with us, Son of God?" (verse 29). Nobody had referred to Jesus as the Son of God in public before. (The devil had called him that as he tempted Jesus in Matthew 4—but he and Jesus were by themselves.)

The demons knew Jesus had power over them, so they begged to be cast into the herd of swine. "All right, go!" Jesus commanded (verse 32). Immediately, the demons went into the pigs, and the pigs ran off some steep cliffs and flew into the sea. So see? Pigs can fly. But more important, Jesus has power over everything on earth and in heaven.

QUIZ: GET TOGETHER

Animals like to hang out in groups. Sometimes those groups have funny names. Draw a line from the animal to its group name. Then check your answers to see how many you got right.

Animal	Name of Group
Cow	Mob
Goose	Pod
Whale	Gaggle
Crow	Herd
Kangaroo	Pack
Monkey	Troop
Wolf	Murder
Lion	Pride

✝ PRAY

Thank God that the power that is inside you—that's the Holy Spirit—is greater than anything in the world.

Life's Guidebook Says
Jesus came and told his disciples, "I have been given all authority in heaven and on earth." MATTHEW 28:18

Answers: Cow—Herd; Goose—Gaggle; Whale—Pod; Crow—Murder; Kangaroo—Mob; Monkey—Troop; Wolf—Pack; Lion—Pride

WHY CAN'T WE GET ALONG?

YOU'VE PROBABLY HEARD THE SAYING, "Fighting like cats and dogs." Cats and dogs don't normally get along, especially if the cat is a cheetah. Cheetahs are fast and ferocious. They can run faster than 70 miles per hour and have sharp teeth to devour their prey.

But at the Cincinnati Zoo, cheetahs and dogs *do* get along in amazing ways. For more than 10 years, a cheetah named Sahara and an Anatolian shepherd named Alexa have been best buds. They grew up together as part of the zoo's Cat Ambassador Program. This program helps educate farmers in Africa on how dogs can protect their livestock. Many times farmers in Namibia and South Africa shoot cheetahs—which are endangered—to save their livestock. But a shepherd dog can protect the animals by keeping away these dangerous cats. That way nobody gets hurt.

The Bible tells us numerous times how God protects us. He not only guards us from dangers, but he can help us get along with our enemies. The prophet Isaiah said when a little child (that's Jesus) is in charge, then "the leopard will lie down with the baby goat" (Isaiah 11:6). Normally, a leopard looks at a baby goat as breakfast. But when the Lord rules, he makes peace between enemies. And that's a much better way to live.

PUZZLE IT OUT: MISSING WORD
Look closely at the words below. One letter that is present in the first word is missing from the second word in each pair. Write that letter in order in the spaces below to discover the missing word from the verse.

1. pastry   trays
2. cakes   sack
3. measure   resume
4. cape   ape
5. loaves   ovals

"Do all that you can to live in __ __ __ __ __ with everyone." —Romans 12:18
                                  1 2 3 4 5

✞ PRAY
Praise God that he'll come back to rule the world and make peace between enemies. And ask him to help you be a peacemaker.

Life's Guidebook Says
In that day the wolf and the lamb will live together; the leopard will lie down with the baby goat. The calf and the yearling will be safe with the lion, and a little child will lead them all. ISAIAH 11:6

Answer: peace

SNAKE IN THE GRASS

SOME SNAKES JUST LOOK SCARY. When a king cobra rises up and displays its diamond-shaped hood, you naturally want to run. Other snakes *sound* mean. You *never* want to be close enough to hear a rattlesnake shake its tail. Then there are the colorful snakes. These striped serpents can be deadly, like the coral snake, or perfectly harmless, like the scarlet king snake. A good rule to follow if you see a red, black, and yellow striped snake is "Red next to yellow kills a fellow. Red next to black is a friend to Jack." So unless you're an expert, it's probably best not to pick up snakes no matter what color they are.

But if you ever hear a snake talk to you, here's a good bit of advice: run! That's what Eve should've done. She didn't. She listened to the serpent's slick tongue, and it cost her life—and all of ours. You probably know the story in Genesis about how God created the beautiful Garden of Eden and told Adam he could eat from any tree except the tree of the knowledge of good and evil. Well, the serpent (you may know him better as Satan) tempted Eve into eating from the tree, saying, "Your eyes will be opened as soon as you eat [the fruit], and you will be like God, knowing both good and evil" (Genesis 3:5). Of course, it was a lie. Eve and Adam both disobeyed God, fell for the temptation, and ate the fruit. The consequences were huge. It messed up their relationship with God, and they were kicked out of the Garden. The created ones—us—can never be equal to the Creator God.

PUZZLE IT OUT: SNAKES IN A GAME

Look for these dangerous snakes in the grass. Search up, down, across, diagonally, and backward.

T	B	L	A	C	K	M	A	M	B	A
A	I	T	R	A	S	K	B	V	G	D
I	V	G	W	R	I	U	P	N	W	D
P	T	I	E	J	K	V	A	C	O	O
A	D	D	E	R	A	L	I	T	C	R
N	E	K	A	N	S	L	A	R	O	C
O	X	A	C	M	P	N	U	S	B	P
C	T	Q	O	B	N	M	A	L	R	L
K	W	O	R	P	S	P	E	K	A	E
Z	B	L	A	N	K	V	I	P	E	R
R	A	T	T	L	E	S	N	A	K	E

Adder
Black Mamba
Cobra
Taipan
Viper
Asp
Boomslang
Coral Snake
Tiger Snake
Rattlesnake

✝ PRAY

Thank God for being your Creator and Savior. Tell him that you want to follow him—not be equal to him.

Life's Guidebook Says

"You won't die!" the serpent replied to the woman. "God knows that your eyes will be opened as soon as you eat it, and you will be like God, knowing both good and evil." GENESIS 3:4-5

IT'S NOT EASY BEING GREEN

DO YOUR PARENTS LET you jump on your bed? Or maybe you have a trampoline in your house or yard. How high can you jump? *Jump, jump, jump!*

Frogs are amazing jumpers. A bullfrog can jump more than six feet. And the Fuji tree frog spins 180 degrees in the air every time it jumps!

In the Old Testament, God called Moses to go to Egypt and tell Pharaoh to free the Israelites. Pharaoh refused to listen, so God sent ten plagues—or bad things—to demonstrate his power and convince Pharaoh to let his people go. In Exodus 8:1-2, Moses tells Pharaoh that frogs will cover the land if he doesn't let God's people go. Pharaoh says no . . . so then come the frogs!

There were frogs in the river. Frogs jumping in the oven. Frogs in the cooking bowls. Frogs in the palace. Even frogs jumping on Pharaoh's bed.

Do you think Pharaoh hopped up with the frogs and had fun jumping on his bed? Probably not. Pharaoh was mad. He told Moses to ask the Lord to take the frogs from his land. Then he would free God's people. Moses prayed, and all the frogs in the houses and fields died. So many frogs died that the people scooped them up in big, smelly piles. *Gross!* Now the frog problem was gone. But instead of keeping his word, Pharaoh decided not to let God's people go.

Do you always keep a promise? How does it feel when friends promise to do something and then go back on their word?

That's exactly how Moses felt. But God wasn't done yet. He would still get his people free.

WACKY LAUGHS

Q. A duck, a frog, and a skunk went to the dollar movies. Which one couldn't get in?

A. The skunk. The duck had a bill; the frog had a greenback; but the skunk had only a scent.

Q. What is a frog's favorite season?

A. Spring!

Q. Why was the frog so happy?

A. It ate everything that bugged it.

✝ PRAY

Ask God to help you be a young man who keeps his promises. When you give your word, make sure to keep it.

Life's Guidebook Says

When Pharaoh saw that relief had come, he became stubborn. He refused to listen to Moses and Aaron, just as the Lord had predicted. EXODUS 8:15

DANCING GOATS

WOULD YOU GLOAT if a goat sang a note from its throat in a boat that did float in a moat?

Don't bother answering that question. Everybody knows it's not nice to gloat. But if you read Isaiah 13, it almost seems like the animals are gloating at Babylon's fall.

The Babylonian Empire was one of the most powerful during Old Testament times. These people are first mentioned in Genesis and come up in many Bible stories, such as the fiery furnace and when Daniel slept with lions. At times, God used the Babylonians to accomplish his purposes. But then Babylon started thinking too highly of itself. The leaders gloated in their power.

About 600 years before Jesus was born, God gave Isaiah a message for Babylon, and it didn't say, "You're doing a great job." God said Babylon would be judged for its wicked actions. The people were sinful, proud, and arrogant. So God would allow another army to conquer Babylon and devastate the city, just like God destroyed Sodom and Gomorrah. And once the city crumbled, wild animals would move in. "Owls will live among the ruins, and wild goats will go there to dance. . . . Babylon's days are numbered; its time of destruction will soon arrive" (Isaiah 13:21-22).

Can you picture a dancing goat? There are more than 60 kinds of goats in the world. Isaiah is probably talking about an ibex. Unlike domestic goats that you see on a lot of farms, the ibex has three-foot-long horns and is an excellent climber. But you'd want to stay away if you saw one dancing; those horns would be dangerous!

AWESOME ACTIVITY: HOUSE OF CARDS

The Bible is clear: it's God who blesses nations or allows them to fall. He controls everything that happens. If a nation—or even your own life—isn't built on God, it's doomed to fall . . . just like a house of cards.

Try to create your own card house. Get some playing cards and start building. You can look online for card-building tips. See if you can make a three-story-high card house before it falls down.

✝ PRAY

Praise God for his power. Ask him to give you wisdom as you live for him.

Life's Guidebook Says

[God] controls the course of world events; he removes kings and sets up other kings. He gives wisdom to the wise and knowledge to the scholars. DANIEL 2:21

BE A DEER

HAVE YOU EVER BEEN really thirsty? Not the kind of thirst that comes from forgetting a juice box in your lunch. This is the kind of thirst that comes after you eat a whole bowl of salty popcorn. Or the lip-cracking thirst that develops after playing a soccer game on a hot summer day. Get the idea?

At times like that, what would you do for a glass of cool, refreshing water? Would you hop on one foot while singing "Mary Had a Little Lamb"? Would you bark like a dog or do a double somersault? When you're really thirsty, you want a drink even more than you want your Xbox. And it's that kind of desire that God wants you to have when it comes to your relationship with him.

Psalm 42 begins with these words: "As the deer longs for streams of water, so I long for you, O God." The Holy Land is a pretty dry place. When the psalmist wrote these words, he may have been looking out at a desert. Deer that live in the desert get really thirsty. They often drink more than six gallons of water a day!

God wants you to act like a deer when it comes to following him. Thirst after God. Drink deeply from his Word. Seek out the refreshment that comes only from a growing relationship with your heavenly Father.

EXPERIMENT: REINDEER CHOW

This snack mix is both sweet and salty. Mix up a batch and then pour yourself a glass of milk or water.

Stuff You Need

- ☞ 12-ounce package of semisweet chocolate morsels
- ☞ 1 cup peanut butter
- ☞ Large bowl
- ☞ Spoon
- ☞ 5 cups of crispy cereal like Chex or Crispix
- ☞ 1-gallon sealable bag
- ☞ Powdered sugar

Try It

1. Melt chocolate in a bowl in microwave. Put on high for one minute at a time. Stir and repeat until melted.
2. Add peanut butter to melted chocolate and mix well.
3. In a large bowl, add the chocolate-peanut butter mixture on top of the cereal. Stir to coat cereal.
4. Put cereal in a one-gallon resealable bag. Add powdered sugar, seal the bag and shake well. Once the cereal is coated, open the bag and enjoy.

✟ PRAY

Tell God that you want to be someone who thirsts after him.

Life's Guidebook Says

As the deer longs for streams of water, so I long for you, O God. PSALM 42:1

NOW THAT'S TALENT

I AM GOOD AT _____.

How did you fill in the blank? God gives everybody different talents. Maybe you put down

- ☞ being kind
- ☞ math
- ☞ making friends
- ☞ singing
- ☞ playing piano
- ☞ being creative
- ☞ being a leader
- ☞ memorizing
- ☞ baseball
- ☞ reading
- ☞ praying
- ☞ juggling
- ☞ making videos
- ☞ writing
- ☞ helping people
- ☞ flying

You probably didn't write down that last one, although being able to fly would be pretty cool. Or maybe you wrote down all those things. If you did, your talent probably isn't being humble. *Ha!* No matter what you wrote in that space, God wants you to use that talent to glorify him. Think about that as you answer these questions:

☞ How can I grow my talent in this area? _____

_____

☞ How can I use this talent for God? _____

_____

How you answer these questions is superimportant. God put you on earth for a purpose. He has big plans for your life. As you develop your talents and use them to glorify and serve him, you're living out part of that purpose. Make the most of your talents, and you'll be amazed at how God can use you.

Now finish this sentence: I want to serve God because _____

_____.

WACKY LAUGHS

Your talent may be telling jokes. Try these out on a family member or friend and see what happens.

Knock, knock.
Who's there?
Pecan.
Pecan who?
Pecan someone your own size.

Q. What do you call a cow that doesn't give milk?
A. A milk dud.

Q. Why did the cat lay on its back with its feet in the air?
A. It was trying to trip birds.

✝ PRAY

Ask God to give you opportunities to serve him with your talents.

Life's Guidebook Says

God's gifts of grace come in many forms. Each of you has received a gift in order to serve others. You should use it faithfully. 1 PETER 4:10, NIrV

A SLING AND A PRAYER

"YOUR GOD IS SO SMELLY that when he plays in a sandbox, cats walk up and try to bury him. And your God is so small that he uses a sock for a sleeping bag."

Nobody knows exactly what Goliath yelled at the Israelites, but it probably wasn't very nice. The Bible says the giant came out to hurl insults at God's people and challenge somebody to fight him. When David visited his brothers at the front lines of the battle, he couldn't believe nobody was willing to fight the giant and shut him up. Maybe it was because Goliath was over nine feet tall. His armor weighed 125 pounds, and his spear was as big around as a person's leg (1 Samuel 17:4-7).

But when David looked at Goliath, he didn't see an unbeatable warrior. He saw a bully who mocked God. He knew God wouldn't let the giant continue spouting off at the mouth. So David went to King Saul and asked to fight. At first Saul refused, but David convinced him. Saul gave David his own armor—"a bronze helmet and a coat of mail." David put it on and strapped on a sword (17:38-39). He tried walking, but the armor was too bulky. He knew armor couldn't protect him; only God could do that.

You know the rest of the story. The young shepherd boy gathered five smooth stones and went out to fight the Philistine. Goliath mocked David, just as he mocked God. But a quick stone to the head ended the fight as soon as it started. David won. God gave him the victory!

EXPERIMENT: SLINGSHOT SURPRISE

David's slingshot looked more like a strap that he swung over his head. Make your own miniature slingshot to play with.

Stuff You Need
- bobby pin (your mom might have one)
- pliers
- scissors
- rubber band
- tiny pieces of paper
- targets (such as plastic cups)

Try It
1. Use the pliers to bend the bobby pin into a Y-shape, like a slingshot.
2. Cut the rubber band and tie it to the arms of the slingshot.
3. Fold up tiny pieces of paper, gather some targets (plastic cups work well), and pretend you're shooting rocks at Goliath.

✝ PRAY
Thank God that he helps you overcome big problems—like Goliath—with ease.

Life's Guidebook Says
[David said,] "The LORD who rescued me from the claws of the lion and the bear will rescue me from this Philistine!" 1 SAMUEL 17:37

THE LORD'S ARMOR

DO YOU EVER LOOK around and think, *That's not fair?*

Maybe you see kids who cheat on their homework get good grades. Other kids might lie to become popular. Sometimes it can feel that being cool is more important than telling the truth. And it can appear that the sneaky kids get rewarded for their wrong actions.

If you've ever felt that way, you're not alone. In the Bible, many people felt that way. The prophet Isaiah was one of them. At times, he felt that honesty had been outlawed (Isaiah 59:14). But Isaiah also knew that God was watching and would make everything right. It was only a matter of time before the Lord would put on his armor and repay his enemies for their evil deeds.

Wait, you might be thinking, *why would the Lord need armor?*

The simple answer is that he doesn't. He's an all-powerful God who's everywhere at once and knows everybody's thoughts and actions. But Isaiah 59:17 tells us, "He put on righteousness as his body armor and placed the helmet of salvation on his head. He clothed himself with a robe of vengeance and wrapped himself in a cloak of divine passion."

Sometimes the Bible's writers describe God in human terms so we can better understand him and picture him in our minds. This is one of those cases. When we read that verse, we can see that no one should mess with God. His righteous body armor is impenetrable. He takes revenge on those who stand against him, while at the same time being compassionate and loving to those who serve him.

And if you really think about it, that's not fair. We don't deserve the Lord's protection and mercy, yet he gives it to us anyway.

PLEXER
See if you can solve this plexer. (If you don't remember what a plexer is, see p. 9.)

armdresorofsedGod

✝ PRAY
Look at today's verse and pick out one of the attributes mentioned: righteousness, salvation, vengeance, or passion. Thank God for showing that characteristic in your life.

Life's Guidebook Says
[The Lord] put on righteousness as his body armor and placed the helmet of salvation on his head. He clothed himself with a robe of vengeance and wrapped himself in a cloak of divine passion. ISAIAH 59:17

Answer: Dressed in the armor of God

BIG MO!

HAVE YOU EVER HAD a coach give you a powerful pep talk before a big game? That's basically what Moses did for God's people in Deuteronomy 33. He'd just finished leading the Israelites through the desert for forty years. Now they stood at the threshold of the Promised Land. Moses was old and tired, and because he'd disobeyed God, he wouldn't be stepping into the Promised Land himself. But instead of being mopey, Moses turned motivational.

He spoke a blessing on the Israelites. He started with the tribe of Reuben and went all the way through to the tribe of Asher, encouraging all of God's people. The journey from Egypt to the Promised Land hadn't been easy. Now the people trusted the Lord to help them take the land. If the journey had been hard before, it was only going to get harder. Moses knew they wouldn't make it unless they relied on God. He ended his blessing on the people with some strong words and a powerful reminder: "How blessed you are, O Israel! Who else is like you, a people saved by the LORD? He is your protecting shield and your triumphant sword!" (Deuteronomy 33:29).

It's kind of cool to think about how God is our protecting shield and triumphant sword. He doesn't change. The same God who did miracles for the Israelites still does miracles today. How's that for a pep talk?

Now get out there and win!

QUIZ: MO FACTS

So much happened during Moses' life. Read this list and figure out which three things he *didn't* do.

1. Float down a river as a baby in a basket
2. Grow up in Pharaoh's palace
3. Speak to God in a burning bush
4. See the Red Sea parted
5. Dunk a basketball
6. Hit a rock and have water come out
7. Bring down the Ten Commandments
8. Ride a whale like a cowboy
9. Die on Mount Nebo
10. Be the first person to step into the Promised Land

✝ PRAY

Ask God to help you motivate the people around you to serve God.

Life's Guidebook Says

[Moses said,] "How blessed you are, O Israel! Who else is like you, a people saved by the LORD? He is your protecting shield and your triumphant sword! Your enemies will cringe before you, and you will stomp on their backs!" DEUTERONOMY 33:29

Answer: 5, 8, and 10

KNIGHT TIME

WOULDN'T IT BE AWESOME to be a knight in shining armor? You'd ride horses. Joust for championships. Fight for the kingdom and be adored by peasants. And you can't beat the uniform: silvery armor, gleaming in the sun. Knights just look cool.

But actually being a knight wasn't too glamorous. A full suit of armor often weighed more than 100 pounds. And there wasn't any air-conditioning in there, so it got hot. Plus, armor isn't flexible. Scientists say it's twice as hard to walk when you're in a suit of armor.

Knights were also expected to live by a very strict code. A Knights Code of Chivalry dates back to the Dark Ages. Just look at this list from *The Song of Roland*, which pretty well represents what was expected from a knight:

- ☞ To fear God and maintain his church
- ☞ To serve the liege lord in valor and faith
- ☞ To protect the weak and defenseless and help widows and orphans
- ☞ To live by honor and for glory
- ☞ To fight for the welfare of all
- ☞ To obey those placed in authority
- ☞ To at all times speak the truth
- ☞ To persevere to the end in any enterprise begun
- ☞ To respect the honor of women
- ☞ To never to turn one's back upon a foe

That sort of sounds like being a Christian, you might be thinking.

And you're right. In fact, God wants you to put on the shining armor of right living (Romans 13:12) and be a modern-day knight for him.

LIFTOFF LIST
Put check marks next to all the ways that you're being a modern-day knight.

___Being friendly to kids who don't have many friends
___Telling the truth to my parents
___Always finishing my homework
___Respecting girls, including with the TV shows I watch and things I see on the Internet
___Honoring my teachers
___Going to church
___Being a leader
___Making decisions that honor God

✝ PRAY
Commit to God that you will remove your "dirty" clothes and put on his shining armor of right living.

Life's Guidebook Says
The day of salvation will soon be here. So remove your dark deeds like dirty clothes, and put on the shining armor of right living. ROMANS 13:12

NOT IN THE DARK

ARE YOU AFRAID OF the dark? Researchers say one in four kids is afraid of something. One of the most common fears is being left alone in the dark.

You probably know there are a lot of Bible verses about fear. God doesn't want you to be afraid. He wants you to trust him and overcome your fears. Isaiah 41:10 says, "Don't be afraid, for I am with you. Don't be discouraged, for I am your God. I will strengthen you and help you." The next time you're afraid, think about that verse, and be encouraged. God can give you the strength to beat your fears.

God also equips you to defeat the dark. In the book of Thessalonians, the apostle Paul tells Christ's followers that they don't belong to the dark. They're the children of the light (1 Thessalonians 5:5). Isn't that cool? You're a child of the light! As a child of the light, you shouldn't have anything to do with darkness. And God provides armor to protect against the dark, including the helmet of salvation (verse 8—see today's verse).

When you believe in Jesus as your Savior, he clothes you in armor. This armor protects you from darkness. It's armor built from faith and love, and it should make you confident to live for Christ. Sure, doubts, fears, and other attacks may come your way. But when they do, be confident of your salvation in Christ, and know that he will always help you.

PUZZLE IT OUT: IT ALL ADDS UP
Solve these math problems and then write in the correct word to discover what Moses told God's people when they were afraid.

" _____ _____ _____. _____ _____ _____ _____ _____ _____
  5x2   8÷4   2x3   15-6   21÷3   13-12   4+4   16÷4   5+6

_____ _____ _____ _____." Exodus 14:13
 6x2   16-13   3+2   16-3

1 = still	4 = watch	7 = stand	10 = Don't
2 = be	5 = you	8 = and	11 = the
3 = rescue	6 = afraid	9 = Just	12 = LORD
			13 = today

✝ PRAY
Thank God for his protective armor, and ask him to give you the courage to not be afraid.

Life's Guidebook Says
Let us who live in the light be clearheaded, protected by the armor of faith and love, and wearing as our helmet the confidence of our salvation.
1 THESSALONIANS 5:8

Answer: "Don't be afraid. Just stand still and watch the LORD rescue you today."

THE BEST OFFENSE

IF YOU PLAY SPORTS, you might have heard a coach say, "A good defense is the best offense." But what exactly does that mean?

Well, if a team can't score against you, it gives you a better chance at victory. Colin's youth basketball team tried that strategy during its basketball season. They worked hard in practice at moving their feet on defense. They learned about staying between their man and the basket. They drilled on getting good position for rebounds. The result? They won one of their games 36–0.

Now that's playing good defense! Just *one* steal and layup would've won the game for Colin's team.

Just like in sports, knights believed in a good defense. A strong shield was just as important—maybe even more important—than a sharp sword. A shield blocked an enemy's attacks from close range and from a distance. A shield was especially effective in stopping arrows.

God knows about the importance of playing defense as you follow him. He gives you armor to protect yourself and the sword of his Word to fight with. But one of the most important things God gives you is the shield of faith (Ephesians 6:16). Your faith in Christ guards you against Satan's attacks of doubt and deception. Hold on tightly to your faith. Use it to shield your mind and body. Your faith isn't just a great defensive tool; you can also use it to go on offense. Shields can be a powerful offensive weapon . . . just ask comic-book hero Captain America.

WEIRD FACTS: SHIELD YOURSELF

- ☞ Shields come in many shapes and sizes. They can be round, oval, square, rectangular, or triangular.
- ☞ Shields often had a design or pattern to represent the soldier's army.
- ☞ If a knight failed to follow his strict code of conduct or acted inappropriately, his shield was hung upside down as a sign of his dishonor.

✝ PRAY

Ask God to fill you with faith to always fight for him.

Life's Guidebook Says

In addition to all of these, hold up the shield of faith to stop the fiery arrows of the devil. EPHESIANS 6:16

UNLOCK YOUR FUTURE

JOHN NEWTON GREW UP riding the waves on huge sailing ships. In the mid-1700s, his father was a ship captain who took John to sea when he was just 11 years old. John's mother had died before he turned seven, and his father wanted to teach him about sailing. John coiled huge ropes, climbed to the top of high masts, and grew strong.

He also grew rebellious. He started cussing and drinking alcohol like the other sailors. Before John's mother died, she had taught him about God's Word and prayed he would become a preacher. But John ran from God. He became the captain of a slave ship and treated people badly.

During one voyage back from Africa, a terrible storm blew up that threatened to sink John's ship. Sailors and supplies washed overboard. Suddenly, John remembered a Bible verse that his mother had taught him. He prayed for God to save his ship. And God answered his prayer. John found a Bible, started reading, and gave his life to God.

Years later, John became a preacher. He traveled around England telling people how God had saved him. John also wrote many famous songs. His most famous is "Amazing Grace," which starts out, "Amazing grace! How sweet the sound that saved a wretch like me."

PUZZLE IT OUT: UNLOCK THE TRUTH

John Newton discovered the true purpose of his life when he gave himself to God. Once he knew the truth, he was free to live the future that God had planned for him.

God has given you many talents and abilities. To get the most out of them and make the biggest difference in the world, you have to use your gifts for God's glory. Unlock your future by figuring out the message on this combination lock. Just "spin" it to the left (L) or right (R) (starting at the letter *O* at the top), and write the correct letters in the spaces below.

L-4, R-1, L-3, R-5, L-6, R-2,   L-6, R-2, L-8

— — — — — —   — — —.

✝ PRAY

Thank God for setting you free, and tell him that you want to use your life for his glory.

Life's Guidebook Says

Jesus said to the people who believed in him, "You are truly my disciples if you remain faithful to my teachings. And you will know the truth, and the truth will set you free." JOHN 8:31-32

Answer: Follow God.

UNLIKELY HERO

WHY ARE THOSE BULLIES always picking on us? Gideon thought.

He shook in his sandals as he hid in a hole from the powerful Midianites. The Midianites had stolen wheat from the Israelites for seven years. Gideon hoped to keep some grain for himself. As he hid, he tossed pieces of wheat up in the air to separate the grain from the part you can't eat, called chaff. But wheat needs a breeze to blow away the chaff. Breezes don't blow in holes in the ground. Things weren't going well for Gideon.

Suddenly, an angel appeared.

"Mighty warrior, the Lord is with you!" the angel said to Gideon.

Gideon looked around. Nobody else was in the hole, so he figured the angel was talking to him.

"Why is God letting our enemies hurt us?" Gideon asked. "Where is he?"

Then the Lord spoke. "I'm sending you."

"I'm so little, from the weakest family in the whole country," Gideon argued.

"I'll be with you," the Lord said.

Gideon wanted proof to be sure he had heard God. He placed meat and bread on a rock as a gift to God. God sent fire to consume the food.

Gideon asked for more signs. He laid a wool fleece (a sheepskin) on the ground. God let dew wet the fleece but not the ground. The next night God kept the fleece dry and wet the ground. Finally, Gideon fought back his fears. He would trust God to help him stand up to the bullies. God gave Gideon the confidence to be a leader. And God wants you to be a leader today.

WACKY LAUGHS

Knock, knock.
Who's there?
Dew?
Dew who?
Dew drop in and visit!

Q. What did the dew say when it formed on the grass?
A. Nothing, it just dew-dled.

✝ PRAY

Ask God to help you be brave and trust him, even if you don't think you are the bravest, strongest, or biggest guy around.

Life's Guidebook Says

"But Lord," Gideon replied, "how can I rescue Israel? My clan is the weakest in the whole tribe of Manasseh, and I am the least in my entire family!" JUDGES 6:15

AND IT'S GOOD FOR YOU, TOO

THE SMELL OF PEPPERONI fills the air. Pizza day in the school cafeteria is the best! You're handed a slice and step into the milk line. *Hmm. What to drink?* You know your mom would want you to choose plain white milk. But the chocolate milk looks so good. You grab a carton of chocolaty goodness and head over to sit with your friends.

Research shows that 7 out of 10 students choose flavored milk over the plain stuff. Flavored milk does taste better, but it's packed with extra sugar. That can be a bad thing . . . unless you're an elite athlete.

Experts say chocolate milk is one of the best things you can drink after a lot of exercise. The mixture of fats, proteins, and sugars helps your muscles feel better faster. Gatorade and other sports drink companies spend lots of money to say their drinks are best. But medical studies show chocolate milk makes highly trained athletes recover quicker after difficult workouts.

Still don't believe it? Well, US gymnast Aly Raisman, who won two gold medals and a bronze at the 2012 Olympics, says she drank chocolate milk after her workouts in preparation for the Games.

AWESOME ACTIVITY: TASTY CHALLENGE

Chocolate milk tastes great and can be good for you too. Want to know something else that's sweet and good for you? The Bible. The writer of Psalm 119:103 said God's words are sweeter than honey. That may sound strange, but as you read more of the Bible, you'll discover that God's laws and God's love truly make life sweet.

Take this challenge: read Psalm 119:97-104 (Psalm 119 is the longest chapter in the Bible, so if you want a superchallenge, read the whole thing), then do 10 push-ups, 20 sit-ups, ride your bike for 10 minutes, and run around your house or apartment building two times. Reward yourself with a glass of chocolate milk. Just remember not to drink too much.

✝ PRAY

Thank God for giving you the Bible so you can grow closer to him.

Life's Guidebook Says

How sweet your words taste to me; they are sweeter than honey. PSALM 119:103

FLOATING FIRE

WHAT WOULD YOU RATHER SEE: a beautiful rainbow in the sky or a flaming torch floating between two halves of a cut-open animal? One of those images is beautiful and inspiring. The other is just plain disgusting.

But in the first book of the Bible, God shows his faithfulness in keeping his promises by using both a rainbow and a floating torch. While these images may stir up very different mental pictures, the meaning is the same for both—God always comes through.

You probably know the story of the rainbow. After God flooded the earth, he put a rainbow in the sky and promised Noah that he'd never flood everything again. In Genesis 9:14-15, God says, "When I send clouds over the earth, the rainbow will appear in the clouds, and I will remember my covenant with you and with all living creatures. Never again will the floodwaters destroy all life." What a beautiful picture!

The picture isn't quite as beautiful six chapters later when God promised Abram that he'd have as many descendants as there were stars in the sky. Even though Abram was old and didn't have any children, he believed God. Abram sacrificed several animals to God, as was the custom of the time, and then at night he saw "a smoking firepot and a flaming torch pass between the halves of the carcasses" (Genesis 15:17). That floating fire confirmed in Abram's heart that God had truly made a covenant with him. To Abram, it was as beautiful as seeing a rainbow.

EXPERIMENT: HOMEMADE RAINBOW

Since it's too dangerous to play with flaming torches, make this rainbow to remember that God always keeps his promises.

Stuff You Need
- ☞ CD
- ☞ flashlight

Try It
1. Go into a dark room.
2. Hold the CD in one hand and the flashlight in the other.
3. Shine the flashlight at the bottom of the CD. Move it around at different angles (and closer to and farther from the CD), and watch a rainbow appear.

✞ PRAY
Praise God for never breaking his promises.

Life's Guidebook Says
[God said,] "No, I will not break my covenant; I will not take back a single word I said." PSALM 89:34

THAT'S ON FIRE

WHOA, CHECK OUT THAT BUSH. *It's totally on fire!* Moses thought. *But wait, it's not actually burning. I must've been in the sun too long tending these sheep.*

"Baaaa!"

"You're right, Fluffy," Moses said. "I'm going in for a closer look."

As Moses approached the burning bush, he heard the voice of God. "Take off your shoes, Moses. This is holy ground."

Moses couldn't believe it. He hid his face, afraid that one peek at God would kill him.

"I've seen my people suffering," God said to Moses. "I'm sending you to Egypt."

"Goody, when do we leave?" Moses said.

Actually, that's not how Moses replied. Even though God had uniquely prepared him by having him grow up in Pharaoh's palace, Moses was scared to go back to Egypt. "Who am I to go?" Moses said. "I don't talk well. What if they don't listen to me?" Instead of relying on the God of the universe, Moses came up with excuses.

God reminded Moses of his power by turning Moses' staff into a snake and then having Moses' hand look severely diseased and healing it (Exodus 4:2-7). But Moses was still afraid.

"Lord, please! Send anyone else," he said.

But God knew Moses was the right man for the job. He convinced Moses to go. Moses went, and the rest is history.

LIFTOFF LIST

Just like he did for Moses, God has special plans for your life. There are some things that he wants all of his followers to do. Other times God has specific tasks just for you. Put a check mark next to everything you think God wants you to do. Then write in a couple of ideas of where you think God might send you.

___ Tell others about God at school or in a homeschool group.

___ Show God's love by doing yard work for a neighbor.

___ Light a neighbor's bush on fire.

___ Show God honor by looking nice at church.

___ Turn my hockey stick into a snake.

___ Go on a mission trip.

___ _____.

___ _____.

✝ PRAY

Tell God you want to do his will for your life—no excuses.

Life's Guidebook Says

God also said to Moses, "Say this to the people of Israel: Yahweh, the God of your ancestors—the God of Abraham, the God of Isaac, and the God of Jacob—has sent me to you." EXODUS 3:15

LIGHT MY WAY

IF YOU'VE EVER BEEN LOST, then you know how cool it is to have GPS. GPS, or Global Positioning System, can find your location at nearly any spot on the planet. GPS works by tapping into a network of 30 satellites that orbit over 12 miles above the earth. The system was originally created for the military, but now anyone can use it. Your parents might have a GPS system in their cars or on their phones where an electronic voice tells them where to turn. But handheld GPS units can save your life if you're lost in the wilderness. And that's where God's people are in Exodus 13.

They're not exactly lost, but they've just left Egypt and are wandering through the wilderness. The Bible says, "The LORD went ahead of them. He guided them during the day with a pillar of cloud, and he provided light at night with a pillar of fire" (Exodus 13:21). How cool is that? It'd be impossible to get lost! A pillar of fire would never lose its satellite signal or have you miss a turn and then say, "Rerouting . . . rerouting."

If you followed a pillar of fire, you'd always know where to go. And here's the cool thing: with the Holy Spirit in your life and God's Word in your hand, you can know exactly where you should go today.

AWESOME ACTIVITY: GREAT GUIDE

Get a bandanna or other blindfold. Then find a friend, sibling, or parent and have them cover your eyes so you can't see. Have that person guide you from one room to another with just their voice. (Example: "Go forward three steps and stop. Now turn right and walk forward two steps.") See if you can make it without getting hurt. Then put your hand on your guide's shoulder and, without any talking, go where you are led. Take turns guiding each other, and then discuss these questions:

☞ What was easier to follow—instructions by voice or by touch?
☞ What were the challenges of each method?
☞ Was it hard to trust the person guiding you?
☞ How does God guide us?

✞ PRAY

Thank God that you have the Bible and the Holy Spirit to show you where to go.

Life's Guidebook Says
Your word is a lamp to guide my feet and a light for my path. PSALM 119:105

BURNT OFFERINGS

Whoosh!

Fire flashed down from heaven. It burned up all the offerings and sacrifices made to God. Flames wrapped around Temple pillars and flooded hallways and rooms. People could see the flames from miles away.

Were they scared, worried, or upset? Actually, they felt the exact opposite emotion. They were thrilled!

Second Chronicles 7 tells the story of Israel dedicating Solomon's Temple to the Lord. The people had spent seven years constructing the most glorious Temple imaginable. There's no accurate way to estimate how much the Temple cost to build or the wealth it contained. But the Bible tells us it had gold, silver, bronze, precious stones, artwork, and beautiful cedar timbers. The Temple even housed the priceless Ark of the Covenant, which contained the pieces of the Ten Commandments. In today's dollars, the Temple would've been worth billions and billions. The people wanted to give their best to God. So when his presence descended from heaven in the form of fire and filled the Temple, the people fell facedown on the ground and worshiped, saying, "He is good! His faithful love endures forever!" (2 Chronicles 7:3).

The presence of the Lord was so powerful in the Temple that the priests couldn't go inside. The people were so happy that they celebrated for seven days. Now that's a party!

What's the most excited that you've been about God? Write down your response:

_____

_____

QUIZ: WHO SAID IT?

If you can figure out who said one of these famous quotes from the Bible, you can figure out who said them all.

_____ "Fools think their own way is right."

_____ "Cut the living child in two, and give half to one woman and half to the other!"

_____ "As iron sharpens iron, so a friend sharpens a friend."

_____ "Rivers run into the sea, but the sea is never full."

_____ "A triple-braided cord is not easily broken."

✝ PRAY

Thank God for sending his presence so you can experience his love on earth.

Life's Guidebook Says

[Solomon] prayed, "O LORD, God of Israel, there is no God like you in all of heaven and earth. You keep your covenant and show unfailing love to all who walk before you in wholehearted devotion." 2 CHRONICLES 6:14

Answer: King Solomon said them all (see Proverbs 12:15; 1 Kings 3:25; Proverbs 27:17; Ecclesiastes 1:7; 4:12). He is considered one of the wisest men of all time.

SAVED FROM THE FIRE

POLICE INVESTIGATION—600 BC

Detective: What can you tell me about the deaths that occurred here last night?

King Nebuchadnezzar: I can tell you one thing—the wrong guys died.

Detective: So you admit that you intended to kill someone?

King: Of course. I'm the king—my word is law, and my law was broken. I decreed that when the music played, everybody had to bow down and worship the golden statue.

Detective: That seems like a weird law.

King: Well, it seemed like a good idea at the time.

Detective: So what happened if somebody didn't bow?

King: They'd be thrown into the fiery furnace.

Detective: That seems kind of harsh.

King: I am the king.

Detective: Good point. So what happened?

King: Shadrach, Meshach, and Abednego refused to bow. I really liked those guys. But they said they would worship only the one true God.

Detective: What did you do?

King: I got mad! I had the furnace heated seven times hotter than normal.

Detective: It seems like you have some anger management issues. But certainly those guys were toast. Case closed.

King: That's what I thought. But when my strongest soldiers threw Shadrach, Meshach, and Abednego into the furnace, fire consumed my men and yet *they* were unharmed.

Detective: Say what?

King: Shadrach, Meshach, and Abednego walked around in the furnace like they were at the beach. Then I saw a *fourth* man with them. And he looked like a god.

Detective: Sounds like you've had a rough night. I'm just going to mark this one down as "miracle" and try to forget the whole thing.

King: Thanks, Detective.

WACKY LAUGHS

Q. If King Nebuchadnezzar was a dog, what would he build?

A. A roaring bone-fire

Q. Why do ducks have webbed feet?

A. To stomp out fires

Q. Why do elephants have round feet?

A. To stomp out flaming ducks

Q. What food never gets hot?

A. Chili

✝ PRAY

Praise God that he has the power to save us from anything, even fiery situations.

Life's Guidebook Says

"Look!" Nebuchadnezzar shouted. "I see four men, unbound, walking around in the fire unharmed! And the fourth looks like a god!" DANIEL 3:25

WATCH YOUR TONGUE

Go to a mirror and stick out your tongue. *How rude!* Now keep it stuck out and move it around. Can you touch your nose with your tongue? Try it. Studies show about one out of 10 people can. As you try, look at the underside of your tongue. It's kind of gross, with purple veins and stringy, hanging stuff.

But do you know what can be grosser than the underside of your tongue? The words that your tongue forms. Just check out this conversation:

Brent: I heard you were like Beethoven on the math test.

Jeremy: What do you mean? Beethoven did music, not math.

Brent: Yeah, but you were *dumb, dumb, dumb, dummmmb*.

Mark: *Ohh*, burn!

There's a reason some people say "burn" after a hurtful comment. That's because words hurt, even burn.

The Bible says the tongue is a flame that can set your whole life on fire (see today's verse). James 3:4-5 compares the tongue to the rudder of a ship. The rudder may be small, but it steers the whole ship. In the same way, your tongue is small but steers your life.

Go back to the mirror and stick out your tongue again. This time grab the tip of it and say, "I'm not going to let you burn the people around me." You may sound silly, and that's okay. It's better to sound silly than talk mean.

WEIRD FACTS: TERRIFIC TONGUE

☞ Most people have around 10,000 taste buds on their tongue.

☞ You taste sweetness on the tip of your tongue, while bitter things are sensed more in the back of the tongue.

☞ The blue whale has the largest tongue in the world, weighing 5,400 pounds— that's as much as a midsize car!

☞ The tube-lipped nectar bat has the longest tongue of any animal, compared to its size. The bat is about 2.5 inches long, but its tongue is 3.5 inches long. If your tongue were like this bat's and you were four feet tall, your tongue would be nearly six feet long.

☦ PRAY

Tell God you want to be a fireman and put out the fire in your mouth.

Life's Guidebook Says

The tongue is a flame of fire. It is a whole world of wickedness, corrupting your entire body. It can set your whole life on fire. JAMES 3:6

READY? FIRE!

WHAT'S THE BEST PART about going camping? If you asked 10 boys, 8 of them might say, "The campfire." Imagine yourself sitting in front of a campfire. You see the flames curl around the logs. You hear the crackling of the wood. You smell the smoky scent. Maybe you even taste the s'mores. *Yum!*

As fire consumes the logs, it creates both light and heat. For thousands of years, people have used fire to cook food, warm their homes, and light up the night. Fire has played an important role in all of human history. Fire also plays a key part in your life as a Christian.

Starting all the way back in Deuteronomy 4:24, God is called a "devouring fire." Scientists who study fire have discovered that it's a self-perpetuating chemical reaction. To put that in understandable terms, the heat from fire helps the flame continue to burn as long as there's enough fuel (wood) and oxygen (air).

Think about your relationship with Christ. What fuels it? Maybe it's hanging out with other Christians, listening to Christian music, or doing daily devotions. What breathes life into your faith? Maybe it's seeing God answer prayers or feeling connected to him as you sing worship songs. Make sure you're fueling your fire and providing it with air, so God can totally consume your life.

AWESOME ACTIVITY: COLOR TEST

Have you memorized all the colors of a rainbow? A lot of kids do it by remembering the acronym ROY G. BIV (Red, Orange, Yellow, Green, Blue, Indigo, Violet). The next time you see a rainbow, check and see if that's correct.

And the next time you're near a fire, look at the different colors of the flame. White is usually closest to the source, and it's the hottest. Then come yellow, orange, and finally red. If you ever see blue flame, it's even hotter than white.

Come up with your own sentence where the first letter of each word stands for the colors of flame from hottest to least hot. How about "Boys with young orangutans rock" (blue, white, yellow, orange, red)? Now write your own:

_____

✝ PRAY

Ask God to help fuel your fire for him.

Life's Guidebook Says
Since we are receiving a kingdom that cannot be shaken, let us hold on to grace. By it, we may serve God acceptably, with reverence and awe, for our God is a consuming fire. HEBREWS 12:28-29, HCSB

SWIFTER THAN HORSES

HAVE YOU EVER TRIED to outrun a cat or dog? It's nearly impossible. They run fast. You could never beat them in a short race, but maybe you could win if you raced for a mile. Horses gallop even faster and take longer to get tired. *Yee-haw!* Yet the Bible tells a cool story about how the prophet Elijah easily outran a horse-drawn chariot in a storm.

Three years before this famous race, Elijah had told wicked King Ahab that no rain or dew would wet the ground until Elijah spoke the words for the rain to return. God used the drought to let Ahab know that he was judging Ahab's wicked ways (1 Kings 17:1).

After three years without a drop of rain, crops withered and the land dried up. God told Elijah that he planned to send rain. Elijah sent a message to Ahab to meet with him. A puny cloud that looked like a fluffy cotton ball formed over the sea. It certainly didn't look like a rain cloud, but Elijah told the king to hurry and get back to the city of Jezreel before the big storm started. Suddenly the sky grew dark, the winds blew, and a heavy rain drenched the land.

Elijah sprinted past Ahab's chariot and reached the city first. He had super-powered running ability that day, outrunning a horse in a race that lasted more than 15 miles! (You can read all about it in 1 Kings 18:41-46, NIrv.) God gave Elijah the power to run faster than horses and the storm. God can give you all the power you need.

WACKY LAUGHS

Q. Why did the ballerina stop running?

A. Because she was tutu slow.

Q. Why do barbers win races?

A. They know the shortcuts.

Q. Who won the online race?

A. The e-raser

✝ PRAY

Ask God to give you awesome power when you need it.

Life's Guidebook Says

The LORD gave special strength to Elijah. He tucked his cloak into his belt and ran ahead of Ahab's chariot all the way to the entrance of Jezreel. 1 KINGS 18:46

WISE COACH

"STAY STRONG!" "PACE YOURSELF." "Keep your eye on the goal."

Coaches give advice on exercise, mental focus, and even diet to help athletes win. The apostle Paul gave advice to runners. In 1 Corinthians 9:24-26, he wrote that he had trained his body and brought it under control. Racers should do the same. He said racers should run to win by keeping their eyes on the goal.

Athletes can get distracted if they watch other players, listen to the crowd, or even worry about the weather or an upcoming test. They need to stay focused on the game and their performance.

Athletes need to remember a number of rules and strategies to do their best. For example, did you know soda and sugary beverages can weaken an athlete, while water hydrates athletes and keeps their blood cells working at their peak?

Paul may have written about runners, but he was more concerned about people using the same concepts to think about heaven. He said the heavenly prize is a crown that doesn't break or rust. It's imperishable, and everyone can be a winner. But you need to keep your eyes fixed on God and stay spiritually fit.

LIFTOFF LIST

Check off what you do to stay spiritually fit and physically fit.

__ I exercise at least three times a week.
__ I play a sport.
__ I go to youth group or Sunday school.
__ I read my Bible.
__ I eat healthy most of the time.
__ I get plenty of sleep.
__ I keep my eyes on God and not on temptations.
__ I talk to God.
__ I have good friends who also follow Jesus.

✝ PRAY

Ask God to help you stay focused on him and make friends with other Christians.

Life's Guidebook Says
Don't you realize that in a race everyone runs, but only one person gets the prize? So run to win! 1 CORINTHIANS 9:24

AMAZING RUN

THE MARATHON DES SABLES is ranked by many experts as the most difficult footrace in the world. What else would you call a six-day run across the Moroccan Sahara desert? Runners must carry supplies on their backs, including sleeping gear, food, a flashlight, and even antivenin in case of snakebites. *Yikes!* A race is hard enough without possibly encountering poisonous snakes. Only water and a place to sleep in a tent are provided to runners. Temperatures can reach more than 120 degrees Fahrenheit. Since the beginning of the race in 1986, more than 12,000 runners have participated. Two helicopters monitor the race and pick up runners in distress. Runners trek up rolling sand dunes, facing unexpected windstorms and dehydration from the hot sun, but they willingly confront these challenges to test their endurance and toughness.

Think about how it feels when you run at your top speed. You plow into the wind and feel the breeze against your chest. Your heart starts pounding, but you lift your legs and continue. Running feels good. At some point you tire and have to stop to catch your breath. On a long race, you might wonder if you'll ever reach the finish line as your legs start to feel heavier and breathing gets harder.

Imagine running and never getting tired. The prophet Isaiah said that one day we will run without tiring. We will soar like eagles. Distance will not be a problem, even if that's running more than 150 miles through a desert!

PLEXER

Solve this puzzle as a reminder of what God can do to help you be a winner. (If you don't remember what a plexer is, see p. 9.)

New new UR strength

PRAY

Ask God to give you strength for sports and other activities.

Life's Guidebook Says

Those who trust in the LORD will find new strength. They will soar high on wings like eagles. They will run and not grow weary. They will walk and not faint. ISAIAH 40:31

Answer: Renew your strength.

RUNNING AWAY

"No," Michael said.

"Come on," Josh said. "One time's not going to hurt you. It'll just make you feel weird."

"Don't you like to have fun?" Edward added.

"I *do* like to have fun," Michael said. "But drugs aren't fun. They're dangerous."

"Let's get out of here," Josh said to Edward. "He's a loser."

Michael stopped hanging out with those friends. He was lonely for a while, but he made new friends, grew up, and served in the air force. He felt sad for his old friends, who continued making bad choices and wasted their lives using drugs.

Sometimes running away from trouble is the best choice. That's what the Bible shows us. And that's what Joseph did in the Old Testament. He had been taken to Egypt and forced to work for Potiphar. One day his boss's wife wanted him to do something wrong, but Joseph refused to sin against God. She grabbed his coat as he rushed off. Joseph ended up in trouble with his boss, but it was not his fault. Potiphar's wife lied to make her husband angry, and Potiphar tossed Joseph into prison (Genesis 39:19-20). Joseph didn't give a list of excuses—just accepted the punishment.

Years later, God allowed Joseph to be released from prison, and Joseph ended up in a great place with lots of money and power. God had better plans for Joseph than Joseph could have dreamed of, even though he went through years of difficulties and problems first.

Sometimes we have to turn from trouble and run. We can trust God to be with us and bring new friends and better situations into our lives.

LIFTOFF LIST

Check off the temptations you run from. Then pray about the things that tempt you and are harder to run from.

____ Cheating on tests

____ Cheating in games

____ Bad language

____ Teasing a friend or sibling

____ Disobeying parents

____ Using drugs

____ Spending too much time playing video games

____ Being lazy

____ Telling "little white lies" or stretching the truth

✝ PRAY

Ask God to give you wisdom to run from evil.

Life's Guidebook Says

Run from all these evil things. Pursue righteousness and a godly life, along with faith, love, perseverance, and gentleness. 1 TIMOTHY 6:11

RACE TO THE TOMB

PETER GLANCED OVER HIS SHOULDER. He was beating John! Both of Jesus' disciples were breathing hard as John pulled even with Peter and they ran neck and neck. Then, with a burst of energy, John sped ahead and dashed to the entrance of the tomb. John stopped and stared inside the tomb at the empty linen wrappings that had once covered Jesus. Peter caught up and ran inside the tomb first. John followed Peter. They looked around. Until then they hadn't understood that Jesus must rise from the dead, but now they believed. Then they both turned and left for their own homes without saying a word.

That may seem like a strange race, but it was the most unusual and eventful day in history. Jesus rose from the grave on Easter morning. The linens and empty tomb provided clues about what happened. The first clue had come earlier, when Mary Magdalene had told the disciples about the empty tomb. Peter and John ran to check it out for themselves.

Later that evening Jesus entered the room where John, Peter, and other disciples had gathered. The door to the room was locked, but Jesus simply appeared. This time all of Jesus' followers rejoiced because they saw the living Christ and believed he had risen from the dead. Jesus told them that he was sending them to tell others about him. There were a lot more races left to run!

AWESOME ACTIVITY: AMAZING MOVING FEAT OF FEET

Enjoy racing cardboard feet on a string.

Stuff You Need
- ☞ Index cards
- ☞ Scissors
- ☞ Pen
- ☞ String
- ☞ Chair with legs

Try It
1. Cut out leg and foot shapes from index cards.
2. Poke a hole in the middle of the leg with your scissors.
3. Run a long string through the hole, from back to front. Make sure the cardboard leg can slide on the string.
4. Tie the back end of the string to a chair leg, letting the foot touch the floor.
5. Tug on the front of the string. Bounce it up and down to get the foot to move forward toward your hand.
6. Have a friend make one and tie it to the next chair leg so you can have a footrace.

✞ PRAY

Ask God to help you think deeply about what you read in God's Word and help you believe what you read.

Life's Guidebook Says
[Jesus] said, "Peace be with you. As the Father has sent me, so I am sending you." JOHN 20:21

SECRET RUNNING CODE

THE FOOTBALL COACH SIGNALED to his quarterback. The quarterback quickly called a play as the players changed formation. *Hut, hut, hike!* The quarterback took the ball, dropped back, and threw a perfect pass. The receiver knew right where to be, so he caught the ball and scored a touchdown. The team won the game!

Signals make a big difference in football. Signals can also be the difference between life and death. Obeying traffic signals saves lives. The military uses signals as part of its strategy.

In the Old Testament, Jonathan and David used an unusual signal. Jonathan practiced his archery skills and could easily hit a target. He knew his dad, King Saul, hated his best friend, David, and wanted David dead. It's superhard when there's a problem between your dad and your pal. You want your friends to like your parents and enjoy hanging out with them, and vice versa. That's what Jonathan wanted.

Jonathan told David that if he shot arrows and told his helper to go pick them up close by, it meant that David was safe and could come out of hiding. If Jonathan shot arrows far away and told the helper the arrows were beyond him, it would mean David needed to run far away (1 Samuel 20:20-22). Jonathan's dad stayed angry, so Jonathan shot the arrows past the target to let David know to run away.

Look for God's signals. He may use his Word or one of your close friends to help you.

PUZZLE IT OUT: SECRET MAZE CODE

Starting at the number one and going to 13, find words that match each number in order to form a message. The answer gives a good tip on how to prepare for a race.

1 Two	2 to	3 three	4 plus	5 shoes
2 to	4 days	5 water	5 drink	6 to
3 three	4 days	5 before	6 from	7 of
4 cups	5 a	6 a	7 race	8 drink
5 of	7 drink	7 water	8 sleep	9 lots
6 water	7 of	10 of	11 water	10 of
9 before	12 to	13 hydrate	12 to	13 sleep

✝ PRAY

Thank God for good friends who help keep you safe.

Life's Guidebook Says

Where there is no guidance, a people falls, but in an abundance of counselors there is safety. PROVERBS 11:14, ESV

Answer: Two to three days before a race drink lots of water to hydrate.

REASON TO CELEBRATE

WHAT'S YOUR FAVORITE HOLIDAY? The reasons we celebrate different holidays are pretty obvious. Christmas honors Jesus Christ's birth. Easter remembers his death. Valentine's Day celebrates love . . . and chocolate. Presidents' Day honors great past presidents. And Independence Day commemorates the signing of the Declaration of Independence, which declared the United States free from England.

Many cultures celebrate different holidays—for instance, Presidents' Day isn't a big deal in Canada. Every year around this time, Jewish people celebrate Purim. You can read all about how this festival began in the book of Esther. After Haman's evil plot was defeated and the Jews were saved, Mordecai (that's Esther's cousin) told the people "to celebrate these days with feasting and gladness and by giving gifts of food to each other and presents to the poor. This would commemorate a time when the Jews gained relief from their enemies, when their sorrow was turned into gladness and their mourning into joy" (Esther 9:22). Today, the most important event at Purim is the reading of the book of Esther. People hiss and boo every time Haman's name is read. They send gifts to charity and eat a big meal. Many families also make special triangle-shaped cookies called *hamantaschen*, which are filled with delicious fruit jelly.

Aren't you glad God turns your sorrow into gladness? Next time you feel down, celebrate that you serve an awesome God who saves his people.

WACKY LAUGHS

Q. What did the porcupine say at the party?

A. "I look sharp!"

Q. What do you get when a cow and a duck throw a party together?

A. Milk and quackers.

Q. Why did the banana go to the party with a prune?

A. It couldn't find a date.

✟ PRAY

Thank God for turning your mourning into joy. Tell him that you're going to find your joy in him.

Life's Guidebook Says

[Mordecai told the Jews] to celebrate these days with feasting and gladness and by giving gifts of food to each other and presents to the poor. This would commemorate a time when the Jews gained relief from their enemies, when their sorrow was turned into gladness and their mourning into joy. ESTHER 9:22

THE RACE OF YOUR LIFE

Tiffany Williams could run fast and jump high. She started running the hurdles at age 12, and became one of the top hurdlers in the United States. In 2007 and 2008, she won the US National Championships and even qualified to take part in the 2008 Summer Olympics in China. But things didn't go the way she hoped. She advanced through the early rounds and made it to the finals. But just before the race, Tiffany tore a hamstring muscle. She competed in the finals but couldn't run her normal time She crossed the finish line in last place as the world's eighth fastest hurdler—a setback that would crush many athletes. But Tiffany doesn't define herself by wins and losses; she is a Christian and knows God loves her no matter what. The most important race she runs is the daily one of living to honor Christ. She led youth choir and a Bible study as a teen. And she believes in raising her children to follow Jesus.

While Tiffany was training to make the Olympics, her commitment and perseverance showed as she ran and exercised every day for hours. It also helped that she belonged to an athletic club, which included champion runners and jumpers. The friendships and the challenge of running with others helped her improve and do her best.

Achieving the plans God has for us also takes commitment and perseverance. You may have to do chores, homework, tests, and sports or club activities. Sometimes it can be hard to keep up and still make time for prayer and devotions. It may help to know many other Christians have had the same problem. Make sure you study about past great believers and surround yourself with Christian friends, because they will help you stick close to God.

AWESOME ACTIVITY: RUNNING FASTER

Try these tips and exercises to improve the speed of your feet:

- ☞ Don't lean back while you run.
- ☞ Practice breathing to help your endurance. Oxygen powers your blood and body. Breathe in and out fast, 30 seconds at a time.
- ☞ Keep your form. Hold your body straight. Don't rock your head or swing your arms sideways or sway from side to side.
- ☞ If you want to try hurdles, start by jumping over boxes and leading with one leg.
- ☞ Relax your upper body. Avoid making fists or tightening your hands.
- ☞ Build your endurance by running easy for 5 minutes. Then speed up for 10 to 15 minutes. End with a slower pace to cool down for the last 5 or 10 minutes.

✝ PRAY

Ask God to help you prepare well before playing sports or racing.

Life's Guidebook Says

Since we are surrounded by such a huge crowd of witnesses to the life of faith, let us strip off every weight that slows us down, especially the sin that so easily trips us up. And let us run with endurance the race God has set before us.
HEBREWS 12:1

TWISTED WORDS

FLICK, FLICK! A snake constantly flicks its tongue in and out of its mouth. It might seem weird to you that snakes slither around tasting dirt. But snakes don't taste with their tongues; they smell with them. A snake's forked tongue collects airborne particles and pulls them into its mouth, where special organs sense what's around. The forked part helps a snake determine what direction the scent is coming from.

Snakes aren't the only animals with talented tongues. A chameleon's tongue can be twice as long as a chameleon's body and shoots out of its mouth faster than your eye can see. The tip of its tongue is covered in mucus that sticks to a bug and pulls it into the chameleon's mouth. A giant anteater's tongue can be two feet long! It also is covered with sticky saliva that traps ants.

Have you ever been licked by a cat? Their rough tongues are covered with backward-facing hooks called *papillae*. These hooks make a cat's fur look *purr*fect when it has been licked clean.

Our tongues tend to have the opposite effect—they make us dirty. Our tongues lie, make excuses, blame others, call people names, and say curse words. The Bible says our words can be as deadly as a serpent.

Twisting the truth and blaming others are not good choices. Don't let your tongue become poisonous. Think before you speak. Stop before you utter words that might hurt someone.

TWISTY TONGUE TWISTERS

Try to say these tongue twisters 10 times without stopping.

A sneaky slithering snake schemes, spinning sly sinful speeches.
Truthful thoughts topple untruthful tales.
A curious calico cat licked cream from a can.

✝ PRAY

Ask God for wisdom to think before you speak and to have your words be helpful—not harmful.

Life's Guidebook Says

Their tongues are as deadly as the tongue of a serpent. The words from their lips are like the poison of a snake. PSALM 140:3, NIrV

SNAKEBIT!

CRASH! Strong winds tore apart the boat. *Splash!* Huge waves knocked men overboard. The apostle Paul, his friend Luke, sailors, and guards all ended up fighting for their lives in the sea. But just as God had promised them, they all made it safely to the small island of Malta after the shipwreck. The people who lived there built a fire and treated the men kindly. Paul went to put more wood on the fire. Suddenly, a poisonous snake shot out of the wood and bit Paul on the hand. Everybody waited for him to die, but nothing happened. *Whoa!* Now the people on Malta wanted to know more about Paul. They thought he might be a god.

Luke goes on to write, in Acts 28, that the people took Paul to the island's leader. Paul prayed for the leader's sick father. God healed him. The news spread and more people came to Paul for healing. He prayed, and God healed them all.

Paul didn't worry about his situation, whether he was on a sinking ship or being bitten by a snake. He always trusted God. And he let his actions show his faith.

WEIRD FACTS: SNAKE STATS

☞ A herpetologist is someone who studies reptiles.

☞ The world's longest snake, a reticulated python, can grow nearly 33 feet long.

☞ The fastest snake in the world is the black mamba. It can slither along at 14.9 miles per hour.

☞ The carpet viper has killed more people than any other snake in the world. It lives anywhere from West Africa to India.

☞ The hognose snake and the spitting cobra fool enemies with bad breath. They flip upside down and play dead. Then they stick out their tongues to give off a foul smell.

☞ Cobras dance to music even though they can't hear. They feel the vibrations.

✝ PRAY

Ask God to help you trust him regardless of your situation. Pray that your actions show your faith.

Life's Guidebook Says

As Paul gathered an armful of sticks and was laying them on the fire, a poisonous snake, driven out by the heat, bit him on the hand. . . . But Paul shook off the snake into the fire and was unharmed. ACTS 28:3, 5

STAFF OF POWER

"NOTHING UP MY SLEEVE," the magician said with a flourish of his arms. "Presto!"

Magicians often divert people's attention by moving their hands so the audience will look away from what is really happening. That way they can make things look like they've appeared, disappeared, or changed by magic. When Moses came back to Egypt, Pharaoh thought he had learned some magic tricks. Moses' brother, Aaron, grabbed his long walking stick, called a staff, to show Pharaoh that God had sent him. God turned the staff into a snake. Pharaoh called his magicians and had them do the same trick. *Ha!* Their staffs turned into snakes too. His magicians were as good as God's man.

Wrong! Aaron's snake-staff slithered over and swallowed up the other snakes. Moses wasn't doing a slick trick. God knew that the Egyptians worshiped snakes. Pharaoh wore a headpiece that included a golden snake spitting venom at its enemies to represent his power. This test with snakes was really to teach Pharaoh to wise up and realize his power would never match God's power.

Stubborn Pharaoh didn't learn this lesson. He and his people would have to suffer through some terrible plagues before he would admit that God was more powerful than the gods of the Egyptians.

EXPERIMENT: SLIMY SNAKE SNACKS

Transform some snack foods into a sweet snake treat.

Stuff You Need
- ☞ Oreo cookies
- ☞ Plastic sandwich bag
- ☞ Hammer or rolling pin
- ☞ Paper cup for each snack
- ☞ Gummy worms, or cut out worms from fruit roll snacks

Try It
1. Place cookies in sandwich bag. Seal securely.
2. Use the hammer or the rolling pin to crush the cookies.
3. Place crushed cookies in cup. Stir in "worms." Now you have snakes in a cup of dirt.

Make some to share with friends or family!

✝ PRAY
Ask God to help you not be stubborn and be able to see his truth and power.

Life's Guidebook Says
[Pharoah's magicians] threw down their staffs, which also became serpents! But then Aaron's staff swallowed up their staffs. EXODUS 7:12

WHAT A FEAST!

DOES YOUR FAMILY SIT DOWN for a special meal at Easter? What's your favorite food to eat? Check everything you like, and then circle your favorite.

__ Ham	__ Jell-O salad	__ Sweet potatoes
__ Turkey	__ Rolls	__ Gravy
__ Mashed potatoes	__ Olives	__ Peeps
__ Green bean casserole	__ Hard-boiled eggs	__ Chocolate eggs

Easter is the perfect time to get together and feast with your family. Just before Jesus went to the cross, he had a big dinner with his disciples. You've probably heard it called the Last Supper. Jesus and his friends went to an upper room and ate the Passover meal together.

After the meal, Jesus said and did some things that might have seemed strange to the disciples. First, he broke some bread and told his friends that his body would be broken for them. Then he took some wine and said his blood would be poured out as a sacrifice for them. Finally, he said that somebody sitting around the table would betray him.

Jesus would do anything for his friends—even friends who would betray him. His sacrifice was for all people who believe in him. As Jesus' friends, we sometimes mess up. But he always forgives and has prepared a place for us with him in heaven. And when we get to his Kingdom, there will be plenty of eating and drinking (Luke 22:29-30).

PUZZLE IT OUT: *MMM*, FOOD
See if you can find all these foods mentioned in the Bible. Look up, down, across, diagonally, and backward.

C	G	F	I	G	S	S	H
H	B	R	E	A	D	N	O
E	N	Y	A	N	B	I	L
E	O	Z	O	P	V	S	I
S	H	M	L	Q	E	I	V
E	L	F	I	S	H	A	E
A	L	I	A	U	Q	R	S

Figs
Olives
Bread
Fish
Quail
Cheese
Grape
Raisins

✝ PRAY
Praise Jesus that he came as a sacrifice for everybody who believes.

Life's Guidebook Says
Just as my Father has granted me a Kingdom, I now grant you the right to eat and drink at my table in my Kingdom. LUKE 22:29-30

· IT'S NO RIOT

IT'S EASY FOR LARGE GROUPS of people to get out of control. Maybe you've seen videos of Black Friday sales on the day after Thanksgiving as people rioted to rush through doors and get a good deal on a TV.

There weren't any TVs when Jesus walked the earth, but his trial almost caused a riot. After the Jewish leaders condemned Jesus to die, he went before the Roman governor, Pontius Pilate. As Pilate sat on the judgment seat, his wife sent him an urgent message: "Leave that innocent man alone. I suffered through a terrible nightmare about him last night" (Matthew 27:19). Pilate wanted to let Jesus go, but the crowds demanded his death.

"What crime has he committed?" Pilate shouted.

The crowd ignored him and shouted even louder, "Crucify him!"

Before the mob of angry people could turn into a riot, Pilate washed his hands to demonstrate that he was "innocent of this man's blood." Then he turned Jesus over to Roman soldiers to be flogged and killed.

Do you think Pilate's actions were right? He was both right and wrong. He was right that Jesus was innocent of the charges brought against him. But he was wrong that he was innocent of Jesus' death. God's Son died because of our sin. So in reality, we're all responsible for his death on the cross.

QUIZ: AT THE CROSS

How much do you know about Jesus Christ's death and resurrection? (Answers are found in Matthew 27–28.)

1. When soldiers mocked and beat Jesus, they put a crown of _____ on his head.
2. Who did soldiers force to carry Jesus' cross when he became too weak?
3. Jesus told his followers that he'd rise from the dead in _____ days.
4. On what day of the week did Jesus rise from the dead?
5. What was the angel sitting on when the two women came to Jesus' empty tomb?

✝ PRAY

As you celebrate Easter this year, thank God for dying for your sins.

Life's Guidebook Says

As Pilate was sitting on the judgment seat, his wife sent him this message: "Leave that innocent man alone. I suffered through a terrible nightmare about him last night." MATTHEW 27:19

Answers: 1. thorns; 2. Simon of Cyrene; 3. three; 4. Sunday; 5. the stone

HEALED BY A SNAKE

PIT VIPERS ARE AMONG the most dangerous snakes in the world. Their fangs are like needles. If one bites you on the arm and injects its venom, you will almost immediately start to feel a burning sensation. Soon your arm will begin to swell. Eventually, the venom will affect your heart, which will beat more slowly.

Vipers bite more people than any other venomous snake, so many antivenins were created to help people survive snakebites. But do you want to hear something even more cool? Forty years ago, scientists figured out they could use pit viper venom to make blood pressure medication.

People have been using venom-based cures since before Jesus walked the earth. Today, scientists study venoms and how they are formed to find new ways to treat diseases. One study found that venom from copperhead snakes may help stop the growth of cancer tumors. Research at the Mayo Clinic in Minnesota uses venom from the mamba snake to find ways to help people who have heart attacks.

In Old Testament times, people didn't have a lot of antivenom. But God sent a special instant healing to save the Israelites from deadly snakebites. He had Moses make a bronze snake and stick it on a pole. One look at it and the bitten person lived. That's a fast cure with no needles or time in a hospital! God made the snakes, venom and all, so he knows how to cure people of snakebites and knew that one day we'd find a way to put venom to good use.

PLEXER

Solve this plexer to find out the name of a poisonous creature. (If you don't remember what a plexer is, see p. 9.)

```
CO
 P  P
 ER
  S
   N
    A
     K
   E
```

☦ PRAY

Ask God to help scientists find new cures to help people with heart problems or cancer.

Life's Guidebook Says

Moses made a snake out of bronze and attached it to a pole. Then anyone who was bitten by a snake could look at the bronze snake and be healed!
NUMBERS 21:9

Answer: Copperhead snake

SLIPPERY WONDER

HAVE YOU EVER WATCHED a snake glide over a rock or up a cliff? It has no arms or legs to grab on to a slippery surface, so you might think it would just slide off. But some snakes can even climb trees. That seems amazing, because we can't see how they pull themselves up or move.

King Solomon is known as the wisest man who ever lived. He wrote that one of the mysteries he didn't understand was how a snake moves on a smooth rock (see today's verse). Solomon wrote that 900 years before Jesus was born. And it's taken a long time for scientists to figure out how snakes move.

Snakes' muscles run the whole length of the snakes' bodies. When they shift their weight, they can move their bodies backward, forward, or sideways. That's called slithering. Their bodies can also flex left and right, which helps them swim. This is called undulation. They also use sidewinding, a type of rolling, by keeping part of their bodies in touch with the ground while they lift up other parts of their bodies. There is also a movement called rectilinear locomotion, in which snakes lift their scales and move them forward to pull their bodies along.

God created many amazing creatures and gave them different abilities to move. Three out of the four things Solomon didn't understand deal with motion. He was amazed by slithering snakes, gliding eagles, and sailing ships. But the love between a man and a woman also was beyond his comprehension. Think about those four things today.

WACKY LAUGHS

Q. What's so good about snakes?
A. They have poison-ality.

Q. What did the boa constrictor say to its prey?
A. "You're my latest crush!"

✝ PRAY

Thank God for making snakes and other creatures. Thank him also for the beautiful love between a man and a woman that one day you'll share with your wife.

Life's Guidebook Says

There are three things that amaze me—no, four things that I don't understand: how an eagle glides through the sky, how a snake slithers on a rock, how a ship navigates the ocean, how a man loves a woman. PROVERBS 30:18-19

STRONGER THAN CHAINS

HIGH IN THE SKY on a cloudless afternoon in August 2013, several men pushed a coffin with a man inside—a live man—out of an airplane. While falling almost three miles through the air, escape artist Anthony Martin worked to free himself from handcuffs, a chain, and the locked coffin. Two parachutes kept the coffin balanced while a large crowd watched the skydiving feat from the ground.

Anthony worked fast to undo the handcuffs, escape the chains, and get out of the box before crashing into the ground. Once freed, he opened his parachute and glided effortlessly to the earth in front of a cheering audience. Anthony didn't do this stunt just for the fun of it. He'd been practicing picking locks since he was six. He could escape handcuffs at age 10. He has performed numerous dangerous escapes over the years, including escaping from cages under freezing water. But Anthony doesn't just want to entertain people, he wants to see them saved. He uses his daring escapes to explain how Jesus helps us escape from death and gives us eternal life.

Jesus was no magician. He was God's Son. He amazed people after he died by rising from the dead. The disciples discovered that chains, locks, and doors were not strong enough to keep Jesus out. A week after Jesus rose from the grave, he appeared in a room with a locked door. *Poof!* He stood in the middle of a group of his friends. He didn't need to open the door or walk through the wall. No matter where you are, you can be sure if you call on Jesus that he'll be right there with you, too.

TWISTY TONGUE TWISTERS

Try to say these tongue twisters 10 times without stopping.

God's carefully chosen guys cheer.
Chains cannot contain Christ.

PRAY

Thank Jesus for saving you from death and giving you eternal life in heaven.

Life's Guidebook Says

Eight days later the disciples were together again, and this time Thomas was with them. The doors were locked; but suddenly, as before, Jesus was standing among them. "Peace be with you," he said. JOHN 20:26

STRONG HAIR

No haircut for that boy! An angel of the Lord told Samson's mother that she would have a special son. He would be very strong, and God would use him to be a special helper for the Israelites. But he must never get his hair cut, shave, or drink alcohol. The hair part sounds pretty weird, but Samson made a bold fashion statement wherever he went.

His actions were also bold. God used Samson to fight the Philistines. Ropes couldn't hold him. Neither could city gates. Once the people in the town of Gaza planned to kill him, but Samson lifted the city gates—poles and all—and carried them to the top of a hill.

Samson was strong, but he had a weakness for women. He made bad choices when it came to women, including getting involved with one named Delilah.

The Philistines paid Delilah to find out the source of Samson's strength so they would have a chance at beating him. Once Delilah discovered Samson's hair was the root of his strength, she lulled him to sleep and had his head shaved. Then the Philistines poked out Samson's eyes and chained him to the pillars of their stronghold, a temple.

Samson was surrounded by more than 3,000 people mocking him. He prayed for God to give him super strength just one more time. He realized his strength came from God—not his hair. Samson pushed apart the pillars of the temple and toppled the building. He wiped out more enemies than ever before. He died doing it, but he taught the enemy a lesson: God gives people strength when they need it.

WEIRD FACTS: FEATS OF STRENGTH

☞ Rhinoceros beetles can carry 850 times their own weight. For their size, they are one of the strongest creatures God created.

☞ The African crowned eagle can fly while carrying four times its own weight.

☞ Exercise makes a heart strong, while sitting too much makes a heart weak.

☞ Scientists think they have found a bacteria that makes the world's strongest glue—and it's made from sugar molecules! The bacterium *Caulobacter crescentus* makes a sticky substance that works underwater.

✝ PRAY

Ask God to give you strength and also wisdom to use your strength wisely.

Life's Guidebook Says
Samson shared his secret with [Delilah]. "My hair has never been cut," he confessed, "for I was dedicated to God as a Nazirite from birth. If my head were shaved, my strength would leave me, and I would become as weak as anyone else." JUDGES 16:17

POWERFUL DRONE FORCE

BUZZ! ZAP! Modern-day drone airplanes whirl through the sky and strike enemy forces with unexpected power.

When God's people went into the Promised Land, there was nothing like today's high-tech drone strike force. Instead God used actual drones to win battles for his people. Male bees and hornets are called drones, and God used these tiny dive-bombers to attack the enemy. Swarms of hornets charged from the sky and stung the Israelites' enemies (Joshua 24:12, NIV84).

While God provided firepower from the air, Joshua led his people from the ground. Joshua wasn't your typical leader; he was born a slave and then helped Moses for 40 years. Also, the Israelites had no time to build weapons. God gave them unusual weapons like a swarm of hornets or horns whose blasts could break down walls. Not normal battle strategies, but God's way showed the people their victories were not due to their own strength or weapons.

God's first words to Joshua were, "Be strong and courageous" (Deuteronomy 31:23). He told Joshua to obey his commands. God promised to be with Joshua wherever he went. That great pep talk let Joshua know he could count on God's help.

Joshua led the army and won many battles as he relied on God's strength.

LIFTOFF LIST

Strength is more than muscle power. For example, it takes strength of character to keep trying to learn something, even when people tease. Strength is more than having the most powerful weapon. It's having a strong faith in a mighty God. Check off these passages as you read them.

___ Noah worked 100 years to build the ark in a place without water. That's strong perseverance, especially when neighbors would have thought he was strange. (Genesis 5:32; 6:10-14; 7:6)

___ Food from angels gave the prophet Elijah strength for 40 days. (1 Kings 19:7-8)

___ Waiting on God can bring strength. (Isaiah 40:31)

___ The Holy Spirit gives people inner strength. (Ephesians 3:16)

___ Don't let sin rule your mind. Have a strong mind controlled by God's Spirit. (Romans 8:6)

___ I'm strong because God is with me. (2 Corinthians 12:9)

✞ PRAY

Ask God for inner strength and a strong faith.

Life's Guidebook Says

[God said,] "This is my command—be strong and courageous! Do not be afraid or discouraged. For the LORD your God is with you wherever you go." JOSHUA 1:9

STRONG MOTHER

"No!" Mrs. Turner yelled. "You will not cut off my son's leg."

The protective mother refused to listen to the doctor who wanted to amputate the infected leg. Her son, James, lay feverish and wounded after the Battle of Guilford in North Carolina during the American Revolution. Mrs. Turner rode on horseback 200 miles to nurse her son back to health. She drilled holes in a large tub and hung it from the ceiling over her son's bed. This let cool water drip on the leg and her son's head. The water kept him cool and lowered his fever. Doctors feared the infection in James's leg would spread to the rest of his body and Mrs. Turner's son would die. Medicine in 1781 was nowhere near as good as it is today.

Mrs. Turner made a tough decision. She loved her son. She wanted him to live *and* keep his leg. She cared for him day and night, until the infection went away. Soon doctors copied her idea to save other men's limbs. Mrs. Turner not only helped doctors, she helped army generals, too, by passing messages as a spy. Enemies never suspected the old woman.

Strength comes from more than just muscles. It's the courage to face danger and try something different. Mrs. Turner cared deeply about her son. Strong families and friends help one another and don't give up when problems come.

AWESOME ACTIVITY: HELP YOUR FAMILY BE STRONGER

Help your family be strong with these tips:

- ☞ Be man enough to give your mom a hug every day.
- ☞ Spend time with family members.
- ☞ Listen and encourage family members to follow their dreams.
- ☞ Pray with and for your family.
- ☞ Communicate and let your family know your plans, feelings, and dreams.
- ☞ Thank family members for their actions and even for listening.
- ☞ Forgive family members who hurt you.
- ☞ Pitch in to help around the house.

✞ PRAY

Ask God to give your mother strength and courage.

Life's Guidebook Says

She opens her mouth with wisdom, and the teaching of kindness is on her tongue.
She looks well to the ways of her household and does not eat the bread of idleness.
Her children rise up and call her blessed. PROVERBS 31:26-28, ESV

GROWING STRONGER

"IT'S TOO HARD." Nael couldn't keep his arm up long enough to perform a five-minute puppet show. Sounds wimpy. But try holding a heavy can of food over your head for five minutes straight. It's not as easy as it sounds.

Nael learned that being a puppeteer also required him to move a puppet's mouth to match its words, use rods to move the hands, keep the puppet's eyes focused on the audience, and hold the puppet at a certain height. At first he wanted to give up. But he loved hearing the audience laugh and knew puppets were a great way to teach younger kids about Jesus. Nael started lifting weights and practicing with his puppet. He also prayed for God's help.

Some things look easy until you try them, like treading water for several minutes or working a heavy puppet. You can build strong muscles through exercise. The Bible tells us that Jesus grew in strength (see today's verse, below). Since his dad worked as a carpenter, Jesus probably helped carry wood, saw it, and lift the plows and furniture they made. Daily work helped Jesus' body grow physically strong. You can follow Jesus' example to grow stronger too.

AWESOME ACTIVITY: STRENGTHEN UP

☞ Use water bottles as weights and practice lifting them. Hold them straight at your sides and then curl them up to work your biceps. You can also raise them directly in front of you or to the side with your arms straight to develop your shoulder muscles.

☞ Have fun testing your strength with arm and finger wrestling.

- Finger wrestling—Test your thumb strength and eye-hand coordination. Make an open fist, with thumb up and loose. Link fingers with your opponent. Count together, "One . . . two . . . three . . . go," and then try to pin your opponent's thumb down.
- Arm wrestling—The shorter the distance between your body and your hand, the more power you can create. Most arm-wrestling matches end within 10 seconds, so the one who makes the first strong move often wins.

✝ PRAY

Thank God that you are growing stronger. Ask God to help your muscles grow as you exercise.

Life's Guidebook Says

[Jesus] grew up healthy and strong. He was filled with wisdom, and God's favor was on him. LUKE 2:40

·SMILE POWER

EXPERTS SAY IT TAKES fewer muscles to smile than to frown. That means smiling is easy. But it's not easy for everyone. There are 43 muscles in your face; about half of them work together when you smile. Some people are born with fewer facial muscles. Others suffer from facial paralysis, which means their muscles don't work and they aren't able to frown or smile. These people may also have trouble eating and swallowing. That'd be a tough way to live, so scientists have worked to find ways to help children and adults get those muscles to move.

Sensors placed on the face target certain muscles and reward a person for using them to smile. It's called electromyography therapy. For one child, a DVD played each time he smiled. Two months of the therapy helped another boy hold a smile for over one minute. Those are miracles for these children. It took a lot of hard work and great muscle control to have them smile.

God gave us muscles in our face so we could smile, grin, frown, and make lots of different faces. Use your facial muscles today, and see if you can make someone around you smile.

AWESOME ACTIVITY: EXERCISES IN THE CAR

When you sit, you can smile. You can also exercise other muscles for flexibility and strength. Try these:

- ☞ Weightlifting. Lift a filled water bottle from your lap to your shoulder or straight out in front of you. Do sets of 20. Try it with your palm up and then with your palm down, to strengthen different muscles.
- ☞ Lock your arms together over your head, grasping your hands just below each elbow. Swing your locked arms from side to side, stretching as much as possible.
- ☞ Curl your toes up toward your legs, then flex them down, pointing them straight out. Do sets of 20.
- ☞ Smile or make funny faces at other passengers in your car.

✝ PRAY

Ask God to give you true joy as you smile at other people.

Life's Guidebook Says

Work with a smile on your face, always keeping in mind that no matter who happens to be giving the orders, you're really serving God.
EPHESIANS 6:7, *THE MESSAGE*

STRENGTH IN NUMBERS

TRY BREAKING A PIECE of thread or string. If you pull hard enough, you can probably do it. Now twist or braid three pieces of the same thread or string together. Try to break it again. Can you do it? Probably not. There's power in numbers. Working together multiplies strength. On a team, everybody's strength works toward a common goal. That's why 11 people play together on a football or soccer team, or why hauling furniture takes more than one person.

The right materials also make a rope stronger. Wet spaghetti may look like string but isn't very strong. Scientists measure the strength of materials to figure out what works best. The amount of force needed to pull and break a rope is called tensile strength. Tensile strength is also used to measure the strength of steel and other materials. Scientists who studied tensile strength recently developed a new type of steel. This steel, used in armored vehicles, resists explosions and keeps the people inside safer. The scientists teamed up a different combination of materials and created a stronger metal.

You can team up with a friend for strength. You are also stronger when God is with you. When you and another person work together with God, there's even greater strength.

PUZZLE IT OUT: CODE OF SYMBOLS

Use the code below to find out what Jesus said in Matthew 18:19 about the power of teaming up with others in prayer to God.

α = A	π = F	Σ = K	$\sim$ = P	= = U	# = Z
β = B	ω = G	< = L	$\vee$ = Q	$\div$ = V	
γ = C	Ω = H	$\leq$ = M	+ = R	$\pm$ = W	
δ = D	Δ = I	$/.$ = N	$-$ = S	$\emptyset$ = X	
μ = E	∇ = J	$\leqslant$ = O	$\times$ = T	∞ = Y	

"Suppose ___ ___ of you on ___ ___ ___ ___ ___ ___ ___ about
       $\times$ $\pm$ $\leqslant$ μ α + $\times$ Ω α ω + μ μ

___ ___ ___ ___ ___ ___ you ___ ___ ___ ___ ___ ___. My ___ ___ ___ ___ ___ ___ in
α $/.$ ∞ $\times$ Ω Δ $/.$ ω α $-$ Σ π $\leqslant$ + π α $\times$ Ω μ +

___ ___ ___ ___ ___ ___ ___ ___ ___ for ___ ___ ___." (NIrV)
Ω μ α $\div$ μ $/.$ $\pm$ Δ < < δ $\leq$ Δ $\times$ ∞ $\leqslant$ =

✝ PRAY

Ask God to give you good Christian friends to form a strong team.

Life's Guidebook Says

A person standing alone can be attacked and defeated, but two can stand back-to-back and conquer. Three are even better, for a triple-braided cord is not easily broken. ECCLESIASTES 4:12

Answer: *"Suppose two of you on earth agree about anything you ask for.*
My Father in heaven will do it for you."

STRENGTHENING OTHERS

COCK-A-DOODLE-DOO! Roosters are God's natural alarm clocks. They start crowing a few hours before the sun rises. They also crow anytime a noise startles them.

Before Jesus went to the Cross, he used a rooster to wake up Simon Peter. Peter said he'd be willing to die for Jesus, but Jesus knew Peter's faith was weak. The Lord told Peter that he would deny him three times before the rooster crowed.

"No way," Peter said.

But after Jesus was arrested, Peter followed him to the high priest's home. Guards stood around a fire as Peter crept closer. Suddenly a servant girl pointed and said, "This man was one of Jesus' followers!"

"I don't even know him!" Peter shouted back, trying to save his own skin. In just a few hours, Peter denied Jesus twice more. Then he heard, *Cock-a-doodle-doo!*

Jesus used the crowing like an alarm to wake Peter up to his failure and warn him to change.

Failure reminds us we are not perfect. We need God to help us be strong. If you fail like Peter, do what Peter did, and change for the better. That will inspire people. Learning from mistakes and admitting when we fail will help us succeed in the future.

A great inventor named George Washington Carver said, "Ninety-nine percent of the failures come from people who have the habit of making excuses." George didn't make excuses for past failures, instead he worked hard to succeed. He woke up at four o'clock every morning and walked into the woods to pray before he started work. He explored the power of the peanut when God told him to and developed more than 300 uses for peanuts.

Peter followed Jesus again with a stronger heart for God. He became a leader who preached about Jesus and encouraged many people to believe in Jesus as Savior.

PLEXER

Solve the plexer to find a muscle that improves with faith. (If you don't remember what a plexer is, see p. 9.)

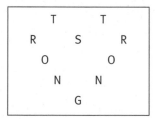

✞ PRAY

Ask God to help you use your weaknesses and failures to help others.

Life's Guidebook Says
[Jesus said,] "I have pleaded in prayer for you, Simon, that your faith should not fail. So when you have repented and turned to me again, strengthen your brothers." LUKE 22:32

Answer: Strong heart

NOISY BATTLE

GIDEON SNUCK into the Midianite camp to spy. He and his soldiers were terribly out-numbered—300 versus more than 100,000. But Gideon and his men had the Lord on their side. Gideon crept close to a tent and overheard a soldier tell his friend about a dream. In the dream the man saw a loaf of barley bread knock over a Midianite tent. *Hooray!* Gideon knew that God had sent the dream as a sign of victory for the Israelites.

Gideon returned to his men and shouted, "Get up! God has given us the victory!" They prepared for a midnight raid by going to grab their weapons. But instead of spears and shields, Gideon gave the men horns and torches inside clay jars. Gideon split his men into three groups. The men followed Gideon and surrounded the Midianite camp. Gideon blew his trumpet and smashed his jar. He grabbed the torch and held it high.

All Gideon's men shouted, "A sword for the Lord and for Gideon!" and smashed their jars. *Crash!* The noise woke the enemy; it sounded like a huge army surrounded them. The Midianites shook in their sleeping bags. When they peeked out of their tents, they saw bright flashes of light from the torches. Now they were sure a huge army was coming after them.

The Midianites grabbed their swords and stabbed at anything near them. *Oops!* They even stabbed one another. Terrified by all the noise and chaos, they ran away. God's chosen men had won the battle, thanks to the Lord!

WACKY LAUGHS

Q. Why did bread falling on a tent worry the Midianites?
A. They thought they would be sandwiched.

Q. What did the Midianites say after they lost the battle?
A. "What a jarring experience!"

Q. When did modern sound systems begin?
A. In Bible days. Gideon used surround sound to win a battle.

✝ PRAY

Ask God to help you win in spite of struggles.

Life's Guidebook Says

It was just after midnight, after the changing of the guard, when Gideon and the 100 men with him reached the edge of the Midianite camp. Suddenly, they blew the rams' horns and broke their clay jars. JUDGES 7:19

GOOD VIBRATIONS

THE CITY OF JERICHO looked impenetrable. Its walls were nearly 6 feet thick and over 20 feet tall. The city could withstand an attack from a great army. But it couldn't stand before God. God told his people to walk around the city once a day for six long days. On the seventh day, they marched around the city seven times and blew trumpets. On the seventh trip around, they shouted.

Blast! The good vibrations tumbled the wall surrounding the city. Bricks rolled and crashed together like an avalanche. *Rumble! Boom!* The Israelites jumped over the piles of rubble into the city and won the battle.

When some people read that story in Joshua 6, they didn't believe it. Over time, sand had buried the remains of Jericho. Archaeologists have been digging in Jericho since the mid-1800s. In the last 150 years, they've made some amazing discoveries that support the Bible's story. They found heaps of bricks from the wall. They also found a portion of the mudbrick wall on the north side that had never collapsed. That's probably where Rahab lived. She had hidden Israelite spies before the battle, and they promised to save her if she stayed inside her home (Joshua 2:15-18). Archaeologists also found burned grain supplies and other items, just like the Bible says (Joshua 6:24).

The Bible tells some amazing stories. Some of them don't sound possible, but nothing is impossible with God. He created everything and can do anything. When you read something in the Bible, you can trust that it's true.

WEIRD FACTS: BATTLE PLANS

- ☞ A huge wooden horse was used to win a battle during the times of the ancient Greeks. It is called the Trojan horse.
- ☞ Russia once made a circular battleship that could spin like a top to fire in any direction. It was too hard to steer and was never used!
- ☞ Uruguay soldiers fought with cheese in a war with Brazil. They ran out of cannonballs, so they loaded cheese into the cannons. One cheese ball even hit the mast of a ship and killed two enemy sailors.

✝ PRAY

Thank God for his Word always being true.

Life's Guidebook Says

When the people heard the sound of the rams' horns, they shouted as loud as they could. Suddenly, the walls of Jericho collapsed, and the Israelites charged straight into the town and captured it. JOSHUA 6:20

COURAGE TO ACT

Do YOU EVER TALK around the dinner table with your family? You might share a high-five moment of the day or tell your parents about a problem. Queen Esther, a Jew, chose the dinner table to share a huge problem.

Haman, a wicked leader in Persia, plotted to have all Jews in the country killed. Queen Esther's cousin Mordecai heard about the plot and asked her to plead with her husband, the king, to save the Jews. But walking up to the king uninvited was a big problem. He could have the person who did that executed. Queen Esther asked her people to pray and fast for three days. Then she approached the king.

Esther knew that entering the king's presence without being summoned might be the last thing she ever did. But the king loved Esther and asked what she wanted. She invited him and wicked Haman to dinner. They both came, and she asked them to come again the next night. Finally, she revealed Haman's plot. The king was furious and ordered his men to execute Haman. Esther's people were saved!

Jews still celebrate Esther's courage every year. The celebration is called Purim.

PUZZLE IT OUT: GOD'S HEROES REVIEW

Use the names at the right to match the heroes with the clues below.

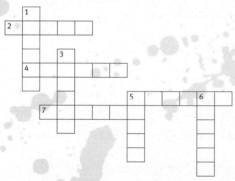

Gideon (Judges 7)
David (1 Samuel 16:1, 11-13; 17:32-51)
Daniel (Daniel 6:16-22)
Esther (Esther 7–8)
Joseph (Genesis 45:4-11)
Moses (Exodus 3:10; 12:31-42)
Joshua (Joshua 3; 6)
Philip (Acts 8:26-40)

1. He saved his family from famine in Egypt.
2. He brought the Israelites out of Pharaoh's land.
3. He led an army of just 300 men.
4. He led an Ethiopian to God.
5. (across) He walked in the lions' den.
5. (down) He was a shepherd who defeated Goliath and became a great king.
6. She saved her people after she invited the king to dinner.
7. He led the people into the Promised Land and in the battle at Jericho.

✝ PRAY

Ask God to give you courage to do the right thing when you face difficult circumstances.

Life's Guidebook Says

This Festival of Purim would never cease to be celebrated among the Jews.   ESTHER 9:28

Answers 1. Joseph; 2. Moses; 3. Gideon; 4. Philip; 5. (across) Daniel; 5. (down) David; 6. Esther; 7. Joshua

CHEERS FOR THE NEW LEADER

MARCHING BANDS, banners, huge balloons, and fancy floats pass by in a parade. Parades have been around about as long as people have had reasons to celebrate. Many countries celebrate a new leader coming into power with a parade.

In the Old Testament, King David ordered one of the loudest parades to celebrate a new king (see 1 Kings 1). Tons of people paraded behind Zadok the priest, Nathan the prophet, and King David's son Solomon. The people shouted with joy as the priest crowned Solomon as the new king. They played music and made so much noise that the earth shook. But this wasn't a scary earthquake. It was a happy one.

After the celebration, David had a father-son talk with Solomon (see 1 Kings 2). He told him to follow God and keep God's rules. He reminded Solomon to be kind and wise. Later, God asked Solomon to tell him his biggest wish (see 1 Kings 3). Solomon could've asked for riches or power. Instead, he asked for wisdom. This pleased God, and he answered Solomon's prayer. Solomon became the wisest man who ever lived.

EXPERIMENT: SQUAWKING STRING
Make happy musical noise with string.

Stuff You Need
- ☞ String (cotton string or thread) cut into 3-foot pieces
- ☞ Paper clips
- ☞ Paper cup (It's more fun with a few different-size cups.)
- ☞ Paper towel
- ☞ Scissors

Try It
1. Tie one end of the string around a paper clip.
2. Poke a slit in the bottom of a paper cup with the scissors and slide the paper clip inside the cup.
3. Twist the string and clip so the paper clip lies flat at the bottom of the cup (you may have to pull the clip to the top of the cup and then slide it back down).
4. Wet the paper towel (slightly damp is fine).
5. Hold the cup in one hand. Wrap the paper towel around the end of the string.
6. Pull the string tight and then loosen it. Continue pulling and loosening the string and listen to the honking sounds! Pull faster for a giggling sound. This works because the string vibrates, and that causes the paper clip to vibrate. The cup acts like an amplifier so you can hear it.

✞ PRAY
Rejoice and praise God for all he has done for you. Pray for God to give your leaders wisdom.

Life's Guidebook Says
All the people followed Solomon into Jerusalem, playing flutes and shouting for joy. The celebration was so joyous and noisy that the earth shook with the sound. 1 KINGS 1:40

ALL FOR THE WALL

"YOU CAN'T MAKE SOMETHING out of that heap of rubbish and burned stones!" Sanballat taunted.

"You're a bunch of poor, feeble Jews," Tobiah said. "The stone wall will collapse if a fox climbs on it."

Sanballat and Tobiah were bullies. They teased the Israelites that they could never rebuild the city wall around Jerusalem. The rubble had sat for many years and no one had fixed any part of it.

Babylonians had destroyed Jerusalem, the city where the Israelites worshiped God. They marched the people to a foreign land and made them serve as slaves. But finally, the king of Babylon had allowed some of God's people to return.

Hoorah! The Israelites rebuilt the Temple. *Boo!* The city wall had remained a pile of rubble 70 years after the Temple was rebuilt. Cities needed walls as protection from enemies and wild animals. The king let Nehemiah go to Jerusalem and lead the people in rebuilding the wall.

Nehemiah ignored Sanballat's and Tobiah's teasing and threats. The people worked hard and completed the wall in 52 days.

Even though the people had worked together to build the wall, Nehemiah noticed the richer people taking advantage of the poorer families. Other families bickered with each other. Nehemiah had the priests read the Scriptures and hold a revival. The people agreed to get along. They chose to dedicate the restored wall and their hearts to God. On the dedication day, the people marched on the wall and held a great celebration to thank God for helping them. (You can read all about these stories in the book of Nehemiah.)

LIFTOFF LIST

You may never have to fight with swords, but you probably have a lot of other battles, especially spiritual ones. Check off things you can do when you have to fight back and stand for God.

___ Praise God.
___ Sing praise songs.
___ Listen to praise music.
___ Scream.
___ Listen to God's directions in the Scriptures and in my heart.
___ Pray.
___ Surround the enemy with God's light. (That means reading God's Word out loud!)
___ Say Bible verses that I know by heart.

✝ PRAY

Rejoice that God's Word changes hearts and holds real power.

Life's Guidebook Says

Many sacrifices were offered on that joyous day, for God had given the people cause for great joy. The women and children also participated in the celebration, and the joy of the people of Jerusalem could be heard far away. NEHEMIAH 12:43

FREEDOM CELEBRATION

BRIGHT-COLORED FIREWORKS filled the sky. The boom of cannons, dances, parties, and feasts created a noisy celebration. So what was the big deal? In October 1783, the colonists celebrated America's freedom.

They had fought a difficult battle against the greatest army and navy on earth to win the American Revolution. Now they partied joyfully. They also stopped to thank God. Every celebration began with a church service that praised God for his goodness. The leaders of the new country made a proclamation and set two dates aside to thank God for freedom. The first took place on December 11, 1783, and the other the following year on October 19, 1784. The proclamation included these words:

> *The United States in Congress assembled do recommend it to the several States, to set apart the second Thursday in December next, as a day of public thanksgiving, that all the people may then assemble to celebrate with grateful hearts and united voices, the praises of their Supreme and all Bountiful Benefactor, for his numberless favors and mercies.*

Jesus spoke even greater words about freedom. He said that truth makes us free. He also told us he is the truth. Our freedom comes from Jesus, and we can celebrate that every day.

PUZZLE IT OUT: MAKES SENSE

Different types of US coins and dollar bills have the face of a famous American. Many helped the United States be free. Use the letter next to each type of coin or bill to fill in the blanks next to the names of the Americans pictured on that coin or bill. Then read down the columns to discover the message.

Penny = D	Quarter = N	$10 = S	$100 = U
Nickel = G	$1= R	$20 = T	$5,000 = E
Dime = I	$5 = O	$50 = W	

____ Franklin Roosevelt	____ Lincoln coin	____ Washington bill
____ Washington coin	____ Grant	____ Ben Franklin
____ Jefferson	____ Madison	____ Hamilton
____ Lincoln bill	____ Jackson	____ Jackson

✝ PRAY

Thank God for freedom, including the freedom to worship.

Life's Guidebook Says
He saved us from our enemies. His faithful love endures forever. PSALM 136:24

Clues: 1¢ = Lincoln; 5¢ = Jefferson; 10¢ = Roosevelt; 25¢ = Washington; $1 = Washington; $5 = Lincoln; $10 = Hamilton; $20 = Jackson; $50 = Grant; $100 = Franklin; $5,000 = Madison.
Answer: In God we trust.

RATTLING BONES

YOU'VE LOST SOME BONES. Seriously! But don't worry. They aren't lying around somewhere. It's how God designed you. You were born with 300 bones. But as you've grown, some of your bones—especially in your skull—have fused together and become stronger. Right now you probably have 206 bones. That means you've lost 94 bones! That's a lot of bones. But it's nowhere near the number of bones the prophet Ezekiel saw in a strange vision.

Ezekiel saw a valley full of bones. God told him to speak to the bones, so he did: "Dry bones, listen to the word of the LORD!" (Ezekiel 37:4). Suddenly, the bones rattled and moved. *Yikes! Clank! Clink! Rattle!* The bones came together and formed complete skeletons. God told Ezekiel to speak over the bones again. Muscles grew onto the bones, and then skin grew. Then God told Ezekiel to say, "Come, O breath, from the four winds! Breathe into these dead bodies so they may live again" (verse 9). The bones came to life and formed a great army.

That story may give you the creeps, but God used it to bring hope to his people. Enemies had captured the Israelites. God's people had given up hope and said to one another, "We have become old, dry bones" (37:11).

God can breathe his spirit of life into us when we feel depressed or think we have failed and nothing will get better. If you feel down with lazy bones, ask God to breathe life into your spirit.

AWESOME ACTIVITY: CANDY-ADE

Ezekiel shared that God would replace people's hard hearts with new ones that would not be like hearts of stone. Soften hard candy for a sweet drink.

Stuff You Need
- ☞ 3 pieces of hard candy
- ☞ Plastic resealable bag
- ☞ Hammer
- ☞ Glass of water
- ☞ Baking soda and lemon juice (optional)

Try It
1. Place candies in a resealable bag.
2. Hammer candies to crush them into a powder.
3. Mix candies in a glass of water. This makes a sweet drink.
4. Stir in ½ teaspoon baking soda and 1 tablespoon lemon juice to make the drink fizz.

✝ PRAY
Ask God to fill your spirit with hope and joy.

Life's Guidebook Says
"I will put my Spirit in you, and you will live again and return home to your own land. Then you will know that I, the LORD, have spoken, and I have done what I said." EZEKIEL 37:14

THE FINAL BATTLE

KABOOM! CRASH! Think of the loudest noise you've ever heard. It might have been a thunderstorm, music turned up too loud, a zooming plane, a speeding racecar, or shouting at a sporting event. Maybe you've even been told to quiet down because you were making lots of noise. All those sounds will seem like whispers compared to a future crowd making cheerful noises to God.

Jesus spoke about the end of times while he was on earth. God even gave the apostle John a glimpse of Jesus Christ's triumphal return. John wrote about his visions in the book of Revelation. In it, there's a huge battle scene. The most evil city ever, called Babylon, is thrown into the sea. *Roar!* After Babylon is destroyed, the believers will roar with joy. *Alleluia!* They will shout praises to God.

On that day, it will sound like rushing waters and thunder. With so many believers cheering, it'll be a big noise. And that's just the beginning. After Jesus' victory, there will be a wedding and a big banquet to continue the celebration.

If anybody ever tells you that God doesn't like to have fun, you can confidently tell them they're wrong. God loves to celebrate. He loves to hear us shout with joy—even when those shouts sound like thunder.

EXPERIMENT: CREATE SOUND EFFECTS
Try making sound effects with items around the house. Here are some ideas:

- ☞ Snap carrots to make a bone-cracking sound.
- ☞ Create the sound of a fire crackling by wrinkling cellophane and snapping twigs.
- ☞ Drop a sack of potatoes for the sound of somebody tripping and hitting the floor.
- ☞ Flap heavy work gloves to create the sound of birds flapping their wings.
- ☞ Fill a box with rocks to drop for crashing sounds.
- ☞ Blow through a straw in a glass of water to create the sound of boiling water.

✟ PRAY
Thank God that he's preparing his people for the final battle . . . and celebration.

Life's Guidebook Says
I heard again what sounded like the shout of a vast crowd or the roar of mighty ocean waves or the crash of loud thunder: "Praise the LORD! For the Lord our God, the Almighty, reigns." REVELATION 19:6

APRIL

APRIL FISH

IF YOU'RE LEFT-HANDED, you know how difficult life can be. You need special left-handed scissors; writing in a spiral notebook is nearly impossible; and if you play baseball, you're pretty much stuck playing first base, right field, or pitcher. That's why on this day in 1998, Burger King took out a full-page advertisement in *USA Today* newspaper announcing that it had created a left-handed Whopper. All of the ingredients were rotated 180 degrees, so left-handed people could properly enjoy their hamburgers.

Families immediately began to flock to Burger King to order the left-handed Whopper. Just one problem: it didn't exist! Did you notice the date today? It's April Fools' Day! Burger King took out the ad as a joke.

Nobody knows exactly when April Fools' Day began. Some experts say it dates back to France in 1582. That's when the country changed the start of a new year from the end of March to January 1. Some people forgot, so kids taped paper fish on their backs and shouted, "*Poisson d'avril!*" Translated, that means "April fish," which stands for a young, gullible fish that's easily caught.

Today, someone may try to catch you in an April Fools' Day prank. King Solomon wrote that there's a proper time to cry, laugh, grieve, and dance (Ecclesiastes 3:4). Now's the time to laugh. No foolin'.

AWESOME ACTIVITY: JUST FOOLIN'
Pulling a prank on someone can be fun; just make sure everybody laughs. Try these ideas and then jump out to say, "April Fools'."

- ☞ Cereal box switch-up—Carefully switch around the cereal bags into different boxes. When people go to pour their favorite cereal, they'll get a surprise.
- ☞ Shrinking shoes—Stuff cotton balls or toilet paper into the toes of someone's shoes. When she goes to put them on, she'll think her shoes have shrunk or her feet have grown.
- ☞ Turned upside down—Sneak into a family member's room and turn some of his stuff upside down: books, stuffed animals, pictures. (Just make sure not to break anything.)
- ☞ Terrible toothbrush—Sprinkle a tiny amount of salt on someone's toothbrush. When he goes to brush his teeth, he'll be minty and salty fresh. *Yuck!*

✝ PRAY
Thank God for laughter and for the joy he brings to your life through family and friends.

Life's Guidebook Says
[There is] a time to cry and a time to laugh. A time to grieve and a time to dance.
ECCLESIASTES 3:4

ROLLED AWAY

DID YOU EVER GET an A on a test when you weren't prepared? Or has your dad announced he has tickets to the sold-out game to see your favorite team play? Think of some news you've received that excited you and yet made you a little afraid, because it was so amazing it felt like it couldn't be true.

That's how some women felt when they went to Jesus' tomb on Sunday morning. They went expecting to find their Teacher and Savior lying dead in the tomb. Instead an angel whose face shone like lightning greeted them. The huge stone was rolled away from the entrance of the grave. All of the mighty soldiers guarding the tomb had scattered.

The women didn't know what had happened. They were afraid. Then the angel said, "Go quickly and tell his disciples that he has risen from the dead, and he is going ahead of you to Galilee. You will see him there" (Matthew 28:7).

We'll see Jesus again. Could it be true?! The news filled the women with fear and joy. It seemed impossible, yet they knew deep down that nothing was impossible for God. Their hearts filled with hope. They turned and quickly ran away from the tomb to tell the disciples what they had seen. The stone had been rolled away! God's power had raised Jesus from the dead.

PUZZLE IT OUT: WHEEL CODE

Look at the letters rolling around on this wheel. In the code below, each letter needs to be switched with the one above or below it in the wheel to solve for the message. For example, A=Q, and Q=A.

What did the angel tell the women?

" __ __ __ __ __ __ __ __ __ __ __.
   X U   Y C   K L D   X U B U

__ __ __ __ __ __ __ __ __."
X U   Y C   B Y C U K

—Matthew 28:6, (NIrV)

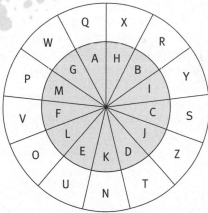

✝ PRAY

Ask God to help you move obstacles out of your way. Tell him you want to spread his Good News.

Life's Guidebook Says
The women ran quickly from the tomb. They were very frightened but also filled with great joy, and they rushed to give the disciples the angel's message. MATTHEW 28:8

Answer: "He is not here. He is risen."

YOU'RE INVITED

WHAT ARE THE BEST PARTS of going to church? Write down a few ideas:

1. _____
2. _____
3. _____

You may have written: seeing my friends, learning about God, watching videos, or the snacks.

Church can be a lot of fun. But you might have noticed that many of your friends don't go to church. Have you ever wondered why? A recent study found that two out of three people would be willing to go to church if somebody they knew invited them. Think about one or two people you know, and make a point of inviting them to church with your family. At this time of year, there are usually lots of special events to celebrate Jesus' rising from the dead. Easter is a perfect time to invite your friends to join in the fun.

When Jesus came to earth, he encouraged his followers to hang out together and learn more about him. (What does that remind you of?) And he's our example in how we should live. Jesus' close friend, the apostle John, wrote, "Those who say they live in God should live their lives as Jesus did" (1 John 2:6). Jesus wasn't shy talking about his heavenly Father and helping other people. You can do both of those things by inviting your friends to church.

WEIRD FACTS: GOD'S HOUSE

☞ More than 60 million people in the United States go to church every week.

☞ On the island of Malta—where the apostle Paul got shipwrecked—75 percent of people attend church.

☞ The largest church in the world is in South Korea. It has seven services in one day in a building that holds 21,000 people. That means 200,000 people come to church in one day!

☞ After Jesus died on the cross and rose from the grave, early Christians held church services in their houses.

☦ PRAY

Ask God to bring friends to mind that you can invite to church. Then do it.

Life's Guidebook Says
Those who say they live in God should live their lives as Jesus did.   1 JOHN 2:6

COOL CRUISE

CRUISE SHIPS JUST KEEP getting bigger and better. At the time the *Oasis of the Seas* motored into the ocean in October 2009, it was the world's largest passenger ship. More than 6,000 people could fit on this floating fun park—and that doesn't count the 2,394 crew members. The ship is more than three football fields long, 20 stories high, and over 200 feet wide.

While the sheer size of the *Oasis of the Seas* is impressive, what it holds is even better! There's a carousel, a zip line, two surfing wave pools, a mini golf course, a basketball court, two rock-climbing walls, a kids' waterpark, and an ice-skating rink. More than 3,000 construction workers took about two years to finish this ship at a cost of $1.5 billion.

The Bible talks about a great ship. But instead of being built for fun, it was built for survival. In Genesis, God tells Noah that the world is so evil that he's going to send a flood to kill every living thing that breathes (Genesis 6:17). He gave Noah plans to build an ark. The Bible doesn't say exactly how long it took him to build it, but it was probably at least 50 years! Even though the ark was massive—450 feet long, 75 feet wide, and 45 feet high—and held two of every animal, it was less than half the size of today's cruise ships. Of course, it held only eight people, not 8,000!

Noah built the ark just as God instructed. It kept him, his family, and all the animals safe when water covered the earth for 150 days.

LIFTOFF LIST

Noah showed obedience to God's command by building a huge boat in a dry place. Do you think people made fun of him? How do you show obedience to God?

___ I go to church.
___ I obey my parents.
___ I pray every day.
___ I thank God for everything he gives me.
___ I treat people with kindness.
___ I show respect to teachers and other adults.
___ I tell my friends about Jesus.

✝ PRAY

Ask God to help you obey his commands, even if they don't make sense to you.

Life's Guidebook Says

God wiped out every living thing on the earth—people, livestock, small animals that scurry along the ground, and the birds of the sky. All were destroyed. The only people who survived were Noah and those with him in the boat.
GENESIS 7:23

HOPE ON A ROPE

HAVE YOU EVER HAD to try to climb up a rope in gym class or scale a climbing wall like Spider-Man? It's not easy. You have to possess superstrong hand and forearm muscles to grip tightly and climb safely.

Before God's people went into the Promised Land, Joshua sent two spies to scope things out near Jericho (Joshua 2:1). The spies snuck into the city, but Jericho's king found out and wanted them captured. Soldiers searched for the spies and learned they'd visited a woman named Rahab. Rahab told the soldiers that the spies had left the city, but they were actually trapped on her roof. Once the king's men were gone, Rahab tied a rope securely in her home and lowered it through the city wall all the way to the ground.

"I know the Lord has given you this land," she said to the spies. "We are afraid of you. So when you capture the city, swear you'll save me and my family." (You can read the whole story in Joshua 2:1-24.)

The spies agreed and quickly climbed down the rope to safety. They returned to Joshua and told him, "All the people in the land are terrified of us" (Joshua 2:24). They also explained to Joshua how Rahab had saved them from being captured and the promise they made to her. Joshua honored that promise after the walls around Jericho fell.

AWESOME ACTIVITY: CLIMB ON

If you want to become an excellent climber, try these easy exercises to strengthen the muscles you use for climbing.

- ☞ Grip strength helps you hold things. Find an old tennis ball or racquetball. Squeeze it 15 times with each hand. Repeat three times.
- ☞ Flexibility is key for climbers. See if you can stand and touch your toes. Hold for seven seconds.
- ☞ Strong shoulders help you hold yourself up. Grab two full gallon-size milk jugs. Hold them at your sides. Shrug your shoulders straight up, and hold for a few seconds. Lower them straight down. Do 10 repetitions.
- ☞ Build your core strength with sit-ups, crunches, or planks. A good core helps with every activity.

✝ PRAY

Thank God that he can win battles for us before they even start and that he always provides a way of escape from temptation.

Life's Guidebook Says
Since Rahab's house was built into the town wall, she let them down by a rope through the window. JOSHUA 2:15

NO LION

KING DARIUS KNEW SOMETHING about delegating. One man can't run a huge kingdom. He must have trusted advisors. But when one of Darius's administrators was thrown into a lions' den, the police came to investigate.

Detective: Your lions look pretty full.

King Darius: They should be. They just ate several of my advisors and their families.

Detective: Really? I thought you'd thrown *Daniel* into the lions' den.

King Darius: I did. My other advisors tricked me. They had me sign a law saying that nobody could pray to anyone or anything but me for 30 days.

Detective: You must think highly of yourself.

King Darius: I'm the king.

Detective: That's true. So what happened?

King Darius: My most trusted administrator, Daniel, refused to stop praying to his God. That's one thing I love about Daniel—he's reliable.

Detective: But you threw him into the lions' den anyway.

King Darius: I had to. It was the law. But I hoped his God would save him. And he did!

Detective: So where is Daniel now?

King Darius: Probably praying and thanking his God for saving him. He said his God sent an angel to shut the lions' mouths.

Detective: But the lions' mouths certainly weren't shut when you threw in your other advisors.

King Darius: Yeah, they won't be tricking me again.

WACKY LAUGHS

Q. What was Daniel's favorite flower?
A. The dande-lion.

Knock, knock.
Who's there?
Lionel.
Lionel who?
Lionel roar if you tease it.

Q. Why did the lion spit out the clown?
A. Because he tasted funny.

Q. Why did the tiger not trust its friend?
A. Because it was lion.

✝ PRAY

Tell God that you want to pray to him more often. Make a plan to pray at least once a day.

Life's Guidebook Says
When Daniel learned that the law had been signed, he went home and knelt down as usual in his upstairs room, with its windows open toward Jerusalem. He prayed three times a day, just as he had always done, giving thanks to his God.
DANIEL 6:10

FIRE PROTECTION

WHEN FIREFIGHTERS RUSH into burning buildings, they wear special suits to help them stay safe. These suits can protect them in temperatures of nearly 600 degrees. That's pretty amazing. But the shiny, heavy suits aren't flameproof, and they don't provide much protection against other fire dangers, such as smoke. That's why firemen also carry compressed air into fires to help them breathe. Firefighting is a dangerous job, so thank these brave men and women whenever you see them.

When Shadrach, Meshach, and Abednego were thrown into the fiery furnace, they were not wearing fireproof suits. The Bible tells us they were tied up and thrown into the fire wearing pants, turbans, robes, and other clothing (Daniel 3:21). Sounds like they'd immediately burst into flames. But you probably know what really happened. Their ropes burned away, and they walked around unharmed. So what saved them?

In a word: God.

Before Nebuchadnezzar tossed Shadrach, Meshach, and Abednego into the fire, they said that the God they served could save them. Then they said these amazing words, "Even if he doesn't, we want to make it clear to you, Your Majesty, that we will never serve your gods" (Daniel 3:18). These brave young men were willing to die for their faith. They knew God could do anything. And the almighty God saved them. Now that's the ultimate fire protection!

WEIRD FACTS: THAT'S HOT!

- ☞ Candle flames burn at 1,800 degrees Fahrenheit.
- ☞ Fires need heat, fuel, and oxygen to burn.
- ☞ You should check the batteries in smoke alarms twice a year.
- ☞ Red fire is around 1,500 degrees Fahrenheit. Orange-colored flames are around 2,000 degrees Fahrenheit. White flames can be 2,600 degrees Fahrenheit or more!
- ☞ Always have an escape plan from your home in case of a fire. Talk to your parents about making a plan.

✝ PRAY

Ask God to give you the courage to stand up for your beliefs—no matter the consequences.

Life's Guidebook Says

Then Nebuchadnezzar said, "Praise to the God of Shadrach, Meshach, and Abednego! He sent his angel to rescue his servants who trusted in him. They defied the king's command and were willing to die rather than serve or worship any god except their own God." DANIEL 3:28

HOMECOMING GONE WRONG

JESUS WAS BACK! Reports of his miraculous healings and his powerful words spread throughout the land. And now he was coming back to teach in his hometown of Nazareth. Everybody knew him in Nazareth—Jesus, the carpenter's son. As usual, when the Sabbath came, Jesus went to the synagogue. They handed him a scroll, and he read from the prophet Isaiah. He amazed all in attendance with his gracious words.

But then something went wrong. One moment they were praising Jesus, and the next they were mad at him. Jesus had said that a prophet was never accepted in his hometown. *Ouch!* That hurt the people's feelings. They became so angry that they forced Jesus out of the synagogue and to the edge of a cliff near Nazareth. They planned to push Jesus over the cliff.

Jesus knew their plans. He could see the anger in their faces. He used his power to walk right through the middle of the crowd and escaped unharmed (Luke 4:30). How'd he do it? We don't know. But nothing was impossible for him.

Have you ever visited a friend that you haven't seen in a while? Did you treat that friend with anger or excitement? At first, the people in Nazareth were happy to see Jesus. But their excitement quickly turned to anger when he spoke the truth to them in the synagogue. What a strange homecoming.

QUIZ: THAT'S PROPHETIC

When Jesus spoke in the synagogue, he read from the prophet Isaiah. Isaiah wrote many prophecies that Jesus fulfilled. Experts say Jesus fulfilled more than 300 prophecies in his life. Look up these verses, and draw a line to the fulfilled prophecy.

Isaiah 7:14 and Matthew 1:20-21   Jesus healed the deaf and the blind.

Isaiah 11:10 and Matthew 1:1-6   Jesus was born to a virgin mother.

Isaiah 29:18 and Luke 7:21-22   Jesus was in the line of King David.

✝ PRAY

Praise Jesus for being the fulfillment of so many Old Testament prophecies.

Life's Guidebook Says

[Jesus said,] "The Spirit of the LORD is upon me, for he has anointed me to bring Good News to the poor. He has sent me to proclaim that captives will be released, that the blind will see." LUKE 4:18

JEREMY TAKES THE WHEEL

ON THIS DAY IN 2012, a bus ride to school turned dangerous for Jeremy Wuitschick and his friends at Surprise Lake Middle School.

The morning started like any other. Students sat on Bus 29 talking about homework and sports. But then the bus driver started making gagging noises. Suddenly, the bus began drifting onto a curb and toward a church as the driver slumped over in his seat. While students filled the bus with screams, Jeremy jumped into action. The thirteen-year-old ran up the aisle, grabbed the wheel, and steered the bus back onto the road. Then he took the keys out of the ignition. The bus eventually slowed down and came to a stop near the school.

Jeremy wasn't trying to be a hero when he took the wheel; he was just living out Paul's command in Philippians 2:4, "Don't look out only for your own interests, but take an interest in others, too." Even right after the accident, as his friends thanked him for keeping them safe, he prayed for the driver and thanked God. "God protected us," Jeremy said. "I know that for sure."

Jeremy didn't want the attention on himself; he wanted God to get the glory for his actions. That's why when newspapers and national news shows talked to him, he tried to always mention his Savior.

"I'm a Christian, so I didn't want the bus to hit a church," Jeremy said when he was interviewed on the *TODAY* show.

And thanks to Jeremy, it didn't.

LIFTOFF LIST
Put an **X** next to ways you can look out for other people's interests.

___ Sharing my lunch with a friend who forgot his
___ Sitting next to somebody who doesn't have a lot of friends
___ Inviting the new kid to play a game
___ Doing an extra chore around the house without being asked
___ Helping a younger sibling with homework
___ Standing up for someone who's being bullied

✝ PRAY
Ask God to give you opportunities where you can serve others and tell people about him.

Life's Guidebook Says
Don't look out only for your own interests, but take an interest in others, too.
PHILIPPIANS 2:4

KNOCK IN THE NIGHT

KNOCK, KNOCK.

"Who's there?"

"Peter."

"Peter who?"

"This is no joke," Peter said. "An angel just broke me out of prison!"

Over the centuries, there have been many innovative prison escapes. During World War II, British pilot Roger Bushell organized an amazing escape from a German prison by digging tunnels. A French criminal, Pascal Payet, escaped two high-security prisons in the same way—by hijacking a helicopter—both times! In the 1500s, a priest named John Gerard escaped the Tower of London by hacking away at the stones that held his cell closed, sneaking past the guards, and lowering himself down a huge wall on a rope into a boat in a moat. Gerard planned the whole thing with friends by sending them letters with secret messages written in orange juice, which became invisible.

While all of those escapes are impressive, they can't compare to the apostle Peter's miraculous escape from prison. Acts 12:6-16 says the night before Peter was going to be placed on trial by King Herod Agrippa, he was chained to two guards deep inside a prison. Other guards stood outside his cell door and at the prison gates. Suddenly, light filled the dark cell as an angel of the Lord stood before Peter. The angel woke Peter up, had the chains fall from his wrists, and said, "Put on your coat and follow me!"

At first Peter thought he was dreaming as he walked past the guards. But once he left the prison and walked through the streets, the angel disappeared, and Peter realized that he was free. He rushed to a home where people were praying for him. He knocked on the door, and everybody celebrated his escape.

QUIZ: ANGELIC VISITOR

An angel saved Peter. Answer true or false to these statements about angels.

1. People turn into angels when they die.   **T or F**
2. The word *angel* means "messenger."   **T or F**
3. It's a good idea to pray to angels.   **T or F**
4. God sends angels to help people.   **T or F**

✞ PRAY

Thank God for his angels, who watch over and protect you.

Life's Guidebook Says

"It's really true!" [Peter] said. "The Lord has sent his angel and saved me from Herod and from what the Jewish leaders had planned to do to me!"   ACTS 12:11

Answers: 1. F; 2. T; 3. F; 4. T

EAT YOUR VEGGIES

Have you heard about Joey McBean
Who refused to eat anything green?
His parents tried to make him eat peas.
But he blew them off with a big sneeze.
He said no grapes, kale, and Brussels sprouts.
Eating candy was what he was about.
But when Joey went outside to play,
He noticed that his skin looked all gray.
He couldn't run and his arms were not strong.
That's when he realized that something was wrong.
He went inside and made a big salad.
This tastes good, he thought. And so ends this ballad.

HAVE YOU EVER HAD a parent or family member tell you to eat your vegetables? And, no, french fries and Tater Tots don't count. Some kids just don't like the taste of vegetables. Others think they look weird. But the truth is when God created the earth, he made vegetables and fruit so we could eat them and be healthy.

Food fuels our bodies. Sometimes we only have time for some fast food. Other times we can sit and enjoy a full meal with our families. But all the time, we should try to make good choices when it comes to what we put in our bodies. When we eat food in the closest form to how God made it—not all processed or taken from a box and put in the microwave—we're sure to live healthier lives.

WEIRD FACTS: GOOD EATIN'

According to nutrition experts, these are some of the healthiest foods you can eat:

☞ Broccoli—It contains tons of vitamins K and C, which help build strong bones.
☞ Blueberries—They are rich in fiber and phytonutrients. Both help keep your body working properly.
☞ Sweet potatoes—They boost your immune system with lots of vitamin A.
☞ Apples—It's true what they say: "An apple a day keeps the doctor away."
☞ Spinach—It makes your eyes strong and fights off diseases.
☞ Kiwifruit—It's packed with more vitamin C than oranges have.

✝ PRAY

Thank God for creating fruits and vegetables to keep you healthy.

Life's Guidebook Says
God said, "Look! I have given you every seed-bearing plant throughout the earth and all the fruit trees for your food." GENESIS 1:29

THE BEAT GOES ON

TURN OVER YOUR LEFT HAND, so your palm faces the ceiling. Now take two fingers from your right hand and place them on your left wrist near your thumb. What do you feel?

You should feel the consistent beat of your heart. Okay, you're actually feeling your pulse as your heart pumps blood throughout your body. Your pulse is probably around 80 beats a minute. Without your heart, you'd have no pulse . . . and that'd be a bad thing.

Your heart is key to your life. That's why God designed your body to protect it. Your heart is located behind and just to the left of your breastbone. This solid bone and your ribs act as a cage around your heart, which is also surrounded by a tough, double-layered sac called the pericardium. A gooey liquid between the two layers protects the heart from jarring. This protective sac also guards your heart from infections in the body.

Just like God created your body to protect your physical heart, the Bible says we should guard our spiritual hearts from inappropriate pictures and language, because our hearts reflect who we truly are. Keeping our spiritual hearts clean and healthy isn't easy. You may have to tell your friends that you don't want to listen to certain songs, play certain video games, or watch certain movies. They might make fun of you for being a Goody Two-shoes. But a little teasing is worth it to protect your heart.

EXPERIMENT: HEART MONITOR
If you had trouble taking your pulse, create this pulse meter.

Stuff You Need
- ☞ Play-Doh
- ☞ Toothpick
- ☞ Watch or clock with a second hand

Try It
1. Get a small amount of Play-Doh, and flatten into a quarter-inch-thick circle.
2. Insert a toothpick into the Play-Doh, so it stands straight up.
3. Place one arm on a table, with your palm up.
4. Put the Play-Doh on the inside of your wrist, just below your thumb.
5. Watch the toothpick shake as your heart beats.
6. Count how many times the toothpick moves in a minute to figure out your resting heart rate.
7. Now run around or do 50 jumping jacks. Sit down and count your pulse again.

✟ PRAY
Praise God for how he created your heart. Then tell him you're going to protect it.

Life's Guidebook Says
As a face is reflected in water, so the heart reflects the real person.
PROVERBS 27:19

LAME FAME

DO YOU WATCH A LOT OF TV? Studies show that most kids watch more than 30 hours a week. Write down some of your favorite shows:

1. _____
2. _____
3. _____

Have you ever thought about the messages those shows teach you? While a lot of TV can seem like harmless entertainment, most shows have an underlying message they're trying to get across. In 2011, a study by the Children's Digital Media Center@Los Angeles looked at 40 years of popular TV shows for kids. Starting in 1967, researchers looked at the top character qualities that these programs showcased. These qualities included everything from being popular to helping out your community. Years ago the top character qualities were doing good, helping others, and following traditions. But in 2007, the number one trait taught in children's shows was the importance of fame. In the 1960s, 70s, 80s, and 90s, fame ranked 13th or lower, but in the last decade it jumped to the top and has stayed there. Other top traits in 2007 included personal achievement, popularity, and image.

What matters most to you? Is it fame, popularity, and looking cool? Or is it helping others, serving God, and being kind? You'll have to work extra hard to accomplish what God wants for your life if the shows you're watching are influencing you the opposite way. Earthly fame is fleeting—Disney teen stars come and go; reality stars are soon forgotten. But the Bible says God's fame lasts forever. And that's what you need to focus on.

PLEXER

See if you can solve this plexer. (If you don't remember what a plexer is, see p. 9.)

FAME

✝ PRAY

Ask God to help you live for his glory, not for your own fame.

Life's Guidebook Says
Human pride will be brought down, and human arrogance will be humbled. Only the LORD will be exalted on that day of judgment. ISAIAH 2:11

Answer: Fading fame

BEARS OF CONSEQUENCE

CALLING SOMEBODY NAMES CAN be hazardous to your health. Don't believe it? Just yell, "Hey, megaloser!" to the bully at your school and see what happens. Wait. That's a bad idea. Instead, check out this scene that happened in 2 Kings 2:23-24:

Elisha (thinking): *Wow, it's a long way from Jericho to Bethel. My feet hurt.*
Group of Boys: Go away, baldy!
Elisha: Are you talking to an eagle? Because name-calling isn't nice.
Group of Boys: We're talking to you. Go away, baldy!
Elisha: You guys aren't very creative. You just yelled that a second ago.
Group of Boys: Baldy, baldy.
Elisha: God, those boys shouldn't be making fun of your prophet.
Group of Boys: Baldy, baldy.
Elisha: You guys are about to learn a painful lesson.
Group of Boys: Ha, ha. Very funny, baldy.
Two Bears: Grrrrrr.
Group of Boys: Run for your lives!

The rest of the story gets kind of gruesome. Two bears run out of the woods and maul 42 of the boys. *Ouch!* Those boys were probably thinking, *Sticks and stones may break my bones. And bears will always hurt me.*

What a crazy story! Sounds kind of harsh, huh? But God takes what comes out of your mouth very seriously.

PUZZLE IT OUT: RUNAWAY ANIMALS

Bears played a big part in today's Bible story. See if you can find all of these animals mentioned in the Bible. Look up, down, across, diagonally, and backward.

A	B	E	S	R	O	H
D	O	N	K	E	Y	K
Z	O	M	R	A	I	L
C	R	G	E	G	U	I
Q	E	O	F	L	A	C
B	E	A	R	E	M	E
X	D	T	L	I	O	N

Bear
Donkey
Goat
Calf
Dog
Horse
Deer
Eagle
Lion

✝ PRAY

Tell God you're going to watch what you say and make sure your words honor him.

Life's Guidebook Says

[Jesus said,] "You have heard that our ancestors were told, 'You must not murder. If you commit murder, you are subject to judgment.' But I say, if you are even angry with someone, you are subject to judgment! If you call someone an idiot, you are in danger of being brought before the court. And if you curse someone, you are in danger of the fires of hell." MATTHEW 5:21-22

SO THIRSTY

SAMSON WAS THIRSTY. Really thirsty.

He was so thirsty that he thought he might die. So what did he do to work up such a mighty thirst? Did he . . .

a. play basketball for two hours in the hot sun?
b. wrestle a lion?
c. defeat 1,000 men?
d. mow the lawn by cutting each blade of grass with nail clippers?
e. all of the above?

The answer is *c*. (But try doing *d* and see how thirsty you get.)

Samson performed phenomenal acts of power. God gave him amazing strength to fight for his people and defeat the Philistines. One time Samson agreed to be tied up with two brand-new ropes and handed over to the Philistines. When the Philistines saw him tied up and helpless, they cheered in triumph. That's when the Spirit of the Lord allowed Samson to snap the ropes. He ran over to a dead donkey, grabbed its jawbone, and charged into the pack of Philistines.

Whack, hack, smack! Samson swung the jawbone wildly. Man after man fell down dead. Samson kept attacking the Philistines until he'd killed 1,000 men. He finally threw away the jawbone and cried out in victory. Then it hit him—he was really thirsty.

"Must I now die of thirst and fall into the hands of these pagans?" Samson cried out to the Lord (Judges 15:18). God heard Samson's plea. And the same God who gave Samson strength gave him refreshment. Water started pouring from a hole in the ground. Samson drank and drank, until his thirst was quenched.

WEIRD FACTS: DRINK IT UP

Water is the second most popular drink in the United States behind soda, but it's way more healthy for you. Check out these fluid facts:

☞ Your body is more than 60 percent water. Drinking water helps you have enough saliva, moves nutrients around your body, and maintains your body temperature.
☞ Water energizes your muscles.
☞ Water helps your skin look good.
☞ Water keeps your kidneys and other organs working right.

✝ PRAY

Thank God that he can give you strength and quench your thirst.

Life's Guidebook Says
God caused water to gush out of a hollow in the ground at Lehi, and Samson was revived as he drank. JUDGES 15:19

BABY PRAYERS

HAVE YOU EVER PEEKED when your family prays around the dinner table? Be honest. Everyone's head is bowed, but you look around to see what your family is doing. Maybe you saw your dad with his eyes closed as he asked the blessing. Perhaps you caught your brother sneaking a bite of chicken.

In the Old Testament, Eli the priest peeked over as Hannah prayed in the Tabernacle, and he knew something was wrong. Her mouth moved, but no words came out. Her eyes were closed, yet tears flowed down her cheeks and onto the ground. She even swayed as she prayed and looked a little unbalanced. Eli couldn't believe it—somebody had come into the Tabernacle after drinking too much alcohol!

"Must you come here drunk?" Eli said, running up to her. "Throw away your wine!" (1 Samuel 1:14). Hannah assured the priest that she hadn't been drinking. She was just really sad and praying for God to give her a son. Eli quickly realized she was being honest and told Hannah not to worry and that he hoped God would grant her request. In her prayer, Hannah promised God that she'd give her son to the Lord to serve in the Tabernacle.

Sure enough, God said yes to Hannah's request, and she had a baby. Just as she'd promised, Hannah brought little Samuel to Eli to serve God for all of his life. Hannah loved Samuel with all of her heart, but she gave her beloved son to the God who answered her prayers.

PUZZLE IT OUT: MISSING WORD

First Thessalonians 5:17 is one of the shortest and most powerful verses in the Bible. Look at the words below. One letter is missing from the second set of words. Write that letter in the correct space to discover the missing word from that verse.

1. pecan   cape
2. cream   cram
3. over   ore
4. floor   fool

"__ __ __ __ __ stop praying." —1 Thessalonians 5:17
   1   2   3   2   4

✝ PRAY

Tell God you'd be willing to give him anything, even what you prize the most.

Life's Guidebook Says
"In that case," Eli said, "go in peace! May the God of Israel grant the request you have asked of him." 1 SAMUEL 1:17

Answer: Never

GET UP!

Ryan: Welcome to *Joppa Alive!*, the top show in the Mediterranean Sea area. I'm your host, Ryan Seaside. Today we have a very special guest, the apostle Peter. You probably know him from his three denials of Jesus. But today God is using him in amazing ways. He recently healed a paralytic man in Lydda. And just yesterday, he raised a woman from the dead in our city! Thanks for joining us, Peter.

Peter: Thanks, Ryan, but it wasn't me who raised Tabitha from the dead. It was the Lord's amazing answer to prayer.

Ryan: Now, you're not a doctor and have no formal medical training.

Peter: That's correct. I'm a fisherman by trade. But Luke, who's standing over there, is a doctor. He's writing down all of these events.

Ryan: So you're sure Tabitha was dead and not just sleeping.

Peter: Oh yeah. She died when I was in Lydda. Two men came to get me. Everybody knew Tabitha was a great woman. She always treated people kindly and even made clothes for the poor.

Ryan: If she was already dead, why did you bother coming?

Peter: Because God can do anything. Jesus rose from the dead, and he raised people back to life when he walked the earth.

Ryan: Tell us exactly what happened.

Peter: Well, I got to her house and they took me to an upstairs room. Many widows were crying. I asked everybody to leave, closed the door, knelt down, and prayed for a miracle.

Ryan: Then what?

Peter: I turned and said, "Get up, Tabitha!" She opened her eyes and sat up. Everybody rejoiced when they saw her.

Ryan: And we rejoice with you today on *Joppa Alive!*

AWESOME ACTIVITY: PRAYER KEEPER

God is a prayer keeper. He always hears and answers your prayers. Sometimes he answers yes right away. Sometimes he says no. Sometimes he asks you to wait. As followers, we have to trust that God's timing is perfect.

Get a spiral notebook to keep track of your prayers. Write down the date and what you pray. After a while, look back and write down how God answered your prayers. Share with others how he answered your prayers and then watch your faith—and theirs—grow stronger.

✝ PRAY

Praise God for showing his power when you pray.

Life's Guidebook Says
The news spread through the whole town, and many believed in the Lord.
ACTS 9:42

BLINDSIDED BY PRAYER

IF YOU THINK ABOUT IT, fast food is amazing. You pull up to a speaker and shout that you want a double cheeseburger with no pickles and a chocolate shake. By the time your parents pull forward in the car, your order is ready. *Yum!*

Sadly, many people treat God like a fast-food restaurant. They say a quick prayer, wait a couple of moments, and expect to have their prayer answered immediately. Does this scene sound familiar? You're sitting in class before a big test. As your teacher hands out the papers, you pray, *Dear God, please help me do well on this test even though I didn't study enough. Amen.* When you don't do well, you get mad at God for not answering your prayer.

While God doesn't answer prayers like a fast-food restaurant takes orders, sometimes he does answer prayers right away. In the Old Testament, God gave Elisha special knowledge about the king of Aram's plans against the Israelites. The king got so mad that he marched his soldiers to Dothan to capture Elisha. As the army marched toward Elisha, he prayed to God to blind the enemy (2 Kings 6:18). *Zap!* Suddenly, none of the soldiers could see. "You're in the wrong city," Elisha said to the blind soldiers. "Follow me, and I'll take you where you should go."

Elisha led the Aramean army to Samaria, where their sight was restored. Israelite soldiers surrounded them. But instead of killing the Arameans, they fed them a great feast and sent them home.

LIFT-OFF LIST

As a prophet, Elisha had a special relationship with God. God let Elisha know things that would happen in the future. And God amazingly answered his prayers. When you pray to God, remember this helpful acrostic that spells P-R-A-Y.

__ **P**raise. Start by praising God for his power and goodness.
__ **R**epent. Admit to God that you're a sinner and ask for forgiveness.
__ **A**sk. Tell God how you'd like to see him work in your life.
__ **Y**ield. Let God know that you want his will done—not your own.

✝ PRAY

Tell God you trust him to answer your prayers at the perfect time.

Life's Guidebook Says

As the Aramean army advanced toward him, Elisha prayed, "O LORD, please make them blind." So the LORD struck them with blindness as Elisha had asked.
2 KINGS 6:18

PLAGUE STOPPER

In the mid-1300s, one of the worst diseases to ever hit earth spread throughout Europe. Called the "Black Death" because of the strange black boils that appeared on people's bodies, this plague killed more than 20 million people. The disease spread through the air, but also could be contracted by being bitten by fleas and rats. Great numbers of these pests lived in Europe at that time. Nearly 700 years ago, people didn't understand this plague or know how to fight against it. Medicine wasn't very advanced. Doctors even refused to see patients, because they were afraid of getting sick.

The book of Numbers also talks about a terrible plague, but this plague came from God's judgment against the Israelites. God's people had stopped in an area of Moab on their way to the Promised Land. Instead of staying at their camp, the Israelite men started following Moabite women and worshiping their gods. God doesn't want to be one of many gods we worship. He's the one true God. He deserves to be the only God we serve. He even says that we should have no gods before him. He told Moses that the men sinning against him needed to be put to death. Phinehas, the great-nephew of Moses, heard this command. Phinehas was a priest. Some translations of the Bible say Phinehas prayed to God and then took action. He thrust a spear that killed a man and a woman who were sinning against the Lord (Numbers 25:8). Then the plague stopped. But still, 24,000 people died.

PLEXER

Solve this plexer to fill in the missing words of this Bible verse. (If you don't remember what a plexer is, see p. 9.)

(If you don't remember what a plexer is, see p. 9.)

> called
> the lord

"Out of my distress I _____ ____ _____ _____; the LORD answered me and set me free." —PSALM 118:5, ESV

✝ PRAY

Thank God that he's a just God. He sends judgment and takes it away.

Life's Guidebook Says

Phinehas had the courage to intervene, and the plague was stopped.
PSALM 106:30

Answer: Called on the Lord

MOVE THAT MOUNTAIN

AN OLD SAYING GOES, "No prayer, no power. Little prayer, little power. Much prayer, much power." The meaning of that saying is sort of obvious. If you don't pray for something, you're missing out on a lot of power. That's why you should share prayer requests and ask other people to pray for you.

While this saying makes an important point, it's missing a key fact. Your words don't matter much to God. Your faith does. Words can be empty if you don't believe what's coming from your mind and mouth. But when you have faith that God hears your words and answers prayers, it makes your words more powerful.

Jesus told his disciples in Matthew 17:20 that if they had just the tiniest bit of faith, nothing would be impossible for them. They could even move mountains! Asking to move a mountain would be kind of a weird prayer. What's the purpose? (Unless you were a settler moving across America in the 1840s and ran into the Rocky Mountains.)

When you pray, remember what Jesus said: Have faith and pray with the power to move mountains.

WEIRD FACTS: PEAK PEAKS
Check out these massive mountains:

- ☞ At 29,035 feet, Mount Everest is the tallest mountain on earth. Formed by tectonic plates, Everest grows about one-quarter inch per year.
- ☞ Olympus Mons on Mars is 16 miles high—making it the tallest mountain on any planet in the solar system. More than three Mount Everests could fit in this phenomenal peak.
- ☞ The Andes is the longest mountain range, stretching nearly 4,350 miles along South America's western coast.
- ☞ The tallest mountain on earth measured from base to top isn't Mount Everest. Mauna Kea, on the Big Island of Hawaii, stands 33,474 feet from the bottom of the Pacific Ocean to its peak. But only 13,796 feet of this inactive volcano stick up above land.

✝ PRAY
Praise God for the power of prayer. Ask him to give you faith when you pray.

Life's Guidebook Says
[Jesus said,] "Truly, I say to you, if you have faith like a grain of mustard seed, you will say to this mountain, 'Move from here to there,' and it will move, and nothing will be impossible for you." MATTHEW 17:20, ESV

LET IT SNOW

WHEN YOU THINK ABOUT APRIL, you probably picture blooming flowers and refreshing rains. But April has also seen its share of epic snowstorms.

Between April 19 and 21, 1893, over 30 inches of snow fell on St. Cloud, Minnesota. Twenty-four inches of snow fell in a single day. The wet, heavy snow closed down trains and made roads nearly impassable. Of course, people didn't drive cars until the 1900s, so horses could still sort of get around.

More recently, nearly three feet of snow fell from April 5 to 7, 2008, in South Dakota, Minnesota, and Wisconsin. Gusty winds made drifts more than six feet high and closed down schools and businesses for days.

It doesn't snow too often in the Holy Land, and usually only the mountains get any accumulation. But in Psalm 51, David writes about the snow. David was a man after God's own heart, but he also made plenty of mistakes. In this psalm, David asks for God's mercy. He says that the times he's disobeyed God's commands make him feel terrible and keep him up at night. He tells the Lord that he's a sinner and that he wants his joy back. And he writes these amazing words: "Wash me, and I will be whiter than snow" (Psalm 51:7). When God forgives your sins, you become as pure as newly fallen snow.

EXPERIMENT: KEEP IT CLEAN

The Lord purifies you from your sins and washes you whiter than snow. He also takes your sins as far away from you as the east is from the west (Psalm 103:12). Try this experiment as a way to see how God cleans up your life.

Stuff You Need
- ☞ Bowl of water
- ☞ Pepper
- ☞ Dish-washing soap

Try It
1. Fill a bowl half full with water.
2. Sprinkle pepper all over the surface of the water. The more the better. The pepper represents sin in your life.
3. Put a drop of dish-washing soap on your finger. The soap stands for the Lord.
4. Dip your soapy finger into the bowl. What happens to the surface of the water? When the Lord comes into your life, that's how clean you become.

✞ PRAY
Thank God that he forgives your sins.

Life's Guidebook Says
Purify me from my sins, and I will be clean; wash me, and I will be whiter than snow. PSALM 51:7

HEAVENLY PLACE

CLOSE YOUR EYES and picture your perfect paradise. What did you see—a beach? An amusement park? A room full of video games? A soccer field? A classroom piled with textbooks? (Just kidding about the last one, but school can be a really cool place.)

When you picture your favorite place, you're safe, happy, and having fun. You probably don't picture a hospital room or a funeral home. Those places are usually filled with sickness and sadness.

We don't know exactly what heaven's going to look like. Words can't describe how beautiful, joyful, and fun it will be. But we do know some things about heaven that the apostle John wrote down in the book of Revelation. For one, heaven will be your perfect paradise—no matter what you pictured. We also know that heaven is a place where there's no more death, sorrow, crying, or pain (Revelation 21:4). In your forever home with God, sadness is gone forever and joy rules every day!

AWESOME ACTIVITY: HEAVEN BOUND

Have you ever told God that you believe in him and asked Jesus to forgive your sins? There's only one way to get to heaven—and it's only a prayer away. You can't earn entry into God's Kingdom. It's a free gift from him. If you want to guarantee that you'll see God in heaven, just pray something like this:

> *Jesus, I know I've disobeyed your rules. Thank you for taking the punishment on the cross for my mistakes. I believe you died and rose from the dead. I accept your gift of forgiveness and ask you to be the Lord of my life. I want to follow you on earth and look forward to seeing you in heaven. Amen.*

If you just prayed this prayer, tell your parents, a pastor, or the person who gave you this book. They'll be happy to hear that you're heaven bound. Then keep reading this book to learn all you can about your relationship with God.

✝ PRAY

If you've already prayed to ask Jesus to be your Savior, thank God for making such a beautiful place where you'll be able to spend eternity with him.

Life's Guidebook Says

[God] will wipe every tear from their eyes, and there will be no more death or sorrow or crying or pain. All these things are gone forever. REVELATION 21:4

ROCK-HARD ABS . . . AND MORE

DO YOU EVER GET FRUSTRATED with your body? Maybe you wish you could throw a football like an NFL quarterback. Or perhaps you'd love to have a huge lung capacity, so you could be a great swimmer and swim across the English Channel. Maybe you'd just like to be more coordinated, so you wouldn't trip all the time.

Your body will change through the years. Many of those changes will occur when you're a teenager, when you'll grow (choose just one)

a. at least several inches.
b. a deeper voice.
c. more body hair.
d. a third arm.
e. all the above except *d*.

The answer is *e*. But your body will continue to change long past your teen years. The Bible tells us one of the greatest changes happens when we die. That can sound scary. But as followers of Christ, when we die, our bodies are transformed from physical bodies to spiritual bodies. First Corinthians 15:43 says our bodies are "buried in weakness, but they will be raised in strength." No matter how well our bodies perform here on earth, we'll have amazingly powerful bodies when we get to heaven.

AWESOME ACTIVITY: CORE TRAINING

What's the situation with your abs? While worrying about having six-pack abs isn't a great idea at your age, you can work on having a strong core with these exercises:

☞ Bicycles—Lie on your back with your fingers laced together behind your head. Lift up your head slightly as you raise your feet and move your legs in a bicycle motion. Do three repetitions of 10.

☞ V-sit—Lie on your back and then try to raise your feet and upper body together. It's difficult. But if you can do it correctly, you'll end up sitting in a V shape. Hold for five seconds and go down. Try to do 10 repetitions.

☞ Swimmers—Lie on your stomach with your arms and legs stretched out as far as they'll go. Raise up your left arm and right leg. As you put those down, lift your right arm and left leg. Do 20 repetitions, and it'll look like you're swimming.

✝ PRAY

Thank God that he gives you a perfectly strong body when you get to heaven.

Life's Guidebook Says
Let me reveal to you a wonderful secret. We will not all die, but we will all be transformed! 1 CORINTHIANS 15:51

SCI-FI IN THE BIBLE

THINK OF THE FIRST TIME you saw something new and different. What words did you use to describe it? If you lived in the middle of a jungle and saw a hot-air balloon for the first time, what would you say to help your friends understand what it looked like? Write your answer here: _____

_____.

Your description might sound like something from a fantasy or sci-fi movie. Perhaps you'd say it was a magical floating egg without wings that carried people and spit fire.

Puzzling descriptions fill the book of Revelation. Sometimes what you read can sound like an odd gadget or a weird creature in a sci-fi movie. The apostle John described strange, evil locusts that looked like horses with tails like snakes that stung and hurt people. One modern scholar thought that sounded sort of like a military helicopter. John, who wrote the book of Revelation, had never seen automobiles, helicopters, or other modern vehicles. He would have had trouble describing unknown future technology. He used things he knew—like chariots, horses galloping, and swarms of locusts in the sky—to describe the things that God showed him in a vision.

Bible experts still don't understand all the descriptions in Revelation. John may have even described science that hasn't been invented yet. But in the midst of all the strange descriptions in Revelation, we can know that God controls the future and he wins in the end.

PUZZLE IT OUT: UNTWIST THE MESSAGE
The Bible verse below looks puzzling, but the words are just scrambled. Untwist each word to discover how the apostle John describes the place you'll go in the future as one of God's followers.

"The twelve gates were made of pearls—each gate from a single pearl!

Adn   eht   mina   srttee   aws   peur   dlog,

_____ _____ _____ _____ _____ _____ _____,

sa   crlea   sa   sglsa.

____ _____ ___ _____." REVELATION 21:21

✝ PRAY
Praise God that he knows the future, even if you can't totally understand it.

Life's Guidebook Says
The power of the horses was in their mouths and in their tails. The tails were like snakes whose heads could bite. REVELATION 9:19, NIrV

Answer: And the main street was pure gold, as clear as glass.

MASSIVE MANSION

How MANY ROOMS are in your home? Count all the closets and bathrooms. The largest private home built in the United States has a mind-blowing 250 rooms! Beginning in 1889, around 1,000 craftsmen from around the country came to Asheville, North Carolina, to work on the construction. Building such a massive, elaborate property took six years. But when it was finished, the Biltmore House had 35 bedrooms, 43 bathrooms, 65 fireplaces, three kitchens, an indoor swimming pool, and a bowling alley. The dining room table was so large that 64 guests could easily enjoy a meal together. A hidden passageway from the library to the guest rooms allowed people to sneak down for a book.

Today, anybody can pay to tour this magnificent house. That's not the case with the house that Jesus talked about in the Gospel of John. He'd just finished eating the Last Supper with his disciples, where he told them that someone would betray him and predicted Peter would deny him three times. After such alarming news, the disciples were worried, so Jesus told them, in John 14:1-2, "Don't let your hearts be troubled. . . . There is more than enough room in my Father's home. If this were not so, would I have told you that I am going to prepare a place for you?"

The disciples didn't understand what Jesus meant. But in a few days—after Jesus' arrest, trial, death on a cross, and rising from the dead—they knew Jesus was in heaven, preparing a place for them. He's preparing a special place in an amazing mansion for you, too.

WACKY LAUGHS

Knock, knock.
Who's there?
Ima.
Ima who?
Ima going to heaven!

Q. What do you call a bunny's home?
A. A rabbitat.

Q. What two fish can you find in heaven?
A. The angelfish and sole.

✝ PRAY

Thank Jesus that he knows you so well that he's making a special place for you in his Father's house.

Life's Guidebook Says

[Jesus said,] "There is more than enough room in my Father's home. If this were not so, would I have told you that I am going to prepare a place for you?"
JOHN 14:2

BABY IN A BASKET

NORMALLY, THE BIRTH of a baby is a time for celebration. Experts say four babies are born every second around the world. That's a lot of celebrating!

But when Jochebed and Amram had a baby, they didn't celebrate at all. They were too afraid for their baby's life. In those days, the Israelites lived as slaves in Egypt. Pharaoh feared the Israelites would become too strong, so he ordered that all their baby boys be killed. Jochebed hid her baby for three months, but then things became too dangerous. She got a basket, covered the bottom with tar, put her baby inside, and placed the basket in the Nile River. Now, the Nile River is no place for a baby. It's filled with crocodiles and dangerous currents. But the basket stayed safely in the reeds.

You probably know what happened next. Pharaoh's daughter came down to bathe and discovered the basket. She picked up the baby, decided to raise him as her own, and named him Moses (Exodus 2:10).

From the time of his birth, Moses had a special relationship with God. God kept him safe in the basket, safe wandering across the desert, and safe when he came back to free his people from Pharaoh. God even allowed Moses to perform amazing miracles, such as parting the Red Sea and bringing water out of a rock.

The same God that had a relationship with Moses wants a close relationship with you. Now that's a reason to celebrate!

PLEXER

See if you can solve this plexer. (If you don't remember what a plexer is, see p. 9.)

NibasleRiketver

✝ PRAY

Praise God for his awesome power and ability to do miracles . . . even today.

Life's Guidebook Says

The LORD replied, "Listen, I am making a covenant with you in the presence of all your people. I will perform miracles that have never been performed anywhere in all the earth or in any nation. And all the people around you will see the power of the LORD—the awesome power I will display for you." EXODUS 34:10

Answer: Basket in the Nile River

LIGHT THE WORLD

THE SUN IS HOT. How hot? Well, the temperature at its core is 27 million degrees Fahrenheit. That's too hot to even comprehend. As the closest star to earth, the sun heats our planet and gives us light. Although the sun is 93 million miles away, it takes just eight minutes for light to get to us over that distance.

The sun is powerful, too. Scientists estimate you'd have to explode 100 billion tons of dynamite every second to equal the energy produced by the sun. Without the sun, life on earth couldn't exist. But when it comes to power, the sun can't even come close to competing with God's Son.

First, God created the sun. A created thing can never compare to its creator. Plus, the book of Revelation tells us that with God around there's no need for a sun. Revelation 21:23 says heaven won't have a sun or moon, because the Lamb (that's Jesus) will provide the light. Think about that fact. When we get to heaven, God's power will be so obvious that light from him will illuminate everything. Nothing is hidden from God in heaven or on earth. In John 8:12, Jesus says that he's the light of the world. Later, in 1 John 1:5, the apostle John writes, "God is light, and there is no darkness in him at all."

Unlike the sun, which we sometimes can't see, God's power and light always surround us.

WEIRD FACTS: SUN SPOTS
Check out these amazing facts about the sun:

- ☞ The sun is so big that one million earths could fit inside it.
- ☞ Because of the difference in gravity, if you weigh 75 pounds on earth, you'd weigh 2,100 pounds on the sun!
- ☞ Every planet in our solar system rotates around the sun in the same direction—counterclockwise.
- ☞ The sun rotates much more slowly than the earth. While the earth rotates once every 24 hours, it takes the sun 609 hours to completely rotate.

✝ PRAY
Tell God you want to live in the light—even when the sun is down and it's dark outside.

Life's Guidebook Says
The city has no need of sun or moon, for the glory of God illuminates the city, and the Lamb is its light.   REVELATION 21:23

AMAZING WONDERS

GOD DID AWESOME THINGS in the apostle Paul's life. The Lord blinded Paul and restored his sight. He sent Paul all over the known world and provided food, shelter, and all his needs as he spread the Good News about Jesus. Paul performed and saw numerous miracles. If anybody had a reason to brag about his relationship with God, it was Paul. But Paul said he wouldn't boast (although he probably did . . . a little).

God even showed Paul a vision of heaven. In the beginning of 2 Corinthians 12, Paul writes that he was caught up to heaven and heard things that were too astounding to be put into words. What do you think Paul saw and heard? Write down some ideas:

_____

_____

Now go back and read your ideas. You're probably wrong, because Paul said it was *too* amazing to express in words, and you just used words. *Ha!*

But seriously, heaven will be an amazing place. The Bible gives us hints of what it'll be like, but we won't know the full extent of its glory until we're there. Then we can agree with Paul that he was right.

QUIZ: ALL ABOUT PAUL

Look at each statement below. Did Paul do it? Answer true or false, and then check your answers.

1. Was bitten by a poisonous snake and lived   **T or F**
2. Was known for always wearing a Los Angeles Angels baseball hat   **T or F**
3. Survived a shipwreck by swimming to the island of Malta   **T or F**
4. Had a band of followers known as the Fantastic Pharisees Merry Men   **T or F**
5. Built a wooden ship to hold two of every animal   **T or F**
6. Traveled over 10,000 miles to tell people about Jesus Christ   **T or F**
7. Was dragged out of a city, hit with stones, and left for dead but came back and kept preaching   **T or F**
8. Wrote, "I can do everything through Christ, who gives me strength."   **T or F**

✞ PRAY

Thank God that you'll get to spend eternity in a place that's too astounding for words.

Life's Guidebook Says
I was caught up to paradise and heard things so astounding that they cannot be expressed in words.   2 CORINTHIANS 12:4

Answers: 1. T; 2. F; 3. T; 4. F; 5. F; 6. T; 7. T; 8. T

TRACK IT DOWN

Tommy had never been hunting with his dad before. So when Dad invited him to go turkey hunting, he jumped at the chance. After camping all night near a field, they woke up early and walked to find a good spot to hide. As they hiked, Dad pointed out deer tracks. They even saw a fresh set of bear tracks. Finally, Dad found a good place to settle down and call in the turkeys.

"Getting just the right clucks and purrs is important to bring in the turkeys," Dad said, taking out his turkey caller. He showed Tommy how to do it and then handed the caller to Tommy. He tried to imitate his dad's call, but all that came out was a silly sound. "Good try," Dad said, laughing. "But you still need some practice."

Tommy practiced and Dad laughed for most of the morning. They didn't see many turkeys, but they had a great time together.

As Christians, we're called to imitate Christ—not a turkey call. Deuteronomy 13:4 commands us to follow, worship, and remain faithful to the Lord. Just like Tommy and his dad saw deer tracks, we should look for where God is going and follow him. When we remain focused on Christ, we will always be hunting down the right path.

EXPERIMENT: ANIMAL TRACKER

Think of one thing you can do to stay on track for Jesus. Then find an open space near your home to track some animals.

Stuff You Need
☞ Measuring tape
☞ Small wooden stakes or chopsticks
☞ String (optional)

Try It
1. Look for a patch of land near your home that's mainly dirt.
2. Measure a three-foot square.
3. Mark the corners with the wooden stakes. You can tie a string around all the stakes next to the ground or make a line in the dirt with your foot.
4. Smooth out all the dirt in the square.
5. Come back in a day or two. Check to see what prints an animal or insect has made in your square. You may want to take a photo and match the prints to pictures online to see what kind of animal you tracked.

✝ PRAY

Commit to following God—no matter where he leads you.

Life's Guidebook Says
You must follow the Lord your God and fear Him. You must keep His commands and listen to His voice; you must worship Him and remain faithful to Him.
DEUTERONOMY 13:4, HCSB

ALL SKINNED UP

WHEN SOMEBODY SAYS you're "thick skinned," it means that you don't let little things bother you. How would you react in these situations?

a. Somebody cuts in front of you at the water fountain.
b. You accidentally drop your backpack and someone laughs.
c. Your mom forgets to wash your favorite T-shirt.

If you answered (a) "So what," (b) "It's no big deal," and (c) "Not a problem," then you're probably pretty thick skinned. And as a boy, you're naturally thick skinned. A man's skin is about 25 percent thicker than a woman's. Your skin is also rougher than a girl's, and oilier. That means boys tend to need more frequent showers than girls.

Being thick skinned can help you, especially in your relationships with friends. Whenever you hang out with somebody for a long time, you're bound to eventually say something you regret or do something stupid. Maybe you've had a friend make fun of you when you accidentally dropped your lunch in the lunchroom. Or perhaps a close friend didn't invite you over for a sleepover when a lot of other guys were invited. Instead of getting mad or holding a grudge, the Bible tells us to be forgiving. King Solomon put it this way in Proverbs 19:11: "Sensible people control their temper; they earn respect by overlooking wrongs."

Being thick skinned doesn't mean you store up anger until you explode. It means you let the little things go and concentrate on more important things—like being a good friend.

WACKY LAUGHS

Q. Why couldn't the prisoner call a friend?
A. He didn't have a cell phone.

Q. On what kind of boat does everyone get along?
A. A friend-ship.

Q. Why doesn't anyone want to be friends with a clock?
A. Because all it does is *tock, tock, tock.*

✝ PRAY

Ask God to help you be patient with your friends and forgive the little things that bother you.

Life's Guidebook Says
Sensible people control their temper; they earn respect by overlooking wrongs.
PROVERBS 19:11

LOST AND FOUND

A SHEPHERD BOY IN ISRAEL searched for a lost goat along crumbling cliffs near the Dead Sea. Suddenly, he spied a cave. Maybe you've had fun rock climbing with harnesses and strong ropes, but it's much scarier without places to grip and when rocks disintegrate as you try to grab them. The shepherd boy climbed to the mouth of the cave and tossed a rock inside. *Crash!* He heard something break. He left to tend his flocks and returned later with a friend. That's when they made an amazing discovery.

The boys entered the cave and found old jars they hoped contained great treasures. *Oomph!* They opened a tall clay jar and discovered old scrolls wrapped in linen. When Bible experts learned about the discovery, they rushed to the caves of Qumram. These ancient papers, called the Dead Sea Scrolls, turned out to be the oldest fragments of the Scriptures ever discovered.

When God's Word is found, it's a time to celebrate. In the Old Testament, King Josiah took over the throne after his father, evil King Amon, was killed. The people had forgotten God's Word and even lost the Scriptures, the Law of Moses. As Josiah's workers restored the Temple, they found the Law of Moses. Josiah read it and tore his clothes to show that he felt bad that he and his people had not followed God's Word. Josiah made changes and led his people in following God again. Just like Josiah, you should treat your Bible as a special treasure.

WEIRD FACTS: ARCHAEOLOGY AND THE BIBLE

- ☞ It's believed that a group called the Essenes produced the Dead Sea Scrolls from 200 BC to AD 68. Many are written on animal skins.
- ☞ More than 168,000 Bibles are sold or given away every day.
- ☞ The Bible has been translated into more than 1,200 languages.
- ☞ In 2009, archaeologists dug up Egyptian coins with the name and picture of Joseph.
- ☞ A stone tablet, called the Mesha Stele, tells the story of some of the kings of Israel.
- ☞ Archaeologists found the palace at Samaria where kings of Israel lived.

✝ PRAY

Thank God that the Bible has been preserved so well.

Life's Guidebook Says

While they were bringing out the money collected at the LORD's Temple, Hilkiah the priest found the Book of the Law of the LORD that was written by Moses.
2 CHRONICLES 34:14

CUT AND BURNED

RIP! CRACKLE! KING JEHOIAKIM listened to the words God gave the prophet Jeremiah. Then he grabbed the scroll, cut it into pieces, and threw them in the fire (Jeremiah 36:23). He burned other copies of words that God had told Jeremiah to write. He didn't like hearing God's message, because it pointed out that he was wicked. *No problem!* he thought. *I'll just wipe out God's Word.*

Do you think his plan worked? Well, Jehoiakim remained a king only a little over three years after that. The book of Jeremiah, on the other hand, can still be found thousands of years later in our Bible.

Modern leaders have also burned God's Word. In 1379, John Wycliffe and his friends began translating the Bible into English. Within four years, they had distributed thousands of copies to the people. However, this angered church leaders, who tried to hunt down and burn every copy. They thought only the church should own Bibles—not common people. They did terrible things, like burning people to death for hiding a copy of God's Word. Wycliffe also lost his life. But his work was not lost. He wanted everybody to be able to have a Bible so they could study God's Word for themselves. Today, there are still over 150 original copies of the Wycliffe Bible left.

God said his Word would last forever, and he keeps proving it.

EXPERIMENT: REAPPEARING WORDS

God's Word has spread everywhere, even when men have tried to get rid of it. Enjoy this experiment as a reminder that God's Word will survive.

Stuff You Need

- ☞ 2 blank pieces of paper
- ☞ Water
- ☞ Hard surface (glass or countertop)
- ☞ Ballpoint pen

Try It

1. Soak one piece of paper and lay it flat on the hard surface.
2. Cover it with the dry piece of paper and write a message. The impression of your message will appear on the wet paper.
3. When the paper dries, the message disappears. Wet the paper again and you'll see the message again.

✝ PRAY

Ask God to help you memorize Scriptures, so no one can take God's Word from you.

Life's Guidebook Says

The grass withers and the flowers fade, but the word of our God stands forever.
ISAIAH 40:8

BREAKING WORDS

CRASH! MOSES SMASHED the stone tablets with the Ten Commandments written on them. He was shocked and angry to walk down the mountain and find the people worshiping a golden calf they had made instead of waiting to hear from the one true God (Exodus 32:19). The Israelites had seen the smoke on top of the mountain that showed them God's presence, but they grew tired of waiting for Moses to return with God's message. Instead they made an idol and worshiped it.

God had promised Israel would become a great nation, but only if the people followed his rules. God forgave the people and instructed Moses to write the laws on another set of tablets, and Israel became a great nation. Many years later, however, the nation fell when it again turned away from following God. God's truth teaches leaders and people everywhere how to be wise and great.

Write down the two biggest lessons you've learned from the Bible:

1. _____
2. _____

Near the beginning of the 20th century, the president of Brazil asked businessman and philanthropist Roger Babson to explain why America became so much greater than Brazil when they had the same resources. Babson replied, "North America was largely founded by people seeking God. South America was founded by men seeking gold." You can help keep your country great by following God's rules. Countries fail when they fall away from God. Let the Bible's commands guide your heart and mind, and you can be wise too.

WACKY LAUGHS

Q. Who was the biggest sinner in the Bible?

A. Moses, because he broke all the Ten Commandments at once.

Q. If Moses came back to earth, why wouldn't he want to talk to former president George W. Bush?

A. Because the last time he spoke to a bush, he ended up wandering in the desert for 40 years.

✝ PRAY

Pray for your country and its citizens to follow God.

Life's Guidebook Says

Blessed is the nation whose God is the LORD, the people whom he has chosen as his heritage! PSALM 33:12, ESV

THE LAST WORD

EXTINCT! ROMAN EMPEROR DIOCLETIAN wanted to rid Christianity from the world. His soldiers searched high and low to destroy every copy of God's words and any portion of Scripture. He imprisoned and killed Christians in the largest and bloodiest persecution in the history of the Roman Empire. In the year AD 303, his men built a column of victory over the embers of the last Bible they burned. Diocletian ordered his men to inscribe the words *Extincto nomine Christianorum* on the column. That means "Extinct is the name of Christians."

Wrong! Three years later, Constantine became emperor of the known world. More important, during his reign Constantine became a Christian. He offered a reward for any copies of the New Testament people could find. Within 24 hours people presented him with 50 copies. Constantine made Christianity the official religion of the Roman Empire. What a huge turnaround!

Today, there are still unbelievers who try to stop Christians from talking about Jesus. Both the Old and New Testaments tell us that what God says will last forever. When people try to stop the spread of Christianity, it fails. God always wins.

PUZZLE IT OUT: HIDDEN MESSAGE

Decode this puzzle to see what Jesus said about God's Word lasting.

To find the real letter for each word, use the chart. Each two-letter code is from the column word *LOST* and then the row word *WORDS*. So LR = G.

	W	O	R	D	S
L	M	R	G	L	A
O	O	S	W	V	B
S	D	N	E	Y	T
T	B	I	H	P	U

"__ __ __ __ __ __ __ __ __ __ __ __ __ __ __ __
TR SR LS OD SR SO   LS SO SW   SR LS LO SS TR

__ __ __ __   __ __ __ __ __ __ __ __ __ __ ,
OR TO LD LD   SW TO OO LS TD TD SR LS LO

__ __ __ __ __ __ __ __ __ __ __
TW TS SS LW SD   OR OW LO SW OO

__ __ __ __ __ __ __ __ __
OR TO LD LD   SO SR OD SR LO

__ __ __ __ __ __ __ __ ."
SW TO OO LS TD TD SR LS LO

✝ PRAY

Thank God that you can trust his words will remain forever. Ask him to give you the courage to keep sharing Scriptures.

Life's Guidebook Says

[Jesus said,] "I tell you the truth, until heaven and earth disappear, not even the smallest detail of God's law will disappear until its purpose is achieved."
MATTHEW 5:18

Answer: Luke 21:33: "Heaven and earth will disappear, but my words will never disappear."

EAT YOUR WORDS!

THINK OF YOUR FAVORITE dessert or snack. It might be ice cream or gooey chocolate. It's probably sweet and certainly yummy. Psalm 119:103 mentions that God's Word is sweeter than honey. Ezekiel actually ate God's words and said that they did taste as sweet as honey (Ezekiel 3:1-3). The Bible says the apostle Peter said God's Word is solid food (Hebrews 5:12-14). That means it leaves you feeling full and your stomach happy. One town believed those exact ideas.

Around the time of World War I, a patient treated at an American hospital in Turkey received a Bible. He returned home and showed it to friends, although he lived in an area with no Christians. Someone became very angry that he owned a Bible. *Rip!* The man grabbed the book, tore it to pieces, and tossed them into the street. A butcher came by and picked up the papers. He used them to wrap small items such as olives and bits of cheese. Villagers who read the wrapping asked the butcher for more. Sometime later a salesman came to the village and found 100 people all eager to buy a Bible. The little taste they'd had of the Bible made them hungry to have all of it. Crack open your Bible and get a taste of it today. You'll soon want more.

AWESOME ACTIVITY: SWEET SURPRISE KISSES
Make sweet chocolate kisses with a sweeter surprise.

Stuff You Need
- ☞ Foil
- ☞ Scissors
- ☞ Glass and pencil (optional)
- ☞ Tape
- ☞ Empty egg carton
- ☞ Chocolate chips
- ☞ Microwave-safe dish
- ☞ Small nuts or chopped-up pieces of caramel

Try It
1. Cut foil into two-inch circles. You can trace a glass to make it easier. Cut into the center of each circle. Overlap the center cut edges of foil to make a cone or funnel shape. Tape closed on outside. Place the cone point down in an egg carton. These are molds for making the kisses.
2. Melt chocolate in a microwave-safe dish (follow instructions on package).
3. Pour chocolate into cones, leaving room at opening.
4. Drop in a nut or piece of caramel.
5. Cool (place in freezer to cool it faster).
6. Remove candies from foil and enjoy.

✝ PRAY
Pray for more people to read the Bible and believe in Jesus.

Life's Guidebook Says
"Fill your stomach with this," [God] said. And when I [Ezekiel] ate it, it tasted as sweet as honey in my mouth. EZEKIEL 3:3

SWORDS THAT CUT DEEP

WHAT CUTS DEEPLY and divides the flesh?

a. A laser
b. A sword
c. The Bible
d. A balloon
e. A roll of French bread

Just remember your ABCs, because all of those letters are correct. (*E* could also work if the bread is *really* old.)

The Bible describes the precision with which God's Word can cut into our lives. His Word is sharper than a double-edged sword (Hebrews 4:12). It can pierce our innermost being. But while God's Word can hurt, it also always brings healing.

Modern science has created lasers that can both hurt and heal. A laser is a specially focused light beam where all the light is one color and the light waves all travel in the same direction. The light beam concentrates on one tiny spot, so the energy is powerful. CDs and DVDs are read with lasers. Lasers can also accurately cut hard metals, and doctors use them in surgery for delicate operations.

That's impressive, but God's Word is even more powerful. When you read your Bible, it changes who you are. It brings new life and helps you understand the truth. It pierces deep inside you and judges your thoughts and desires. And it's a lot safer to handle than a metal sword or a laser.

AWESOME ACTIVITY: BALLOON SWORD FIGHT
Blow up long balloons and enjoy a balloon battle. Consider some techniques used in sword fights and have fun.

☞ "Drawing the sword" is when you remove it from the scabbard strapped to your body. Practice starting with the balloon sword at your side and drawing it upward.
☞ Your body needs to be balanced to fight. Watch where you place each foot.
☞ It's best to stand perpendicular (at a right angle) to your opponent, so less of your body is exposed.
☞ *En garde* means to ready your weapon.
☞ To "block" is to stop a blow from an opponent.
☞ To "lunge" is to thrust the sword forward toward your opponent's chest.

✝ PRAY
Ask God to help you not be afraid to dig deeply into his Word. The truth may hurt a little, but God always brings healing.

Life's Guidebook Says
The word of God is alive and powerful. It is sharper than the sharpest two-edged sword, cutting between soul and spirit, between joint and marrow. It exposes our innermost thoughts and desires. HEBREWS 4:12

LIVE IT, WEAR IT, LOVE IT

DO YOU EVER READ T-SHIRTS? Some have funny sayings, like "If history repeats itself, I am so getting a dinosaur" or a camel saying, "Guess what day it is!"

Lots of Christians wear T-shirts so people know what they believe. This gear can also include words and messages. Maybe you've seen the classic *WWJD?* (which stands for *What Would Jesus Do?*). Or perhaps you've found shirts with fun sayings like "Gopher this, gopher that, gopher Jesus." Other shirts just feature long passages from the Bible. While wearing your faith on your chest may seem new, it actually started a long time ago.

In the book of Deuteronomy, God told his people to wear his words as symbols on their hands and to bind them on their foreheads. No, God's people didn't run out and get tattooed. (Leviticus 19:28 says not to print any marks on your body.) But they did wear little boxes on their foreheads that contained tiny scrolls. God hoped the boxes would remind them to live out his words. Many of the people made a big show of wearing God's words, but, sadly, they didn't follow them.

That's true today. Just because you wear a shirt with God's Word or a message about Jesus, it doesn't mean you're living out your faith. Some people put on a tee and act mean and choose to disobey God.

What God really wants is to have his words lived out and written on our hearts. That means memorizing and treasuring Scripture, so it becomes part of who you are and all the choices you make. More than having his Word surround us, God wants it to be a part of us that we live every day.

PLEXER
Solve this plexer to see what God wants to break out. (If you don't remember what a plexer is, see p. 9.)

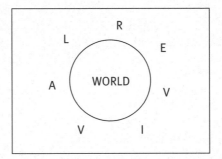

✞ PRAY
Ask God to help you know and live his words so people will want to know him.

Life's Guidebook Says
Tie them to your hands and wear them on your forehead as reminders. Write them on the doorposts of your house and on your gates. DEUTERONOMY 6:8-9

Answer: Revival around the world

CAPTIVE WORDS

WHACK! Eighteen-year-old James Smith was great with an axe. In 1755, you had to be. Swinging an axe helped you clear roads and build houses. As James and a friend rode out to clear some trees for a road in the wilderness of Pennsylvania, they heard a frightening noise.

Whoop! Whoop! A war cry sounded. Before James could grab his rifle, Indians dragged him off. They tortured him before eventually inviting him to join their tribe and learn their ways. James was adopted by an Indian family, but he never forgot his faith. During his captivity, he was given a Bible that Indians found in a raid. He treasured the Bible and read it continually.

When James escaped four years later, life was much different from what he remembered. The girl he loved had married someone else. His family was excited to see him but surprised by how much he looked and acted like an Indian. He married and had seven children. As tensions in the frontier grew, he trained a group of men, called "Smith's Rangers," to fight. They dressed, acted, and fought like Indians. They warred against hostile Indians and also fought traders who took advantage of peaceful tribes.

When James's first wife died, he spent Sunday afternoons sitting beside her grave reading the Bible. He married again and moved to Kentucky, a new frontier. James forgave the Indians who had kidnapped him and became a missionary to share his greatest treasure—God—with those who had once been his captors.

QUIZ: WHAT WOULD YOU RATHER DO?
Would you rather . . .

- ☞ play a game or read the Bible?
- ☞ spend time with a friend or your dad?
- ☞ go to church or sleep late on Sunday?
- ☞ read a comic book or the Bible?

You may have found that reading the Bible is not the number one thing you want to do. But reading God's Word always has great benefits. Check out this next group of questions to see if you treasure God's Word:

Do you have a favorite Bible verse or story?
When you have a problem, do you talk to God about it?
Do you know where your Bible is right now?

Answering yes to these questions shows that you treasure God's Word and that it's important in your life.

✝ PRAY
Thank God for your Bible, and ask him to help you memorize Scriptures.

Life's Guidebook Says
Store your treasures in heaven, where moths and rust cannot destroy, and thieves do not break in and steal. MATTHEW 6:20

HOORAY FOR MOMS!

LIST THREE THINGS you love about your mom:

1. _____
2. _____
3. _____

You may have written that she's a good cook, plays games with you, or lets your friends hang out at your home. These are all good reasons to be thankful for your mom. Your mother does many things. She probably drives you places, washes your clothes, helps with homework, and feeds you. The Bible gives a list of what an excellent mom does that includes preparing meals, helping the poor, earning money, and making clothes for her family. Following the list, it says, "Her children stand and bless her" (Proverbs 31:28). Mother's Day is a great time to thank and praise your mom for what she does and to show you love her.

Paul praised two mothers, but not for their cooking, beauty, or hard work. He praised Lois and Eunice, the mother and grandmother of Timothy, for teaching Timothy about God. These moms shared their love of God. Can you remember your mom reading Bible stories to you when you were little? Do you remember your favorite one? Paul honored Timothy's mother with words of praise and reminded Timothy that he was blessed to know the Scriptures as a child (2 Timothy 3:14-15).

Thank God for your mom, and thank your mom for sharing her faith with you.

AWESOME ACTIVITY: HONOR YOUR MOTHER

Choose a few ways to honor your mom this week.

☞ Give her a hug every hour on Mother's Day.
☞ Make a list of 10 reasons you love her.
☞ Make a card or write a poem for her.
☞ Cook her a meal or snack.
☞ Buy or make a gift for her.
☞ Do something with her, like watch a movie, take a walk, or tell her jokes.
☞ Give her a neck or back massage.
☞ Pray for her.
☞ Thank her for teaching you about Jesus.

✚ PRAY

Ask God to bless your mom with good health and a good future.

Life's Guidebook Says

I remember your genuine faith, for you share the faith that first filled your grandmother Lois and your mother, Eunice. And I know that same faith continues strong in you. 2 TIMOTHY 1:5

BULLY ZAPPER

"WEAKLING! LOSER! You can't make anything work."

If you listen to the things bullies yell, they can hurt and make you feel defeated. That's what happened to God's people when they were trying to rebuild the wall around Jerusalem (you can read the whole story in the book of Nehemiah).

Israel's enemies teased and taunted. Finally, the Israelites ignored their words and just continued working. Then the bullies moved on to threatening physical harm. That's when the people responded with a great idea. One person worked while another stood and held a weapon. They prayed and stood up for one another. They didn't confront the bullies, but they focused on their own activities and stuck together.

We would never go around school or other places with weapons, but we can do what God's people did by standing together and sticking up for our friends. Research shows that bullies tend to back down when they see that the person they want to bully is not alone. So sticking with your friends is more fun and safer than being a lone wolf. Chances are a bully is targeting more people than just you. Look around and see who else needs a defender against the bully, and talk with that person about standing together. When you stand and do nothing, you're a bystander. But when you stand against a bully, you're an upstander. Two or more upstanders can make a great team to zap out bullying. Having friends close by also gives you witnesses for when you report bullying to adults.

PLEXER
Solve this plexer. (If you don't remember what a plexer is, see p. 9.)

```
D        stopstop bull eee
N
A
T
S
```

✝ PRAY
Ask God to give you friends who will stick up for you and the strength to stick up for your friends.

Life's Guidebook Says
[Nehemiah said,] "Only half my men worked while the other half stood guard with spears, shields, bows, and coats of mail. The leaders stationed themselves behind the people of Judah. NEHEMIAH 4:16

Answer: Stand up to stop bullies.

A BIG, BAD BULLY

THINK OF THE BIGGEST GUY you've ever seen. Maybe he's a football player or professional wrestler. Now think of the meanest kid you know. Put those two thoughts together and what do you get?

Well, whatever you get, it probably wouldn't compare to nine-foot-tall Goliath. He stood meaner, bigger, and tougher than any other bully. What Goliath had in height, he lacked in intelligence. He had just one move—the old dare-ya trick. He would just yell, "*I dare* the soldiers of Israel to send a man down to fight me." And when you're as big, mean, and scary as Goliath, no man wants to fight you.

But one boy did. God enjoys showing his strength in our weakness, so he sent a boy to accept the giant's dare. David, the young shepherd, wasn't intimidated by that giant dude. He refused to wear heavy armor or even look like a soldier. He was a God-loving shepherd boy and proud of it. He didn't shrink away when Goliath shouted curses. Instead, he told Goliath he was coming in the name of the Lord and that God was the one he'd really have to fight (1 Samuel 17:45). He picked up five stones as his ammunition, but he only needed one. *Swish!* The stone zipped through the air, hit the giant between the eyes, and killed him in one blow. Once David chopped off Goliath's head, the Israelite soldiers gained courage and chased after the army of Philistines.

PUZZLE IT OUT: GET RID OF THE BULLY

Cross out the letters in the word *bully* to find a secret message.

B	I	L	G	L	Y	N	Y	O	L	R	L	E
B	U	N	Y	E	G	A	L	T	L	I	B	V
E	U	W	Y	O	B	R	L	D	L	S	Y	A
U	N	Y	D	L	T	H	B	I	N	Y	K	O
F	G	L	O	D	U	S	W	O	Y	R	D	S

_____

_____

✝ PRAY

Thank God that you don't have to be bigger than a bully to stand up to him, because you serve a big God. Ask God to help you see the truth behind a bully's words.

Life's Guidebook Says

David replied to the Philistine, "You come to me with sword, spear, and javelin, but I come to you in the name of the LORD of Heaven's Armies—the God of the armies of Israel, whom you have defied." 1 SAMUEL 17:45

Answer: Ignore negative words and think of God's words.

GOOD COMEBACKS

EVER FEEL STUMPED and can't think of a good comeback to a tricky question? Religious leaders tried to stump Jesus. They followed him and tried to trap him with clever questions.

Jesus outwitted them every time. He often responded to their questions with a question of his own. When they asked, "Should we pay taxes?" Jesus asked for a coin and answered by saying, "Whose picture is on the coin?"

"Caesar's," they answered.

Jesus said, "Give to Caesar what belongs to Caesar. Give God what belongs to God" (Matthew 22:15-22).

At another point in the Bible, Jesus was eating a Sabbath meal at the home of a leader of the Pharisees. A man in need of healing stood nearby. The Pharisees wanted to see if Jesus would heal the man and therefore break the Old Testament law against "working" on the Sabbath. So Jesus asked them, "Which of you doesn't work on the Sabbath? If your son or your cow falls into a pit, don't you rush to get him out?" (Luke 14:5). They didn't reply, because they knew they would help. Jesus healed the man.

Jesus used God's wisdom to leave his bullies puzzled, with their mouths hanging open. He had the wisdom to know what questions to ask.

Jesus also used silence. When Jesus was questioned by Herod, he remained silent (Luke 23:9). Herod wanted to see Jesus perform a miracle. Jesus knew Herod's heart. Jesus also knew his words and actions had already spoken for him.

AWESOME ACTIVITY: RESPONSES TO TEASING

The best response to a bully can be silence (then going and reporting the bullying to an adult). No one likes to be called a tattletale, but this is the best way to save both yourself and others from being bullied. If a bully thinks nobody will tell, it makes him believe he can continue to bully people. Memorize these verses and think about them if someone teases you.

☞ The one who has knowledge uses words with restraint, and whoever has understanding is even-tempered. (PROVERBS 17:27, NIV)

☞ Do not be quick with your mouth, do not be hasty in your heart to utter anything before God. God is in heaven and you are on earth, so let your words be few. (ECCLESIASTES 5:2, NIV)

✝ PRAY

Ask God to help you live in such a way that your words and actions speak of your belief in Jesus Christ.

Life's Guidebook Says
[Herod] asked Jesus question after question, but Jesus refused to answer.
LUKE 23:9

INVISIBLE ENEMIES

HAVE YOU EVER SEEN a floating finger? Just hold your pointer fingers an inch or so in front of your eyes and a few inches apart. Stare straight ahead, slightly unfocus your eyes, and you'll see part of a finger appear in midair! Move your fingers closer together and farther apart to change the size of the floating finger. You can also wiggle your two fingers up and down to make the "finger" move. Of course, you didn't magically grow a floating finger. It's an optical illusion that tricks our eyes.

Our eyes don't see everything. The apostle Paul tells us invisible enemies surround us (Ephesians 6:12). He is talking about Satan and his demons. The good news is God's invisible angels also battle for us. Demonic bullies don't frighten angels. Light is always greater than darkness. Angels are ready to bring on the fight.

Thinking about invisible powers can seem scary. But you should always remember that God's power is mightier than Satan's. You can call out for God's help through prayer. God knows how to help you. Paul also reminds us in Ephesians to be prepared. God's way of being prepared is to put on the right types of armor and carry the right weapons. These include truth, prayer, and God's Word.

EXPERIMENT: UNSEEN HELP

Air pressure, even if we cannot see it, can help us. Try this experiment to learn about unseen help, and remember that God's invisible angels lift you up.

Stuff You Need

☞ Plastic bag
☞ Books

Try It

1. Place the bag on a table with the open end hanging over the edge.
2. Put a book or two on top of the bag.
3. Hold the opening almost closed, and blow air into the opening. This is like blowing up a big balloon. Blow air into the bag until the books rise off the table.

✝ PRAY

Ask God to help you against unseen evil forces.

Life's Guidebook Says

We are not fighting against flesh-and-blood enemies, but against evil rulers and authorities of the unseen world, against mighty powers in this dark world, and against evil spirits in the heavenly places. EPHESIANS 6:12

WARNING! WARNING!

Has your mom or dad ever said, "How many times do I have to tell you to stop doing that?" What did you do? Did you keep doing the same behavior or heed their warning?

In the Old Testament, Pharaoh received numerous warnings from God, but he ignored every one. Moses asked Pharaoh again and again to let God's people go. Each time Pharaoh said no.

God sent 10 plagues on Pharaoh's land to get his attention and change his mind. Through God's power, Moses turned water to blood; sent frogs, gnats and flies, disease, and a hailstorm; and created other major problems. God wanted to show Pharaoh the might of the one true God. Each time, Pharaoh would ask Moses to stop the plague and promise to let the people go. Moses kept his word, but then Pharaoh changed his mind and continued to keep the people as slaves.

God and Moses never gave in to the bully. God eventually sent an angel of death to take the lives of the firstborn sons in Egypt. Finally, Pharaoh let the people go. But even then he tried one last time to win and chased after the Israelites. That's when God used the Red Sea to swallow up the Egyptian army. Pharaoh didn't know the Lord or understand his power (Exodus 5:2). As followers of Christ, we know God's power. So when we get a warning about our behavior, we need to be ready to change.

WEIRD FACTS: BULLY FOR YOU

☞ The word *bully* has changed meanings over hundreds of years:
- In the early 1900s, President Teddy Roosevelt used the term to mean "first rate." He would say, "Bully for you," to people who did a good job.
- In 1530 *bully* meant "sweetheart"—from the Dutch *boel*, meaning "lover" or "brother."
- Around the 17th century, the people used it to mean "fine fellow," but it eventually turned to "harasser of the weak" (which is what we think of when we use the word today).

☞ According to research by Fight Crime/Invest in Kids, by age 24, 60 percent of young men who bullied others from first through ninth grade had been convicted of at least one crime.

✝ PRAY

Tell God you're going to listen for his warnings, and be ready to change your behavior.

Life's Guidebook Says

"Is that so?" retorted Pharaoh. "And who is the Lord? Why should I listen to him and let Israel go? I don't know the Lord, and I will not let Israel go."
EXODUS 5:2

MAKES US STRONGER

SOME MEN JUMPED ANDREW as he walked along a crowded street in Egypt. They kept hitting his head and kicking him. Andrew thought he was going to die, but the entire time he prayed and felt God's peace. Finally the police showed up. *Whew!* Wait. *Oh, no!* They threw *Andrew* in jail! As Andrew regained his strength, he found many other Christians in prison, and they prayed together. Once Andrew was released, God sent people who helped him recover.

How had Andrew ended up in Egypt? Well, he had taken a year off from college in 2011 to serve as a missionary in Africa. Most of the time he lived with people who did not believe in Jesus. Andrew worked with them and got to know them. They listened with respect when Andrew spoke about Jesus. He was traveling through Egypt while a riot broke out, and that's where people beat him and imprisoned him. He discovered through his problems that God is with him no matter what happens. He became stronger inside and out because of what happened to him. Being a missionary isn't easy, but Andrew wants to continue serving God in this way. He returned to college but plans to go back to the mission field after graduation.

Jesus said we are blessed when people bully us for our faith. We may get teased, hurt, or lied about. Our response to being persecuted can help us grow, make us stronger, and empower our faith.

PUZZLE IT OUT: THE SHAPE OF THINGS

Unscramble each word in the shapes and then arrange them to find how God helped one man.

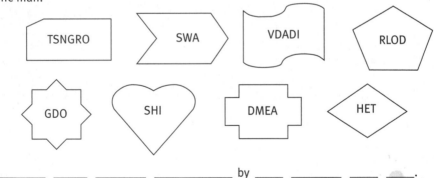

TSNGRO   SWA   VDADI   RLOD

GDO   SHI   DMEA   HET

_____ ____ _____ by ___ _____ ___ ____.

✝ PRAY

Ask God to help you to learn from tough times to be a better and stronger man.

Life's Guidebook Says

God blesses you when people mock you and persecute you and lie about you and say all sorts of evil things against you because you are my followers. Be happy about it! Be very glad! For a great reward awaits you in heaven. And remember, the ancient prophets were persecuted in the same way. MATTHEW 5:11-12

Answer: David was made strong by the Lord his God.

GANGBUSTERS

KING AHAB and his wife, Jezebel, were among the cruelest, meanest bullies that ever lived. The Bible says that Ahab sold himself to what was evil (1 Kings 21:25). This couple formed their own little gang and decided to kill off all God's prophets they could find. But one of their servants, named Obadiah, hid a hundred prophets in two caves and snuck water and food to save them.

Jezebel really wanted to get God's number-one prophet, Elijah. She hated the prophet so much that he topped her list of people to bully. She threatened Elijah's life. She even used witchcraft to try to curse Elijah, threatening to take his life. Her words hurt Elijah's spirit, and he felt depressed and overwhelmed. He cried to God. God spoke to him in a soft voice and renewed his spirit to help him face Jezebel. (You can read the whole story in 1 Kings 19.)

God also had a message for Jezebel, but it wasn't nearly as encouraging. Through Elijah, God let Jezebel know that she'd die soon and dogs would eat her remains (1 Kings 21:23). *Gross!* But that's exactly what happened to this evil queen.

Following God doesn't mean we will always feel great or be happy. Bullies can hurt our feelings and make us depressed. But like Elijah, we can turn to God, listen for his voice, and renew our strength.

LIFTOFF LIST
It's normal to feel sad, angry, and even alone at times. We need to turn to God, friends, and other people who love us to help us feel better. Check off things that help you feel better when you're feeling down:

___ Talking to a friend
___ Playing a video game
___ Watching a funny movie
___ Praying
___ Telling jokes
___ Reading the Bible or thinking about a favorite Scripture verse
___ Going for a run or bike ride

✝ PRAY
Tell God your problems, especially with bullies. Ask him to take care of the trouble.

Life's Guidebook Says
After the earthquake there was a fire, but the LORD was not in the fire. And after the fire there was the sound of a gentle whisper. When Elijah heard it, he wrapped his face in his cloak and went out and stood at the entrance of the cave.
1 KINGS 19:12-13

GOD'S GUYS LOOK DEEP

JESUS WAS TIRED from walking all day. He rested by a well as his disciples went to get food. When a woman came to get water, Jesus spoke to her. *Eww, cooties!*

In those days, Jewish men didn't talk to Samaritan women, especially a woman who was considered to have a bad reputation. But Jesus asked this woman to give him some water. He wanted to tell her something important and help her look beyond her daily chore of fetching water at the well. Jesus told her a great truth. He said he could give her lasting water that would bubble up inside her all the time. No, she wouldn't be a walking river of H_2O. He meant a different type of water. He could give her the Holy Spirit to quench her soul, so she'd never be spiritually thirsty again (John 4:13-14).

Some stories in the Bible seem hard to understand. God wants us to look deeper than the words and think about truth we can learn from his Word. The woman finally understood Jesus was the Messiah as he continued to talk and shared what he knew about her. She raced off to tell all the people in her village about Jesus.

Jesus wants us to discuss truth with him and share truth with our friends. Don't just read a Bible verse. Start looking deeper to find out what Jesus wants you to know.

LIFTOFF LIST
Put your faith into action. Check off these deep "watery" thoughts as you do them or learn about them.

____ I'll offer drinks when friends come to visit. Jesus said something cool about giving water to a child. (Matthew 10:42, NIV)

____ I want to let God's Word water my soul today, so I'll spend time thinking about today's verse.

____ I have someone I can talk with and ask questions about portions of the Bible I don't understand.

____ I understand what my church believes about baptism.

____ I know a way I can save water today (without being stinky).

____ The Holy Spirit teaches me and whets my appetite to understand more about God. (John 14:26)

✝ PRAY

Ask God for living water—that's his Holy Spirit—to fill you.

Life's Guidebook Says
[Jesus said,] "Those who drink the water I give will never be thirsty again. It becomes a fresh, bubbling spring within them, giving them eternal life."
JOHN 4:14

WELL-BEING

OH, MY ACHING HEAD! you think as you walk dizzily around the park. *Ouch! Now my stomach hurts too.*

If that ever happened to you, you'd probably think that you were getting sick. But it might be something even more dangerous—dehydration. When you don't drink enough water or other fluids, your body can shut down. So if you're being really active on a hot day, make sure you drink plenty of water, and watch out for those early warning signs of dehydration.

Water is used for drinking, washing, and cooking. Plants need it. Animals need it. And you need it. It's important to drink enough water. In Bible days, people lived in the desert, where they couldn't find water easily. They dug deep in the ground to make wells. Finding water made them so happy they named the wells, such as *Beer-lahai-roi*, which means "well of the Living One who sees me" (Genesis 16:14); *Beersheba*, meaning "well of the oath" (Genesis 21:30-31); *Esek*, which means "argument" (Genesis 26:20); and *Rehoboth*, meaning "open space" (Genesis 26:22). The names showed that people knew God supplied the water.

God is able to give us what we need. We often forget that and think science, doctors, or our own efforts can give us answers. Many people think that with enough money they can buy all they need.

Remember the real truth that God has power over everything. His words can keep you from becoming spiritually dehydrated, so "drink" from the Bible every day.

QUIZ: GOD'S WATER POWER
See what blanks you can fill in without looking up the verse. Then read the verses to check the answers.

___ Jesus had control over storms. He _____ the wind and waves.
(Matthew 8:23-27)
___ Jesus changed water into _____. (John 2:1-10)
___ Moses changed water into _____. (Exodus 7:17-25)
___ Moses made bitter water taste sweet by throwing a piece of _____ into it.
(Exodus 15:22-25)
___ God gave his people water from a _____. (Exodus 17:1-7)
___ God saved his people when he _____ the Red Sea.
(Exodus 14:21-29, NIrv)

✝ PRAY
Thank God for providing rain and water . . . and for water for your soul.

Life's Guidebook Says
I lift my hands to you in prayer. I thirst for you as parched land thirsts for rain.
PSALM 143:6

Answers: rebuked, wine, blood, wood, rock, parted

WATER FIGHTS

SPLASH! YOU MIGHT ENJOY water fights with friends when it's hot. Squirting water at each other or throwing water balloons is a great way to cool off.

Water fights can be fun. But in the book of Genesis, Isaac had a water fight that wasn't fun at all. God had blessed Isaac with bountiful crops and huge flocks of sheep and goats. His Philistine neighbors were jealous, so they filled Isaac's wells with dirt. The king told Isaac to move. He did, and he dug another well. This time his neighbors came and claimed the water was theirs. Rather than fight, Isaac let them have the well. He moved again and dug a new well. Again there was a dispute. Isaac trusted God to show him where to dig the next well. This time there was no argument, and Isaac prospered. (You can read the story in Genesis 26:12-22.)

In Bible times, wells gave life. They also became local meeting places where people talked and exchanged information. You and your friends may have a favorite hang-out where you can talk. It might be somebody's basement, a tree fort, or your church. Hopefully, it's a place where you can talk about deep, important things and share what God's been doing in your lives. He may not be leading you to a new place to dig a well, but God guides you every day.

WEIRD FACTS: WELL, WELL, WELL WELLS

☞ Jacob's well is the oldest continuously used artifact on earth today. (An artifact is a man-made object.) Jacob's well is 100 feet deep.

☞ About 15 out of every 100 families in the United States use well water.

☞ In some places, drills must dig 1,000 feet to find underground water.

☞ A dripping faucet can waste almost 20 gallons of water a week.

☞ Letting the water run while you brush your teeth wastes two gallons of water a minute.

☞ A bath uses three times more water than a shower.

✞ PRAY

Ask God for friends to meet with, enjoy, and talk about faith.

Life's Guidebook Says

Isaac moved on and dug another well. This time there was no dispute over it, so Isaac named the place Rehoboth (which means "open space"), for he said, "At last the LORD has created enough space for us to prosper in this land."
GENESIS 26:22

BUBBLES OF JOY

JERRY STEPPED IN THE SHOWER and turned the handles. *Hiss!* He heard a sound, but no water flowed out. The well had run dry! Jerry and his sister had to haul water from neighbors' houses so his family—plus the chickens, dog, cats, and even the parakeets—could drink. Finally, Jerry asked his uncle, "Can I hook a hose up to your faucet and add enough hoses to reach my back door?" His uncle agreed. Jerry screwed together the ends of hoses he borrowed from neighbors until he reached his house. That provided the water to keep his family and animals alive until they dug a deeper well.

The Israelites knew something about wells. God's people lived in deserts. They understood drought, thirst, and burning sand where grass doesn't grow. God sent a prophet to tell them about his plans for their future. He promised that one day the deserts would be filled with bubbling springs of water and that lush, green plants would cover the land (Isaiah 35:7).

God added that when these springs came, his followers would be filled with joy, and sadness would flee away (35:10). Sometimes our joy seems to dry up because we don't dig deep enough into our relationship with God. He wants to bless us. And when our souls have dry and thirsty days, it's easier for us to be thankful for the blessings he sends.

AWESOME ACTIVITY: BUBBLY WASHCLOTH

A little soap and water, plus blowing hot air, can produce bubbles that burst out of a cloth.

Stuff You Need
☞ Water
☞ Soap
☞ Washcloth

Try It
1. Wet the soap and washcloth.
2. Rub the soap back and forth across one side of the washcloth.
3. Flip over the washcloth and blow through the cloth—bubbles will pop out on the soapy side.
4. Keep blowing on it, and it will soon look like a white beard. Hold it up to your chin for a bearded look.
5. To impress friends, rub the cloth with soap and let it dry. Then add a little water in front of your friends and start blowing to make bubbles appear like magic.

✝ PRAY
Pray for God to fill your heart with love, so you feel bubbly with joy inside.

Life's Guidebook Says
The burning sand will become a pool, the thirsty ground bubbling springs. In the haunts where jackals once lay, grass and reeds and papyrus will grow.
ISAIAH 35:7, NIV

WATER FOR THE THIRSTY

"THE PEOPLE OF KENYA need fresh drinking water, and we're going to help."

The youth pastor at Kelly Forsha's church in Pennsylvania spoke passionately about helping others. Kelly knew she wanted to do something. The 12-year-old couldn't imagine walking miles every day just to get clean water. She helped raise money for the church's project, but then she wanted to do more. She talked to her parents and her school and formed her own organization, Digging Wells for Hope (DW4H). She sold pencils at school and other places to raise money to dig wells in Haiti. She knew that fewer than one out of three people in Haiti had access to clean drinking water.

By the end of 2013, almost four years after starting her project, Kelly had helped dig 12 wells in Haiti. The deepest is 350 feet deep. All of her wells provide clean water to thousands of people every year.

The earth has lots of water, but 97 percent is salt water. Clean drinking water is hard to find in some places. Many organizations are reaching out to help people drill new wells, including DW4H.

God made the entire earth. Some people are blessed to live in a land with plenty of water, food, and other resources. God calls those with plenty to share what we have. Youth groups, school organizations, and other groups of kids are helping. You can follow Kelly's example by grabbing a few friends and doing something to raise money for wells in poor countries. Then you'll be helping children around the world.

WACKY LAUGHS

Q. What Christmas carol did the Israelites sing in the desert?

A. "No-well, no-well, no-well . . ."

Q. What did the man say when his wife asked, "Why don't you go dig that well and then cross it off the to-do list?

A. "I'd rather be well-to-do!"

✝ PRAY

Ask God to give you ideas of how you can reach out to help the poor.

Life's Guidebook Says
If you help the poor, you are lending to the LORD—and he will repay you!
PROVERBS 19:17

THIRSTY CAMELS

HAVE YOU HEARD of the gallon challenge? It's popular among teens and college kids . . . and it can be dangerous. The idea is to drink an entire gallon of milk in one hour. Here's the problem: your body can't handle that much liquid at one time. Whatever milk goes in usually gets vomited out. Plus, you could get diarrhea and cramps. *Gross!*

God made camels very different from humans. The humps probably make that obvious. Camels would have no problem with the gallon challenge, because they can drink over 25 gallons at one time. In the Old Testament, Abraham sent one of his servants out on camels to find a wife for his son Isaac. When the servant stopped at a well, a girl named Rebekah offered him water. Then she gave water to the man's ten camels. That's a lot of water to haul from a well! The man had prayed and asked God to have a woman offer to water the camels so he would know she was the right wife for Isaac. Rebekah was an answer to prayer!

Rebekah showed compassion for the thirsty and tired traveler with her generous offer to do much more than asked. Some kids do only the little bit that's asked of them. Others help generously when they see a need. Look around today and see where you can help without being asked.

AWESOME ACTIVITY: WELL-MEANING WELLS

Look up each Bible verse to find out why each well was given its name. On the lines write the name of the well.

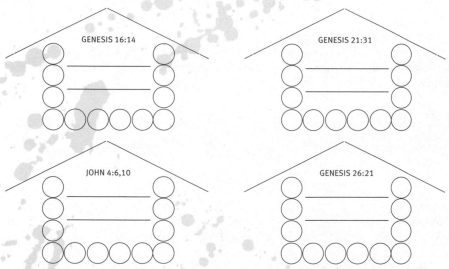

GENESIS 16:14

GENESIS 21:31

JOHN 4:6,10

GENESIS 26:21

✝ PRAY

Thank God for animals he made, and tell God you will help care for animals.

Life's Guidebook Says

[Rebekah] quickly emptied her jug into the watering trough and ran back to the well to draw water for all his camels. GENESIS 24:20

Answers: 1. Well of the Living; 2. Well of the Oath; 3. Jacob's well; 4. Enmity

DEEP THINKING

YOU MAY NOT FEEL like it, but right now you're standing on a ball that's spinning at 1,000 miles per hour. The earth is a gigantic orb that spins through space. You don't go flying off it because gravity holds you down. And because the sky, ground, and buildings all spin at the same speed, you can't feel any movement.

Less than 1,000 years ago, most people believed the earth was flat. But thousands of years ago, the prophet Isaiah wrote, "God sits above the circle of the earth" (Isaiah 40:22). God gave his prophet the wisdom to know the earth was round. The truth is, the Bible holds tons of wisdom that has inspired many people to study science and other subjects.

In the early 1800s, Matthew Maury sailed around the world during his time in the United States Navy. He studied many sea charts. When he almost died from an illness, his daughter read Psalm 8:6-8 to him. These verses describe how God gave man charge over creation, including whatever passes through the "paths of the seas" (verse 8, KJV). The thought grabbed Matthew's attention.

Once healed, Matthew spent the rest of his life mapping the ocean's currents and conducting experiments to discover their speed and direction. He put notes in bottles asking people to send him responses if they found the bottles. He added weights to the bottles so they would drift underwater in the currents, and he labeled each note. Many people returned the bottles and answered the questions of where and when they found them. Matthew used the information to make maps of the ocean.

Matthew is called the "pathfinder of the seas" and "father of oceanography." His work helped people find the fastest and safest routes to sail. In the 1850s, his maps saved US shipowners over $2 million a year.

God wants wisdom to live deep inside you. Ask questions and ponder what God means in the verses you read. If you read closely, you might unlock deep secrets hidden in his Word.

PLEXER

Solve this plexer to see how Jesus traveled. (If you don't remember what a plexer is, see p. 9.)

walked
H_2O

✝ PRAY

Ask God to help you understand when you ponder the Scriptures.

Life's Guidebook Says
I know that you want truth to be in my heart. You teach me wisdom deep down inside me. PSALM 51:6, NIrV

Answer: Walked on water

FREAKY STORMS

THUNDER ROARED and lightning flashed. Suddenly, a huge *crackle* and *pop* sounded. The house shook. It lifted James off his bed and bounced him back down. His video game stopped and the lights went out. The lightning strike did an amazing amount of damage, cracking a water pipe and causing a leak in the bathroom.

Maybe you've heard that lightning doesn't strike the same place twice, but this was the fifth time James had gotten caught in a house that was struck by lightning. Once it burned a hole in the garage roof, and mice invaded before anyone saw the opening with the blackened edges. At his grandpa's home, it melted the motor in a vacuum in the closet, opened the garage door, cracked the toilet, and tossed the doorbell 20 feet into the woods. Researchers say boys are about five times more likely to be hit by lightning than girls. That's mainly because guys tend to be outside more, and that's where lightning is the most dangerous—especially if you're holding a metal bat or golf club.

Lightning is uncontrolled electrical power. When storms come, it's good to follow safety rules such as avoiding water, open spaces, and high places. Staying inside is best.

Lightning has been hitting our planet since it was formed. Studying lightning led to the discovery of electricity. Imagine your life without electricity. James may want to forget about it, but electricity powers where you live . . . just like God powers your life.

QUIZ: SIGNS IN THE SKY

1. Westerly winds
2. Dark clouds
3. Red sky at sunset
4. Easterly winds
5. Dark, greenish sky
6. Leaves on oak or maple trees are curly
7. Smoke from a campfire swirls and descends
8. Dew on the ground, and it didn't rain during the night
9. Birds are quiet and flying low or sitting on lines
10. Cold, and there's a halo around the moon

A. Expect heavy rain
B. Tornado may be coming
C. Fair weather
D. High humidity; expect heavy rain
E. Low pressure, expect rain
F. Storm front coming
G. Expect rain
H. Expect snow power

✝ PRAY

Ask God to protect you when storms come.

Life's Guidebook Says

Your thunder roared from the whirlwind; the lightning lit up the world! The earth trembled and shook. PSALM 77:18

Answers: 1. FC; 2. BG; 3. AC; 4. CF; 5. B; 6. D; 7. E; 8. F; 9. G; 10. H

ROCKS FROM THE SKY

"COME OUT TO THE PORCH. It's hailing!" Jerry yelled.

His sister and brother dashed out as their mom yelled, "Be careful. Hail is hard like rocks!"

Ping! Ping! The three siblings stood near the house and listened to the pinging of ice balls hitting the roof. Jerry reached out and tried to grab a piece of hail as it fell.

Ouch! It stung his hand. His sister reached down and picked up several marble-sized pieces from the ground. She smashed them together to make a bigger ice ball. Although the storm only lasted about 15 minutes, hail covered the yard and made it look like there had been a snowstorm. Then the sun shone again, and the hail quickly melted.

Hail can cause lots of damage. *Crash!* One six-inch diameter hailstone caved in the roof of a car in Oklahoma. In 2003 in Nebraska, the largest hailstone ever recorded—nearly the size of a soccer ball—hit the ground. You'd never want to do a header with that ball!

As Joshua led God's people to take over the Promised Land, the Lord used hail to win a battle. *Wham! Zap!* The Amorites had marched to kill the Israelites. But God threw hail from the sky so large that the icy rocks killed many soldiers. God's power won the day as he sent hail from the sky. (You can read the whole story in Joshua 10.) God's power is still on display today in hailstorms and other natural wonders.

WEIRD FACTS: WEATHER WONDERS

- ☞ The average snowflake falls at 5.5 feet per second.
- ☞ The fastest winds recorded were in a tornado funnel, going at more than 300 miles per hour.
- ☞ The United States has 100,000 thunderstorms a year.
- ☞ Small whirlwinds can form over the water, causing it to hiss and bubble.
- ☞ Colored lights sometimes flash above the clouds. Pilots have seen blue jets and red sprites.
- ☞ In Europe, the frost of 1709 was so cold that trees exploded.

✟ PRAY

Praise the Lord that he controls the weather and can use it to help his people.

Life's Guidebook Says

The Amorites ran away as Israel marched toward them. They ran down the road from Beth Horon to Azekah. As they ran, the LORD threw large hailstones down on them from the sky. The hailstones killed more of them than the swords of the men of Israel did. JOSHUA 10:11, NIrV

BLASTED

HURRICANE ANDREW POUNDED the Florida coast for hours as Michael, his siblings, and his mom huddled in a closet to stay safe from the storm. What a bad time for Dad to be away on military orders! Mom kept reading the Bible with a flashlight. As she read, they talked about the verses and prayed for safety.

Finally, Mom read about Jesus calming the storm. They prayed again. Silence filled the air. Michael heard only the sound of his baby brother's breathing.

"Mom," he said, "you should have read that one first."

They laughed. Then Michael, his older sister, and their mom carefully walked out. The bedroom looked fine. But when they reached the stairs, they looked down and saw broken glass and pictures floating in water that flooded the living room. The front doors blew back and forth in the wind, and most of the furniture had slammed into the far wall. *What a mess!* Thankfully, God had kept them safe during one of the worst hurricanes in US history.

Being in a house during a hurricane would be scary. Being in a boat during a big storm would be terrifying. That's where Jesus and his disciples were when a storm blew up on the Sea of Galilee. The disciples were scared silly, but Jesus slept peacefully. Just when they thought they might drown, the disciples woke up Jesus. The Lord quickly calmed the storm (Matthew 8:26).

Having power over the waves can seem amazing. Nothing is beyond God's power. He doesn't always act, but when he does, even the wind and waves obey his words. We should do the same.

WACKY LAUGHS

Q. What weather likes to meet people?
A. Hailstones. They come with a greeting.

Q. What did the lightning say to the thunder?
A. Nothing. He just bolted when the thunder clapped.

Q. How are a needle and a hurricane alike?
A. They both have eyes but can't see.

✝ PRAY

Thank God for gentle breezes and ask for protection from strong storm winds.

Life's Guidebook Says
Jesus responded, "Why are you afraid? You have so little faith!" Then he got up and rebuked the wind and waves, and suddenly there was a great calm. MATTHEW 8:26

LIFE-CHANGING WIND

ONE DAY A $20 BILL blew out of Ken's hand as he walked to the ice-cream shop. He tried to chase it down, but he couldn't catch it. What a bummer! So much for the big ice-cream cone he had planned to buy. Since it was already gone, Ken prayed his lost money would help someone.

A few years later Ken deeply needed money. As he walked across a field, he prayed for God to provide for his needs.

Wham! A $20 bill blew right into his face. Ken grabbed it. He looked all around, but didn't see anybody. He smiled and thanked God for sending such a blessing.

Wind can do strange things. The Bible tells us God controls the wind. Maybe he even kept that $20 bill blowing around until Ken really needed some cash. That's kind of fun to think about.

Getting $20 in the wind is cool, but the biggest windy blessing came days after Jesus returned to heaven. *Swish!* A sound came from the sky. The disciples turned and saw fire descending toward them. *Yikes!* But the fire didn't burn the house or even singe their hair. It separated into tongues and rested on each of them. They got burned, but not with flaming fire. Their hearts burned inside with power, joy, and passion. They were filled with the Holy Spirit. *Wow!* God's followers wanted to tell everyone about Jesus, and they did! That day was Pentecost, the birthday of the Christian church.

You may not see the Holy Spirit descend on you like fire. But as God's follower, you have his Spirit working inside you every day.

AWESOME ACTIVITY: IT'S A SIGN

Wouldn't it be great if you could put up signs in the sky for the weather to obey? Imagine . . .

- ☞ a *Stop* sign that can stop a tornado.
- ☞ a *U-turn* sign to direct a hurricane back into the ocean.
- ☞ a *Yield* sign to tell a twister to yield to your town and not destroy it.
- ☞ a *No Parking* sign to tell the rain not to stay too long.
- ☞ a *One Way* sign to blow money and blessings your way.

What other signs would you like to have for the weather?

✝ PRAY

Ask God to put a fire inside you to want to share his love.

Life's Guidebook Says
Suddenly, there was a sound from heaven like the roaring of a mighty windstorm, and it filled the house where they were sitting. . . . And everyone present was filled with the Holy Spirit. ACTS 2:2, 4

SIGNS IN THE SKY

Red sky at night, sailors delight.
Red sky in the morning, sailors take warning.

SAILORS NEED TO KNOW when bad weather is coming. Many sailors learn this rhyme as a way to read weather signs in the sky. A red sky at sunset develops when a high pressure system moves toward an area. It means the next day will be clear and sunny. A red sky in the morning foretells a storm, because it shows the high pressure system has passed by and low pressure is coming to bring wind and rain. Meteorologists use changes in air pressure, clouds, and other signs to predict the weather.

James's dad worked in the Coast Guard and sailed a lot. Several years earlier, James stood next to his dad as they took shelter under an awning during a storm. They had ridden their two-seater bicycle to a store and needed to wait out the storm before pedaling home. His dad pointed out a change in the wind direction and said, "Look, there's a rainbow in the east. That means the rain is on the way out. It should be gone in about 10 minutes." Sure enough, 10 minutes later the sun peeked out, and they rode off.

Jesus spoke about signs in the sky that forecast weather (Luke 12:54-56). The Lord wants us to be aware of our surroundings and look for signs to keep us safe.

LIFTOFF LIST

Check off ways to prepare yourself for a storm:

____ Collect rain gear.
____ Put together a hurricane or storm kit.
____ Keep a working flashlight with extra batteries or one that uses solar power.
____ Memorize Scriptures that calm you when you're scared.
____ Trust God even if the circumstances are hard.
____ Be sure you have warm snow clothes.
____ Keep a shovel ready.
____ Know clouds and other signs to tell if a storm is coming.

✟ PRAY

Thank God for warning signs. Ask him to help you be aware, so you can prepare for the storms of life.

Life's Guidebook Says

Jesus turned to the crowd and said, "When you see clouds beginning to form in the west, you say, 'Here comes a shower.' And you are right."   LUKE 12:54

WAS IT A VOLCANO?

KABOOM! On May 18, 1980, Mount St. Helens erupted. The massive mountain, located around 90 miles from Seattle, Washington, had been threatening to blow for months. Steam oozed out of the mountain, and earthquakes rumbled. Then on the morning of May 18, the mountaintop exploded with the power of 20 atomic bombs!

The volcanic eruption created the largest avalanche of debris in history. Enough rocks, trees, and lava rolled down the mountain, to fill one million Olympic-sized swimming pools. Fiery red lava flowed for miles. Ash and hot gases slid down the slope and crushed homes, cars, trees, and animals.

The landscape changed in an instant. And over the next few years, scientists saw changes happen that they had believed took millions of years to occur. New canyons formed. Rivers changed course. Mount St. Helens showed that Creation could've happened just like it says in the Bible—in days—instead of over millions of years.

The prophet Nahum describes another mountain that shook, melted, and burned (see today's verse). The description matches a volcanic eruption, but these mountains shook because they were in God's presence. God is a loving heavenly Father, but he's also the most powerful force in the universe.

EXPERIMENT: UNDERWATER VOLCANO
Create an underwater eruption to understand how volcanoes happen.

Stuff You Need
- ☞ Large clear glass bowl or tall jar
- ☞ Small clear jar with a lip
- ☞ Yarn or string
- ☞ Hot water
- ☞ Blue food coloring

Try It
1. Fill the large container with cold water higher than the height of the small container.
2. Tie yarn around the lip of the small container to form a handle.
3. Fill the small container with hot water. Add a few drops of blue food coloring.
4. Lower the small container into the large one. Watch the volcano erupt. The hot water is lighter than the cold water, so it rises up.

✟ PRAY
Ask God to help you understand science and how he created the world around you.

Life's Guidebook Says
In his presence the mountains quake, and the hills melt away; the earth trembles, and its people are destroyed. Who can stand before his fierce anger? Who can survive his burning fury? His rage blazes forth like fire, and the mountains crumble to dust in his presence. NAHUM 1:5-6

TWISTED TALE

SEEING A TORNADO can be scary. People say twisters scream across the ground like a freight train. But what if that freight train was on fire? *Yikes!* Fire tornadoes are much rarer than other tornadoes. Also called fire whirls, these natural phenomena form when intense hot air rises inside a wildfire. A fire twister can lift smoke, ash, and debris high in the air and spread the fire fast. As the air twirls and spins, it can grow and become larger and more dangerous. Fortunately, just like other tornadoes, fire tornadoes usually last only a couple of minutes.

In the Bible the prophet Ezekiel described a strange, fiery windstorm (see today's verse). The windstorm Ezekiel saw sounds like a fire whirl. People rarely see them, although forest rangers may catch a glimpse of one more frequently. Ezekiel said that the center of the fire looked like glowing metal. If you've ever watched a blacksmith on a video or at a historic site put iron in a hot fire, you know the metal glows as though it is on fire. That's like the glowing metal Ezekiel saw. This was the beginning of a vision God gave Ezekiel to reveal his glory and power.

God spoke to Ezekiel in this fiery vision. He called Ezekiel to be a prophet and to speak his words to the people. God may never speak to you in a fiery vision, but he communicates with you in many other ways. You can hear God in his Word, through advice you get from a grandparent, and in your heart from the Holy Spirit. Plus, you can see God's power in nature. It may not be in an awesome fire tornado, but God's power is evident even in a simple rainstorm.

TWISTY TONGUE TWISTERS

Try saying each of these 10 times fast.

- ☞ We'll weather weird weather.
- ☞ Sunsets miss sunshine.
- ☞ Ships safely sailed in strong storms.

✝ PRAY

Ask God to protect people and homes from tornadoes. Ask God to protect your home from weird weather.

Life's Guidebook Says

[Ezekiel said,] "I looked up and saw a windstorm coming from the north. I saw a huge cloud. The fire of lightning was flashing out of it. Bright light surrounded it. The center of the fire looked like glowing metal. EZEKIEL 1:4, NIrV

HIDDEN SUN

ONE MINUTE THE SUN SHONE. The next, everything went dark. Although it was only noon, the sun disappeared for three hours. But that was only part of the weird weather. At 3 o'clock, the earth shook. Even the curtain in the Temple tore in half from top to bottom.

All of this happened on the day Jesus died. Some historians say evidence puts this darkness at Friday, April 3, AD 33. A partial solar eclipse was recorded for this date and time. But a partial eclipse doesn't explain all the strange happenings. When Jesus died on the cross, God's power was on display.

The Jewish religious leaders and the Romans thought they were in charge when they had Jesus crucified. But nothing was beyond God's control. God sent his Son as a sacrifice for our sins. We have new life because Jesus rose from the dead. Not only were all the historic details controlled by God, but he also controlled the sky and weather. It was his will for Jesus to die at that moment. He hid the sun to show his mourning for the death of his Son and to warn people that Jesus was no ordinary person. Soldiers who had not followed Jesus observed the weird weather and said, "This man truly was the Son of God!" (Matthew 27:54). When we look at all of the evidence around Jesus' life, death, and resurrection, that should be our response too.

PLEXER
Find the weather descriptions in these plexers. (If you don't remember what a plexer is, see p. 9.)

✝ PRAY
Thank God for sending Jesus and putting signs in the sky to show his power and truth.

Life's Guidebook Says
At noon, darkness fell across the whole land until three o'clock. . . . At that moment the curtain in the sanctuary of the Temple was torn in two, from top to bottom. The earth shook, rocks split apart. MATTHEW 27:45, 51

Answers: Twist-her / The sun hiding behind clouds

JUNE

SHINING DIAMOND

WHAT DO YOU LIKE to do during summer vacation? How does finding a diamond worth thousands of dollars sound? Not too bad, huh?

During the summer of 2013, Michael Dettlaff's family traveled to Crater of Diamonds State Park in Arkansas and plunked down several dollars a person to search for precious stones. The 12-year-old didn't have to look for long. After just 10 minutes, Michael plucked out a 5.16-carat, honey-brown diamond. Officials said the diamond was the 27th largest ever found at the park. Experts estimated the diamond could be worth as much as $15,000! Thrilled by his discovery, the Boy Scout from North Carolina called his gem "God's Glory Diamond."

As a follower of Jesus, everything you do should be for God's glory—whether that's going to school, hanging out with friends, playing sports or music . . . even searching for diamonds. Jesus talked a lot about treasure. In one of his parables, he said heaven is more valuable than anything on earth (Matthew 13:44). God's Son knows that how we spend our money speaks loudly about what's going on in our hearts. Our eternity in heaven and relationship with him are far more valuable than any earthly treasure. Put your time, talent, money, and efforts into something that lasts forever in God's Kingdom. Then your life will be like a diamond.

QUIZ: DIAMONDS IN THE ROUGH

Answer these questions and fill in the correct numbers to discover how many diamonds have been found at Crater of Diamonds State Park.

1. How many days are in Creation (including the day of rest)?
2. How many loaves of bread did Jesus use to feed 5,000 people?
3. How many idols are more powerful than God?
4. How many books of the Bible begin with X?
5. How many arks did Moses build?

1	2	3	4	5

✝ PRAY

Tell God you'd give everything for his Kingdom—and mean it!

Life's Guidebook Says
[Jesus said,] "The Kingdom of Heaven is like a treasure that a man discovered hidden in a field. In his excitement, he hid it again and sold everything he owned to get enough money to buy the field." MATTHEW 13:44

Answer: 75,000

WHAT A CHORE!

"BACK WHEN I WAS A KID, I had to walk to school. And it was uphill . . . both ways!"

Have your parents ever told you stories from their childhood that showed life was harder when they were kids? It's probably true. Research shows that kids do fewer chores today than they did 15 years ago. As a boy, you probably do even less, because parents assign more housework to girls than boys. Studies say kids spend less than 30 minutes a day cleaning and doing other housework.

How much time do you usually spend helping your family around the house? Is it 30 minutes or more? Nobody likes doing chores. But by doing some dirty work, you may actually "clean up" your character. Experts say that when you help your family, you develop responsibility, organization skills, and empathy. Those are all good things. Not only do you become a stronger person by doing chores, but you strengthen your family as well.

In Galatians 6:5, Paul says we are responsible for our own conduct. That means you can choose to be lazy or decide to work hard. The Bible also says you shouldn't compare your workload to a friend's or sibling's. Just because your older brother doesn't do much to help, that doesn't give you an excuse to avoid chores. In a family, there's no freeloading. Everybody needs to work together.

LIFTOFF LIST

Instead of waiting for your parents to assign you chores, volunteer to pick up some responsibilities. What are you ready to take over? (Mark all that apply.)

___ Taking out trash

___ Putting dirty clothes in the hamper

___ Filling cups or glasses with drinks before meals

___ Picking up toys each day

___ Cleaning fine china

___ Vacuuming

___ Cleaning up after my cat/dog

___ Taking my dog/cat for a walk

✝ PRAY

Thank God for your family, and ask God to give you opportunities to serve them this summer.

Life's Guidebook Says

We are each responsible for our own conduct.   GALATIANS 6:5

HEAR ALL ABOUT IT

"EXTRA! EXTRA! Read all about it!"

Years ago boys stood on street corners shouting for people to come buy newspapers. Today, with the Internet and iPads, not many people read papers to get their news. And here's a sad fact: statistics show that 50 percent of the world's population can't read very well. So even if they had a newspaper or tablet, they still wouldn't get the truth of what's happening!

That's something especially important to think about as you try to share God's Good News with the people around you. Romans 10:17 says, "Faith comes from hearing, that is, hearing the Good News about Christ." That means you need to talk about Jesus.

Think about your friends and family members who don't know Jesus. Do they go to church? How many of them listen to Christian music or radio? Probably not many, which means they're not *hearing* about Jesus. As you play with your friends or hang out with family members, look for ways to bring up what God is doing in your life. Memorize Scripture, and share God's wisdom when people close to you don't know what to do about a situation in their lives. Let your friends know you're praying for them during difficult times. Don't hide your relationship with Christ. Boldly speak about the difference he's made in your life so others will believe.

WACKY LAUGHS

Kyle: I lost my pet dog yesterday.
Matt: Why don't you put an ad in the newspaper?
Kyle: Don't be silly. My dog can't read.

Q. How do cats tell each other about Jesus?
A. By sharing the good *mews*.

Q. What does ice do when it hears a funny joke?
A. It cracks up!

Q. If you grilled a steak for Jesus, how would he want it?
A. Well done, thou good and faithful servant.

✝ PRAY

Ask God to give you opportunities to be a bold witness for him with your words.

Life's Guidebook Says
Faith comes from hearing, that is, hearing the Good News about Christ.
ROMANS 10:17

WOODEN LIES

HAVE YOU EVER TOLD a lie to stay out of trouble? Many kids do. You're tossing around a Nerf football in the living room with your friends when an errant pass knocks over a family picture and breaks the glass in the frame. Instead of owning up to the mistake, you tell your parents, "It was so crazy. My friends and I were just sitting in the living room reading books when an escaped orangutan busted into our house and broke the picture."

Okay, that's not a very believable story. Your lies are probably better. The Gibeonites in the Old Testament certainly told more believable lies. The book of Joshua explains that the Gibeonites were afraid of God's people. Joshua had just led the Israelites into the Promised Land and easily conquered Jericho and Ai. Many of the local kings banded together to fight the Israelites, but the Gibeonites had a different plan. Even though they lived nearby, they sent ambassadors dressed in old ragged clothes. Their saddles were patched. Their bread was old and moldy. When they arrived at the Israelite camp, they said they'd come from a far-off land to make a peace treaty with Joshua (Joshua 9:6). The Israelites inspected the bread and believed their story. But they forgot to ask God what he thought about it (Joshua 9:14). Joshua signed the peace treaty.

Three days later the Israelites realized the lie. The Gibeonites lived just a short distance away! Joshua was angry. Many of the Israelites wanted to kill the Gibeonites, but the leaders said they should honor the treaty. Still, the Gibeonites' lie couldn't be rewarded. Joshua went to the Gibeonites and said they'd have to serve Israel by cutting wood and carrying water.

How's that for a punishment?

PLEXER
What's the worst punishment you've received? Solve this plexer to figure out what teachers would do to a student in the 1900s who behaved badly in class. (If you don't remember what a plexer is, see p. 9.)

<table>
<tr><td>Stand</td></tr>
</table>

✝ PRAY
Tell God you want to tell the truth, even if there are consequences.

Life's Guidebook Says
The LORD detests lying lips, but he delights in those who tell the truth.
PROVERBS 12:22

Answer: Stand in the corner

GOOD JOB

WHAT DO YOU WANT to be when you grow up?

Every year a popular magazine ranks the best jobs. Recently, the top jobs included dentist, nurse, pharmacist, computer analyst, physician, and software designer. (Sorry, *ninja* wasn't on the list.) By doing well in school and studying hard in college, you can pursue nearly any career you'd like.

But that wasn't the case when Jesus grew up. In Bible times, boys nearly always followed the same career path as their fathers. So during Jesus' ministry, when he showed up in his hometown of Nazareth and taught about God's Word, people were confused. They were impressed by his teaching but couldn't believe it was coming from the carpenter's son (Matthew 13:55). After all, carpenters' sons are good at woodworking—not preaching. Because they had a limited view of Jesus, they didn't believe his wise words.

Is anything limiting your view of Jesus? Maybe you've heard people say that he was just a good teacher and not God's Son. Don't be misled. Jesus is exactly who he claimed to be. And you can take that—along with your paycheck—to the bank (which didn't make the list but could be a good place to work).

AWESOME ACTIVITY: IT'S A PLANE!

This carpentry project turns Popsicle sticks into a plane.

Stuff You Need
- ☞ Popsicle sticks
- ☞ Glue
- ☞ Scissors
- ☞ Markers

Try It
1. Lay a Popsicle stick on the table. Put a dot of glue about two inches from one end. Place a stick on top of the glue to form a cross shape. Flip over the cross and glue another stick directly under the second stick to make wings.
3. With a parent's help, cut a Popsicle stick in half with scissors or a sharp blade. Cut one of the halves in half again.
4. Glue the longer piece near the back of the plane as a horizontal stabilizer.
5. Color the short, rounded quarter of a stick. Glue it standing up on the horizontal stabilizer as a tail.
6. Let your plane dry, and then use the markers to make it look cool.

✝ PRAY

Thank God for giving you the faith to believe that Jesus is way, way more than "just the carpenter's son."

Life's Guidebook Says
[The townspeople] scoffed, "He's just the carpenter's son, and we know Mary, his mother, and his brothers—James, Joseph, Simon, and Judas." MATTHEW 13:55

THE MASTER'S HANDS

HAVE YOU EVER WATCHED a potter work at a potting wheel? A master potter can turn a simple lump of clay into a beautiful creation. With just a slight squeeze of his hands, he can make a beautiful vase, useful bowl, or galloping pony. (Okay, he can't make a real pony.) But a potter's skill shows in everything he makes.

In the book of Jeremiah, the Lord tells his prophet to go down to the potter's shop. At the shop, Jeremiah watches as the potter makes a jar. But the jar doesn't turn out the way the potter wants, so he smashes the clay back into a lump and starts again. Then the Lord says to Jeremiah, "Can I not do to you as this potter has done to his clay? As the clay is in the potter's hand, so are you in my hand" (Jeremiah 18:6).

When you allow God to work in your life, he forms you into something beautiful to be used in his Kingdom. It may take some pounding, squeezing, and spinning, but God is making you into something amazing. Does the clay tell the potter what to do? No. Does the clay complain that it wants to be a pot and not a pony? No.

As clay in the Master Potter's hands, we need to trust God with our futures . . . and our lives.

EXPERIMENT: SLIMY SENSATION
Make your own claylike slime.

Stuff You Need
- White glue
- Water
- Two bowls
- Borax laundry booster
- Food coloring
- Large spoon
- Ziploc bag

Try It
1. Mix four ounces of glue with a half-cup of water. Stir in a couple drops of food coloring.
2. In another bowl, dissolve one teaspoon of Borax in one cup of water.
3. Stir the glue mixture into the Borax mixture. Keep stirring until your slime forms.
4. Remove the slime from the water and start playing. Store slime in a Ziploc bag.

✝ PRAY
Praise God that he's the Master Potter. Tell him that you trust him to make you what you should be.

Life's Guidebook Says
The LORD gave me this message: "O Israel, can I not do to you as this potter has done to his clay? As the clay is in the potter's hand, so are you in my hand."
JEREMIAH 18:5-6

POWERFUL SEAS

VISITING THE CITY DUMP can be gross . . . and fun, as you hunt for treasures among the junk. But there's nothing fun about the Great Pacific garbage patch. This big area in the Pacific Ocean is filled with floating plastics, sludge, and other garbage.

When David de Rothschild heard about how much plastic was floating in the ocean, he wanted to make people aware of the problem. So he built a boat. No, he wasn't going to float out and pick up trash. He wanted to sail across the Pacific Ocean in a special boat made only of plastic bottles. David spent years building his boat out of 12,500 plastic bottles. He called his boat *The Plastiki*. Then on March 20, 2010, David and his five-man crew set sail from San Francisco, California. They battled through storms and 70-mile-per-hour winds. But four months later, they docked safely in Sydney, Australia.

David experienced the power of the sea firsthand. He used the wind and ocean currents to make it safely to his destination. In the book of Psalms, it says some people went to sea and saw the Lord's power in action. Whether it's an ocean wave or a strong wind, God's might is always there for us to see.

EXPERIMENT: WHIRLPOOL IN A BOTTLE
You can't contain God's power, but you can create a powerful whirlpool.

Stuff You Need
- ☞ Two one-liter bottles
- ☞ Water
- ☞ Dish-washing soap
- ☞ Food coloring
- ☞ Large rubber washer
- ☞ Duct tape

Try It
1. Take the labels off both bottles, and fill one with water.
2. Put a couple drops of food coloring and dish-washing soap in that bottle.
3. Place a rubber washer that's the same size as the bottle's opening on the water-filled bottle.
4. Put the other bottle on top, opening to opening, and tape in place. Use lots of duct tape to make sure the bottles are firmly taped together.
5. Swirl the bottles around in a circular motion, and then turn them over. Watch a bubbly, colorful whirlpool appear as the water flows from one bottle to the other.

✝ PRAY
Praise God for his power displayed on earth. Commit to taking care of his creation.

Life's Guidebook Says
They, too, observed the LORD's power in action, his impressive works on the deepest seas. PSALM 107:24

FOLLOWING COMMANDS

WHEN YOUR PARENTS tell you to do something, what do they expect to happen? For the task to get done, right? That's the way it works in a lot of homes.

The military works that way too. When a commanding officer tells a soldier to make his bed, he expects the bed to be made perfectly and immediately. Without obedience, an army wouldn't work. Just check out this scene:

General: Go over there and protect those people.

Soldier: Nah, I'm going to get something to eat.

During Jesus' ministry on earth, he came face-to-face with a powerful Roman military officer. The officer's young servant was sick and unable to move. Jesus offered to come and heal the servant. But the officer said, "Lord, I am not worthy to have you come into my home. Just say the word from where you are, and my servant will be healed" (Matthew 8:8).

The officer knew the power of a command. When he told his soldiers to go, they went. When he said, "Jump," they asked, "How high?" So the officer knew if Jesus commanded the servant to get better that he would be healed. Jesus was amazed at the officer's trust. He turned to his followers and said, "I tell you the truth, I haven't seen faith like this in all Israel!" (Matthew 8:10). Then Jesus told the officer to go home, because his servant was healed. And at that exact time the servant became well, because God's word always accomplishes its purpose.

PUZZLE IT OUT: KEY TO SUCCESS

Answer these math problems and fill in the correct word to complete Proverbs 13:13:

"People who despise advice are asking for trouble; _____ _____

11-9   1+2

_____ ____ _____ ____ _____."

1 x 1   2 x 3   49÷7   15-11   45÷9

1. respect	3. who	5. succeed	7. command
2. those	4. will	6. a	

✝ PRAY

Tell God you're going to follow his commands and trust his promises to come true.

Life's Guidebook Says

The officer said, "Lord, I am not worthy to have you come into my home. Just say the word from where you are, and my servant will be healed." MATTHEW 8:8

Answer: Those who respect a command will succeed.

· GOOD WORK

DEEP IN THE TENNESSEE WOODS sits the world's largest tree house. Actually, it's not sitting—it's growing. Horace Burgess isn't done building yet. For more than 15 years, Horace has hammered together his amazing creation. The tree house is 97 feet tall and measures over 15,000 square feet—that's as big as a castle! There's a basketball court, a bell tower, a praise chapel, and tons of little rooms and passageways.

Horace started building the tree house after God gave him a vision one day as he prayed. He felt the Lord tell him, *If you build a tree house for me, you'll never run out of wood*. And it's been true. The tree house is made from donated recycled wood. Wood keeps coming in, so Horace keeps building.

"This is God's tree house," Horace said. "And I want everybody to know about him."

The apostle Paul made tents instead of tree houses, but his goal was the same as Horace's. He wanted everybody to know about Jesus. In Acts 18, it says Paul went to Corinth and stayed with Priscilla and Aquila. They worked together making tents. But on the weekends, Paul would go to the synagogue, the Jewish place of worship, to try to convince the Jews and Greeks about the lifesaving truth of Jesus Christ (Acts 18:4). Paul worked hard at both of his jobs—making tents and telling others about God.

LIFTOFF LIST
What jobs do you have? Do you work hard at all of them? Mark off everything that you work at.

___ Getting good grades at school

___ Being a good brother

___ Learning an instrument

___ Playing a sport

___ Growing closer to God

___ Telling others about Jesus

___ Taking care of my pet

___ Keeping my room clean

___ Learning everything in Wikipedia

___ Obeying my parents

✝ PRAY
Ask God to give you the opportunity to tell others about him.

Life's Guidebook Says
Each Sabbath found Paul at the synagogue, trying to convince the Jews and Greeks alike. ACTS 18:4

KEEP IT SIMPLE

WHAT HAPPENS to a black rock that's thrown into the Red Sea?

It gets wet.

What happens to an angry, sick general who's dunked in the Jordan River seven times?

He gets healed.

It's true. You can read the whole story in 2 Kings 5. Naaman was a mighty Aramean army commander. He had guided his troops to great victories over the Israelites. His wife even had a young Israelite girl for a slave. As powerful as Naaman was, his body felt weak because he suffered from leprosy. Leprosy is a disease that causes muscle weakness, yucky sores, and the loss of feeling in your arms and legs. One day the slave girl told Naaman's wife about the prophet Elisha in Samaria. She knew Elisha could heal her master. Naaman talked to the Aramean king and got his permission to go to Israel to talk with Elisha. But instead of coming out to speak with Naaman, Elisha sent a messenger to say, "Go dunk seven times in the Jordan River. Then you will be healed."

The news should have excited Naaman, but it didn't. It made him mad. He had expected Elisha to come out, wave his hand, and heal him. Dipping in the dirty Jordan River did not sound like the recipe for healing. But before Naaman could rush back to Aram, his officers said, "If the prophet had told you to do something very difficult, wouldn't you have done it? So you should certainly obey him when he says simply, 'Go and wash and be cured!'" (2 Kings 5:13). Naaman couldn't argue against that reasoning. He went. He washed. He was cured. And he worshiped God (verse 15).

QUIZ: DOUBLY TOUGH

Sometimes we're willing to do something doubly tough for God, but we won't do the simple things he asks us to do (such as reading his Word, praying, and treating others with kindness). Naaman learned that simple obedience can produce miracles. See if you can solve these questions using only words with double vowels:

1. What do you use to clean the carpet?
2. What ant-eating mammal has a long nose and tongue?
3. What do you get by mixing blue and yellow?

✝ PRAY

Tell God you're going to do the little things for him.

Life's Guidebook Says

Naaman said, "Now I know that there is no God in all the world except in Israel."
2 KINGS 5:15

Answers: 1. Vacuum; 2. Aardvark; 3. Green

BEST BUILDERS

WHAT'S YOUR FAVORITE TYPE of craft project? Papier-mâché? Popsicle-stick towers? Paper airplanes? Some guys are great at working with their hands. That was definitely true for Bezalel and Oholiab (call them Bez and Oli). Out of all of God's people, the Lord told Moses to put those two in charge of constructing the Tabernacle, the Ark of the Covenant, and a number of other holy objects. God had given specific instructions on how each piece should look. For instance, he said the altar for burning incense should be 18 inches square and 36 inches high with horns at the corners carved from the same piece of wood. The top, sides, and horns should all be covered with gold. A decorative gold molding should go around the entire altar. Then two gold rings had to be made so two golden acacia wood poles could be put through them (Exodus 30:2-5). Wow, that's a lot of instructions.

Bez and Oli didn't shy away from God's instructions. They paid careful attention and created everything just as God commanded. The Bible says God filled Bez with his Spirit and gave him great ability in all kinds of crafts (Exodus 31:3). What has God filled you with? Are you an artist, a musician, an athlete, or a star student? By paying careful attention to God's instructions, you can create something beautiful with your talents . . . and your life.

AWESOME ACTIVITY: POP GOES THE PAPER
This craft shoots high on the fun scale.

Stuff You Need
- ☞ Empty yogurt cup
- ☞ 12-inch balloon
- ☞ Scissors
- ☞ Piece of paper

Try It
1. Clean and then carefully cut off the bottom one-third of the yogurt cup to make a tube.
2. Tie a knot in the balloon and cut off the other end.
3. Stretch the open end of the balloon over the rim of the cup.
4. Rip off a strip of paper and wad it into a ball.
5. Put the paper ball into the cup, pull back on the balloon knot, let go, and watch the paper fly!

✝ PRAY
Ask God to help you learn the little details of the Bible.

Life's Guidebook Says
[God said,] "I have filled him with the Spirit of God, giving him great wisdom, ability, and expertise in all kinds of crafts." EXODUS 31:3

RECORD-BREAKING FISH

GREG BERNAL WAS ABOUT to call it a day and go home.

One last cast, he thought. He threw his fishing line into the Missouri River and waited. That's what fishermen do. They wait. And Greg was a good fisherman. In 1995, he had caught a state-record catfish in Illinois that weighed more than 95 pounds. But on this hot July afternoon in 2010, Greg was about to reel in a giant.

Thirty minutes after his bait hit the water, the reel took off. Greg kept pressure on the line and tried to work the fish to the surface. When the catfish's head finally popped out of the water, Greg knew he had a record breaker. He landed the massive fish and got it weighed. The blue catfish tipped the scales at 130 pounds and was 57 inches long!

The Bible tells a story about a record-breaking catch too. After Jesus died on the cross and rose from the dead, his disciples went out fishing. They fished all night, but caught nothing. Just as they were about to give up, they saw a man on the beach. "Throw out your net on the right-hand side of the boat," the man yelled. Many of the disciples were trained fishermen—what did this man know? But they tossed over the net and couldn't pull it back in because there were too many fish (John 21:6). Suddenly, John realized that the man on the beach was the risen Lord.

Sometimes you might hear a message from God that doesn't make sense, such as "Throw your net on the right side" or "Be kind to those who treat you badly." But when you obey his commands, you'll always make a great catch.

PUZZLE IT OUT: FRESH FISH

H	S	I	F	N	U	S	L
B	G	A	T	S	P	L	J
A	C	A	T	F	I	S	H
S	T	O	U	G	K	E	T
C	R	A	E	A	E	C	R
E	N	U	H	R	A	K	O
R	L	A	C	J	R	I	U
B	A	S	S	T	C	Z	T
T	W	A	L	L	E	Y	E

Bass
Bluegill
Catfish
Gar
Pike
Sunfish
Trout
Walleye

✝ PRAY

Tell God you're never going to give up following his instructions.

Life's Guidebook Says

[Jesus said,] "Throw out your net on the right-hand side of the boat, and you'll get some!" So they did, and they couldn't haul in the net because there were so many fish in it. JOHN 21:6

NOTHING UP MY SLEEVE—*PRESTO!*

DO YOU LIKE watching magicians? They can pull a rabbit out of an "empty" hat. They can disappear from stage and suddenly reappear in the audience. They can even guess which card you pull from the deck. But all of their tricks are just that—tricks. They fool your eye with misdirection and sleight of hand.

God doesn't do tricks. He performs miracles. Thousands of years ago, the Israelites lived as slaves in Egypt. They called out to God, and God called Moses to go free his people. Just one problem: Moses didn't want to go. He didn't think the Egyptians would listen to him. After all, he'd fled Egypt after killing a man. Plus, he didn't speak well. God didn't listen to Moses' excuses. He simply told Moses to toss his staff on the ground. *Hiss!* It turned into a snake. Then he told Moses to pick up the snake by the tail. *Presto!* It was a shepherd's staff again. Next, God told Moses to put his hand into his cloak. When he pulled it out, he was holding a beautiful bouquet of flowers. *Wrong!* His hand was actually white with disease. Moses put his hand back into his cloak, and this time it came out perfectly healed.

The Lord told Moses, "If they do not believe you and are not convinced by the first miraculous sign, they will be convinced by the second sign" (Exodus 4:8). God knew Moses was the right man for the job. He wasn't concerned about Moses' *ability*; he wanted Moses' *availability* to follow him. And that's the same thing God wants from you.

PLEXER

Solve this plexer to figure out the first of the 10 plagues to hit Egypt. (If you don't remember what a plexer is, see p. 9.)

✝ PRAY

Tell God you want to make yourself available to do what he wants you to do.

Life's Guidebook Says

The LORD asked Moses, "Who makes a person's mouth? Who decides whether people speak or do not speak, hear or do not hear, see or do not see? Is it not I, the LORD?" EXODUS 4:11

Answer: Water turns to blood.

AWESOME DADS

WHEN RICK HOYT WAS 15, he entered his first race—a five-mile run. Five miles was pretty far for Rick, especially since he couldn't even walk. A lack of oxygen to Rick's brain at birth had resulted in his being diagnosed as a spastic quadriplegic with cerebral palsy. Doctors had told Rick's parents to put him in an institution, but they refused. Instead they brought Rick home and discovered that their son was very intelligent. Although he couldn't speak, he could communicate with his eyes. The Hoyts worked with engineers to develop a computer that could track Rick's eyes and help him communicate by selecting letters and words on a computer screen.

Rick wanted to compete in the race to benefit a lacrosse player who'd been paralyzed in an accident. Rick's father, Dick, agreed to push him in a wheelchair. They came in second to last, but Rick told his dad, "When I'm running, it feels like I'm not handicapped." Since that time, they've run more than 1,000 races, including marathons and Ironman Triathlons. In 1992, the pair even ran across the United States in just 45 days!

This month we celebrate Father's Day. Many dads would do anything for their sons and make great sacrifices for their families. Our heavenly Father even gave his one and only Son as a sacrifice for us. Jesus once asked a group of fathers, "If your children ask for a fish, do you give them a snake instead?" (see today's verse). Of course not. Fathers want to give good gifts. Our heavenly Father gives even better ones.

AWESOME ACTIVITY: CHIP OFF THE OLD BLOCK
Make this gift to give to your dad.

Stuff You Need
- ☞ Block of wood
- ☞ Sandpaper
- ☞ Photo of yourself
- ☞ Glue
- ☞ Marker

Try It
1. Make sure your photo will fit on the block of wood.
2. Smooth the wood by sanding any edges that might splinter.
3. Glue your photo to the wood, leaving some room for a message.
4. Next to your photo, write, "Chip off the Old Block."
5. On the back of the wood, write your dad a message to tell him you love him.

✝ PRAY
Praise God for being the ultimate Father and ask him to bless your dad.

Life's Guidebook Says
You fathers—if your children ask for a fish, do you give them a snake instead?" LUKE 11:11

OIL WELL

Sandy: SANDY DESERT HERE, the top reporter with *Old Testament News*. I'm joined today by a widow who struck oil. But not the kind that runs cars, because those won't be invented for thousands of years. *Ha!* This widow's sons were about to be sold as slaves because she couldn't pay her bills. Now she's an oil tycoon. Let's hear the rest of her story.

Widow: Thanks, Sandy. It's a story I'm happy to tell because it shows God's power. And telling people about God was something my late husband loved to do.

Sandy: Sorry to hear about your loss. Your husband sounds like a good man.

Widow: He was. But when he died, I didn't have any money and fell behind on my bills.

Sandy: That's when a creditor came and demanded payment, right?

Widow: Exactly. He said if I couldn't pay, he'd take my two sons as slaves.

Sandy: That sounds kind of harsh. What did you do?

Widow: I called out to the prophet Elisha. He asked me what I had of value in the house. All I had was a small jar of olive oil.

Sandy: That's not much.

Widow: It's not. But Elisha said to ask my neighbors and friends for empty jars. I started pouring oil from the tiny flask, and it kept filling jar after jar.

Sandy: But that's impossible!

Widow: Nothing's impossible with God. The oil filled every jar I had before running out. Then Elisha told me to sell the oil, so my sons and I could keep living together.

Sandy: There you have it—an amazing miracle. And a new oil baroness.

AWESOME ACTIVITY: MIRACLE TRACKER

Sometimes it can feel as if we don't have much. Just a small jar of oil. But God can multiple our little and turn it into a lot. Get a piece of paper and a pencil. Write down any time you can remember when God turned your little efforts into big rewards. When you're done, ask your parents and grandparents if they have any stories of God "multiplying oil."

✝ PRAY

Offer God your "little" and ask him to make it a "lot."

Life's Guidebook Says

Her sons kept bringing jars to her, and she filled one after another. Soon every container was full to the brim! 2 KINGS 4:5-6

WATER, WATER EVERYWHERE

NAPOLEON BONAPARTE WAS a great military commander. In the early 1800s, he led French armies in conquering much of Europe. He understood military strategy and planning. He also understood the importance of food. Napoleon is credited with saying, "An army marches on its stomach" (which is sort of weird, because an army marches on its feet). But in a way Napoleon was right; a well-fed army can be very effective.

As important as food is to an army, water is even more vital. Experts say you can live without food for three weeks, but you can live without water for only three days. During a big battle in the Old Testament, Israel's army was in desperate need of water. The kings of Judah, Israel, and Edom had joined forces to fight against Moab. For seven days, they marched their armies through the wilderness, where there was no water, so they could make a surprise attack. You can probably see a problem here. Without water, the men and animals were about to die. The kings came to the prophet Elisha for help. At first, Elisha wasn't going to do anything. But out of respect for King Jehoshaphat of Judah, Elisha went to the Lord. God told him that water would fill the dry valley. No rain would come down—water would rise up (2 Kings 3:17). In the morning, after an offering to the Lord, water appeared! All the soldiers and animals drank their fill. Now they were ready for the fight, and God gave them the victory.

WACKY LAUGHS

Q. What has holes but can hold water?
A. A sponge.

Patient: Is it all right to swim on a full stomach?
Doctor: No, it's better to swim on the water.

Q. What runs but never walks?
A. Water.

Q. What do you call a cat that floats in the water?
A. A bobcat.

✞ PRAY

Are you experiencing a dry spell with God? Ask him to make you thirsty for him.

Life's Guidebook Says
The next day at about the time when the morning sacrifice was offered, water suddenly appeared! 2 KINGS 3:20

CAUGHT IN A QUAKE

LIVING IN JAPAN as a missionary, Brianah had seen some strange things, like superfast trains, passionfruit-flavored KIT KAT bars, and people eating raw fish. But nothing could prepare her for what she saw on March 11, 2011. That's when a magnitude 9.0 earthquake—one of the largest in history—hit northern Japan. The house shook and power lines swayed. Brianah thought the earth might open up and swallow her house. Her family ran outside. Everything shook. Brianah watched in shock as her family's car bounced up and down like a basketball.

The earthquake was so huge that it also caused a massive tidal wave that wiped out entire cities. In all, more than 15,000 people died in this terrible disaster.

When God's people left Egypt, they wandered for years through the desert. One day, a man named Korah tried to form a rebellion against Moses. He complained that Moses had promised the people a land flowing with milk and honey. Instead all they got was sand. God's anger burned against Korah and his friends. He wanted the people to know that Moses was his chosen leader. Moses stood in front of the people and said, "If nothing happens to Korah and his men or they die a natural death, then you'll know the Lord hasn't sent me. But if the ground opens up and swallows these men, then you'll know they have shown contempt toward God" (Numbers 16:29-30). Moses had barely finished speaking when the ground shook, split open, and swallowed Korah and the other families who followed him.

This is a scary story, but it shows the importance of knowing who you're following. Do your leaders serve God, something else, or themselves?

WEIRD FACTS: EARTHSHAKING RECORDS
- ☞ The most powerful earthquake ever recorded hit Valdivia, Chile, in 1960. It measured 9.5 on the Richter scale.
- ☞ The Richter scale is named after Charles Francis Richter.
- ☞ Because of shifting tectonic plates, earthquakes happen all the time.
- ☞ You can't feel earthquakes that measure less than 2.0 on the Richter scale. As the numbers get higher, the intensity multiplies exponentially. Earthquakes that measure 7.0 or more are huge.

✝ PRAY
Ask God to help you follow and trust the right leaders.

Life's Guidebook Says
The earth opened its mouth and swallowed the men, along with their households and all their followers who were standing with them, and everything they owned. NUMBERS 16:32

BIG DREAMS

HAVE YOU EVER DREAMED you could fly? Not like Superman—more like being able to lift off the ground and soar above your everyday life? Flying dreams are fun and surprisingly common. Researchers say people in every culture around the world experience dreams of flight. They also say these dreams make us feel powerful and peaceful.

The first book of the Bible tells us about a dream that Joseph had that caused anything but peace. Joseph was his father, Jacob's, favorite. Everybody knew it, especially Joseph's brothers. Then Jacob made it really obvious by giving Joseph a robe of many colors. Rather than being embarrassed by the extra attention, Joseph seemed to rub it in his brothers' faces. One day Joseph had a dream that symbolized all of his brothers bowing down before him (Genesis 37:6-7). Instead of keeping quiet, Joseph told his brothers all about it. Their negative response didn't stop Joseph from sharing another, similar dream he had a short time later (verses 8-9). You may know what happened next. Joseph's brothers threw him in a pit, sold him into slavery, and acted like he was dead. Too bad Joseph didn't have a flying dream to share with his brothers. They might have liked that one.

Joseph went on to have many more dreams. God actually gave him the ability to understand and interpret dreams. Many of Joseph's dreams came true, including the one about his brothers bowing before him. Many years later Joseph became a mighty leader in Egypt and his brothers came to him (although they didn't recognize him) to beg for food. Joseph reunited with his family—and that was a dream even he couldn't have imagined.

PUZZLE IT OUT: NAME GAME

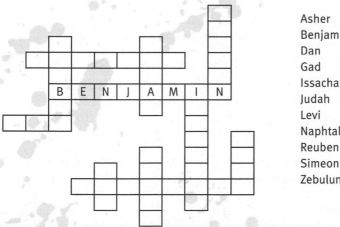

Asher
Benjamin
Dan
Gad
Issachar
Judah
Levi
Naphtali
Reuben
Simeon
Zebulun

✞ PRAY

Thank God for your family, even brothers and sisters who you may fight with every once in a while.

Life's Guidebook Says

"Listen to this dream," [Joseph] said. "We were out in the field, tying up bundles of grain. Suddenly my bundle stood up, and your bundles all gathered around and bowed low before mine!" GENESIS 37:6-7

EAR ALL ABOUT IT

ROBOTS ARE TAKING over the world! No, not really. But everywhere you look, there's a robot. On TV . . . robots. Movies . . . robots. LEGOs . . . robots. Toys . . . robots. Hospitals . . . robots.

Doctors use robots to do surgery from across the country. Robots can be used to do dangerous surgeries where a steady hand is superimportant. Many experts say ear surgery may be the most difficult procedure after brain surgery, so a doctor in South Korea developed ESOBOT (Ear Surgical Robot). This robot uses 3-D imaging technology to help surgeons perform delicate procedures without hitting nerves. When doctors get too close to a nerve, the robot beeps and refuses to move forward.

Jesus didn't have an ESOBOT, but he still performed an amazing ear surgery. When Temple guards came to arrest God's Son on the Mount of Olives, Peter wasn't going to go down without a fight. He pulled out his sword and slashed wildly through the air. His blade hit a servant on the head and sliced off his right ear. Before a battle could break out, Jesus calmed everybody down, grabbed the severed ear, and put it back on the man's head. Immediately, the man was healed. (You can read all about the incident in Luke 22:47-53.)

Jesus didn't need a robot, because he knows the inner workings of every person. He healed the man with a touch. And he has the same healing powers today.

WACKY LAUGHS

Q. How does corn smile?

A. From ear to ear.

Q. What is the most amazing drum in the orchestra?

A. The eardrum.

Jamie: Mommy, Mommy! There's a pickle coming out of my ear!

Mom: Don't worry, honey. We'll use a cuke-tip.

Q. How much did the pirate pay to get her ears pierced?

A. A buccaneer.

✝ PRAY

Do you have friends or family members who are not feeling well? Pray for them to experience God's healing power. He's called the Great Physician for a reason.

Life's Guidebook Says
Jesus said, "No more of this." And he touched the man's ear and healed him.
LUKE 22:51

DREAMS MAY COME

HAVE YOU EVER HAD a bad dream? Everybody has. The most common nightmares include dreams about monsters, falling, bugs, mean animals, and being trapped. Can you imagine having a dream about falling next to a monster with bugs flying all around, while you're trapped in a cage? *Yikes!* Now that would be a bad dream.

In the Old Testament, Joseph ran into a couple of guys who'd just had bad dreams. Joseph was serving in an Egyptian prison after being falsely accused of a crime. He didn't complain. He just did his job. One morning he noticed that Pharaoh's cup-bearer and baker (who were also in prison) looked worried. They'd both had bad dreams. Joseph told them interpreting dreams was God's business, so they should share their dreams with him (Genesis 40:8).

The cup-bearer's dream had grapes and vines and ended with his putting a cup into Pharaoh's hand. Joseph explained the dream meant in three days the cup-bearer would be released from prison and get his old job back. In the baker's dream, he was carrying pastries on his head. But before he could give them to Pharaoh, birds came and ate the pastries. Joseph didn't have good news for the baker. His dream meant that he'd be killed in three days. Both of Joseph's interpretations came true.

Sometimes you can have dreams about your future at night or when you're thinking about what you'd like to do in years to come. As you dream about the future, remember that the Lord directs your steps. God had a great plan for Joseph, and he delights in every detail of your life (Psalm 37:23). It's good for us to plan, but we also have to watch for God's guidance.

EXPERIMENT: POP GOES THE BAG
Bakers use baking soda in recipes. You can use it in this explosive experiment:

Stuff You Need
- ☞ Ziploc sandwich bag
- ☞ ¼ cup warm water
- ☞ ½ cup vinegar
- ☞ 1 tablespoon baking soda
- ☞ Kleenex

Try It
1. Go outside to a large, open area.
2. Pour the water and vinegar into the bag.
3. Fold up the baking soda inside the tissue.
4. Carefully place the tissue inside the bag, and quickly seal it.
5. Run far away from the bag, then turn to watch it explode!

✝ PRAY
Ask God to be in your dreams—both day and night.

Life's Guidebook Says
The LORD directs the steps of the godly. He delights in every detail of their lives.
PSALM 37:23

GREATEST WISH

As JASON AND HIS DAD walked along the beach, an old oil lamp washed up in front of them. Jason ran to pick up the rusty object.

"Maybe we can shine that up a bit to see if it's worth anything," Dad said.

Jason rubbed the lamp with the bottom of his T-shirt. Suddenly, smoke poured from the opening and a genie appeared. Jason dropped the lamp in surprise.

"What is your wish, my master?" the genie said.

Of course, this is a made-up story. You've probably even read something like it in other books or seen scenes like this in a movie. While the situation is fictitious, the question is a good one: What do you wish for?

Write down your top three wishes here:

1. _____
2. _____
3. _____

Now circle your number-one wish. When Solomon took over as king for his father, David, a very strange thing happened. One night the Lord appeared to Solomon in a dream and said, "What do you want? Ask, and I will give it to you!" (1 Kings 3:5). God doesn't do this with everybody, but he wanted to see what Solomon would say. Solomon asked for wisdom so he could properly lead God's people. God was so pleased with Solomon's wish that he gave the new king wisdom—plus riches and fame.

Go back and look at your list. What was your top wish? Did it help you or help God? No matter what you're given, whether it's talent, money, intellect, or wishes, make sure you use it to bring glory to God.

PLEXER

Solve this plexer to find out what God wishes for you to do. (If you don't remember what a plexer is, see p. 9.)

HgrowIM

✝ PRAY

Tell God you want to be like Solomon and know the difference between right and wrong.

Life's Guidebook Says

[Solomon said,] "Give me an understanding heart so that I can govern your people well and know the difference between right and wrong." 1 KINGS 3:9

Answer: Grow in him.

M-O-O-O-VING DREAM

YOU HAVE DOZENS of dreams every night. Doctors say that humans dream about every 90 minutes. So during your lifetime, you'll have more than 100,000 dreams. Dreams can be cool, but we don't always remember what we've dreamed.

When Joseph was imprisoned in Egypt, Pharaoh had a weird dream that he did remember—and it bothered him. His dream showed seven healthy cows coming out of the Nile River to graze on marsh grasses. Then seven scrawny cows came out of the river and stood by the fat cows. Suddenly, the thin cows ate the healthy cows. *Gross!* Pharaoh woke up and immediately asked his magicians and wise men what his dream meant. Nobody could tell him. Finally, Pharaoh's cup-bearer remembered Joseph. Joseph had interpreted one of the cup-bearer's dreams in prison. The cup-bearer was supposed to tell Pharaoh about Joseph a couple of years earlier, but he forgot. Now Pharaoh sent for Joseph. Joseph knew God could easily interpret the dream (see today's verse). Pharaoh told him the dream about the cows. Immediately, Joseph knew the dream meant that there would be seven years of plenty in Egypt, followed by seven years of terrible famine. Joseph told Pharaoh to find a wise man to help store food while it was plentiful, so they'd have enough when the famine hit.

Pharaoh did exactly that. Because Joseph was filled with the Spirit of God, Pharaoh put Joseph in charge of the entire land of Egypt. Now more of Joseph's dreams were about to come true.

WEIRD FACTS: CATTLE TATTLE

God used cows in Pharaoh's dream as a warning about the future. Pharaoh listened and God blessed Egypt. Check out these cow facts:

- ☞ Cows chew an average of 50 times a minute.
- ☞ Dairy cows can produce eight gallons of milk and 125 pounds of saliva each day!
- ☞ Cows can smell something from six miles away, which helps them stay safe from predators.
- ☞ Holstein cows' markings are like fingerprints. No two Holsteins have exactly the same black-and-white pattern.

✟ PRAY

Ask God to help you see warnings in your life and then make the right decisions.

Life's Guidebook Says

"It is beyond my power to do this," Joseph replied. "But God can tell you what it means and set you at ease." GENESIS 41:16

NAME THAT DREAM

IMAGINE YOUR MOM WALKING into the kitchen and saying, "What did I dream last night?"

"I have no idea," you might answer.

"Well, if you can't tell me, you're grounded for a month!"

Sounds unreasonable, right? People wouldn't actually expect you to know *their* dreams. But that's exactly what happened to Daniel.

King Nebuchadnezzar had a disturbing dream. When he woke up, he couldn't totally remember it. He called his magicians and wise men together and demanded they tell him about his dream and what it meant (Daniel 2:2-3). Nobody could do it. Nebuchadnezzar got so angry that he ordered all the wise men in Babylon killed. One of the king's guards went to execute Daniel and his friends, who weren't with the king when he first asked about his dream. Daniel wanted a little time to get back to the king. The guard agreed, so Daniel told his friends to pray to God. That night God came to Daniel in a vision and showed him the king's dream and its meaning. When Daniel went before the king, he said that no wise man could do what the king wanted. However, there are no secrets from God. Then Daniel explained the king's dream and what it meant.

Have you ever had a dream at night that disturbed you? If so, ask God to give you peace and show you if it had any meaning. When you personally know God, you have a connection to the greatest source of wisdom in the universe.

PUZZLE IT OUT: WHAT'S THE WORD?

Look closely at the words below. One letter is missing from the second word in each pair. Write that letter in order on the spaces below to discover the missing word from what Daniel said to God in Daniel 2:20.

1. pastry   trays
2. loaves   slave
3. warm   arm
4. cape   cap
5. flour   foul

"Praise the name of God forever and ever, for he has all wisdom and __ __ __ __ __."

    1 2 3 4 5

✝ PRAY

Tell God you don't want to keep secrets from him, because he knows everything already.

Life's Guidebook Says
Daniel replied, "There are no wise men, enchanters, magicians, or fortune-tellers who can reveal the king's secret. But there is a God in heaven who reveals secrets." DANIEL 2:27-28

Answer: power

WISE SNAKES

A TENTACLED SNAKE in Southeast Asia tricks fish to capture them. The snake uses slight body movements to make the fish go the direction it wants. Tentacled snakes calculate where the fish will swim *next*, and then make body adjustments. Then they move their heads faster than you can blink to capture their prey. It almost looks like the fish swim right into the snake's mouth.

Fish usually make speedy turns and dart away when a predator swims into sight. But with this snake, fish are tricked to turn into trouble.

When Jesus sent out his 12 disciples, he told them to be wise as snakes.

The tentacled snake is pretty smart, but the Antiguan racer snake showed it was really wise when it escaped its enemy. In the early 1900s, European settlers on the island of Antigua wanted to get rid of the rats. They imported mongooses to eat the pests. Bad idea! Mongooses sleep at night when rats are awake. Instead of eating rats, the mongooses ate birds and snakes, especially the Antiguan racer snake. They gobbled them all up, and people thought the snakes had vanished.

But in the early 1990s, scientists discovered that a few wise Antiguan snakes had made their way to a tiny island near Antigua that was free of the mongoose. People started a project to help the Antiguan racer build up a bigger population.

God wants us to be as wise as snakes to help us survive any problems. That's why he gave us creative minds and his Holy Spirit to escape danger and find wisdom.

LIFTOFF LIST

√ Check off good things you can think about that keep you out of trouble.
X Cross out bad thoughts you should not think about.

___ Fishing
___ Learning something new as I read the Bible
___ Bad names to call someone
___ Helping someone
___ Praying for other people
___ Computer games that are not violent
___ TV shows that have mean jokes or lots of violence
___ Other countries and places I want to visit
___ Friends and things to do together
___ Excuses to get out of work
___ New games I can invent

✝ PRAY

Ask God to make you wise like a snake so you can survive problems.

Life's Guidebook Says

[Jesus said,] "I am sending you out like sheep among wolves. So be as wise as snakes and as harmless as doves." MATTHEW 10:16, NIrV

STAMPEDE!

IN THE EARLY 1920S, Notre Dame had one of the best college football teams of all time. In three years, they lost only two games. Their quarterback and running backs were so good and so feared that people called them the "Four Horsemen of Notre Dame." These four players ran all over the field and trampled the competition.

But those four "horsemen" were nowhere near as feared as the four horsemen that the apostle John describes in the book of Revelation. These horsemen, who ride on a white horse, red horse, black horse, and pale horse, are part of God's final judgment on earth. They're called the "Four Horsemen of the Apocalypse." This scary stampede of horses will bring war, famine, and death (Revelation 6:1-8).

In the future, God will judge all people. Only those who are perfectly holy through their relationship with Jesus will go into the new heaven and inhabit the new earth. When some people read the book of Revelation, they get confused and scared. Some of the events John describes are frightening. But when you know Jesus as your Savior, there's nothing to fear. The apostle John makes it clear—Jesus wins in the end. Only God is victorious! He never loses a game. He's undefeated and unbeatable . . . which is way better than Notre Dame's four horsemen.

WACKY LAUGHS

Q. What is a horse's favorite salad dressing?
A. Ranch.

Q. What is a horse's favorite book of the Bible?
A. *Neigh*-amiah.

Q. What did the pig say to the horse?
A. "Why the long face?"

Q. What kind of horse can you ride by moonlight?
A. A night-mare.

Q. Why are wild horses wealthy?
A. They make big bucks.

✞ PRAY

Thank God that his goodness is more powerful than any evil in the world. Praise him because he'll win the last battle.

Life's Guidebook Says
I looked up and saw a horse whose color was pale green. Its rider was named Death, and his companion was the Grave. REVELATION 6:8

JESUS TAKES A RIDE

IN ABOUT THREE WEEKS, professional football teams will come together to start training for the upcoming season. During this same time, experts will try to predict which teams will make it to the Super Bowl. These prognosticators will try to look into the future to see which team is best before the season even starts. They look at statistics, matchups, coaches, and players to make their best predictions.

God's prophets in the Old Testament didn't have a lot of data to interpret. But they did have something that none of these football gurus have: God's Spirit. Football experts guess who's going to be the best in just a few months, and they're often wrong. God's prophets made predictions hundreds—even thousands—of years before something happened, and they were never wrong. That's because God's Spirit was guiding what they wrote.

Nearly 500 years before Jesus' birth, the prophet Zechariah made some statements about Israel's coming King. He wrote, "Shout in triumph, O people of Jerusalem! Look, your king is coming to you. He is righteous and victorious, yet he is humble, riding on a donkey—riding on a donkey's colt" (Zechariah 9:9). Does that sound like anybody you know? If you said, "Jesus," then you're correct. Hundreds of years later, Jesus rode into Jerusalem on a donkey's colt to fulfill this prophecy.

Go back and look at the words that Zechariah used to describe Jesus. He said he was *righteous*, *victorious*, and *humble*. What a great description! Take a few minutes today to write down a few more words that describe your Savior:

_____

_____

QUIZ: HOW CUTE!
A baby donkey is called a colt. Draw a line to match these animals and their offspring.

Bear	Kit
Deer	Joey
Dog	Chick
Fox	Cub
Goat	Pup
Kangaroo	Calf
Penguin	Kid
Whale	Fawn

✝ PRAY
Praise Jesus for being righteous, victorious, and humble.

Life's Guidebook Says
Tell the people of Jerusalem, "Look, your King is coming to you. He is humble, riding on a donkey—riding on a donkey's colt." MATTHEW 21:5

Answers: Bear—Cub; Deer—Fawn; Dog—Pup; Fox—Kit; Goat—Kid;
Kangaroo—Joey; Penguin—Chick; Whale—Calf

RACING THE CLOCK

WHAT CAN YOU NEVER CATCH no matter how fast you run? Here's a hint: the thing you're chasing always runs at the same speed.

If you guessed "time," you're right! The clock keeps ticking steadily ahead. It can seem slow when you're waiting for school to end, or waiting for a birthday or Christmas to come. Or it can seem fast when you're having fun playing a game or hanging out with friends. But the truth is time never changes.

Jonas Cattel couldn't outrun time, but he did save the day.

In 1777, the British locked up the 18-year-old for breaking curfew—staying out too late—during the Revolutionary War. During the night, he overheard a plan between the British and Hessian soldiers to attack Fort Mercer. In the morning they released the teenager, and that's when Jonas made an amazing run.

Jonas was a trailblazer. He made trails throughout New Jersey and knew them well. He raced through shortcuts, twisted along little-known paths, and ran 10 miles at top speed to get to Fort Mercer and let the Continental army know about the plot. The army moved their cannons into position at Red Bank and surprised the British, who quickly surrendered. Every year, from Haddonfield to Red Bank, New Jersey, there's a historic 10-mile footrace to celebrate when Jonas made great time to save the day.

Time may go on and on, but you shouldn't let a day go by without letting others know about the saving power of Jesus.

TWISTY TONGUE TWISTERS

Try to say these tongue twisters 10 times without stopping.

Thirty thieves thought 'twas time to try tricky tricks.
Running free, running far, racing round rocks and rubble.

✝ PRAY

Thank God for the time he gives you. Ask God to help you be patient when you need to wait and help you move fast when it's important.

Life's Guidebook Says

This is all the more urgent, for you know how late it is; time is running out. Wake up, for our salvation is nearer now than when we first believed. ROMANS 13:11

CITY OF PROMISE

HAVE YOU EVER VISITED an Old West ghost town? You look around at falling-down build-ings and empty dirt streets. Tumbleweeds blow across the road. Lizards scamper under wooden sidewalks to find shade. You can tell that this was once an exciting place to live, but not anymore. Those glory days of gold, glamour, and parties are long gone. Many old towns eventually disappear, never to be seen again.

During Zechariah's life in the Old Testament, visiting Jerusalem was kind of like visiting a ghost town. You could tell the city had been something special, but it wasn't anymore. The city walls were knocked down. The Temple had been destroyed. With their capital gone, Jewish people were spread all over the Middle East. But God gave his prophet an amazing promise. Instead of Jerusalem disappearing into the sand, the Lord of Heaven's Armies said the city would be restored. Old men would walk and talk in the city square. Children would play in the streets (Zechariah 8:4-5). God knew the few people living in Jerusalem probably wouldn't believe him, because the living conditions were so unsafe and depressing. So he told Zechariah that he'd bring his people from the east and west and once again they'd live safely. "All this may seem impossible to you now," the Lord said. "But is it impossible for me?" (see today's verse).

Think about that question: Is it impossible for God? Of course not! Nothing is impos-sible for the all-powerful Master and Creator of the universe. Next time you face a seem-ingly impossible situation, remember God's words to Zechariah.

PLEXER

Solve this plexer to find out what God wanted his people to build to protect Jerusalem. (If you don't remember what a plexer is, see p. 9.)

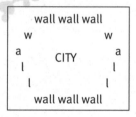

✝ PRAY

Thank God that nothing is impossible for him.

Life's Guidebook Says
This is what the LORD of Heaven's Armies says: All this may seem impossible to you now, a small remnant of God's people. But is it impossible for me?
ZECHARIAH 8:6

Answer: Walls around the city

STAND-UP STUNTMAN

ALLEN ROBINSON knows something about surviving dangerous situations. During his lifetime, he's fallen off buildings, been set on fire, crashed countless cars, hung from hot air balloons, and been blasted by explosions. But don't worry—it's all part of a day's work as a stuntman in Hollywood. Allen has appeared in some of the biggest TV shows and movies. He's worked with the top A-list actors. And through it all, he's lived out his faith in Jesus Christ.

"As a Christian working in Hollywood, you're definitely a minority," Allen says. "I like that challenge."

Allen doesn't beat people over the head with a Bible, but he doesn't hide his faith either. Before big stunts, he'll often bow his head and pray for safety. If somebody tells a crude joke, he'll walk away instead of laughing with everybody else. On a movie set, you're with about 150 people every day for a few months. After watching Allen for a while, people start to notice there's something different about him. He doesn't cuss. He seems peaceful and happy.

What would your friends say about you? Would they notice something different about you because you're a follower of Jesus Christ? Or would you blend in with everybody else? Allen grew up loving adventure and taking risks. Try a risk that's worth taking by shining for Jesus with your words and actions.

AWESOME ACTIVITY: WE ALL FALL DOWN

Stuntmen stay safe while performing dangerous tricks. One of the first things stuntmen learn is how to fall correctly. Take some time to practice this skill on a soft surface. Just follow these steps . . . and don't hurt yourself.

Try It

1. Make sure your head doesn't hit the ground. If you're falling backward, tuck your chin into your chest. If you fall forward, turn your head to the side.
2. Slap your palms against the ground as you fall forward, but don't try to catch yourself, which might result in a wrist injury.
3. Exhale as you fall.
4. Bend your knees and try to "fold" yourself onto the ground.
5. Roll as you hit the ground, instead of hitting straight on.

✝ PRAY

Ask God to help you be a light for him in your everyday life.

Life's Guidebook Says

Let your good deeds shine out for all to see, so that everyone will praise your heavenly Father. MATTHEW 5:16

A GOOD NAME

EVERYTHING THAT HAPPENS to us on earth feels real. And it is. But sometimes we can forget that there's an even more important spiritual dimension to our lives. The book of Job reminds us of that fact. The Bible says Job feared God and stayed away from evil (Job 1:1). And God blessed him for his actions. Job had 10 children, 7,000 sheep, 3,000 camels, and tons of servants and was one of the richest men in the land.

Job didn't keep his money to himself. He helped others. He gave to the poor and assisted orphans in need of help (Job 29:11-12). People respected Job because of the way he treated others. While everybody else was impressed with Job, Satan wasn't. Satan told God that the only reason Job served him was because God always protected and blessed him. So God allowed Satan to test Job. Job lost his animals, his servants, his health, and even his children. Satan thought Job would curse God if he lost everything. But Job didn't. He said, "Should we accept only good things from the hand of God and never anything bad?" (Job 2:10). Job continued to serve God and others. Later in his life, God blessed Job more than he had before. God gave him 14,000 sheep, 6,000 camels, and 10 more children.

You can learn a lot from Job's life. He praised God in the tough times. He understood life wasn't about riches; it was about serving God. And he used his blessings to bless others.

WEIRD FACTS: IT'S GOOD TO HELP

Researchers have found that helping others has surprising benefits—and not only for the people you help. Volunteering . . .

- ☞ allows you to make new friends.
- ☞ helps you overcome shyness and develop good social skills.
- ☞ increases your self-confidence.
- ☞ makes you feel happier.

✝ PRAY

Pray for God to provide you with opportunities to serve others.

Life's Guidebook Says

[Job said,] "All who heard me praised me. All who saw me spoke well of me. For I assisted the poor in their need and the orphans who required help."
JOB 29:11-12

JULY

WORKING FOR FREEDOM

BANG! WHACK! TROMP, TROMP! Young boys and old men hammered wood as they listened to marching soldiers practice their drills. Boys of all ages helped build places where soldiers could sleep as the whole city of Baltimore, Maryland, prepared for the British attack in the War of 1812.

In August of 1813, people chose to work together to fight for freedom. Women and girls rolled bandages and cooked. Merchants brought supplies. Men joined the army. City leaders met daily with General Samuel Smith. The citizens trusted the general to keep them free and win against the British, led by General Robert Ross. As they worked, the people often sang this song:

> The gen'ral gave orders for the troops to march down,
> To meet the proud Ross, and to check his ambition;
> To inform him we have decreed in our town
> That here he can't enter without our permission.
> And if life he regards, he will not press too hard,
> For Baltimore freemen are ever prepared
> To check the presumptuous, whoever they be,
> That may rashly attempt to evade our decree.

By working together, the people helped win the Battle of Baltimore over the more powerful British forces. The morning after the battle, when Francis Scott Key saw the American flag still flying above the town, he wrote the words of "The Star-Spangled Banner," the national anthem of the United States. You're never too young to be patriotic. Hang a flag or wear your country's colors this week as a symbol of freedom.

WEIRD FACTS: FLAGS
- ☞ An upside-down flag is a distress signal.
- ☞ Other names for a flag are *banner* and *standard*.
- ☞ Early flags were made of metal and called *vexilloids* (meaning flag-like).
- ☞ In the Middle Ages, knights carried flags to share information, such as which king they served.
- ☞ The military uses signal flags to communicate messages. There is a flag for each letter of the alphabet.

✝ PRAY
Ask God to keep our country free and bring freedom to people everywhere.

Life's Guidebook Says
You have been called to live in freedom, my brothers and sisters. But don't use your freedom to satisfy your sinful nature. Instead, use your freedom to serve one another in love. GALATIANS 5:13

IT WAS NO PICNIC!

ABIGAIL ADAMS and her eight-year-old son, John Quincy, sat together on a grassy hill. She didn't plan a picnic that day. She wanted John to watch courageous men fight for freedom at the Battle of Bunker Hill.

Young John watched men charge with guns and swords. He heard the roar of cannons and saw men fall from wounds. Red blood covered the battlefield. Years later he described that day:

> *I saw with my own eyes those fires, and heard Britannia's thunders in the battle of Bunker Hill, and witnessed the tears of my mother and mingled them with my own, at the fall of Warren, a dear friend of my father, and a beloved Physician to me. He had been our family physician and surgeon, and had saved my forefinger from amputation under a very bad fracture.*

John felt sad for the deaths but celebrated when the colonies won the American Revolution. Years later, he sailed to France to make peace with England and end another war, the War of 1812. Eventually he became the sixth president of the United States. John read several chapters of the Bible every morning. He tried to end slavery, believing all people should be free.

War is no picnic. It's messy and bloody. Many soldiers have fought so we can have the freedom to worship and make our own choices on how to live. Jesus, the Prince of Peace, will someday come and bring complete peace to every place on earth. When Jesus rules the new earth, there won't be any more wars.

LIFTOFF LIST

Take steps to live at peace with others. You can disagree, but do it peacefully. Try these ideas to settle problems:

____ Release anger in acceptable ways (run, jump, write about it).
____ Calm down before talking about the problem.
____ Pray and think about how Jesus would respond.
____ Calmly tell the person involved what he did that upset you.
____ Listen and think before acting.
____ Meet to discuss possible solutions and list people's reasons for their choices.
____ Pray together and forgive the people involved.
____ Choose a solution, then try to set a time to talk about how it is working.

✝ PRAY

Ask God to help you settle differences without arguing or fighting.

Life's Guidebook Says

Do all that you can to live in peace with everyone.   ROMANS 12:18

YOUNG PATRIOTS

"Mother, I think I can get letters to the soldiers." Mary Redmond, nicknamed the "Little Black-Eyed Rebel," had come up with a plan. She often played with a boy named Billy, who came to Philadelphia from an area near where the Continental army had camped. Mary discovered Billy was loyal to the colonists in the fight for freedom from England.

Some of Mary's relatives remained true to England, but she and her family supported the Revolution. Billy agreed to her plan and hid letters in the lining of his jacket. She traded the letters to loved ones for spy messages that gave information about the British troops.

One day Mary noticed soldiers watching Billy. She knew they sometimes searched him. Mary pretended to play with Billy. They raced around and tagged one another. When no one was looking, Mary covered Billy with her shawl and they swapped papers.

Months later, when Mary learned that the British general had surrendered, she wanted to scream for joy but knew people loyal to the British king were watching her. So she stuck her head up the chimney and cheered to celebrate the victory of American General Gates.

You don't have to hide your excitement about serving Christ. He's won the ultimate victory over death and in your life. So lift up your head and shout. You can praise God and thank him loudly for freedom.

AWESOME ACTIVITY: MASKING A MESSAGE
During the American Revolution, "masks" were used to send secret messages. A mask is a shape with cutout openings. Make your own to talk with a friend.

Stuff You Need
- ☞ Index cards
- ☞ Hole punch
- ☞ Sheet of paper
- ☞ Pencil

Try It
1. Hold the index cards together, and punch the same holes in both. Make several holes around the paper. (See the diagram for how it might look.)
2. Place one mask on top of a clean sheet of paper, and write letters in each hole to create a message.
3. Lift up the mask and add letters to make words and create a fake letter.
4. Pass the letter to a friend with the other mask, so he can read the real message.

✝ PRAY
Thank God for freedom. Sing a song to praise him.

Life's Guidebook Says
If the Son sets you free, you are truly free.   JOHN 8:36

CELEBRATING FREEDOM

HOORAY! CHEERS FILLED THE AIR as towns from New Hampshire to Georgia celebrated victory in the American Revolution on October 23, 1781. *Boom! Crackle!* Soldiers fired cannons and towns held parties with firework displays and bonfires. *Rat-a-tat-tat.* Drum rolls, displays of patriotic colors, and shouting added to the joy. Some places even burned large stuffed figures of Benedict Arnold.

Patriot leaders had signed the Declaration of Independence on July 4, 1776, but the first celebration for the victory took place five years and a few months later. The celebrations started with church services to thank God for his help. On October 18, 1783, after the official signing of the peace treaty, the United States' early leaders made a special proclamation to thank God:

> *The United States in Congress assembled do recommend it to the several States, to set apart the second Thursday in December next, as a day of public thanksgiving, that all the people may then assemble to celebrate, with grateful hearts and united voices, the praises of their Supreme and all bountiful Benefactor, for his numberless favors and mercies.*

Throughout the newly formed country, people came together to thank God on December 11 and spent the day praying and listening to sermons.

Thousands of years before and thousands of miles away, another nation, Israel, also took time to thank God for its freedom and victories. With Moses, the people held a huge party and sang a song of praise (Exodus 15:1-21). They understood that it's God's blessing that makes a nation great. When you score high on a test, win a game, or learn a new skill, stop and thank God for helping you be a winner too.

WACKY LAUGHS

Q. What were the scribbles drawn by early American children called?
A. Yankee doodles.

Q. What did the banner say when Francis Scott Key saw it?
A. Nothing. It just waved.

Q. What is a patriotic cow's motto?
A. "United we stand. Divided we're steak."

✟ PRAY

Thank God for your latest victory or achievement.

Life's Guidebook Says

The LORD your God is going with you! He will fight for you against your enemies, and he will give you victory! DEUTERONOMY 20:4

WELLS FOR THIRSTY PEOPLE

RYAN HRELJAC was in first grade when he first heard about people dying from thirst in Africa. It amazed him to learn that people walked hours to fill buckets with water. *Swish! Gulp! Gulp!* He counted one, two, three . . . ten steps to a water fountain where he could easily get a drink.

Ryan wanted to do something. He begged his parents to let him do extra chores to earn money to build a well in Africa. *Clink! Clink!* Chores only earned small change. Digging a well in Africa costs thousands of dollars, because it takes big drills to dig deep. The wells also need to use parts that can be easily fixed if something breaks. Ryan started speaking to groups to ask for money. He looked for more ways to raise funds and began Ryan's Well Foundation.

In a few years, he did it! He raised enough money for one well. But he didn't stop with one. After 10 years, his organization had raised over one million dollars. Ryan now speaks at churches and many other places to encourage people to give money to help people have fresh water.

Ryan works hard to provide water for people who are thirsty. Think of ways you and your friends can help raise money for a well . . . or another project that's close to your heart. Jesus said when you help people in need, it's like you're helping him directly—that's how much the Lord cares for the needy.

EXPERIMENT: THIRSTY POPPING PEAS

Dehydrated peas thirst for water. Add water and watch them pop with joy!

Stuff You Need
- ☞ Glass (a wineglass shape works best)
- ☞ Dried peas
- ☞ Water
- ☞ Plate

Try It
1. Fill glass to overflowing with dried peas.
2. Pour water in the glass to the brim.
3. Place the glass on a plate. As the peas absorb water through their skin, they swell and stretch. Soon the peas will rise, overflow, and clatter onto the plate. As they fall, you'll hear a popping noise.

✝ PRAY

Ask God what he wants you to do to help other people. Thank him for clean drinking water.

Life's Guidebook Says
[Jesus said,] "I was hungry, and you fed me. I was thirsty, and you gave me a drink. I was a stranger, and you invited me into your home. MATTHEW 25:35

CHAMPION SWIMMER

JOSH DAVIS didn't start out as a world-class swimmer. One coach even told him to give up competitive swimming. But Josh loved the sport. He didn't give up. He kept working hard and found another coach who showed him techniques to improve his strokes, turns, and dives into the pool. Josh practiced hard and earned a swimming scholarship to one of the top programs in the United States.

Then, at the 1996 Summer Olympics, Josh took home three gold medals. He was the only man to win three golds in Atlanta. At the 2000 Summer Games, Josh was the captain of the swim team and earned two silver medals. However, he didn't win at everything.

When he first went to college, Josh partied a lot and made bad choices. He became very ill and realized he was not happy. For two weeks, he was stuck in bed. Lying flat on his back, Josh decided that he needed someone to help him make better choices. He chose Jesus to be his life coach. He returned to college and started to attend Bible studies and hang out with Christian friends.

After the fame Josh earned at the Olympics, he went on to teach clinics on how to swim well. He also shared his faith and the importance of choosing Jesus as your coach to be an eternal winner.

Long ago, God separated the land from the water to form oceans. He created sea creatures such as fish that could swim. People also learned to swim. Can you swim? If so, go to a pool, jump in, and enjoy a race with a friend. And remember to thank God for creating water to be a great way to cool off and have fun in the summer.

LIFTOFF LIST

Check off your abilities with water.

____ I can swim well.
____ I wear a life jacket when boating.
____ I have enjoyed a water park.
____ I practice holding my breath underwater.
____ I snorkel.
____ I am on a swim team.

✝ PRAY

Ask God to be your life coach, and tell him you want to follow his commands.

Life's Guidebook Says

God said, "Let the waters beneath the sky flow together into one place, so dry ground may appear." And that is what happened. GENESIS 1:9

SEA SAWS

YOU'VE PROBABLY HEARD about God parting the Red Sea and allowing Moses to lead his people across. That's also when God stopped Pharaoh and his soldiers with a big splash by letting the waters fall back down. But that wasn't the only time God showed his power by parting water.

God stopped the waters of the Jordan River from flowing so his people could cross into the Promised Land. The gurgling and rushing of the river halted, and the water rose up in a high heap. A riverbed is usually muddy on the bottom, but the Bible says the people walked on dry ground. God dried the slimy mud. This time they weren't fleeing from an enemy. They were crossing to enter the land God had promised to give them, which is now the modern-day country of Israel.

The parting of the Jordan happened 40 years after God parted the Red Sea. All the adults who crossed the Red Sea had died except for Caleb and Joshua. The people had probably heard about the miracle as their parents or grandparents told them the story when they were children. Now God's people saw and experienced his power themselves. They watched the water swirl up and then slide back down after they crossed.

God continues to show people miracles and answer their prayers. Listen to your parents and grandparents share answers to prayers and miracles they have experienced. Trust that God will answer your prayers too.

PLEXER

See if you can solve this plexer. (If you don't remember what a plexer is, see p. 9.)

Jordan God River

✞ PRAY

Thank God for being faithful to your parents and grandparents. Ask God to let you experience some of the amazing things you've heard about.

Life's Guidebook Says

The priests who were carrying the Ark of the LORD's Covenant stood on dry ground in the middle of the riverbed as the people passed by. They waited there until the whole nation of Israel had crossed the Jordan on dry ground. JOSHUA 3:17

Answer: God parts the Jordan River.

ALMOST DROWNED

POWERFUL WAVES POUNDED Josh McQuoid. The fast-flowing current pulled him away from the shore. Just minutes before, the 12-year-old had been enjoying a day at the beach in New Zealand. Now he was struggling for his life!

Crash! First, a wave hit him and dragged him into the sea. Then more waves came and flipped him around. Josh was held underwater for nearly 20 seconds. When he fought his way to the surface, he saw help coming. A group of people had formed a human chain, holding hands and stepping into the swirling water to grasp the hand of the struggling boy. Two police officers had started the chain and called for more people to join them. Those on the shore stood on steady ground while others felt the harsh splash of waves beat against them. Each person supported the next one as the team worked together.

Once rescuers pulled Josh onto the land, they used CPR to get him breathing again. Medics quickly arrived and took Josh to the hospital. All of that happened in 2013, but Josh is still thankful for the people who saved his life.

Teamwork makes a difference. Without a team of people working together, Josh probably wouldn't be alive today. Think of how you cooperate at home, school, or church. Are you a good teammate? How does your work make a difference to the people around you?

WEIRD FACTS: WATER SAFETY TIPS

- ☞ Never swim alone. Make sure there's an adult nearby or lifeguard on duty.
- ☞ Learn CPR.
- ☞ Watch the weather report for riptides or strong currents.
- ☞ Be aware of waves.
- ☞ Understand what an undertow is and how to escape it.
- ☞ Swim in areas that are labeled safe.
- ☞ Wear a life jacket when boating.
- ☞ Learn to tread water.
- ☞ Get out of the water if you hear thunder or see lightning.
- ☞ Take breaks to drink plenty of fresh water when you swim.
- ☞ Enter the water feet first to make sure it's safe.

✝ PRAY

Thank God for friends and other people who are willing to help you when you are in trouble.

Life's Guidebook Says

[Jonah] said, "I cried out to the LORD in my great trouble, and he answered me.
I called to you from the land of the dead, and LORD, you heard me! JONAH 2:2

WATERY CHANGES

WHOOSH! CULLEN JONES zoomed down the waterslide. *Crash! Flip!* Cullen's inner tube hit the water and turned over. At just five years old, Cullen didn't know how to swim. The water was over his head, and his parents couldn't see him. They shouted for help. Lifeguards dove in and rescued Cullen. Wanting to prevent another accident, Cullen's mother enrolled her son in swim lessons the next week. Cullen quickly learned to swim. At eight, he joined a swim team. And in 2008, Cullen won a gold medal in a relay in the Summer Olympics alongside Michael Phelps, Jason Lezak, and Garrett Weber-Gale. He added another gold and two silver medals at the 2012 Summer Olympics.

Cullen became the second African American to win an Olympic gold medal in swimming. He even set a world record in the 50-m. freestyle. But none of that would've happened if he hadn't been willing to work on his weakness and turn it into a strength.

You can change a weakness of yours into a strength too. All it takes is practice, hard work, and a fearless attitude. The Bible tells us to work at improving our faith, which can often be weak. Pump up your faith by building good character, self-control, knowledge, and love (2 Peter 1:4-7). Then think of something you want to be better at . . . and work at it.

PUZZLE IT OUT: CHANGE THE WORDS

Jesus didn't have any weaknesses, but he was good at changing things. Using the code, write the letter of the first number in each problem in the left column. Then solve the math problem and write the letter for the answer in the right column. Read down the columns to discover two things that Jesus changed.

A	B	C	D	E	F	G	H	I	J	K	L	M	N	O	P	Q	R	S	T	U	V	W	X	Y	Z
1	2	3	4	5	6	7	8	9	10	11	12	13	14	15	16	17	18	19	20	21	22	23	24	25	26	27

First change:

___ $23 - 5 + 10 - 2 \cdot 3$ ___

___ $1 + 2 + 10 - 4$ ___

___ $20 - 17 + 3 + 8$ ___

___ $5 \times 5 - 20$ ___

___ $18 + 2 - 13 + 11 + 9$ ___

Next change:

___ $12 + 5 - 15 + 4$ ___

___ $21 - 18 - 1 + 2$ ___

___ $14 \div 14 + 0$ ___

___ $3 \times 6 + 4 - 3$ ___

___ $8 + 15 - 4 + 1$ ___

_____ into _____ and _____ into a _____

Read about those changes in John 2:1-10 and John 6:8-11.

✝ PRAY

Ask God to help you change in an area where you need to improve.

Life's Guidebook Says

Our faces are not covered with a veil. We all display the Lord's glory. We are being changed to become more like him so that we have more and more glory. And the glory comes from the Lord, who is the Holy Spirit.

2 CORINTHIANS 3:18, NIrV

Answers: Water into wine / lunch into a feast

MUD IN YOUR EYES

SWIFTY: SWIFTY HERE, the top reporter with *Pharisee Nightly News*. Reports say Jesus tried to bully this man with me. Sir, I'm following up on problems that Jesus is causing.

Man: Why? He's a great man.

Swifty: We heard he threw mud in your eyes. That sounds nasty, even dangerous.

Man: Well, he did put mud on my eyes, but—

Swifty: That's abuse.

Man: No, it was healing.

Swifty: How can mud heal you?

Man: Jesus spit on some dirt and made mud. It was more like clay.

Swifty: So he spit in your eye and then threw dirt on top of it.

Man: No, you don't understand. I was blind!

Swifty: Of course you were. Dirt in the eye will do that.

Man: No, I was blind *before* Jesus found me.

Swifty: That's even worse. He bullied a blind man.

Man: No, he healed me! He put mud on my eyes and told me to wash in the pool.

Swifty: Was he trying to make you look silly, like a clown?

Man: No, he was helping me. Once I washed off the clay, I could see.

Swifty: That's weird. Where's this dirt? Maybe there's healing power in it.

Man: No, Jesus is the healer. He's healed the deaf, lepers, and even the dead.

Swifty: All with mud and spit?

Man: No, he used only the clay on me. He's the healer. The dirt is just dirt.

Swifty: *Hmm*, I think I'd better start following him and see what else he can do.

PUZZLE IT OUT: FINDING THE TRUTH

It can take people time to understand the truth about Jesus. Find your way through the maze by tracing the path with the letters "Jesus is the real healer."

✝ PRAY

Ask Jesus to heal someone you know who is sick.

Life's Guidebook Says

[Jesus] spit on the ground, made mud with the saliva, and spread the mud over the blind man's eyes. He told him, "Go wash yourself in the pool of Siloam."
JOHN 9:6-7

SPRINKLE LIFE WITH FUN

IF YOU LIKE RUNNING through the sprinkler, you can thank Joseph Lessler of Buffalo, New York. In 1871, he invented the lawn sprinkler. Since that time, sprinklers have changed a lot. But one thing hasn't: it's still a great way to stay cool on a hot summer day.

While running through the sprinklers in the middle of the day is a good idea, watering grass and plants at that time should be avoided. The best time to water plants is early in the morning, because less water evaporates and leaves don't get sunburned. Yes, leaves can sunburn! The water acts like a magnifying glass as it sits on a leaf. But prickly or hairy leaves don't burn, so a cactus can get watered anytime.

Before God sent the first-ever rain, he watered the earth by sending springs up from the earth (Genesis 2:6). He used his built-in sprinkler system to grow life and keep it healthy! God sprinkled the earth and made it beautiful.

You can help keep the world beautiful. Offer to help your family or a neighbor with their yard work. Experts say it's best to water thirsty plants less often, but use more water, because it encourages roots to grow deep. God wants you to have deep roots in him, too. Make sure to sprinkle your day with prayer, reading his Word, and praising him for a beautiful planet.

WACKY LAUGHS

Q. Why did the missionary cross the ocean?
A. To get to the other tide.

Q. What did the Red Sea do as God parted it?
A. It gave a big wave.

Q. What did the dirt say to the rain?
A. "Thanks to you, my name is mud!"

✝ PRAY

Thank God for rain and a beautiful world.

Life's Guidebook Says
Springs came up from the ground and watered all the land. GENESIS 2:6

JESUS WALKED ON WATER

HAVE YOU EVER SKIPPED a stone across a lake? It's amazing to watch it hop before it sinks. Maybe you can do a double or even triple skip. In 2007, a man in Pennsylvania set a world record by throwing a stone and making it skip 51 times! It traveled almost as far as a football field before it plopped into the depths.

More recently, some men made a film that used a hidden platform to make it look like they could skip across the water. They called it liquid mountaineering. They created a video where they took a few running steps on top of the water before sinking in. Of course, they were actually running on the platform—twisting the truth with video tricks.

Jesus didn't need tricks to walk on water. As God, he can control nature. After Jesus fed a crowd of 5,000 with a few loaves and fish, his disciples waited for him at the Sea of Galilee. When he didn't show up, they rowed a few miles into the sea. Late at night, they saw Jesus walking toward them on the water. Peter couldn't believe it, and yet he wanted to imitate Christ.

"Lord, is it you?" Peter asked. "If it is, tell me to come to you on the water." Jesus invited Peter to come. He stepped out of the boat and walked on water, but only for a few steps. He took his eyes off Jesus and started sinking. Jesus reached out his hand, grabbed Peter, and saved him.

The greatest athletes on earth have never been able to do what Jesus did. The disciples saw the miracle and spoke the truth when they said, "You really are the Son of God!" (Matthew 14:33). Because Jesus is God, you can trust that he can do anything. And when you keep your eyes on him, you'll be able to do amazing things too.

TWISTY TONGUE TWISTERS

Try to say these tongue twisters 10 times without stopping.

Wonderful, wet, warm washing water.
Six or seven swift swans swam.
Sailors swam seven shimmery, shiny seas.

✞ PRAY

Thank God for sending his Son to save you. Thank God for being all powerful.

Life's Guidebook Says

[The disciples] had rowed three or four miles when suddenly they saw Jesus walking on the water toward the boat. They were terrified. JOHN 6:19

WILL WORK FOR LIZARD

PETE REALLY WANTED a lizard. "Mom, can I have a leopard gecko?" he asked.

"What?" Mom said. "Look at your room. How can I let you have a pet lizard? With piles of dirty clothes and toys scattered everywhere, a lizard could get lost."

"What if I keep my room clean?" Pete said.

"Well, you'd have to prove you could really keep it clean," Mom said.

Pete agreed to clean his room and keep it clean for six months. He spent four days getting his room clean and then worked a little every day to keep it that way. He also read books on how to care for a lizard and keep it healthy.

At the end of six months, Pete's mother let him choose his lizard and tank. Pete filled the bottom of the tank with fake green carpet and added some cool rocks, a half log, and climbing sticks. He caught bugs and fed his lizard every day. Pete made sure to keep water in a dish. He even sprayed water in the tank every day to make it humid. His leopard gecko seemed to like having Pete take him out and hold him.

Pets can be fun, but they need a lot of care. Many parents want their children to show they can be responsible with little things before they allow them to have the big responsibility of having a pet. Did you know that responsibility was one of the first things that God taught Adam and Eve? In Genesis 1, God made them responsible for the rest of creation. God still wants us to take good care of the world he has given us, including animals. Think of chores you do that show responsibility.

LIFTOFF LIST

How well do you show responsibility and follow your parents' rules for taking care of things and pets?

____ I put my bicycle away after riding it.

____ I feed my pet and give it water.

____ I pick up my toys and games.

____ I make my bed every day.

____ I turn off lights when I am the last person to leave a room.

____ I clean my dishes after eating.

____ I do my chores without being reminded.

____ I do my homework on time.

✝ PRAY

Ask God to help you be responsible.

Life's Guidebook Says

My son, obey your father's commands, and don't neglect your mother's instruction. PROVERBS 6:20

PLANTING SEEDS

THE BOYS DUG into the soil and dropped pea seeds in rows as their grandpa had instructed.

This is taking too long, DeForest thought.

He called over his brother and their cousin. None of them wanted to plant pea seeds. DeForest said they could roll over a big rock, dump the seeds in the hole, and be done fast. They all agreed to the plan.

A few weeks later Grandpa called the three boys to his house. He walked them over to the rock and said, "Funny thing. This here rock appears to be growing a green beard."

He had discovered the boys' trick.

The boys had to dig up all the sprouts and carefully plant them one by one. That was even harder than planting the seeds correctly in the first place.

When they were done, DeForest said, "I don't want to be a farmer when I grow up." He wanted to be a doctor and help people. And he did become a doctor . . . sort of. His full name was DeForest Kelley, and he played Dr. McCoy in the original *Star Trek* TV show and movies. Although he became a famous actor, DeForest still planted gardens of flowers at his home, especially roses.

God's truth can grow into something beautiful. Jesus compared God's Word to a seed. He used a parable about a farmer scattering seed to explain how the word of God can grow in our hearts (Mark 4:1-19). As a child, DeForest's dad, a preacher, planted that seed in his son's heart. He also encouraged DeForest's performing by allowing him to sing Christian songs at church.

Make sure your heart is filled with "good soil." Take out rocky parts and stay away from thorns. Then God's Word will multiply in amazing ways.

QUIZ: THE SEEDS

How much do you know about the seeds and the farmer (see today's verse)?

1. What happened to the seeds in rocky soil? _____
_____
2. The seeds among thorns were _____.
3. Who ate the seeds on the path? _____

✝ PRAY

Tell God you want to keep learning and planting his Word in your heart.

Life's Guidebook Says

The seed that fell on good soil represents those who hear and accept God's word and produce a harvest of thirty, sixty, or even a hundred times as much as had been planted! MARK 4:20

Answers: 1. Grew fast but the sun scorched them; 2. choked; 3. birds

GROSS BUT GOOD

No DOUBT ABOUT IT—maggots are gross. These pale, white, worm-like things seem to always pop up in trash cans and scary movies. For centuries people thought maggots just appeared on dead animals or leftover meat. But as science advanced, people discovered that maggots are fly larvae (basically, baby flies). Flies lay their eggs on garbage or rotting roadkill, then the baby maggots hatch and eat what they're living on. They're like nature's garbage disposals that make unwanted things go away.

Maggots have other uses as well. Fishermen use them as bait. Doctors have used them to eat dead tissue on a person, while the live tissue remains unharmed. Now that's good, but *gross*.

When God's people left Egypt, they ran into a maggot problem. Well, first they ran into a food problem—they didn't have any. So God sent manna from heaven for the people to eat. Families gathered it in the morning. Moses told them to only gather what they'd eat in one day. "Do not keep any of it until morning," he said (Exodus 16:19). But some people didn't listen. They tried to hoard the manna, so they wouldn't have to gather it the next day. But when they woke up, it was filled with maggots.

God wants us to follow his commands. There are no shortcuts. He doesn't want us to be greedy. If you try to hoard what God gives you or try to outsmart the Lord, you'll just end up with a pile of disgusting bugs.

EXPERIMENT: JAR FULL OF MAGGOTS

This experiment is super gross. Make sure to get a parent's permission before you try it.

Stuff You Need
- ☞ Empty pickle jar
- ☞ Some ground beef
- ☞ Paper towel
- ☞ Rubber band

Try It
1. Place the raw beef in the jar, with the lid off, and set it outside where animals can't get to it.
2. Once you notice several flies visit the meat, put the paper towel over the jar and secure it with a rubber band.
3. Check the jar every day until you see maggots.
4. In several days, your jar will fill with maggots. Put the lid on the pickle jar and carefully throw it away.

✝ PRAY

Tell God you're going to listen to his instructions and follow them perfectly.

Life's Guidebook Says
Some of them didn't listen and kept some of it until morning. But by then it was full of maggots and had a terrible smell. EXODUS 16:20

GIANT LIZARDS

THE NAME *DINOSAUR* MEANS "great lizard." The Bible describes a mysterious large animal with a tail like a cedar tree. It's named *Behemoth,* and its description still puzzles people. Many scientists think it sounds like a dinosaur. Behemoth ate grass like an ox. Archaeologists have found dinosaur dung with grass in it. The plant-eating dinosaurs, called Titanosaurs, include the Brachiosaurus. Behemoth dwelt in marshy places and had strong bones, powerful stomach muscles, strong limbs, and tightly knit muscle tissue (Job 40:15-24).

People didn't know about dinosaurs for a long time. Scientists identified the first dinosaur bones in the 1800s. Many of the first discoveries were in Connecticut and the Rocky Mountains. Two men, Othniel Marsh and Edward Cope, competed to dig fossils in the Rockies. Newspapers called this the "Bone Wars." These two paleontologists found 136 types of dinosaurs. But people found large bones that may have been dinosaurs much earlier than the 1800s. Men wrote descriptions of "dragon" bones in Wucheng, China, more than 2,000 years ago.

God knew about dinosaurs long before man found the evidence. He created them and chose their size and abilities. Nothing is a mystery to God. He created you and knows your abilities, even ones you haven't discovered yet.

PUZZLE IT OUT: LOGIC PUZZLE

Try to follow the clues and figure out what bones or dinosaur each paleontologist found. Then, for a harder challenge, see if you can figure out the year each paleontologist made his discovery. Use the chart to help figure it out.

1. Marsh found the stegosaurus.
2. The paleontologist who found bones in 1877 did not find the hadrosaurus and was not Cope.
3. The paleontologist who found triceratops found it later than what Leidy found.
4. Cope did not find the thighbone.
5. The one who found the thighbone found it earlier than Leidy found bones.

	Hadrosaurus	Stegosaurus	Thighbone	Triceratops	1786	1858	1877	1887
Leidy								
Cope								
Marsh	X	yes	X	X				
Wister								

Hint: First cross off what Leidy did not find.

✞ PRAY

Ask God to show you abilities that you have not yet discovered.

Life's Guidebook Says

[Behemoth's] tail is as strong as a cedar. The sinews of its thighs are knit tightly together. JOB 40:17

Answer: Wister found the thighbone in 1786; Leidy found the Hadrosaurus in 1858; Marsh found the Stegosaurus in 1877; Cope found the Triceratops in 1887.

STICKY TOES

LITTLE LIZARDS WIGGLE between rocks, slip inside houses, and squirm into tiny spots. The Bible calls them "small but unusually wise" and mentions that they even live in palaces (Proverbs 30:24, 28). A gecko is one smart lizard. It's the only lizard that can make more than a hissing sound. It can chirp, bark, and click. Geckos have excellent eyesight and can see well in the dark. That's good, since they like to be active at night.

Geckos can stick almost anywhere. Scientists study these amazing animals to learn more about glue and suction. The Namib Desert gecko has webbed feet to walk on sand and burrow in sand dunes. Most geckos have hair-like projections on their feet that act like tiny suction cups so they can scale glass windows and run upside down across ceilings. They use their tails to store food and balance themselves. Plus, they can grow a new tail if they lose one escaping from an enemy.

The stickiness of geckos amazes scientists. They have sticky toe pads, but not like sticky tape. The secret is in the geometry, or shape, of their feet. Ridges cover the toes with tiny triangle-shaped hairs called setae. The endings of the setae create something called a van der Waals force, yet detach in milliseconds. Amazingly, dirt doesn't stick to the geckos' toes—although they can stick to nearly every kind of material whether it is wet or dry. Scientists copied some of God's amazing design to make a new dry adhesive with flexible tangled ends. Take time to watch an animal. You may learn something new about God and his world.

WEIRD FACTS: AMAZING GECKOS
☞ Gecko eyes don't open and close.
☞ Scientists think there are more than 2,000 types of geckos.
☞ Geckos live on every continent except Antarctica.
☞ Geckos eat insects and worms. Larger types eat other animals, like birds and mice.
☞ If a gecko sheds its tail, it may return to eat it since food is stored in the tail.
☞ Geckos have a hard time sticking to Teflon.
☞ Gecko toes bend in the opposite direction from human toes.

✝ PRAY
Thank God for making amazing lizards. Ask him to help you learn from animals.

Life's Guidebook Says
Lizards—they are easy to catch, but they are found even in kings' palaces.
PROVERBS 30:28

GILA MONSTERS HELPING PEOPLE

HOW MUCH DO YOU WEIGH? If you weigh 90 pounds, you might eat a meal that weighs about a pound. (Can anyone say "Happy Meal"?) But if you were a Gila monster (pronounced HEE-luh), you could eat a meal weighing 30 pounds! The Gila monster lives in deserts and can be found in Arizona, Nevada, California, and New Mexico. Because food is scarce, when a Gila monster finds a meal, it eats a lot and stores extra fat in its body and tail. Normally, Gila monsters hide underground or behind rocks. They can grow up to two feet long and are covered with rounded, beaded scales that serve as armor. Gilas move very slowly—but watch out for their bite! This lizard has strong jaws and doesn't let go when its teeth sink in. As it holds on to its prey, venom passes into its jaw and flows into the wound. Scientists say Gila monster venom is as toxic as a western diamondback rattlesnake's. But Gila monsters transfer a lot less poison than snakes do.

Gila monsters are amazing animals, but scientists are especially amazed by a chemical they produce called Exendin-3. Exendin-3 wakes up the pancreas to control blood sugar. It releases insulin, lowers blood glucose (sugar), and slowly empties the stomach to decrease hunger and help with weight loss. Gila monsters produce this chemical because they don't eat very often. Scientists copied the chemical and now use it to help people with diabetes. Diabetes is a growing problem where people have difficulty regulating the sugar levels in their blood. Eating too much sugar is never a good idea . . . even if you're a Gila monster.

God's special designs in animals often give scientists new ideas to help people. It's another sign of the great love God has for his creation, and especially his children.

WACKY LAUGHS

Q. What is the richest lizard?
A. A chameleonaire!

Q. What did the lizard bring to school?
A. A newt-book.

Knock, knock.
Who's there?
Lee.
Lee who?
Leaping lizards are in the garden.

✝ PRAY

Pray for God to show scientists more cures for diseases.

Life's Guidebook Says

God has made everything beautiful for its own time. He has planted eternity in the human heart, but even so, people cannot see the whole scope of God's work from beginning to end. ECCLESIASTES 3:11

ON THE SCENT

WHAT'S THE WORLD'S BIGGEST LIZARD? If you said "dragon," you've been watching too many movies or reading too many fantasy books. But you're actually half right. The Komodo dragon is the world's largest lizard—growing up to 10 feet long! Being a dragon, this lizard eats animals and not plants. The dragon has powerful legs, sharp claws, and jaws like a shark. It lies quietly and watches for a tasty creature to pass by. Then it springs into action and attacks, biting its prey and hanging on. Talk about bad breath—this animal's saliva is full of more than 50 types of nasty bacteria. Plus, its bite is poisonous. If an animal manages to escape, the Komodo simply tracks it by following the scent of the dragon's own saliva. The bitten animal usually dies within 24 hours, and the dragon gets its meal. Komodo dragons are only found living wild on the islands of Indonesia. They can swim from island to island. On land, these dragons can run about 11 miles an hour. But unlike dragons in the movies, they can't fly or breathe fire.

If you think about it, Satan is sort of like a Komodo dragon. God's enemy is patient and waits for the right moment to attack. Satan watches for our weakness. We must be careful, because he often tempts us when we least expect it. If he wounds us as we escape, we'll find Satan slinking around and following, waiting for us to feel discouraged and wanting to give up. When you feel discouraged, pray for God's strength. Tell your parents, and look for a friend to encourage you.

PLEXER

Try to solve this scaly puzzle. (If you don't remember what a plexer is, see p. 9.)

thescentKomododragon

✝ PRAY

Ask God to keep you strong and help you find friends who will encourage you.

Life's Guidebook Says

Stay alert! Watch out for your great enemy, the devil. He prowls around like a roaring lion, looking for someone to devour.   1 PETER 5:8

Answer: Komodo dragon follows the scent.

ONE SMALL STEP

HAVE YOU EVER GONE OUTSIDE on a clear night and stared at the moon? Sometimes it seems so big and so close that you could touch it. Of course, you can't. It's more than 225,000 miles away from earth. But on this day in 1969, two American astronauts landed on the moon!

Buzz Aldrin piloted the lunar module to the surface, and then Neil Armstrong took the first steps on the moon. As Armstrong's foot touched down, he famously said, "That's one small step for a man, one giant leap for mankind." Maybe you've studied the moon landing at school and heard those words before. But Aldrin read some even more famous words a couple of hours *before* Armstrong left the lunar module. And Aldrin's words came directly from Jesus.

As soon as he landed on the moon, Aldrin thanked the Lord by taking Communion. He had brought up a small piece of bread and a tiny vial of wine. On a three-by-five card, he had written out Jesus' words from John 15:5: "I am the vine; you are the branches. Those who remain in me, and I in them, will produce much fruit. For apart from me you can do nothing." As Aldrin asked everybody listening on earth to spend a few moments giving thanks, he read the Bible verse to himself and took Communion.

You probably won't ever walk on the moon, but you will accomplish many amazing things in your life. When you do, remember to take a moment to thank God.

AWESOME ACTIVITY: SPACED OUT
Go outside on a clear, dark night and look at the moon and stars. July is famous for its meteor showers. See if you can find the Big Dipper, the North Star, or a planet. If your family owns a smartphone, download an app such as Google Sky Map and try to spot as many celestial bodies as you can. As you look at the stars, say this verse: "Who created all the stars? . . . Because of his great power and incomparable strength, not a single one is missing" (Isaiah 40:26).

✝ PRAY
Thank God for past accomplishments and for everything he'll help you do in the future.

Life's Guidebook Says
[Jesus said,] "Yes, I am the vine; you are the branches. Those who remain in me, and I in them, will produce much fruit. For apart from me you can do nothing."
JOHN 15:5

TREE-MENDOUS

JESUS WAS HUNGRY. He was 100 percent God and 100 percent man, so when he walked the earth, he had to eat. He walked over to a fig tree. No figs. "May no one ever eat your fruit again!" he said (Mark 11:12-14). Just the next day, as Jesus and the disciples passed the same tree, they noticed that it had dried from the roots up. The branches drooped and limbs easily snapped off (verse 20).

Long before Jesus cursed a fig tree and caused it to wither and die, God spoke about his power over trees. The prophet Ezekiel stood at the city gate and gave a message that God brings down tall trees and makes green, leafy trees wither (see today's verse). The message foretold the capture of the Jewish people and the destruction of their Temple and city. God used many symbols and stories to pass along his truth to the people. And everything God said came true. He is all powerful. God can take away a person's power and riches faster than a tornado can destroy a palace.

Jesus stood at the same spot centuries after Ezekiel when he told the fig tree to wither. God's Son showed the people his power and reminded his disciples that although people celebrated his coming and held a great parade to honor him, it would not last. He would die too. But since God is the one with *tree-mendous*, unlimited power, Jesus would defeat death and rise from the grave. God's power over trees is impressive. His power over death is even more amazing.

QUIZ: BIBLE TREES
1. We get oil from the fruit of this tree. (John 18:1)
2. Noah used wood from this tree to make the ark. (Genesis 6:14, NASB)
3. This type of tree was used to build the Temple. (1 Kings 5:5-6)
4. Zacchaeus climbed this kind of tree. (Luke 19:2-4)
5. Branches from this tree were used in the parade for Jesus. (John 12:13)

✝ PRAY
Thank God for creating trees. Praise him that he is more powerful than nature.

Life's Guidebook Says
"All the trees of the forest will know that I the LORD bring down the tall tree and make the low tree grow tall. I dry up the green tree and make the dry tree flourish. I the LORD have spoken, and I will do it." EZEKIEL 17:24

Answers: 1. Olive; 2. Gopher; 3. Cedar; 4. Sycamore; 5. Palm

TREE TALK

"I'M THE TALLEST," the mighty redwood said. "I stay green all year."

"Well, I grow delicious apples," the apple tree said. "So I'm the best. And if you don't agree, I may start throwing some of my apples at you."

"I'm the best," argued the aspen tree. "Just one of me makes many trees that stretch for miles."

Can you imagine a group of trees arguing? That sounds like a fairy tale or cartoon. Yet thousands of years ago, the prophet Jotham used such tree talk to teach a lesson to the Israelites. He shared a parable where trees tried to choose a king from among themselves (Judges 9:8-15). No tree wanted to do it. Finally, a thorn tree accepted the responsibility. That type of tree produces no fruit and only hurts people with its prickly thorns. That's the type of king the people chose when they picked a man named Abimelech as their king. The parable warned God's people that they were making a bad choice, but they didn't listen.

Unless you like seeking comfort from a thorn bush, this story serves as a good reminder to listen to God and follow good advice. Bad choices can cause problems. The easiest option often isn't the best. When you have to make a big decision, pray to God and seek godly counsel from others. When you make honorable choices, you'll have God and everyone else "rooting" for you.

WEIRD FACTS: TREE SPEAK

☞ Some trees send messages to warn other trees of danger. When insects attack a willow tree, the tree gives off a chemical that warns other trees about the problem. The trees "listen" and then make tannins in their leaves. Tannins are bitter and make it harder for insects to attack.

☞ Acacia trees also talk to nearby trees if giraffes or deer attack. They give off ethylene as a signal. The other trees then create enough tannin to taste yucky.

☞ The branches and trunk of the rainbow eucalyptus tree have stripes of red, orange, yellow, green, purple, and pink, and the rainbow pattern is always changing like a living painting.

✝ PRAY

Tell God you want to listen to him, make good choices, and grow strong.

Life's Guidebook Says

The godly will flourish like palm trees and grow strong like the cedars of Lebanon. PSALM 92:12

· TREE OF LIFE

GEORGE WANDERED OFF the Cape Horn Overlook Trail in Washington while hiking with his friend. He started exploring the woods and quickly realized that he couldn't find his way back. He walked over to the edge of a cliff to get a better view. Suddenly, he started slipping. He reached out and grabbed the nearest object—a tree. He hugged the tree tightly and started yelling for his parents. For nearly an hour, he shouted until his family came and rescued him. Hugging a tree saved his life.

While George is a made-up character, it's a fact that trees are natural helpers from God. They provide shade and food. You may live in a home made of wood, write on paper made from the pulp of trees, and enjoy maple syrup, made from tree sap, on your pancakes. The fruit and nuts from trees are a great source of food. Wood provides many raw materials for making things we use.

God put many amazing trees in the Garden of Eden. He created a very special tree called the tree of life. (That's not the tree that Adam and Eve ate from. They munched on fruit from the tree of the knowledge of good and evil.) But if you know Jesus as your Savior, you will eat the fruit from the tree of life in heaven. It will grow a marvelous fruit that doesn't exist on earth. Can you imagine what it might taste like?

PLEXER
See if you can solve this tree plexer. (If you don't remember what a plexer is, see p. 9.)

	b b
Tree	r r
	a a
	n n
	c c
	h h

✝ PRAY
Thank God for trees and all you have that comes from them.

> ### Life's Guidebook Says
> Anyone with ears to hear must listen to the Spirit and understand what he is saying to the churches. To everyone who is victorious I will give fruit from the tree of life in the paradise of God. REVELATION 2:7

Answer: A tree branches out.

APPLE PICKIN'

"LOOK AT THOSE little red apples!" Johnny picked one and took a bite. *Yuck!* He spit it out. "It's too sour to eat."

"That's a crab apple," Grandpa said. "Not nearly as tasty as many other types of apples." He pointed to another tree. "Try one of those."

Crunch. Johnny bit into a big red apple and said, "*Mmm.* What kind is this?"

"Red delicious."

"That's a good name for it," Johnny said, taking another bite.

Johnny and his grandpa filled a basket with sweet-tasting apples. They carried the apples to a cider press. Johnny helped dump in the apples and turned the press to make cider.

Johnny learned that crab apple trees only make sour apples. These apples can be used in cooking and making jelly, but they aren't good to pick and eat.

Jesus talked about fruit trees. He said that a good tree makes good fruit and a bad one only makes bad fruit. He used this story to remind us that truly sweet things can only come out of a person with a good heart. A person who follows Jesus and works on having a good heart produces good fruits like goodness, peace, joy, and love. These are called fruit of the Spirit. What kind of fruit are you making?

WACKY LAUGHS

Q. What trees do most people like?

A. Poplars.

Q. What tree should you avoid to stay healthy?

A. Sick-a-more.

Q. What tree sends a message to get well?

A. O-live.

Q. Why did the banker climb a tree in Europe?

A. He wanted to go to an overseas branch.

✝ PRAY

Ask God to help you produce the fruit of the Spirit—love, joy, peace, patience, kindness, goodness, faithfulness, gentleness, and self-control (Galatians 5:22-23).

Life's Guidebook Says

A good tree produces good fruit, and a bad tree produces bad fruit.
MATTHEW 7:17

O CHRISTMAS TREE!

WHAT WAS THE FAVORITE gift that you received last Christmas? Do you still use it? The truth is many of the toys and games you got last Christmas are no longer new and exciting. Maybe you're bored with others. You probably haven't thought about Christmas gifts or carols for months.

As of today, Christmas is just five months away. Some people will take today to celebrate Christmas in July—if only they'd give you presents again! Even though you'll have to wait for more gifts, take time to remember the joy of the season. Jesus didn't come so you could have new toys and fill yourself with cookies and turkey. He came to give you himself and to die for you. The purpose for the Christ-child's coming on Christmas is so you could have eternal life. Jesus lay in a wooden manger and later died on a wooden cross.

Long before he came, God talked about trees. The Most High told us he is like the evergreen tree (see today's verse). The real fruit that gives us life comes from God and the gift of Jesus. Eat some pine nuts—that come from evergreen trees—and celebrate the real meaning of Christmas today . . . and every day.

PUZZLE IT OUT: TREE CODE

Start at the top of the tree. Change each letter to the one before it in the alphabet and each number to the one before it numerically (so 4 replaces 5 and B replaces C. Each * is a space between words or numbers. Write the new letters or numbers in order in the spaces below to crack the code.

```
            C
          V U *
        U I F * H P
      E M Z * X J M
    M * G M P V S J T I
  * M J L F * Q B M N *
 U S F F T * B O E * H S P X
* T U S P O H * M J L F * U I F *
D F E B S T * P G * M F C B O P O *
          Q T B
          M N *
        1 0 * 3 *
        * 2 * 3 *
```

" __ __ __   __ __ __   __ __ __ __ __ __   __ __ __ __   __ __ __ __ __ __ __ __   __ __ __ __

__ __ __ __   __ __ __ __ __   __ __ __ __ __   __ __ __ __ __

__ __ __   __ __ __ __ __ __ __   __ __   __ __ __ __ __ __ __ ." __ __ __ __ __ __   __ __ : __ __

✝ PRAY

Praise God for sending Jesus, the gift that lasts.

Life's Guidebook Says

[God said,] "I am the one who answers your prayers and cares for you. I am like a tree that is always green; all your fruit comes from me." HOSEA 14:8

Answer: Look up Psalm 92:12 in the Bible or turn back a few pages to find this verse.

I DON'T DESERVE THIS BAD DAY!

"MOM, THEY STOLE my backpack!" Michael said, looking into the backseat of the car. The windows had been broken. Glass and papers were strewn everywhere. "My new history book was in there, and we have to pay for lost books. How can we do that? Dad doesn't even have a job."

Michael felt like God had let him down. His family was at church when someone broke into their car. Why would God let something bad happen when they were following him and worshiping in church? He hoped the thief would be caught and punished.

The prophet Jonah felt even angrier than Michael. God told Jonah to go to Nineveh. Jonah headed the other way, but was quickly hand-delivered in the belly of a great fish. *Gross.* When Jonah finally obeyed God and told the Ninevites that God planned to destroy their city, he thought God would wipe these terrible people off the planet—and he was happy about it. But the Ninevites told God they were sorry and promised to change. So God forgave them. Jonah complained to God, left Nineveh, and sat down to sulk. What a bad day! Jonah felt so hot and angry that he wanted to die. God reminded him that, as God, he could forgive people and be merciful.

God showed Michael mercy too. Michael prayed and forgave the unknown thief. He found a better backpack on sale in a dollar bin at a store. His little brother prayed daily for Michael to get his book back, and a week later a friend called to say he had found Michael's stolen book in his driveway. What a turnaround! That's the beginning of a great day.

WACKY LAUGHS

Stupid things thieves have actually done:

☞ One thief wore the boots he was accused of stealing to his trial.

☞ A burglar ran from the police by jumping a fence into a prison yard.

☞ A robber left his wallet with his ID in it, making him easy to find.

✞ PRAY

Talk to God when you have a bad day. Forgive people who may have caused any problems.

Life's Guidebook Says
[Jonah said,] "I knew that you are a merciful and compassionate God, slow to get angry and filled with unfailing love. You are eager to turn back from destroying people." JONAH 4:2

BEATEN

DANIEL STARED at the black eye in the mirror. He had five stitches on his face, too. But it wasn't from a fight. A waterslide had beaten him up. The water gushed out so fast that Daniel flipped over and hit his head. So much for his fun day at the water park. Instead, Daniel spent his day in the emergency room. His friends continued playing and having fun without him, while an adult took him to the hospital. It left Daniel feeling like a loser.

Daniel's fun trip certainly took a turn for the worse. Jesus told the story of another trip that went wrong for a man in the Bible. Robbers beat the traveler and left him for dead. The beaten man watched as a priest and a Temple assistant walked by. They didn't seem to care about him but instead hurried to enjoy their day. Finally, a stranger stopped and helped him. The stranger, called the Good Samaritan in Jesus' story, even paid the man's medical bills.

We are not promised that every day as a Christ follower will be wonderful. God tells us there will be trials and times that test us. He blesses those who endure trials and terrible days. The first chapter of the book of James tells us an interesting way to look at things when we have troubles. It says to rejoice and see troubles as an opportunity to show our faith and become better because of it.

LIFTOFF LIST

James gives us some good advice for facing hard times. Check off what you can do, or have done, when you face problems.

____ Know it tests your faith.
____ Be patient.
____ Endure and bear it.
____ Ask God for wisdom to learn from it.
____ Become stronger.
____ Become a better person because you faced a problem.
____ Remember God's promises.
____ Trust in God.
____ Consider the trial a joy.
____ Don't doubt God.

✝ PRAY

Pray for God to use your bad times to help you grow stronger. Ask for his help to get through those times.

Life's Guidebook Says

Dear brothers and sisters, when troubles of any kind come your way, consider it an opportunity for great joy. For you know that when your faith is tested, your endurance has a chance to grow. JAMES 1:2-3

BAD DAY U-TURNS

KERPLAT! When a tornado hit Sean's home, it flattened everything. At first, all seemed lost. Then people came to help. Sean's church friends opened their homes and helped sort through the wreckage. His family had the insurance to rebuild. They lived with friends while they waited for their new house to be finished.

Soon Sean started looking back and being thankful for the tornado. God had kept his family safe. He'd discovered how many people cared for him. Also, Sean now thought more about needy people. He wanted to help others after so many people had helped him. He stopped asking for stuff all the time and started making sandwiches to feed the homeless. Eventually, Sean and his family moved into their new home. He got all new toys, furniture, and clothes. But more important, he received a new perspective on how to live for God.

Sometimes good can come from the worst day. When Jesus died, it seemed like the saddest day of all time. Soldiers whipped him and stuck a crown of thorns onto his head. He lugged a heavy cross through the streets. Then Roman soldiers hammered nails through his hands and feet. Jesus suffered more pain than anyone wants to feel. He did it all for you. Then he rose from the dead and filled his followers with joy (John 20:20). He did it to open the gates of heaven, so you could live forever and gain a new way to look at life.

EXPERIMENT: FLOATING PING-PONG BALLS
You can keep a Ping-Pong ball floating in the air with gravity and air pressure.

Stuff You Need
- ☞ Hair dryer
- ☞ Ping-Pong balls

Try It
1. Set the hair dryer on "cool" and turn it on. Aim the hair dryer so the air blows straight up.
2. Drop a ball into the blowing air. It should float there without flying away or falling. (The ball may get hot, so be careful!)
3. Challenge yourself to try it with two Ping-Pong balls.

✝ PRAY
Ask God to help you see the good that comes from a bad day or problem.

Life's Guidebook Says
As he spoke, [Jesus] showed them the wounds in his hands and his side. They were filled with joy when they saw the Lord! JOHN 20:20

A TERRIBLE DAY IN HEAVEN

"WAR IS A TERRIBLE THING." You've probably heard that before. Maybe you have friends or family members who fought for their country. But that quote comes from General William K. Harrison Jr., one of the bravest soldiers in World War II. He saw men die and understood the wicked plans of the enemy.

It's sad that countries fight. At least in heaven there will always be peace. *Oops!* Look in the Bible again. There will be one last battle in heaven in the future (Revelation 12:7). *Pow!* Angels will battle demons. *Bam! Crash!* Angels will throw Satan, the great dragon, and other demons back to earth. Everyone in heaven will rejoice. *Hooray!* But all won't be bright and sunny. Satan will start a huge war on earth. He will be filled with anger and will gather an army and raise a beast from the sea. These wicked enemies will try again to defeat God, but it won't work. Satan will be bound and tossed into a bottomless pit.

Thankfully, we know the end of the story because God has shown us the future in the Bible. God's Word tells us there will be more wars before the final battle. That's sad. But we always have hope, because we know God will be the ultimate victor.

War is terrible, and so is fighting with friends or against bullies. Whenever you can, choose to live at peace with the people around you.

PLEXER
Solve this plexer to remember you can be a peacemaker. (If you don't remember what a plexer is, see p. 9.)

Upeace

✝ PRAY
Pray for peace and ask God to protect our men and women who serve in the military and their families.

Life's Guidebook Says
There was war in heaven. Michael and his angels fought against the dragon and his angels. REVELATION 12:7

Answer: Peace begins with you.

CHEATED AND TRICKED

A NIGERIAN PRINCE NEEDS your help. Government officials want to take his family's money, so he must transfer it to the United States. All you need to do is set up a bank account with $1,000 and send him your information. Then he'll deposit over $21 million. For your help, you get to keep 10 percent. That's $2.1 million!

Do you believe it? You shouldn't. Thousands of people have received an e-mail describing a situation like the one above. But it is a scam from con men trying to steal money. Instead of putting in $2.1 million, they take the $1,000.

Jacob, grandson of Abraham, was quite a con man. He was the younger twin to his brother, Esau. Esau was hairy and loved to hunt. Jacob stayed at home and was a good cook. One day when Esau came in from hunting, he saw some soup Jacob had made and wanted it. Jacob said Esau could have some soup if he gave up his birthright (that meant twice the inheritance—which was a lot of cattle, sheep, and goats). Esau must've been thinking with his stomach instead of his head, because he took the deal.

Then Jacob's mom helped him pull off an even bigger con. Jacob and Esau's dad, Isaac, was going blind. Jacob put fur skins on his arms so he'd feel hairy like Esau. It fooled Isaac, and he gave Jacob the blessing that was meant for Esau. That made Esau so angry that he planned to kill Jacob. Jacob ran away. It wasn't until years later that the brothers made peace.

Tricking people is never a good idea. Con men get caught. Live truthfully and you never have anything to fear.

EXPERIMENT: AWESOME ICE CUBE TRICK
Catch an ice cube in water with a string.

Stuff You Need
☞ Glass of water with ice cubes
☞ String
☞ Salt

Try It
1. Drop the string on top of the water and sprinkle salt on the ice. The salt causes the ice to melt and soak the string.
2. Once the string is frozen in place, lift the ice cube by pulling the string.

✝ PRAY
Ask God to give you wisdom so people won't cheat you, and try not to cheat others.

Life's Guidebook Says
Esau exclaimed, "No wonder his name is Jacob, for now he has cheated me twice. First he took my rights as the firstborn, and now he has stolen my blessing." GENESIS 27:36

TERRIBLE DAY COMING (KEEP READING ONLY IF YOU DARE)

IT'S SCARIER THAN ANY MOVIE, because it's true. No more sun, great hunger, bugs galore, and earthquakes. Angels pour out plagues worse than the ones sent on Egypt. Hail and fire mixed with blood fall down from heaven. One-third of the trees die. One-third of the sea turns to blood. That's just a glimpse of the terrible, horrible, bad days to come. We know these things will happen, because they are in the Bible. Scripture says that leaders and kings will hide in caves. People will cry to the mountains to fall on them and hide them from God's destruction. They will know God's power through the terrible plagues.

Wait! There's hope. After all the tribulation and terrible days, Jesus will come and bring peace. God will create a new earth. There will be great joy and peace for those who know Christ. We cannot see the future. Sometimes it is hard to understand. But we can have hope and expect good things in the future. Christians always have hope, because God is always there for us.

WEIRD FACTS: END TIMES

Jesus spoke about the end of the world, and the book of Revelation tells us more. Here are some of the facts:

- ☞ Jesus said two people will be together, but suddenly one of them will disappear. (Matthew 24:40)
- ☞ Heavenly bodies (planets, stars) will be burned and dissolved. (2 Peter 3:10-13)
- ☞ Worse days than anyone has ever known, called tribulations, will come. (Matthew 24:21-22)
- ☞ Only God the Father knows when these things will happen. (Mark 13:32)
- ☞ The Mount of Olives will be split in two, and a valley will form between the split. (Zechariah 14:1-5)
- ☞ The sun will be black and the moon will be like blood. (Revelation 6:10-14)

✞ PRAY

Praise God that his true power will be revealed in the future. Tell him that you trust him no matter what happens.

Life's Guidebook Says

That terrible day of the LORD is near. Swiftly it comes—a day of bitter tears, a day when even strong men will cry out. It will be a day when the LORD's anger is poured out—a day of terrible distress and anguish, a day of ruin and desolation, a day of darkness and gloom, a day of clouds and blackness.
ZEPHANIAH 1:14-15

AUGUST

SAFE AND SOUND

How MUCH TIME do you spend playing outside? Studies show kids spend less than half as much time outdoors as they did 20 years ago. Why is that? Are computer games that popular? Maybe. But maybe not.

Every year *Highlights* magazine asks its readers to give their opinions on a wide range of topics in the State of the Kid survey. Then the readers ask the editors for hints on the "hidden object" puzzles. Just kidding! The 2013 survey showed that 50 percent of children believe playing inside is safer than playing outside. So some kids choose to stay inside to feel safe.

Do you feel safe when you play outside? Sure, you need to stay away from busy streets and be careful of strangers. But God wants you to feel safe wherever you are, because he's always there to guard you. In 2 Thessalonians 3:3, the apostle Paul reminds us that the Lord is faithful and always strengthens us. God doesn't want you to put yourself in danger, but he also doesn't want you to miss out on life because you're too afraid.

Don't let fear stop you from getting outside and having fun. Enjoy your summer by joining a sports team, riding your bike, walking your dog, or playing with friends. God created nature for you to enjoy. Discover all you can this summer.

AWESOME ACTIVITY: SUMMER FUN

Have you been sitting around too much this summer? Try these ideas to get outside and have fun:

- ☞ Grab paper and a pencil. Look for textures in nature—maybe tree bark, a leaf, or a rock. Put the paper over the tree or rock and gently rub the pencil back and forth to make an etching.
- ☞ Set up an obstacle course in your backyard. Use a sprinkler, some cones to run around, a box to jump over, or other objects. Invite some friends and compete for the fastest time.
- ☞ Go yard bowling. Find pieces of wood or plastic bottles to set up as pins. Then step back and kick a soccer ball to see how many you can knock down.

✝ PRAY

Thank God for his constant protection.

Life's Guidebook Says
The Lord is faithful; he will strengthen you and guard you from the evil one.
2 THESSALONIANS 3:3

SLIDE THROUGH SUMMER

DO YOU LIKE GOING down slides? What's your favorite—twisty slides, long fast slides, bumpy slides, or waterslides? One slide that you want to stay away from is the "summer slide." Researchers say kids who get on the summer slide lose knowledge and abilities over the summer months. The statistics are startling. Students who jump on the summer slide lose . . .

☞ nearly two months of math skills.

☞ more than two months of reading ability.

☞ some test-taking knowledge.

That means students who slide over the summer start the school year off with less knowledge than when they ended in the spring. Then they have to try to catch up. So how can you stay off the summer slide? Engage your brain!

Even if you don't love to read, try to read a little every day. (Hey, you're reading this book, so you're already training your brain.) Get into God's Word. King Solomon wrote that the purpose of the proverbs was to give us insight and help us live successful lives (Proverbs 1:3-4). That's really the purpose of the entire Bible.

Writing also keeps you sharp. Send a letter to your grandparents. Start a journal. Write about your day, your dreams, or your prayers to God. Plus, you can do a puzzle or play a problem-solving video game. Many video games require logic and quick thinking. (Just make sure you don't play too much.)

If you keep your brain fired up over the summer, you'll be ready to go when school starts again.

PUZZLE IT OUT: ALL FENCED IN

Engage your brain by drawing two rectangles so each of these nine horses has its own corral.

✝ PRAY

Praise God for giving you an incredible brain. Tell him you're going to use it—even over the summer.

Life's Guidebook Says

Their purpose is to teach people to live disciplined and successful lives, to help them do what is right, just, and fair. These proverbs will give insight to the simple, knowledge and discernment to the young. PROVERBS 1:3-4

Answer:

SO EXCITED!

WHAT GETS YOU EXCITED? Is it scoring a goal in soccer, defeating a video game, doing well on a test, or playing perfectly in a band recital? All of those things are reasons to celebrate. Have you ever been so excited that you did a victory dance after notching a goal or scoring a touchdown? A lot of professional athletes do.

Well, that's how excited King David got when he brought the Ark of God back into Jerusalem. This was the Ark that held the Ten Commandments and was a symbol of God's power and presence. Nearly 100 years before David returned the Ark to Jerusalem, it had been taken by the Philistines. The Philistines and the Israelites fought each other for years. Normally, God gave his people the upper hand. But when they tried to use the Ark as a weapon, God allowed them to be defeated and the Ark to be taken away. But the Ark only brought death and pain to the Philistines, so they put it on a cart and sent it away. The Israelites regained the Ark, but never moved it back to their capital. Finally, when David became king, he made plans to bring the Ark to its rightful place.

As the Ark entered Jerusalem, David danced and jumped around in front of it. He was more excited than a little kid dancing around a present-filled Christmas tree. All of God's people shouted with joy and blew horns in celebration.

When you believe in God, his presence is always near to you—even inside of you as the Holy Spirit. That means every day as a Christ follower is a reason to celebrate. What dance will you do?

PLEXER
See if you can solve this plexer. (If you don't remember what a plexer is, see p. 9.)

yHOLYSPIRITou

✝ PRAY
Tell God you're going to celebrate every day, because his presence is always near.

Life's Guidebook Says
David danced before the LORD with all his might, wearing a priestly garment.
2 SAMUEL 6:14

Answer: Holy Spirit inside you

GOOD TO BE GODLY

DEANDRE COULDN'T WAIT for the summer soccer championship game. His team had won every game but one. Only their rivals, the Cobras, had beaten them. And that's who they were facing in the finals. This time they'd win for sure. DeAndre led his team in goals and scored in nearly every game. *God, help me to play my best and use my skills to glorify you*, DeAndre prayed before the game.

When the game started, neither team could gain an advantage. Finally, DeAndre's team earned a corner kick. He cut toward the near post as the ball was struck, but a Cobra defender grabbed his shirt and didn't allow him to score a goal. Even worse, the referee didn't call a penalty. All game long the Cobras tugged on his jersey, tripped him, and bumped him when the ref wasn't looking. Then the unthinkable happened—a Cobra striker got loose on a breakaway and scored a goal. The Cobras won the championship 1–0.

Does that sound fair? Of course not. A team that bends the rules shouldn't win a championship, just like a student who cheats on a test doesn't deserve a good grade. But sometimes it happens. That's the bad news.

Here's the good news: God is in control. Don't fret when cheaters win or evil people gain fame, because God will judge them and bring them down. Psalm 68 tells us that those who hate God will be blown away like smoke. But the godly will rejoice and be filled with joy.

When you see bad people succeed, don't change who you are. Keep following God and doing the right thing. In God's timing, you'll have lots of reasons to celebrate.

WEIRD FACTS: IT'S A KICK
Dribble through these soccer stats:

- ☞ More people play soccer than any other sport in the world. In the United States alone, seven million kids play soccer.
- ☞ Soccer is called *football* all over the world, except in North America. In the United States and Canada, football is the sport played with an oddly shaped leather ball that's thrown or run for touchdowns.
- ☞ A professional soccer player runs about seven miles during a game.

✝ PRAY
Ask God to help you find your joy by following him.

Life's Guidebook Says
Let the godly rejoice. Let them be glad in God's presence. Let them be filled with joy. PSALM 68:3

EXPRESS TRIP TO HEAVEN

NAME SOMEONE in the Bible who never died.

Your first thought might be Jesus. He's the answer to a lot of questions in the Bible. But he's not the answer this time. Jesus did die—and then rose from the dead to conquer death. The Bible tells many stories of God's power raising people from the dead:

- ☞ Paul brought Eutychus back from the dead.
- ☞ Peter raised Dorcas.
- ☞ Jesus raised Lazarus, Jairus's daughter, and others.
- ☞ The prophets Elisha and Elijah also saw people come back from the dead.

Speaking of Elijah, he's one of the people in the Bible who never died. Second Kings 2 tells how God took Elijah into heaven in a whirlwind. But there are *two* people that the Bible says never died. The other is Enoch (pronounced Ee-knock). We don't know much about his life. He was the father of Methuselah; he lived 365 years; he walked in close fellowship with God. And one day he disappeared, because God took him to heaven (Genesis 5:21-24).

Look at those words about Enoch. What stands out to you? Sure, he lived a long time— more than three times longer than the oldest people live today. But the most important words may be "walking in close fellowship with God." Would you like to be described that way?

You can be. When you follow God's laws, read his Word, and pray to him, you can walk in close fellowship with your heavenly Father. What area in your relationship with Christ needs the most improvement? Write it down: _____. Now do your best to grow closer to God.

QUIZ: BIBLE WHO'S WHO

Can you figure out these famous people from the Bible? Think back to what you've learned in Sunday school, from this book, and in God's Word.

1. Was taken up to heaven in a whirlwind: _____
2. Tried to run from God before being swallowed by a great fish: _____
3. Baptized Jesus and ate locusts: _____
4. Popular queen who saved the Jewish people: _____

✝ PRAY

Ask God to help you walk in close fellowship with him.

Life's Guidebook Says
Enoch lived 365 years, walking in close fellowship with God. Then one day he disappeared, because God took him. GENESIS 5:23-24

Answers: 1. Elijah; 2. Jonah; 3. John the Baptist; 4. Queen Esther

POWERFUL STORIES

HAVE YOU EVER HEARD the story about the dog who found a huge chunk of meat? He was so excited that he grabbed it and started running home. But as he crossed a low bridge over some water, he looked down and saw another dog staring at him. That dog also had a huge piece of beef in its mouth. (Obviously, the first dog knew nothing about the reflecting properties of water.) The dog wanted both pieces of meat. He snapped at the other dog. But instead of a tasty treat, he ended up with a mouthful of water. And sadly, he watched as his chunk of beef dropped into the water and disappeared.

There's an obvious lesson in this fable—don't be greedy. When Jesus taught people about God's Kingdom, he often used stories. The Bible records more than 40 parables that teach us truths about God. One of the most famous is the story of the Prodigal Son (Luke 15:11-32). In this story, a younger son demands his inheritance from his father and then spends it foolishly. The son loses everything and ends up eating with the pigs. Finally, he decides to go home and ask for forgiveness. His father sees him coming, runs to his lost son, forgives him, and throws a party. Everybody is happy—except the older brother. He was a good son, but never got a party. The father explains that everything he has belongs to the older brother. But the fact that the lost brother has returned is reason to celebrate.

What lessons do you see in this story? Write down something Jesus was trying to teach:

_____

_____

_____.

Whenever you read one of Jesus' parables, make sure to look for the deeper meaning.

WACKY LAUGHS
Q. How do we know baseball is God's favorite sport?
A. Because Eve stole first, Adam stole second, David struck out Goliath, Gideon rattled the pitchers, and the Prodigal Son made a home run!

Patient: My brother is crazy. He thinks he's a chicken.
Doctor: How long has this been going on?
Patient: For six years.
Doctor: Wow! Why have you waited so long to get help?
Patient: We needed the eggs.

✝ PRAY
Ask God to give you the wisdom to understand his Word.

Life's Guidebook Says
Jesus used many similar stories and illustrations to teach the people as much as they could understand. MARK 4:33

UNFORGIVEN

LOGAN FIDDLED with his hands and looked at the ground. He knew he didn't have the money. He had borrowed $50 from his dad to buy a video game and promised to do extra chores to work off his debt. But that was months ago. All Logan had done was play video games. Now Logan stood in front of Dad.

"We're going to have to sell that video game so you can pay me back," Dad said. "And since it's used now, you'll probably have to sell a few other games to get the money."

"No, please," Logan begged. "I'm sorry. I'll mow the lawn today and pull weeds in the garden. Just give me another week, and I'll work off my debt."

Dad could see Logan was sincere. "Okay," he said, "your debt is forgiven."

Logan couldn't believe it! He was so happy. He skipped out of the living room and ran into his little brother, Lee. Lee owed him a dollar that Logan had given him for candy.

"Where's my money?" Logan demanded.

"I don't have it," Lee said.

Logan ran to Lee's room and grabbed his Nintendo 3DS. "Then this is now mine!" he shouted angrily.

Dad heard all the noise and walked up to his sons. "How could you do this, Logan?" he said. "I forgave a huge debt that you owed me, yet you couldn't forgive your brother just a dollar? Let's go round up your video games. We're selling them all on eBay right now."

What do you think of that story? Jesus used a similar story to teach his followers about forgiveness. Read it in Matthew 18:23-35.

LIFTOFF LIST

Do you have trouble forgiving? See how many items apply to you:

__ I keep track of every wrong ever done to me.

__ I get a gnawing feeling in my stomach whenever I see a friend who treated me poorly.

__ A simple sorry isn't good enough for me. I want the person to pay for what he did.

__ I get angry thinking about an ex-friend who stabbed me in the back.

✞ PRAY

Tell God that you want to forgive others just like he forgives you.

Life's Guidebook Says

[Jesus said,] "That's what my heavenly Father will do to you if you refuse to forgive your brothers and sisters from your heart." MATTHEW 18:35

THAT'S INCREDIBLE

Buck: BUCK COSTO reporting live from the Holy Land for *Total Sports News*. Today we're here to witness a world-record attempt. A camel is going to jump through the eye of a needle! This will take extreme concentration and athletic ability, so let's talk to the camel now. Mr. Camel, what made you want to go for this world record?

Camel: I've always liked jumping. And my mom said I can do anything I put my mind to.

Buck: But you're a full-grown camel.

Camel: Yes, a dromedary, to be exact.

Buck: So you're about eight feet tall and weigh 1,000 pounds—how do you expect to fit through the eye of a needle?

Camel: I'm going to run really, really fast.

Buck: Anything else?

Camel: I don't want to give away any secrets, but I slathered myself with olive oil.

Buck: So that's what I smell?

Camel: Yup, and it makes my coat look fantastic too.

Buck: Well, do your best. This is an amazing feat.

Camel: Thanks, they're size 11.

Buck: I meant . . . oh, never mind. Go finish your preparations.

Camel: No need. I'm ready now.

Buck: The camel is picking up speed. I think he's getting closer to the needle, but it's hard to tell since the needle is so small. He leaps—oh, epic fail! There's just no way he could've fit. How disappointing. Well, that's all for *Total Sports News*; I'm Buck Costo wishing you a good night.

Jesus once said it's easier for a camel to go through the eye of a needle than for a rich person to go to heaven. When you have a lot of money, it's easy to rely on yourself instead of God. Of course, many wealthy people do believe in Jesus, which is why the Lord said several verses later, "Everything is possible with God" (Mark 10:27).

WACKY LAUGHS
Q. Which shirt was the camel's favorite?
A. The camelflage one.

Q. Which camels act like movie stars?
A. Drama-daries.

✝ PRAY
Praise the Lord that everything is possible with him and that anybody who has faith in Jesus can have a relationship with him.

Life's Guidebook Says
[Jesus said,] "It is easier for a camel to go through the eye of a needle than for a rich person to enter the Kingdom of God!" MARK 10:25

BURST OF COLOR

A COLORFUL CREATURE scrambles behind leaves and flowers in a garden. As it scampers away, it changes color. It's a chameleon! These crawling lizards change colors to blend in with their background and communicate what they're feeling.

In the Old Testament, God called chameleons unclean and said, "Don't eat them, and don't even touch them" (Leviticus 11). Back then people didn't have the antibacterial soaps or ways to sterilize food we have now. Many of God's rules prevented disease and helped keep his people healthy. Lizards carry a lot of bacteria that can harm people, including salmonella. The bacteria live in a lizard's stomach and can pass to a person if the lizard touches something and a person puts the item in his or her mouth. So if the lizard crawled on a bowl and food was placed in the bowl and eaten, a person could get sick.

In the New Testament, a vision scared Peter because he saw creepy critters and other unclean animals. Suddenly, he heard a voice tell him to eat them. "No, Lord," Peter declared. "I have never eaten anything that our Jewish laws have declared impure and unclean" (Acts 10:14).

God replied, "Do not call something unclean if God has made it clean" (10:15). That vision changed Peter's thinking (verses 16, 28). God used the vision to help Peter realize that the good news about Jesus dying for our sins is for *all* people. Sometimes we need to change *our* thinking too. Always be willing to reconsider your own ideas and listen to God. He wants you to be open minded when it comes to learning more about him and his laws.

EXPERIMENT: COLOR BURSTS

Stuff You Need
- ☞ Milk that has fat (whole or 2 percent)
- ☞ Bowl
- ☞ Food coloring
- ☞ Liquid soap

Try It
1. Pour a little milk in a bowl.
2. Add drops of a few different colors of food coloring in separate places.
3. Add a drop of liquid soap and watch the colors explode and mix.

✝ PRAY
Ask God to help change your thinking to be more like Christ.

Life's Guidebook Says
Of the small animals that scurry along the ground, these are unclean for you: the mole rat, the rat, large lizards of all kinds, the gecko, the monitor lizard, the common lizard, the sand lizard, and the chameleon. LEVITICUS 11:29-30

PAYDAY!

TREVOR'S DAD NEEDED HELP with yard work. At eight in the morning, he offered Trevor $40 to help mow the lawn, pull weeds, plant flowers, and pick up trash. Trevor wanted the money, so he jumped at the opportunity.

It's sure getting hot out here, Trevor thought at around noon. *But it'll be worth it for the $40.*

Just then, Trevor's best friend, Patrick, walked by.

"Want to go to the pool?" he asked.

"I can't," Trevor said. "Doing work for my dad."

Dad came outside and saw Patrick. "Hey, do you want to help too? I'll pay you."

"Sure," Patrick said as he joined Trevor pulling weeds.

A few hours later, Trevor's neighbor Nate came home with his mom. Dad saw them drive up and went to their house. After a couple of minutes, Nate ran over to help with the yard work.

Just before dinnertime, Trevor's little brother, Miles, walked outside.

"I'm going to put you to work!" Dad said, giving Miles some gloves. He started planting flowers in the ground.

An hour later, it was too dark to work. Dad called all the boys inside.

"Thanks for your help, Miles," Dad said. "Here's $40."

Wow! Trevor thought. *If Miles gets $40 just for an hour's work, how much is Dad going to give me?*

Dad gave the same amount to Nate and Patrick. Then he handed Trevor $40 too.

"That's not fair," Trevor said. "Miles only worked an hour, and he made as much as I did!"

"But I paid you $40, just like I said I would," Dad pointed out. "Can't I be extra generous with my money if I want to be?"

What do you think about that story? Was Trevor treated fairly? Jesus told a similar story in Matthew 20:1-16. God treats everybody graciously. He generously gives his gift of eternal life to children who will serve him all their lives and older people who are about to die. God shows his kindness to all people who believe in him.

PLEXER

See if you can solve this plexer. (If you don't remember what a plexer is, see p. 9.)

> HOT SUN
> working

✝ PRAY

Praise God for his justice and mercy.

Life's Guidebook Says

[The landowner said,] "Is it against the law for me to do what I want with my money? Should you be jealous because I am kind to others?" MATTHEW 20:15

Answer: Working under a hot sun

TRUE RICHES

MONEY CAN BUY you a lot of things: toys, bikes, video games, cool shoes, and electronics. But money can't buy happiness. You've probably heard that before. Maybe you figured someone without much money said it. But a survey of the superwealthy found it was true. Researchers talked with 160 millionaires—120 of the families were worth more than $25 million—and discovered many of them were miserable. Money brought them a lot of material possessions, but it also brought a lot of pressure. The megarich felt like they couldn't complain about life's troubles to their friends and that their loved ones expected them to buy really good presents. Plus, they worried a lot about raising children who weren't lazy and bratty because of growing up so rich.

Jesus didn't own a lot when he walked the earth—really just the clothes on his back. But he was rich in many other ways, including his relationships. Once when he was teaching, a man in the crowd called out and asked Jesus to make his brother divide their father's estate with him. Jesus told the man to watch out for being greedy. Then he shared a story about a rich man who built huge rooms to store his wealth. The man figured if he amassed enough wealth, he wouldn't have to worry about anything in the future. But God told him that he'd die that night and his wealth would be divided among others.

When it comes to wealth, follow Jesus' example. He didn't have a lot of things. But he had good friends, a great reputation, and a wealth of knowledge about God.

LIFTOFF LIST

How are you building a rich relationship with God? Check everything you do:

___ I store God's Word in the vault of my brain.
___ I deposit prayers to heaven.
___ I invest in relationships with other Christ followers.
___ I earn interest by going to church.

✝ PRAY

Tell God you want to invest in having a rich relationship with him.

Life's Guidebook Says
[Jesus said,] "Yes, a person is a fool to store up earthly wealth but not have a rich relationship with God." LUKE 12:21

SWEET WATER

WATER AND SUMMER just seem to go together. Splashing, swimming, boating, fishing, squirting—playing in and being near water can be the perfect way to spend the day. But when chemicals leaked from a storage tank into a river in 2014, some people in West Virginia couldn't drink, wash, or bathe in their water. Trucks brought in bottled water, but it's pretty hard to shower with bottles of water or wash dishes with them instead of using the dishwasher. Hundreds of people became sick, and government leaders closed schools and restaurants. Workers needed to clean the water with safe chemicals before it could be used again.

The Israelites also ran into the lack of clean water in the desert. When they arrived at an oasis and tasted the water from a well, it was too bitter to drink. *Grumble! Grumble!* They complained to Moses, who asked God to help. God told Moses to toss a stick into the water. Moses threw it in and the water became sticky. (*Get it*, sticky. *Ha!*) Actually, through God's power, the water became sweet.

God doesn't want his people to go thirsty. He provides us with drinking water, but he is also our "living water," who quenches all our spiritual needs. Notice how much water your family uses each day, see if there's any way you can save water, and be thankful for clean water. But be especially grateful that you never have to be spiritually thirsty!

AWESOME ACTIVITY: CINNAMON TEA

Throw these sticks into hot water to make it taste great. You don't even need to add sugar. Cinnamon is also one of the healthiest spices.

Stuff You Need
- ☞ 2 cinnamon sticks
- ☞ 1 cup of boiling water
- ☞ Cup

Try It
1. Place cinnamon sticks and water in a cup. Let it sit for 30 minutes.
2. Remove cinnamon pieces and enjoy the sweet taste.

✝ PRAY

Thank God for clean water and tell him you want to drink his "living water."

Life's Guidebook Says
Moses cried out to the LORD. The LORD showed him a stick. Moses threw it into the water. The water became sweet. EXODUS 15:25, NIrV

DISSING DISABILITY

GROWING UP, it took Gabe Murfitt longer to do things than his friends. Eating and writing were a chore. But Gabe was right in the middle of things when it came to riding his scooter, playing soccer, shooting hoops, and practicing the drums.

Sounds pretty ordinary, right?

But one look at Gabe and you know he's extraordinary. Gabe was born with a condition that prevented his arms and legs from growing. His arms are just a few inches long, making it appear as if his hands are coming out of his shoulders. And Gabe's legs are permanently bent at the knee, so he's constantly cross-legged—even when he stands.

Gabe's body is unique and so is his attitude. Instead of feeling sorry for himself or giving up when tasks seem too difficult, Gabe worked extra hard to accomplish the same things as other kids. He loved sports and played point guard for his seventh-grade basketball team. All of his accomplishments caught the attention of TV shows. He appeared on the *Oprah Winfrey Show* and *Good Morning America*.

In high school, Gabe came up with C.L.E.A.R. goals for his life. The letters stood for

Courage
Leadership
Endurance
Attitude
Respect

As a follower of Jesus Christ, Gabe relies on God when things get tough.

"When I'm having rough days, I try to remember that I can do everything by the power of Christ," Gabe said. "Jesus is right there to help me. He can help me overcome any difficulty."

Your challenges may not be as obvious as Gabe's. Maybe you deal with insecurity, anger, doubt, or jealousy. No matter what you're going through, remember that Jesus is right there to help you overcome.

EXPERIMENT: DOUBLE DRIBBLE

Even with three-inch arms, Gabe is a great dribbler. Grab a ball, go outside, and see if you can beat these records:

☞ Pawan Kumar Srivastava of India dribbled for 55 hours and 26 minutes straight! How long can you dribble without messing up?

☞ Joseph Odhiambo of Phoenix, Arizona, set a record by dribbling six basketballs at the same time. How many balls can you dribble at once?

✝ PRAY

Thank God that he's there during the tough times.

Life's Guidebook Says

All glory to God, who is able, through his mighty power at work within us, to accomplish infinitely more than we might ask or think. EPHESIANS 3:20

BROTHER TROUBLE

WHAT'S THE DEAL with biblical brothers? If you're looking for good examples on how to live with your siblings, you may have difficulty finding them in the Bible. Cain and Abel were the first two brothers—and one of them ended up dead. *Yikes!* Then there's Joseph and his brothers. Genesis 37 tells us how Joseph's brothers wanted to kill him because he was their father's favorite. (Those dreams Joseph had about his brothers bowing to him didn't help matters either.) Just before they were about to do the deed, the oldest brother, Reuben, spoke up and said they should throw Joseph into a pit instead. After they threw him into the hole, a group of traders came by on their camels.

"Instead of hurting our brother, let's sell him to those traders," Joseph's brother Judah suggested. So that's what they did. Talk about brotherly *un*love.

If you have brothers or sisters, they probably bother you from time to time. Joseph's brothers focused on all the things they didn't like about him instead of his positive qualities. That caused them to make a very bad decision. Think about your siblings. What do you appreciate the most about them? Write down a few ideas:

1. _____
2. _____
3. _____

God wants us to live in harmony with our brothers. We can do that by remembering that these are lifelong relationships. Your siblings will probably be there for you even longer than your parents. If you fight with your siblings, forgive. If you argue, agree to end things on a good note. And whatever you do, don't act like Joseph's brothers.

QUIZ: OH, BROTHERS
Draw a line to connect the biblical brothers.

Cain	Aaron
Joseph	Andrew
Jacob	Abel
Moses	Esau
Peter	Reuben

✟ PRAY
Ask God to give you the patience and wisdom to live in peace with your siblings.

Life's Guidebook Says
How wonderful and pleasant it is when brothers live together in harmony!
PSALM 133:1

Answers: Cain and Abel, Joseph and Reuben, Jacob and Esau, Moses and Aaron, Peter and Andrew

I DARE YOU

HAS SOMEBODY EVER DARED you to do something? Maybe a friend wanted you to drink a mixture of pickle juice, mustard, animal crackers, and jelly. *Gross!* Or maybe you were dared to drink a frozen slush in one gulp or lick a frozen flagpole. Some dares can be harmless and fun. Others are much more dangerous. Be smart to avoid dangerous dares, especially if they relate to taking drugs or drinking alcohol.

Samson wasn't too smart when it came to dares. God gave Samson amazing strength to fight the Philistines, ancient Israel's number-one enemy. But what Samson boasted in muscle power, he lacked in brain power. Judges 16 tells how he fell in love with a Philistine woman named Delilah. The Philistine rulers found out, and each paid Delilah 1,100 silver pieces to discover the source of Samson's strength.

"I dare you to tell me the source of your strength and how you could be tied up securely," Delilah said to Samson (or something like that).

Samson said that if seven bowstrings bound his arms, he wouldn't be able to move. It wasn't true—Samson was a bit of a jokester. Delilah tied up Samson with seven bowstrings while he slept, but once he woke up, he easily broke them. Delilah kept daring Samson to tell the truth. Two times he made up other stories. Finally, after a lot of begging and nagging, Samson told Delilah the truth about his hair—he would lose his strength if his long, flowing locks were ever cut. He was soon shaved, blinded, and captured, and he died a prisoner not long after.

Giving in to a dare—even if somebody bugs you over and over—is never a good idea . . . unless maybe they're paying for the frozen slush. (Just kidding!)

PUZZLE IT OUT: BIBLE BADDIES

Find these Bible bad guys (and girls) by searching up, down, across, diagonally, and backward.

G	O	L	I	A	T	H	J
N	A	B	N	L	N	E	U
A	D	H	A	I	Z	R	D
M	E	Z	A	E	G	O	A
A	L	C	B	N	O	D	S
H	D	E	L	I	L	A	H
Q	L	J	U	D	I	O	R
P	H	A	R	A	O	H	J

Cain
Delilah
Haman
Herod
Goliath
Jezebel
Judas
Pharaoh

✝ PRAY

Pray for the courage to stand strong and not take dares.

Life's Guidebook Says

Don't do as the wicked do, and don't follow the path of evildoers. Don't even think about it; don't go that way. Turn away and keep moving. PROVERBS 4:14-15

SQUEAKY CLEAN

ZANE AND IAN FINISHED playing basketball in the driveway.

"Let's go inside and get something to drink," Zane said.

The boys ran inside and grabbed two glasses from the sink.

"I washed these this morning," Zane said as he handed Ian a glass.

Zane went to the refrigerator and grabbed some sports punch. As he was about to pour some into Ian's glass, his friend looked inside the cup.

"Gross," Ian said, pulling away. "This glass is caked with dried chocolate milk and orange juice pulp. And I think there're bits of cookie, too."

"Yeah," Zane said. "That's the glass I used to dip my cookies in chocolate milk last night. But the outside is totally clean. Come on, let me pour you some sports punch."

"No way," Ian said, walking back outside.

As silly as it sounds, many kids and adults act exactly like Zane. They're more worried about their outward appearance than the content of their character. Even people in the church act this way.

Jesus often butted heads with the Pharisees, who were religious leaders in biblical times. The Pharisees liked to act spiritual and brag about how holy they were. Jesus wasn't impressed. He knew their hearts were selfish and didn't serve God. Near the end of Jesus' time on earth, he confronted the Pharisees, saying, "You are so careful to clean the outside . . . but inside you are filthy" (see today's verse).

Just like you should pay attention to washing the outside *and* inside of a cup, make sure you're seeking God's help in keeping your heart clean.

WACKY LAUGHS

Q. How do astronauts stay clean?
A. They take meteor showers.

Q. What should you eat to get clean?
A. Shower-kraut.

Q. What happens when you don't clean your mirrors?
A. They give you dirty looks.

✝ PRAY

Tell God that you're going to put more effort into keeping your inside clean than your outside.

Life's Guidebook Says

[Jesus said,] "Hypocrites! For you are so careful to clean the outside of the cup and the dish, but inside you are filthy—full of greed and self-indulgence!"
MATTHEW 23:25

CAUGHT DEAD TO RIGHTS

LIES CAN'T REALLY hurt you, right? You break a lamp and blame it on the dog. You forget your homework and say your dog ate it. You pass gas and look over at your pooch, like he did it. (Hey, why's your dog always taking the blame?)

Anyway, while a lie may help you escape trouble for a moment, it always catches up with you. Yes, always! Sometimes it takes a while. Other times the truth comes out right away. Take the story of Ananias and Sapphira.

In the early church, God's people in Jerusalem shared everything they had with each other. If somebody made dinner, everybody was invited. If a person needed a donkey, another Christ follower would give him one. If somebody came into a lot of money, he shared it with those in need instead of keeping it all for himself. And that's where we find Ananias and Sapphira in Acts 5. They have just sold some land. But instead of giving all the money to the community of God's people, they keep some for themselves. That may be a bit selfish, but it's certainly not the real problem in this story.

The *big* problem is that Ananias goes to Peter and says he's giving *all* the money to God. Peter knows the truth, and catches Ananias in his lie. "The property was yours to sell or not sell, as you wished," Peter says. "And after selling it, the money was also yours to give away. How could you do a thing like this? You weren't lying to us but to God!" (5:4).

As soon as Ananias heard this, he fell to the floor and died. A little while later, Sapphira came in and pretended that they had given all the money too. She also died immediately. *Yikes!*

Who said lying can't hurt you? So make sure to always tell the truth.

PLEXER

See if you can solve this plexer. (If you don't remember what a plexer is, see p. 9.)

$$aC|AUiGHTe$$

✝ PRAY

Ask God to help you always be truthful.

> *Life's Guidebook Says*
> *[Peter said,] "How could you do a thing like this? You weren't lying to us but to God!"* ACTS 5:4

Answer: Caught in a lie

NEPHEW TO THE RESCUE

HAVE YOU EVER HEARD of *fasting*? Maybe you think sprinters do it . . . but that's another kind of fast. In the Bible, God tells his people to fast—or go without food—to humble themselves and grow closer to him. Moses fasted. King David fasted. And Jesus famously fasted for 40 days in the desert. Many kids don't fast because food is so important to a growing body, but as you get older it's a spiritual discipline you may want to learn about.

In the book of Acts, we read about a "fast" that wasn't very spiritual at all. A group of Jews banded together and made an oath to not eat or drink until they had killed the apostle Paul (Acts 23:12). Paul had been arrested numerous times and thrown into prison for telling people about Jesus Christ. But he couldn't keep quiet about his Savior. He knew spreading God's truth was the most important thing he could do as long as he was alive. God even encouraged him to keep on going (verse 11). More than 40 men joined the hunger strike to kill Paul. They hoped he would be transported from one prison to another, so they could kill him as he traveled.

God had other plans. Paul's nephew learned about the plot and ran to the Roman officers to ask them to protect his uncle. The officers took action and quickly moved Paul to a different city to keep him safe.

We don't know the nephew's name, but his quick action saved his uncle. Families stick together and help each other. You probably will never save a family member from a death threat, but when you see a need in your family, do everything you can to help.

AWESOME ACTIVITY: FAMILY TREE

Who's in your family? Sit down with your parents and create a family tree. Try to map out all of your living relatives. You might be amazed at how far your family spreads out.

✝ PRAY

Thank God for your family and for being part of the bigger family of God's children.

Life's Guidebook Says
The Lord appeared to Paul and said, "Be encouraged, Paul. Just as you have been a witness to me here in Jerusalem, you must preach the Good News in Rome as well." ACTS 23:11

BAD-NEWS BEARER

HAVE YOU EVER HAD to stand up to a friend who wasn't acting the right way? It can be hard, because you don't want to ruin a friendship. But a friend's safety and well-being are way more important than safeguarding your relationship. So if you see a friend messing around with inappropriate movies, smoking, or drinking alcohol, you need to encourage him to make better choices (and probably tell a parent, too). If he's a true friend, he'll know your warning comes because you care. The writer of Proverbs knew this when he wrote, "Wounds from a sincere friend are better than many kisses from an enemy" (Proverbs 27:6).

In the Old Testament, God raised up prophets to encourage his people to live for him. Sometimes the prophets brought news of God's laws or foretold future blessings. But many times, the prophets had to bring bad news. The book of Micah is filled with warnings to God's people in Israel and Judah. At this point in history, the people were living for themselves—not God. Merchants were cheating customers. People lied so much that they no longer knew what the truth was (Micah 6:10-12).

God is always loving and ready to forgive. But he's also absolutely just. When his people willfully and knowingly disobeyed his commands and went the other way, God removed his blessing and allowed judgment to come. Micah had to be the bearer of bad news when he said judgment was coming. The people didn't like him very much, but they respected Micah, because they knew he always spoke God's truth.

Your friends might not like it at first when you challenge their behavior. But in the end, it's likely that they'll respect your caring enough to step up and do what is right.

PLEXER

See if you can solve this plexer. (If you don't remember what a plexer is, see p. 9.)

```
              s
    a friend  n
              u
              o
              w
```

✝ PRAY

Ask God for the courage to point out to a friend when he's going the wrong way.

Life's Guidebook Says
Wounds from a sincere friend are better than many kisses from an enemy.
PROVERBS 27:6

Answer: Wounds from a friend

LET'S GO CLIMB A TREE

COLLIN DRAGGED big branches from the woods and piled them in a large circle. He tied some together to form a hut. Then he cut a slit for a window. Collin stood back and admired his hideout. It was perfect! But it wasn't for him. As strange as it sounds, Collin made the hut for his mom. She was a photographer and wanted to snap shots of birds in the yard—but the birds kept flying away. Collin made the lookout big enough for his mom to kneel inside and shoot photos through the long, narrow slit. With Mom tucked safely inside the wooded hideout, the birds never suspected a thing. She snapped lots of photos as birds swooped down to the birdbath or pecked at seeds and berries scattered on the ground. She took close-ups of birds' wings, beaks, and even eyes from her bird's-eye view.

Trees can come in very handy. Long ago, Zacchaeus used a tree as a lookout. He climbed into a tree, thinking no one would see him watching Jesus. *Oops!* Jesus stopped, looked up, and started talking to Zacchaeus. Later, the Lord ate with Zacchaeus, and he became a Christ follower (Luke 19:9-10).

You might be able to trick a bird, but Jesus always knows where you are. That's a good thing, since it means you can talk to Jesus from anywhere. Next time you climb a tree, talk to Jesus—he'll always get the message!

AWESOME ACTIVITY: TREE FUN

Trees breathe in carbon dioxide and breathe out oxygen. The sap inside the tree runs through it like blood runs through our veins. Check out how a tree breathes:

- ☞ Listen to a tree's heartbeat. Put the opening of a glass against the trunk of a tree and you'll hear the beat of the sap moving.
- ☞ On a sunny day, place a clear plastic bag over a clump of leaves. Check the bag in an hour and notice the drops of water in the bag. They form as the plant exhales.

✝ PRAY

Thank God that he always sees you and hears you. Tell him what you are thinking about right now.

Life's Guidebook Says

Jesus responded, "Salvation has come to this home today. . . . For the Son of Man came to seek and save those who are lost." LUKE 19:9-10

ALOHA STATE

ALOHA IS PROBABLY the most spoken word in Hawaii. That's because it has many meanings. It can mean both "hello" and "good-bye." Some people use it as an expression of love. In the Hawaiian language, *aloha* literally means "breath of life." *Alo* means "front" or "face," and *ha* means "breath." Historians point out that in old Hawaiian, *aloha* meant "God in us." Hawaiian words are fun to read and hard to say. The language has only 18 letters—including just eight consonants.

Today is a special day in Hawaii, because it marks the date that Americans said, "Aloha, Hawaii," to welcome it as the 50th state in the United States. On this day in 1959, President Dwight D. Eisenhower signed a proclamation to invite Hawaii into the Union. Many people in Hawaii voted to be part of the United States. Others didn't want to join. But once Eisenhower signed the proclamation, all Hawaiians became official US citizens.

The Bible tells us, "Everyone must submit to governing authorities. For all authority comes from God, and those in positions of authority have been placed there by God" (Romans 13:1). You may not always agree with everything your government officials do, but that doesn't mean you can disregard laws and proclamations you don't like. God puts leaders into power. As a Christ follower, you can pray for godly leaders to be raised up. And you should always show respect to the authorities in your life.

PUZZLE IT OUT: BABY STATES

Fit the last eight states to join the United States into this puzzle. (Hint: Start with the longest state first.)

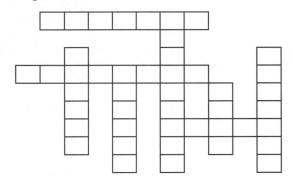

Alaska (January 3, 1959)
Arizona (February 14, 1912)
Hawaii (August 21, 1959)
Idaho (July 3, 1890)
New Mexico (January 6, 1912)
Oklahoma (November 16, 1907)
Utah (January 4, 1896)
Wyoming (July 10, 1890)

✝ PRAY

Ask God to give people wisdom as they vote for governing authorities. Thank God that he's ultimately in control.

Life's Guidebook Says

Everyone must submit to governing authorities. For all authority comes from God, and those in positions of authority have been placed there by God.
ROMANS 13:1

IN THE LEAD

HYENAS CAN BE VICIOUS. If you've seen *The Lion King* movies or watched *Animal Planet*, you know these scavengers attack with great power. Hyenas hunt at night, often coming across an old kill and eating the remains. But hyenas are also smart hunters that go after the weakest animals in a herd. Hyenas have strong jaws and stomachs, which allow them to get nutrients from skin and bones. Really, the only things a hyena can't eat are an animal's hair, horns, and hooves.

As aggressive as hyenas are when they make a kill, they can be surprisingly compassionate while eating it. The most dominant hyenas in a clan get to eat first. But researchers have seen the dominant animals allow sick or younger hyenas the opportunity to go ahead of them. The dominant hyenas often fight off other animals and guard the perimeter of the kill zone so other members of their clan can eat.

Obviously, Jesus is *wa-a-ay* more compassionate than any hyena. But it's amazing to think that even hyenas can show servant leadership. The stronger animals sacrifice and help the weak ones. Have you ever been in a position of leadership? Sometimes it's easy to get caught up in the power. But when Jesus' disciples asked him about ruling, he said, "Whoever wants to be a leader among you must be your servant" (Matthew 20:26). Jesus demonstrated what ultimate servant leadership looks like by dying for us on a cross . . . there's just no way a hyena would ever do that for you.

WEIRD FACTS: NOTHING TO LAUGH ABOUT

Spotted hyenas make many wails, howls, and screams that often sound like laughter. That's where the term "laughing hyena" comes from. Check out these other facts:

- ☞ There are four types of hyenas—spotted, brown, striped, and the aardwolf.
- ☞ Hyenas sleep during the day and hunt at night.
- ☞ Spotted hyenas live in clans that can have as many as 80 members. Females are dominant over the males.
- ☞ In ancient Egypt, hyenas were captured, fattened up, and killed for food.

✞ PRAY

Pray for God to give you the wisdom to be a good leader.

Life's Guidebook Says

[Jesus said,] "Even the Son of Man came not to be served but to serve others and to give his life as a ransom for many." MATTHEW 20:28

SOMETHING TO TALK ABOUT

IF YOU HAD a stuttering problem, what's the last job you'd want to do?

a. Government leader
b. News reporter
c. Performer
d. Any of the above

None of those sound like a good job for someone with a speech impediment. But stutterers have thrived in all of those professions. Christian singer Jason Gray has made more than 10 albums, performed thousands of concerts all over the world, and spoken in front of countless people. But he never wanted to be a performer because of his stuttering problem. When he was growing up, Jason's family went through a painful divorce and other issues that ended up with his mom losing custody of him. That's when Jason's stuttering began.

"It wasn't a speech impediment that I had to overcome [to be a performer] as much as my fear and shame over it," Jason says. "For years and years, I was quiet and embarrassed about it."

Then Jason felt God's calling to be a singer and songwriter. At first, he fought with God. But in the end, God won. (He always does.)

Does Jason's story remind you of anybody in the Bible? Moses was also a stutterer, but God called him to be a spokesman and leader of his people. Moses fought with God, saying, "I get tongue-tied, and my words get tangled" (Exodus 4:10). But God's power is made perfect in our weakness (2 Corinthians 12:9), and Moses excelled as a leader.

Are you embarrassed about anything in your life? Don't let fear hold you back. If you feel God calling you to do something, do it! His strength will make up for any weakness you might have.

WEIRD FACTS: TALK IT OUT

According to the Stuttering Foundation, many high-profile people have overcome speech impediments. Take a look at this list:

☞ James Earl Jones—voice of Darth Vader and Mufasa in *The Lion King*
☞ Darren Sproles—NFL football player
☞ John Stossel—FOX News journalist
☞ Winston Churchill—famous British leader during WWII
☞ Mike Rowe—host of *Shark Week* and narrator of *Deadliest Catch*

✝ PRAY

Ask God to help you overcome shame and live the life he's called you to.

Life's Guidebook Says
Moses pleaded with the LORD, "O Lord, I'm not very good with words. I never have been, and I'm not now, even though you have spoken to me. I get tongue-tied, and my words get tangled." EXODUS 4:10

CUT TO THE TRUTH

"It's my dog!" Jackson yelled.

"No, it's not," Landon said. "He lives at my house."

"But I would know Growler anywhere," Jackson said. "Give him back!"

"Never!" Landon said.

Jackson yanked the puppy from Landon's hands. Landon pushed Jackson down. Just then a policeman walked up to the two boys in the park.

"What's all this fighting about?" the policeman said.

"Jackson doesn't know what he's talking about," Landon said, pulling the dog back. "This is my dog."

"No, it's not," Jackson said.

"Give me the dog," the policeman said. He sat down and pulled out a knife. "Since both of you claim the dog is yours, I'm going to cut it in half and give you each part of it."

"Sounds fair to me," Landon said.

"Don't do it!" Jackson said. "Landon can have the dog."

"Thanks, Jackson," the policeman said. "Actually, I'm giving the dog to you. Only the real owner wouldn't want the dog killed."

What a strange story! But something like this happened in the Bible. Instead of a dog, it was a baby. Two women showed up in front of King Solomon, claiming the same baby was theirs (1 Kings 3:16-28). The king asked for a sword so he could cut the baby in half and give part to each woman. Before he could do it, the real mother told him to spare the child and give it to the other woman. Okay, that's a pretty weird story too.

But the cool part is that King Solomon knew exactly the right questions to ask and actions to take to bring out the truth. God always knows the truth. So when you're in a confusing situation or helping settle a fight between friends, ask for his wisdom in what to do.

WACKY LAUGHS

Q. Why did the dog lay on its back with its feet in the air?
A. It was trying to trip birds.

Q. What is a dog's favorite pizza topping?
A. Pup-Peroni

Q. What do you call a pooch that wakes up too early in the morning?
A. A groggy doggie

✝ PRAY

Pray that you'll be able to say the right thing to help when you see two friends fighting.

Life's Guidebook Says

When all Israel heard the king's decision, the people were in awe of the king, for they saw the wisdom God had given him for rendering justice. 1 KINGS 3:28

BIG, BIG FAMILY

How MANY PEOPLE are in your family? Count every aunt, uncle, cousin, grandparent, and sibling you have. What number did you get? Write it down: _____.

Would you believe that number is actually more than two billion? As a Christian, you're part of God's family—and that's a pretty big group. Christianity is the largest religion in the world. Nearly one out of every three people on the planet claims to be a follower of Jesus Christ. Isn't that amazing?

Christianity started at about the size of a middle school basketball team. There were 12 "players" (the disciples) and one very amazing coach (Jesus Christ). But from those tiny beginnings, the truth about God's love and power spread all over the world. At first, some Christians felt that only Jews could follow Christ. But Jesus said his forgiveness was for all people. In the book of Acts, Peter stands up during a heated argument and lays out the facts: "God knows people's hearts. . . . He made no distinction between us and them, for he cleansed their hearts through faith" (see today's verse).

Faith is what makes you a member of God's family. You weren't born a Christian. But you became one when you believed that Jesus rose from the dead so your sins could be forgiven. Now Jesus is one family member worth following!

TWISTY TONGUE TWISTERS

Try to say these tongue twisters 10 times without stopping.

Flying fish freshly fried for Fred's family.
Bossy brothers blocked Brad's bike.
Christ came to calm our qualms.

✝ PRAY

Praise God for allowing you to be part of his big family.

Life's Guidebook Says

[Peter said,] "God knows people's hearts, and he confirmed that he accepts Gentiles by giving them the Holy Spirit, just as he did to us. He made no distinction between us and them, for he cleansed their hearts through faith." ACTS 15:8-9

GATHERING HOPE

DO YOU EVER NOTICE homeless people who stand near the road holding up signs? In some cities, you can't miss them. Do you ever wonder how they got to their current condition? Did they lose a job, a family member, or their home?

Ruth wasn't homeless, but she certainly needed help. As we meet Ruth in the Old Testament, we learn that her husband, her brother-in-law, and her father-in-law have died. Then her recently widowed sister-in-law goes away, leaving just her and her mother-in-law, Naomi. Naomi is leaving her home in Moab and heading back to Bethlehem. She encourages Ruth to find a new life. But Ruth sticks with Naomi to help take care of her.

When they arrive in Bethlehem, it's time for the barley harvest. They have little to eat, so Ruth picks up leftover grain from the harvesters. She chooses the field of Boaz, a relative of Naomi's late husband. Boaz sees how hard she works and learns her story. He's amazed at Ruth's commitment to Naomi. He's rich enough to give Ruth lots of food and drink. But instead of charity, he feeds Ruth and allows her to work. He even instructs his workers to drop some extra grain (see today's verse).

God blesses Boaz for his kindness, and Boaz ends up marrying Ruth. God blesses us, too, when we help the less fortunate.

EXPERIMENT: PICK IT UP
Rice is the most eaten grain in the world. Check out its power.

Stuff You Need
☞ Small plastic bottle (12 ounces or less)
☞ Uncooked rice (lots of it)
☞ Pencil

Try It
1. Fill the empty bottle with rice. Tap it occasionally to help compact the rice.
2. Slowly push a pencil into the rice as far as you can.
3. Slowly pull it out.
4. Repeat steps 2 and 3. Soon the pencil won't move at all. Then you can lift up the pencil, and the bottle filled with rice will lift up as well.

✝ PRAY
Thank God that he provides for the needy and hurting. Ask him if there's any way you could help someone today.

Life's Guidebook Says
When Ruth went back to work again, Boaz ordered his young men, "Let her gather grain right among the sheaves without stopping her. And pull out some heads of barley from the bundles and drop them on purpose for her. Let her pick them up, and don't give her a hard time!" RUTH 2:15-16

RAISE YOUR HANDS IN VICTORY

ARE YOU READY for some football? Football season is about to kick off. The professionals have played the preseason and college teams have practiced for weeks. Football has a lot of rules, and referees make a lot of signals. Do you know what it means when the referee points both of his hands straight in the air over his head?

    a.   There's a plane flying overhead.
    b.   He forgot to put on deodorant.
    c.   A team scored a touchdown.

The answer, of course, is *c*. But when Moses raised his hands over his head in Exodus 17, it meant something totally different. As Joshua and his men battled the Amalekites, Moses watched from a nearby hill with Aaron and Hur. When Moses raised his hands and his staff over his head, the Israelites did well. But when his hands dropped, the Israelites started losing.

Moses got really tired during the battle, so Aaron and Hur helped keep his hands in the air—and the Israelites claimed the victory. *Score!* Sometimes we need some help from our friends to win the important battles in life.

AWESOME ACTIVITY: YOU'VE GOT SKILLS
Go outside to practice your football skills.

1.   Throw for accuracy. After you warm up your arm, put an empty two-liter bottle on a table or chair. Stand back about 10 yards and try to knock it over with a pass.
2.   Pass for distance. See how far you can throw the ball.
3.   Run the course. Football players have to cut and change direction quickly. Find three tennis balls. Place two of them about 10 yards away from the other one. Stand near the single ball and start a stopwatch. Run and pick up one ball. Sprint back and drop it near the single ball, and pick up that ball. Go back over, drop the ball in your hand and pick up the final ball. Run back to where you started and stop the clock.
4.   Punt for distance. See how far you can punt a football.

✝ PRAY
Ask God for his help in gaining the victory in the things that matter most to him.

Life's Guidebook Says
As long as Moses held up the staff in his hand, the Israelites had the advantage. But whenever he dropped his hand, the Amalekites gained the advantage.
EXODUS 17:11

WINGED MESSENGERS

"A LITTLE BIRDIE TOLD ME."

Have you ever heard that saying? Do you know what it means? Harry Potter and his friends at Hogwarts had owl mail. In the Lord of the Rings books, Sauron used crows to gather information. And in the real world, carrier pigeons have been used to send messages for thousands of years. Also called homing pigeons, these special birds can be trained to always return to the same place—even from hundreds of miles away!

Today, the military still uses carrier pigeons. But they were especially helpful during World War I. Thousands of pigeons flew lifesaving messages through gunfire, rain, and fog. One of the most famous birds, named Cher Ami, saved the 77th Infantry Division when it was trapped behind German lines. American commanders started to attack the area and hit their own people. This brave bird flew a message to US officials to tell them to halt the attack. Twenty minutes later, thanks to Cher Ami, the bombing stopped and the men were saved.

But the saying "A little birdie told me" doesn't have anything to do with actual birds. It comes from the Bible. In Ecclesiastes 10:20, it says: "Don't make fun of the powerful, even in your own bedroom. For a little bird might deliver your message and tell them what you said." In other words, if you say lies or mean words about somebody, don't be surprised if your words make it back to that person. We need to watch what we say. Because once words leave our mouths, who knows where they'll fly?

WEIRD FACTS: PIGEON TALES

Pigeons make amazing messengers. Check out these facts:

- ☞ The dove that Noah sent from the ark to look for dry land was probably a homing pigeon.
- ☞ People have paid more than $130,000 for one homing pigeon.
- ☞ Carrier pigeons can fly 700 miles in a single day.
- ☞ Pigeons fly over 50 miles per hour.

✝ PRAY

Tell God you want to control your tongue and not make fun of other people, even when you're alone.

Life's Guidebook Says

Never make light of the king, even in your thoughts. And don't make fun of the powerful, even in your own bedroom. For a little bird might deliver your message and tell them what you said. ECCLESIASTES 10:20

GOOD TO GIVE

How MUCH MONEY do you give to help people every year? You probably don't have huge piles of cash lying around, but you may drop money in the church offering plate or use some to put together a shoebox for Operation Christmas Child.

Every year a popular money magazine prints a list of the people who gave away the most money. In 2012, businessman and investor Warren Buffett topped the list by donating more than $3 billion. (Yes, that's billion with a *b.*) Second on the list was Facebook creator Mark Zuckerberg, who gave away nearly $500 million. That's a lot of money that can do a lot of good to help needy people.

In the Bible, some people made a big deal about their giving. They wanted everybody to know how generous they were. So before they'd give away their money, they'd blow trumpets to call attention to their act of charity. It's like they were saying: "Look at me. I'm such an awesome person because I'm helping the less fortunate. I'm so rich and cool."

Okay, maybe they weren't saying all of that. But they did want people to notice their kindness and look up to them. Jesus didn't like their attitude. He said when people call attention to their giving, their reward will be on earth—not in heaven. Heavenly rewards are worth so much more. So if you're ever in a place where you can help somebody, follow what Jesus said and "give your gifts in private, and your Father, who sees everything, will reward you" (Matthew 6:4). God's reward can't be beat.

PUZZLE IT OUT: HAPPY TO GIVE

Giving away our money isn't always easy. God looks at our hearts when we give. Solve these math problems to figure out what 2 Corinthians 9:7 says.

"_____ _____ _____ ___ _____ _____ _____ _____."

| 3+4 | 3x2 | 17-12 | 1x1 | 28÷14 | 1+2 | 56÷7 | 11-7 |

1 – a
2 – person
3 – who
4 – cheerfully

5 – loves
6 – God
7 – for
8 – gives

✝ PRAY

Tell God you want to live for heavenly rewards—not honor on the earth.

Life's Guidebook Says
Give your gifts in private, and your Father, who sees everything, will reward you.
MATTHEW 6:4

Answer: "For God loves a person who gives cheerfully."

WHY CAN'T WE BE FRIENDS?

WHEN A FRIEND TELLS you a secret, what do you do?

a. Make a joke about it in a text I send to everybody.
b. Promise not to tell anyone (but if I have a fight with my friend, then I tell anybody I want).
c. Keep my mouth shut (unless my friend's in danger . . . then I'd tell an adult).
d. I don't have any friends.

Hopefully, you didn't answer *d*. But if you answered *a* or *b*, then you'll probably soon be answering *d*, because being trustworthy is an important quality for a friend. When you look for a friend, what qualities do you hope to find? List a few:

1. _____
2. _____
3. _____
4. _____

Look back at that list. Does it describe you? It should. Jesus said, "Do to others as you would like them to do to you" (Luke 6:31). You may have heard that called the "Golden Rule." If you want to make friends, think of how you'd like to be treated and what qualities you'd want a friend to possess. You may want a friend who's funny, shares, is loyal, and likes to play video games. Who wouldn't, right? So if you're grumpy, selfish, and back-stabbing, do you think you'll make many friends? Probably not.

As you look for friends, remember Jesus' advice. Treat other kids how you'd like to be treated. You'll make a lot more friends that way . . . and maybe you'll be able to introduce your new friends to your *best* Friend, Jesus Christ.

LIFTOFF LIST

How do you make friends? See how many items you can check:

___ I ask kids questions about themselves.
___ I introduce myself to new kids at school.
___ I treat people the way I want to be treated.
___ I don't spread rumors.
___ I am loyal.
___ I find kids who like the same things I do.
___ I look for new friends at church.
___ I smile and act friendly.

✞ PRAY

Ask God to help you be a friend and make good friends.

Life's Guidebook Says

[Jesus said,] "Do to others as you would like them to do to you." LUKE 6:31

ARE YOU ORGANIZED?

IF YOU HAVEN'T STARTED school yet, you're about to. That means homework, tests, book reports, and worksheets. It doesn't take rocket science to do well in school. (Unless you're studying to be a rocket scientist.) You just need to pay attention in class, do your homework, take good notes, and turn projects in on time. And a key to excelling in all of those areas is staying organized. Complete this sentence to check your organization skills:

Your teacher gives you a worksheet for homework. You . . .

a. put the worksheet in your homework folder and pull it out of your backpack when you get home to complete it.
b. toss the worksheet in your backpack and remember the assignment on your way to school the next day.
c. leave the worksheet at school, then wad it up and throw it in the trash the next day to practice your basketball skills.

If you want an A, hopefully you answered *a*. By keeping track of assignments and having a special place for homework, you'll be able to do better in school. Staying on top of things helps in all areas of life. In Proverbs it says, "Workers who tend a fig tree are allowed to eat the fruit" (see today's verse). Fig trees need a lot of care. They have to be mulched, pruned, fertilized, and harvested. Each of these things has to be done on a specific schedule. If you're disorganized and don't provide constant care, the crop will suffer.

You have to stay on a specific schedule at school, too. Make sure to tend to the garden of your learning, and in the end you'll reap a bountiful crop on your report card.

WACKY LAUGHS
Q. What did the mother buffalo say to her child when he left for school?
A. "Bison."

Q. What kind of candy do kids like best at school?
A. Recess Pieces

Q. What doctor writes permission slips to be late to school?
A. A tardy-ologist

✝ PRAY
Pray for wisdom to stay organized during the school year.

Life's Guidebook Says
As workers who tend a fig tree are allowed to eat the fruit, so workers who protect their employer's interests will be rewarded. PROVERBS 27:18

SEPTEMBER

REST EASY

JOSEPH FIXED A TRAY with a toaster pastry, orange juice, and some fruit. He carried the tray to his dad, who was still in bed.

"Dad, I made breakfast for you."

"Smells good. Any special reason?"

"It's Labor Day. Time for you to rest, since you work so hard."

"Thanks, Son." Joseph's dad took a bite.

It's sort of funny to call it "Labor Day," since *labor* means "to work" and Labor Day gives workers a day off. Oregon was the first state to celebrate Labor Day. But in 1894, Congress passed an act that made the first Monday in September a legal holiday. It's a day for workers to rest and for you to be thankful for the workers who made the United States great.

God rested on the seventh day after he created the world, plants, creatures, and people. He commanded us to rest on that day to honor him. Rest helps improve our brain's ability to solve problems and concentrate. Rest gives our bodies more energy, helping muscles to grow and allowing bones, muscles, tendons, and ligaments to repair themselves.

So take this Labor Day to lie in a hammock or sit back and do a little growing. Enjoy looking at the results of *your* work—like strong muscles, a clean room, a well-fed pet, and good grades. Balance your life with enough rest and you'll grow great too.

LIFTOFF LIST

Check what you do to rest. Cross off what is not resting.

____ Sit down to just relax.

____ Sleep at least eight hours a night.

____ Avoid too much caffeine (found in chocolate and some sodas). Caffeine can keep me from resting.

____ Keep the same bedtime, so my body is used to a routine.

____ Take a break after school before I start my homework.

____ Stop and think about the good work I did during the day.

____ Run a mile.

____ Wash floors and vacuum.

____ Relax on Sundays (or one other day) each week.

____ Pray and ask God to take care of my problems. Then trust God to help.

✝ PRAY

Ask God to help you let go of your worries so you can rest better.

Life's Guidebook Says

People should eat and drink and enjoy the fruits of their labor, for these are gifts from God. ECCLESIASTES 3:13

LET'S MAKE A DEAL!

WHAT WOULD YOU DO to get your favorite meal or snack?

1. _____
2. _____
3. _____

You may have written: "Clean my room," "Let my brother play with my newest toy," or "Wash the dishes." You might be willing to stand on your head or act like a chicken. You probably would not give up every toy and game you own for one meal. Some ideas sound silly, and others might actually be what your mom tells you to do before you can eat. In the Old Testament, a grown man gave up a lot for one bowl of stew (Genesis 25:27-34).

You might remember the story: Esau spent the day hunting but caught nothing. He walked miles and miles to check traps and waited for hours for an animal to come by. He worked up an appetite and was starving when he returned home. When he stepped inside the tent and took one whiff of his brother's stew, it smelled delicious. All he could think about was eating that stew. "Let me have a swallow of that red stew," he said.

"All right," Jacob replied, "but trade me your rights as firstborn son."

Gulp! That's a big swap! That meant letting Jacob be the leader of the family when their dad died. It also meant Jacob would inherit twice as much as Esau. That's a big price for one measly bowl of red stew. Esau's stomach growled. He agreed to the swap.

Don't be like Esau. Think about the consequences of your decisions in the long run, instead of what you want at the moment.

AWESOME ACTIVITY: LUNCH FOODS
Experiment with new lunch ideas.

Stuff You Need
☞ Pita bread
☞ Cold cuts or tuna salad
☞ Chopped veggies
☞ Grapes or cherries
☞ Nuts

Try It
1. Stuff a pita with meat, veggies, or tuna salad. Add grapes or pitted cherries to sweeten it. Add nuts for more crunch.
2. Or chop up the meat, veggies, fruit, and nuts. Mix it together for a dipping salad. Break the bread into bite-sized pieces. Use bread to scoop up the salad mixture.

✝ PRAY
Ask God to help you wait, think, and make wise choices.

Life's Guidebook Says
The LORD grants wisdom! From his mouth come knowledge and understanding.
PROVERBS 2:6

WHAT'S THAT FOOD?

DOES YOUR MOTHER ever serve something new at dinner? You look, take a sniff, and wonder, *Is that okay to eat?* Maybe you've had to ask, "What is that food?" (Hopefully, you didn't make a face when you asked the question.) It's healthy to try new foods. Maybe when you were little you didn't like the taste of fish. But if you try it again, you may discover that you like it now.

In the Old Testament (Numbers 16, to be precise), God sent some strange-looking food to the Israelites. They had no choice but to eat it, because they were in the middle of the desert with no grocery stores and zero fast-food places.

God promised to send bread to feed his people. The Israelites may have looked forward to some delicious flat bread with olive oil. But in the morning, they looked outside and spotted a strange layer of dew. When the dew melted, they saw little flakes of bread. They called it *manna*, which means "What is it?" They had never before seen anything like it.

Moses said, "It's the food the Lord has given you to eat." He told them to pick it up and eat it. They did. It tasted like honey wafers. *Not bad.* They baked it, boiled it, and found many ways to cook it. *Munch! Munch!* For 40 years, God sent the manna to his people as they wandered in the desert.

In your everyday life, be happy your mom gives you so many things to eat. Thank her, and thank God for your food.

AWESOME ACTIVITY: BANANA ROUNDS
Learn to make this yummy, healthy snack that uses fruit, grain, and milk.

Stuff You Need
- ☞ Sliced bananas
- ☞ Fork
- ☞ Milk
- ☞ Bowls of crushed cereal, crushed nuts, and coconut

Try It
1. Grab a banana slice with the fork. Dip the banana in the milk.
2. Dip the wet banana into a coating of your choice (cereal, nuts, coconut).
3. Make your own concoctions with yogurt, juice, melted chocolate, crushed crackers, or cookie crumbs.

✝ PRAY
Thank God for the huge variety of food that you can eat to stay healthy.

Life's Guidebook Says
The Israelites called the food manna. It was white like coriander seed, and it tasted like honey wafers. EXODUS 16:31

BUGGED

HAVE YOU EVER CHASED fireflies or caught a moth? Maybe you've put bugs in a little cage or a jar with holes poked in the top. You might have counted the legs, checked out the color, and looked for wings. But you probably have never tried to catch bugs to eat them. *Gross!*

In some cultures, people eat bugs as part of their everyday diet. Experts say the average person eats about two pounds of bugs every year! Some are in your foods. Others crawl in your mouth as you sleep. *Gulp!* John the Baptist ate locusts as his main diet (Matthew 3:4). He also ate honey, which sounds much tastier. John may have also eaten beans that grow on the locust tree. These can be crushed and used like flour to make bread. Still, John's diet sounds pretty *boring*.

You probably like lots of different foods, such as sandwiches, pancakes, ice cream, burgers, and chicken. You might have a favorite vegetable, like corn on the cob or tiny raw carrots. It's great that God gave us so many types of food.

There's a saying that some people *live to eat* while others *eat to live*. John the Baptist ate to fuel his body. He didn't think much about food. Knowing God and sharing his faith were more important to John than what he ate. God sent John to prepare people for the coming Messiah and to tell people to be sorry for their sins.

Be sure you spend more time thinking about God than about your next meal or snack.

WACKY LAUGHS
Q. Why did John the Baptist take off his sandals?
A. To save two more soles

Q. What do you give a skeleton for a snack?
A. Short ribs

Q. Why did the spaghetti stick together?
A. Because the cook used tomato paste

✝ PRAY
Pray before each meal to thank God for your food. Ask him to help you share what you've learned from the Bible.

Life's Guidebook Says
Jesus told [Satan], "No! The Scriptures say, 'People do not live by bread alone, but by every word that comes from the mouth of God.'" MATTHEW 4:4

STEWED

HAVE YOU EVER DONE an accidental science experiment in your fridge? You open a container of food and find green mold growing on it. *Gross!* When you see nasty things growing on your food, don't eat it. Toss it in the garbage.

Food is usually great, but there can be problems. Food may spoil when it gets old. Bacteria can grow in foods, especially chicken, causing food poisoning and illness. Some bacteria in food is so dangerous that it kills people. In the Old Testament, a group of prophets sat down to a meal and were accidentally almost poisoned. (You can read the story in 2 Kings 4:38-41.)

The prophet Elisha told a cook to make stew for the men. A young man went into a field to gather herbs to flavor the stew. He also picked some wild gourds. He chopped up the vegetables and added them to the stew without realizing they were poisonous. The men began to eat their meal and cried out, "There's poison in this stew!" It tasted so bad they knew it was poisoned. Elisha calmly asked for some flour and threw it in the pot.

"Now it's all right," he said. "Go ahead and eat."

It tasted fine. No poison remained.

Flour doesn't cure poison, so don't try this at home. But God used it to purify that pot of stew. Elisha listened closely to God, and God used him to perform numerous miracles. Make sure you listen to God and follow his commands too.

WEIRD FACTS: HEALTHIEST FOODS TO EAT

☞ Almonds are a great snack—high in protein for strong muscles and calcium to help grow strong bones.

☞ Apples contain vitamin C and help your body absorb iron to build red blood cells.

☞ Broccoli helps keep your heart healthy.

☞ Spinach contains iron, magnesium, calcium, and vitamins A and C, which are good for you.

☞ Kids who eat a healthier breakfast do better in school, get better test scores, and are able to sit still longer than kids who skip breakfast or eat foods with lots of sugar.

✝ PRAY

Thank God for creating healthy foods. Ask him to help you make good choices on what to eat and to help you resist eating too much sugar.

Life's Guidebook Says

Elisha said, "Bring me some flour." Then he threw it into the pot and said, "Now it's all right; go ahead and eat." And then [the stew] did not harm them.
2 KINGS 4:41

ENDLESS BUFFET

ALL YOU CAN EAT! Sounds great. You can fill your stomach with lots of choices on a long buffet.

Not everyone gets all the food they need. One out of three people in the world are starving. They don't have enough food to keep their bodies alive. Even where you live, statistics show people are hungry. In a small town in Florida, a lady known as Miss Irene collects food for needy people. She hears about families who might need help, then she fills baskets of food and knocks on their doors. One time a woman answered and cried, "I didn't know what I would give my son tonight. I only had one cup of rice in the house. My husband just got a job, but he won't get paid for a week."

Miss Irene hugged the woman and gently scolded her. "We have a food pantry at the church, and there's always plenty. You just call if you need anything."

Hunger is not a new problem. In 1 Kings 17:8-16, the prophet Elijah met a widow gathering sticks. He asked her for water and a little bread.

"I don't have a single piece of bread in the house," she said. "And I have only a handful of flour left in the jar and a little cooking oil in the bottom of the jug. I was just gathering a few sticks to cook this last meal, and then my son and I will die" (17:12).

How sad. Elijah told the woman not to worry. He said her jars of oil and flour would not run out. *Hooray!* The containers didn't run out until the famine ended. She and her son enjoyed an endless bread buffet.

God can supply our needs and also use other people to help. You can help feed the hungry by bringing canned food to a food pantry.

LIFTOFF LIST

Check off ways you can help hungry people.

___ Skip dessert at restaurants or snacks from the vending machine to save money for the poor.

___ Donate canned goods to a food pantry.

___ Volunteer at a food pantry to sort and help package food.

___ Grow vegetables to share with neighbors.

✝ PRAY

Ask God to help you care about those in need like he does.

Life's Guidebook Says

The LORD, the God of Israel, says: There will always be flour and olive oil left in your containers until the time when the LORD sends rain and the crops grow again! 1 KINGS 17:14

GOOD AND PLENTY

SWIFTY: SWIFTY HERE, the top reporter with *Pharisee Nightly News*. I'm checking into a report of an endless buffet for a crowd of thousands that began with a little boy's lunch. I suspect there's a trick involved. Excuse me, may I examine your sack?

Boy: Okay, but it's empty.

Swifty: *Hmm.* Let me feel inside. Not very deep.

Boy: It was big enough for some bread and dried fish.

Swifty: But you supplied the food for a huge crowd. People filled the whole hillside!

Boy: I think there were around 5,000 men. That doesn't include women or children.

Swifty: But everyone ate their fill of food, and there was plenty left over. Are you a magician?

Boy: I'm just a regular kid who gave his lunch to Jesus.

Swifty: Where'd Jesus get the rest of the food? Did he steal it?

Boy: No, he prayed.

Swifty: He prayed? Sounds fishy.

Boy: And bready. *Ha!* But seriously, he broke the bread and asked his helpers to pass out the food.

Swifty: His helpers? They must've been hiding extra food the whole time.

Boy: We would have noticed if they'd been carrying that much food around. Each just had a piece of bread and a fish. They broke what they had and kept passing it out.

Swifty: They must have had some food up their sleeves.

Boy: They didn't. It was a miracle. Jesus prayed and multiplied the food [John 6:1-14].

Swifty: There you have it. I've never known anyone who got such great answers to prayer. I'll be keeping my eye and camera on Jesus. Maybe he'll feed me next time!

PUZZLE IT OUT: REBUS PICTURE PUZZLE

Solve the picture clues to find out more about Jesus.

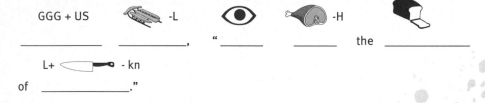

GGG + US   -L   -H

_____ _____, "_____ _____ the _____

L+ _____ - kn

of _____."

✝ PRAY

Thank God that he feeds you both physically and spiritually.

Life's Guidebook Says

Jesus told [Thomas], "You believe because you have seen me. Blessed are those who believe without seeing me." JOHN 20:29

Answer: Jesus said, "I am the bread of life."

BEACH PARTY

WHAT'S YOUR FAVORITE PLACE for a picnic? Some families go to a park or drive to the mountains. If you live near the beach, a picnic can be the perfect way to spend the day. Plenty of food and games to play . . . and some wind to keep the mosquitoes away. Plus, you can swim, build sand castles, play beach volleyball, and enjoy time in the sun.

Stephen lives in Maryland. He likes picnics at the beach, but his favorite thing to do in the ocean is no picnic. During the freezing days of January, Stephen takes an icy dip. No, he's not a fan of hypothermia. He does it to help people by participating in the Polar Bear Plunge. At the beach every year, thousands of people get wet—and cold—to raise money for the Special Olympics. There's also a big carnival with face painting, food, and games.

Jesus and his disciples enjoyed a cool beach party after he rose from the grave. John 21 tells how Jesus started a fire on the beach and waited for his friends. His disciples had been fishing all night, but they hadn't caught anything. As they went by on their boat, Jesus told them to cast their net on the right side. At first they didn't recognize him, but they followed his advice. *Splash!* The net went in the water and filled with fish. *Double splash!* Peter dove in and swam to shore to be with Jesus, who was cooking fish and also had some bread. Water, food, and helping people still go together today.

AWESOME ACTIVITY: MAKE A SLUSHY

Stuff You Need
- ☞ Clear sealable bags, 1 small (sandwich size) and 1 large (food storage size)
- ☞ 3 tablespoons kosher or rock salt
- ☞ Crushed ice to half-fill the larger bag
- ☞ 1 cup of juice
- ☞ Straw

Try It
1. Pour juice into the smaller bag. Seal it.
2. Pour the ice and salt into the large bag.
3. Put the small bag inside the large bag. Seal the large bag.
4. Shake the bag for several minutes.
5. Put the straw in the small bag and take a sip.

✝ PRAY
Ask God to help you find fun ways to help other people.

Life's Guidebook Says
When [the disciples] got [to the beach], they found breakfast waiting for them— fish cooking over a charcoal fire, and some bread. JOHN 21:9

· CHALLENGED

LIST THREE THINGS you've accomplished that you thought would be too hard to do:

1. _____
2. _____
3. _____

Maybe you put down a school project, making a team, learning a skateboard trick, or hiking 10 miles. Congratulations! Challenges push you to try harder and achieve a goal.

Every year students at Heritage High School in Colorado hold Make a Difference Week as a challenge to raise money to help people. In 2013, Nate Novotny and his classmates decided to create a challenge course to raise money for a very special cause. One of the school's past graduates, Navy SEAL Danny Dietz, died serving in Afghanistan. The students chose to raise money for two organizations in his honor. One organization, named after Danny, trains youth to be leaders and understand the importance of teamwork. The other, run by the only survivor of the attack that killed Danny, helps war survivors heal. Nate and his classmates created a course of challenges, such as building marshmallow towers or flinging tennis balls.

Nate and his friends made fun challenges. Other challenges are more difficult. Some people look at Jesus as an obstacle. They don't believe he was God's Son and died for their sins. The Bible calls Jesus a stumbling block (1 Peter 2:8). Some people refuse to trust him and end up stumbling through life. Others trust Jesus to help them overcome problems. When you put your faith in Jesus, he strengthens you to meet the challenges of life.

AWESOME ACTIVITY: TEAM-BUILDING CHALLENGES
Gather friends, divide into teams, and try a few challenges:

- ☞ Give groups egg cartons to build towers that will be tested to see whether they can hold an egg on top without the egg falling and breaking. The tallest tower that passes the test wins.
- ☞ Hide jigsaw puzzle pieces with a colored dot on the back to match team colors. See which team finds all their pieces and completes the puzzle first.
- ☞ Have team members build towers with balloons and static electricity. See who can use the most balloons in their towers.

✝ PRAY
Ask God to help you see problems as a challenge that will help you become a stronger person.

Life's Guidebook Says
"He is the stone that makes people stumble, the rock that makes them fall." They stumble because they do not obey God's word, and so they meet the fate that was planned for them. 1 PETER 2:8

LONG-LASTING HEADACHE

DANIEL'S HEAD started hurting at age 11. This wasn't a little headache that medicine could cure. His head hurt all day and night, month after month, without ever stopping. Doctors ran many tests and tried different medications, but nothing helped. Daniel said it felt like "something is trying to split my head open, and they turned up the volume of the world. Even a whisper hurts. I feel like I'm in a torture chamber in a prison."

Daniel changed to a school that allowed him to work at his own pace and rest his head when he felt like he couldn't do anything. He still got As but spent a lot of time in bed. He graduated and started college with the same headache. He took a few courses at a time, so he could manage his pain.

One night at a church prayer meeting, people prayed for Daniel again. This time his head stopped hurting. For the first time in 11 years, his head didn't hurt. He smiled and laughed and felt good. A few years have passed since God healed Daniel's head, and he still feels good.

Prisons don't always come with bars. Our health or fears can become like a prison. It's hard to trust God when months go by without God answering your prayers. Sometimes you can wonder if he hears you. Joseph, the great-grandson of Abraham, spent years in a real prison, where he continued to trust God (Genesis 39:20-21). His prayers seemed to go unanswered, but God had a plan all along. In God's perfect timing, Joseph was released from prison and became a great leader. God turned bad things into good (Genesis 50:20). God's timing is always perfect, even when we have to wait.

WACKY LAUGHS

Q. How does an elephant climb a tree?
A. It sits on an acorn and waits.

Q. How do you get rid of a headache?
A. Break a window. It will get rid of the pane.

✝ PRAY

Ask God to help you trust even when he takes a long time to answer a prayer. Keep praying.

Life's Guidebook Says
[Joseph said,] "You intended to harm me, but God intended it all for good. He brought me to this position so I could save the lives of many people."
GENESIS 50:20

PATRIOT'S DAY

TODAY WE REMEMBER a sad day in the history of the United States. In 2001, terrorists hijacked airplanes and turned them into weapons. Airplanes hit the Twin Towers in New York City and the Pentagon in Washington, DC. Many people died. But on one hijacked plane, the passengers stood against the attackers and forced the plane to crash into a field in Pennsylvania instead of a building in Washington. They didn't let anyone make them too afraid to stand up and fight.

One of the men on that plane, Todd Beamer, prayed the Lord's Prayer over the phone before he helped lead an attack on the cockpit. Todd believed in God and knew the Lord would take care of his family if he died. After Todd and some other passengers came up with a plan, he quietly said, "Let's roll." His words were some of the last heard from that plane. They overpowered the terrorists that day and brought hope. They showed that we don't have to let fear overcome us. Todd and his fellow passengers knew they would die, but they also knew their choice would save lives.

Celebrate freedom today, and remember the people who died so you could live freely. Today's also a day to pray for peace. The anger in people who want to hurt others reminds us how much everyone needs God.

LIFTOFF LIST
In what ways do you show love for your country?

___ I pray for my country.
___ I wear my country's colors on holidays.
___ I honor the men and women who serve in the military.
___ I show respect to police, firefighters, and others who help people.
___ I display my country's flag.
___ I write letters to my leaders to thank them for their work.
___ I pick up litter to help my country look beautiful.
___ I obey the laws of my country.
___ I read about heroes and heroines who fought for peace.

✝ PRAY
Pray for courage, and pray for God to protect your country and give its leaders wisdom.

Life's Guidebook Says
Do not be afraid of the terrors of the night, nor the arrow that flies in the day.
PSALM 91:5

WHERE THERE'S A WILL, THERE'S A WAY

"HEY, DAD, I want to be a mountain climber when I grow up."

"That's a lofty ambition, Dan, but you need to figure out what to do while you climb mountains."

"Huh? I'll just get to the top."

"Son, most people won't even give you a dollar to climb a mountain. So you need to find a way to earn money as you climb."

Dan Doody thought about his dad's comments. He paced up and down a hill and prayed. He stood at the top of the hill and looked down. Everything looked as pretty as a picture. He thought, *That's it!* He saved money for a camera that he could wear around his head when he climbed. He worked hard at learning how to take great photos. He learned to take photos one at a time as a flower opened or an ant moved a crumb to show the whole process. That's called time-lapse photography.

Dan took such great pictures and learned to climb so well that a magazine hired him to snap pictures on many mountain-climbing trips, including Mount Everest—the highest peak in the world.

Creative thinking helps you find solutions. A few men thought of something new when they wanted Jesus to heal their friend. Jesus was preaching in a house, surrounded by crowds of people. The men couldn't get close to Jesus, so they carried their friend onto the roof, cut a hole, and lowered him down to where Jesus was standing (Mark 2:1-12). Jesus appreciated the friends' creativity and healed the man. As you seek God's will for your life, be creative. You may be amazed at how God blesses you when you put your mind to solving a problem.

PUZZLE IT OUT: REVERSE THINKING

See if you can figure this one out. It reminds you what to do if you need to find a new solution.

> .noitɔɘɿib wɘᴎ ɒ ni ʞoo⅃

Hint: Hold it up to a mirror.

✝ PRAY

Ask God to help you think creatively.

Life's Guidebook Says

They couldn't bring him to Jesus because of the crowd, so they dug a hole through the roof above his head. Then they lowered the man on his mat, right down in front of Jesus. MARK 2:4

FAILURE THAT OPENS DOORS

JAMIE TRIED BUILDING a model of the town library. *Crash!* It collapsed. He kept trying, but his ideas kept failing.

"Mom," Jamie said, "I give up. I'll never finish my school project."

"Do you know enough about the library to write a report?" she asked.

"Yeah, but that's boring. I wanted to show the building."

Jamie thought and thought. Finally, he said, "Maybe I could make something with doors and windows like an advent calendar. Then inside each window I could write a fact about the library." He got red poster board and a white marker to make his poster look like a brick building. Jamie started working and completed the project.

A few days later Jamie rushed in the door. "Mom, I got an A for my library project! The teacher said I should even take it to the library." The librarians loved the poster and hung it in the main entrance, where children could open the doors and windows to learn about the library.

Have you ever run into a project that made you want to give up? Jesus told the story of a man who planted a fig tree but couldn't get it to bear fruit. When he was about to cut it down, the gardener asked for one more year to try some different ideas (Luke 13:8).

Don't quit. Talk about your challenges and look for new ideas. If you have a problem you need to overcome, discuss it with your parents today.

AWESOME ACTIVITY: OPEN-DOOR REPORTS

Stuff You Need
- ☞ Poster board
- ☞ Large piece of paper
- ☞ Pencil
- ☞ Paper
- ☞ Scissors
- ☞ Double-sided tape

Try It
1. Draw a large shape on the poster board. It might be an animal, building, or other shape to show your topic.
2. Cut a matching shape out of paper.
3. On the poster board, draw squares for windows (or eyes, etc., for an animal).
4. Cut three sides of each window, so it can open.
5. Use double-sided tape to attach the poster board over the paper. Don't put tape in the openings.
6. Open each door or window and write a fact inside.

✝ PRAY
Pray for patience and endurance to keep trying new solutions when you fail.

Life's Guidebook Says
The gardener answered, "Sir, give it one more chance. Leave it another year, and I'll give it special attention and plenty of fertilizer." LUKE 13:8

THE FLAME

A FIRE ALMOST KILLED Nassie when he was a boy. While home alone, he had made a mistake that started the fire. He didn't want other children to suffer like he did or burn down their homes, so he started teaching fire safety. He made up a one-man show and called himself The Flame. He wore a red cape and helped firefighters teach kids about the dangers of fire. By the time he finished high school, Nassie had spoken about fire safety to hundreds of groups and schools.

Nassie had received a second chance to live when firefighters saved him. He used his new lease on life to help other people. Jesus loves to see people turn mistakes into opportunities to help others. Jesus told his close friend Peter that Peter would fail him. But Jesus said the failure would become an opportunity for Peter to strengthen Christian brothers (Luke 22:31-34). He knew Peter would deny him. He also knew that once Peter came back to serving the Lord, he would help others be more faithful. *Cock-a-doodle-doo!* Like Jesus foretold, Peter denied him three times before a rooster crowed. Peter wept once he heard the rooster. But instead of wallowing in failure, he made a U-turn and led the early church. He preached and wrote to help others grow in their faith.

If you make a mistake, think of how you can make a U-turn too. Use what you learned to help others.

EXPERIMENT: BUBBLING SALT

Jesus calls Christians to be the salt of the earth. Like the salt in this experiment, we should bubble to the top.

Stuff You Need
- ☞ Empty water bottle or glass
- ☞ Water
- ☞ Cooking oil
- ☞ Food coloring
- ☞ Salt (sea salt is best)

Try It
1. Fill the bottle halfway with water.
2. Add oil almost to the top.
3. Add a few drops of food coloring.
4. Sprinkle a spoonful of salt into the bottle. Watch the salt crystals bubble up and down.

✝ PRAY

Ask God to help you learn from your mistakes and teach others.

Life's Guidebook Says
[Jesus said,] "I have pleaded in prayer for you, Simon, that your faith should not fail. So when you have repented and turned to me again, strengthen your brothers." LUKE 22:32

CARE PACKAGES FOR GRANDMA

CHRISTIAN'S GRANDMA had liver cancer. She wouldn't live long. Christian's home was too far away to visit her. He had spent many summer vacations with her and had lots of fun, so he wanted to show his love. His family decided to send Grandma little presents to open each day. Christian made a special craft with a note that said, "God will watch over you, Grandma." His family filled a box with pictures they drew, letters, photos, a stuffed animal, and other gifts.

Every few weeks they sent another package. Christian's grandpa said it made Grandma smile each day when she opened another little gift. She lived only a few months, but Christian felt glad that he had sent her good-bye gifts. He would always remember the good times they'd had together.

Knowing that someone will die isn't easy. The night before Jesus died, he had supper with his friends, sang a song, and went to a garden to pray. Jesus knew he would die. He also knew he would come back to life. We know that believers will live forever in heaven, but it's still sad to lose someone. This sadness is called grief. Keeping their photos and remembering the good times can be great ways to honor that person.

AWESOME ACTIVITY: STARRY CARDS
When you know someone is sick, send a card . . . and a smile.

Stuff You Need
- ☞ Paper
- ☞ Magazine pictures
- ☞ Markers or colored pencils
- ☞ Star stickers

Try It
1. Fold the paper in half to make a card.
2. Decorate the front with a sky scene. Add star stickers and draw planets.
3. Write, "You make the universe a better place."
4. Inside write a note and add, "I'm praying for you."

✝ PRAY
Pray for people who are sick, especially people you love.

Life's Guidebook Says
Jesus told them, "The Son of Man is going to be betrayed into the hands of his enemies. He will be killed, but on the third day he will be raised from the dead." And the disciples were filled with grief. MATTHEW 17:22-23

COPY THAT

THEODORE TRENDY knew all the coolest things. When everybody had an iPhone, he owned a jPhone—the next generation. He wore dark-wash, organic cotton jeans with T-shirts that were made from recycled plastic bottles. His glasses were imported from Italy. He watched all the entertainment shows and the latest movies to see how Hollywood stars wore their hair.

Theodore looked cool, but he also talked cool. He knew if things were *tight, rad, cray-cray, cool, hot,* or not. Girls liked him and boys wanted to be like him . . . until they tried to have a conversation. All Theodore knew was what it took to be popular. He was cool—but boring.

Maybe you've met kids like Theodore. They've got a good-looking exterior, but are sort of shallow when you get to know them. The Bible says not to copy the world. God doesn't care if you know the latest music or have watched the newest movies. Instead of worrying about being cool, he wants you to concentrate on becoming more like him. When you follow the world, you can get off God's path. That makes it more difficult to follow him. But when you focus on transforming yourself into being more like Jesus, you'll find yourself naturally following God's will for your life.

God has a perfect plan for your life . . . and it's supercool to find it and follow it.

QUIZ: WHAT'S COOL?
Can you match these ways to say "cool" to the decade when they were the popular thing to say?

1. Sweet	a. 1940s
2. Gnarly	b. 1990s
3. Phat	c. 2000s
4. Groovy	d. 1960s
5. Cool	e. 1980s

✝ PRAY
Tell God you don't want to be like the world. Commit to acting and thinking the way he does.

Life's Guidebook Says
Don't copy the behavior and customs of this world, but let God transform you into a new person by changing the way you think. Then you will learn to know God's will for you, which is good and pleasing and perfect. ROMANS 12:2

Answer: 1. c; 2. e; 3. b; 4. d; 5. a

· STICKY GAME

IN KOREA, children play a game called *yut* (sounds like *yoot*) with small sticks they toss in the air. Each stick has a flat side and a round side. Players watch how the sticks land and score points based on how many sticks land flat side up. You score the most points when all four land round side up (called a *mo*). The players move a stone, called a *mal*, along a simple game board they draw. This game began centuries ago and stuck with the culture. Traditionally, in Korea, kids play it on New Year's Day, but it can be enjoyed year-round.

Traditions keep families close. God gave the Israelites traditions and holy days to remind the people that he cares for them. One of these days was Passover, which celebrates God saving the firstborn sons of Israelite families when they were in Egypt. Egyptian children weren't so fortunate. This was the last plague, the one that finally made Pharaoh release God's people. Part of the tradition is to eat standing up, while holding a staff in your hand. Jewish families still celebrate Passover today.

Think of traditions in your family, such as special games you play or holiday activities. Make sure to take photos next time you enjoy a family tradition.

AWESOME ACTIVITY: TALKING STICKS
The Passover tradition includes having the youngest child in a family ask questions to start a conversation about the tradition. Make a talking stick for your family to use to take turns talking about family traditions.

Stuff You Need
- ☞ One foot-long stick
- ☞ Sandpaper
- ☞ Paint or ribbons

Try It
1. Smooth the stick by snapping off sharp points and sanding the ends and rough areas.
2. Decorate the stick by tying on ribbons or painting stripes and designs.
3. To use the stick, sit down with your family. Only the person holding the stick can talk. Let the youngest person in your family hold it first to ask a question about family traditions. Let everyone take turns answering the question.

✝ PRAY
Ask God to help you remember what your parents teach you about him.

Life's Guidebook Says
This is a day to remember. Each year, from generation to generation, you must celebrate it as a special festival to the LORD.   EXODUS 12:14

SHEPHERD'S STAFF

DAVIE POKED the ewe softly with his shepherd's staff. The female sheep that he called Rudi was one of his favorites. He caught Rudi's head in the crook of his staff and gently pulled her head back so she would lie down without getting hurt. She needed to lie down to give birth to woolly twin lambs.

Rudi fought against the staff for a moment. But she trusted the young shepherd and lay down. Soon her babies were safely born, and she began to clean and nuzzle them.

A shepherd's staff has many uses. It can guide a sheep, be used to pull a sheep from a hole, or help a sheep lie down to have her babies.

We can sometimes act like sheep. We don't understand why God would allow us to fall down, or we fight against him when he's trying to guide us away from trouble. We need to trust God. He knows what's best for us . . . just like a shepherd knows what's best for his sheep.

LIFTOFF LIST

Jesus is the Good Shepherd (John 10:11). Check off what you'd like the Good Shepherd to do for you:

___ The shepherd's rod is used to part thick wool to examine the skin and make sure the animal is healthy. I'll let Jesus check my heart for problems.

___ A shepherd's rod is used to drive away wolves and snakes. I will trust God to protect me from enemies.

___ A shepherd does not beat the sheep but gently places the staff against the sheep and applies pressure to guide the sheep in the right direction. I will allow Jesus to guide me.

___ A shepherd uses the staff to pull sheep out of a bramble bush. I know Jesus is the one who can get me out of bad situations when I am stuck.

___ A shepherd's crook pulls the sheep back to safety. Christ can pull me close to him to keep me safe.

✝ PRAY

Ask Jesus to be your shepherd, and commit to following him.

Life's Guidebook Says

The LORD is my shepherd; I have all that I need.   PSALM 23:1

SAVED!

QUESTION: WHAT ARE THE HARDEST three outs to get in baseball?
Answer: The last three.

For nearly 19 years, New York Yankees pitcher Mariano Rivera made his living getting the last three outs. His job as the closer was to enter the game when the Yankees had a small lead and wrap up the victory. It's a role packed with pressure . . . and Mariano thrived in it, thanks to a pitch that God gave him.

You see, Mariano loved to play baseball, but he loved God more. He knew his abilities came from the Lord. Before a game early in his career, Mariano was playing catch with a fellow pitcher. Mariano was fiddling with how he gripped and released the ball. All of a sudden, the other pitcher had trouble catching the ball because it dipped and darted at the last moment. Mariano kept working on that throw until he developed his signature cut fastball.

"That is my miracle pitch," Mariano told pastor Dewey Friedel in an interview. "That's what I call it, because it's God's gifting. I didn't have that pitch before, and nobody taught me that. It came as a miracle."

Mariano threw his cut fastball nearly 90 percent of the time. The best batters in the world knew it was coming, and they still couldn't hit it. On this day in 2011, Mariano broke the all-time saves record by notching his 602nd. He retired from baseball at the end of the 2013 season with 652 saves—that's how many times he saved a game by clinching a New York win.

Just like Mariano always came through for the Yankees, God will always come through for you. He not only saves the game—Jesus saves your life.

PUZZLE IT OUT: MISSING WORD

Look closely at the words below. One letter is missing from the second word in each pair. Write that letter in the spaces to discover the missing word from the verse.

1. lady	day
2. yoke	key
3. drink	kind
4. band	nab

"Believe in the __ __ __ __ Jesus and you will be saved." —Acts 16:31
           1 2 3 4

✝ PRAY

Thank God for saving you.

Life's Guidebook Says

God saved you by his grace when you believed. And you can't take credit for this; it is a gift from God. EPHESIANS 2:8

Answer: Lord

STICKING TOGETHER

"IF YOU HAVE A KNIFE and a little bit of twine, you can survive for days in the forest," Jeremy's dad said. He had been in the Special Forces but now taught survival training. Jeremy and his friends paid attention to every word Dad said and every action he made.

Jeremy's dad showed the boys how to use twine and knots to lash sticks together and make a shelter. "Shelter is key to survival," Dad said. To lash sticks, he demonstrated how to wrap the twine or rope around the sticks and start and end with a clove hitch or square knot. The boys practiced the knots and used small sticks and string to try lashing. Then they gathered long sticks and lashed together tables, benches, and even a tower. Jeremy's dad talked about the importance of finding water and building a fire to stay alive. "And if you're ever lost in the forest," he added, "stay put and build a shelter to keep warm until you're found."

God likes to find things and put them back together. He does that a lot with people. He mends what is broken. In the Old Testament, he told his prophet Ezekiel to find two pieces of wood. On one piece, God instructed Ezekiel to write the names of the tribes who stood with Judah. On the other stick, he wrote Ephraim's names—the tribes of northern Israel. These tribes had argued and split up. God told Ezekiel to join the sticks together to show he wanted his people reunited (Ezekiel 37:15-22).

God wants his followers to be united. God's body works best when it works together. You can show an attitude of togetherness by being cooperative when you work with people and being enthusiastic when you do group projects.

WACKY LAUGHS

Q. What do you call a boomerang that doesn't work?
A. A stick.

Q. Why don't magnets get lost?
A. Because they stick together.

Q. What's brown and sticky?
A. A stick.

Q. What does a stick draw?
A. Stick figures.

✝ PRAY

Ask God for you to get along with other Christians, including ones who attend a different church.

Life's Guidebook Says
Make me truly happy by agreeing wholeheartedly with each other, loving one another, and working together with one mind and purpose.
PHILIPPIANS 2:2

IMPOSSIBLE FLOAT

"I CAN MAKE a rock float," Juan said.

"I don't believe it," Bruce said. "Show me."

Juan tied a rock to a large piece of bark. He set it in the water and it floated.

"That's cheating," Bruce said. "The rock's in a boat."

Juan laughed. "I never said the rock would float on its own."

Heavy objects sink pretty fast. Yet a boat floats and can carry heavy objects without sinking. To float, the object must displace, or push, water out of the way. As this happens, a force called buoyancy pushes upward. A boat may look heavier than water, but to determine whether or not it can float, you need to make many measurements, including the air inside the boat, the total volume, and weight. There's a lot of science in how boats are made.

Some ships are designed to carry huge loads. If you see a tanker full of oil, the hull sinks deeper in the water. Once the oil is unloaded, the ship rides higher, with more of the hull floating out of the water. Naval architects and other experts work together to create amazing floating ships.

A floating miracle occurred in the Old Testament. A worker building a meeting hall dropped an ax head, and it sank into the Jordan River. He cried to the prophet Elisha for help. Elisha threw a stick where the ax had sunk. Suddenly, the ax miraculously floated. The man got back the tool he needed (2 Kings 6:1-7). When you turn to God, he can accomplish wonders that nobody can fathom. Science cannot explain what happened with the ax, but God controls everything and can meet all our needs . . . even the need for the right tool.

EXPERIMENT: MAKE AN EGG RISE

Use salt to change the density of water and lift up an egg.

Stuff You Need

☞ Salt

☞ Glass

☞ Water

☞ Egg

Try It

1. Dump six tablespoons of salt into the bottom of a glass.
2. Slowly add one cup of water without stirring.
3. Lower an egg into the salt water. It will sink. It may take several hours, but the salt will dissolve in the water and the egg will rise.

✝ PRAY

Praise God for his unlimited abilities.

Life's Guidebook Says

Seek the Kingdom of God above all else, and live righteously, and he will give you everything you need. MATTHEW 6:33

STAFF DEVELOPMENT

HAVE YOU EVER SEEN somebody use a walking stick on a long hike? List a few reasons why a walking stick might be a good idea:

1. _____
2. _____
3. _____

Maybe you wrote that it can get rid of spider webs, help when you're tired, or keep you balanced while crossing a stream. You'd be right. A walking stick has many purposes. It can be used to mark your path, draw a tic-tac-toe game in the dirt, and provide protection against a curious animal. If you fall and hurt your ankle, the stick can even become a crutch.

In the Old Testament, God used sticks to show the people his choice for high priest. Some of the Israelites had grumbled and rebelled against Moses and Aaron as their leaders. It was a *sticky* situation. (*Ha, ha.*) God told Moses to write one family name on a staff for each of the 12 tribes. Moses left the 12 rods next to the Ark of the Covenant in the Tabernacle. If a staff grew buds, then that person would be named high priest. The next morning Aaron's staff had sprouted blossoms and even grown ripe almonds (Numbers 17:8)! God instructed Moses to leave Aaron's staff next to the Ark as a warning to those who complained against the Lord's leaders.

God understands your doubts. But when God shows his power time and again, he also wants your trust. Jesus appeared before Thomas and told him to put his finger in the wound in his side. God made Aaron's staff bud and produce almonds. Thousands of pages of manuscripts and museums full of evidence show the Bible is true. Jesus lives up to his claim of being God's Son. Know that your faith is based on fact. And if you see friends starting to rebel or doubt, remind them of God's power . . . even if you don't have a blooming staff.

PLEXER
See if you can solve this plexer. (If you don't remember what a plexer is, see p. 9.)

```
B   B   B
 U   U   U
  D D D
    S
    T
    I
    C
    K
```

✝ PRAY
Thank God for being worthy of your trust and for the plans he has for you.

Life's Guidebook Says
"I know the plans I have for you," says the LORD. "They are plans for good and not for disaster, to give you a future and a hope." JEREMIAH 29:11

Answer: Budding stick

MOVING PLANS

"Chad, this will be your room."

"Wow. It's huge!"

"Let's measure it and you can draw it on your computer at home," Dad said. "That way you can plan where to put your bed and other things."

Chad and his dad each held an end of a long measuring tape. Chad wrote down the lengths of each side of the room, the height of the windowsills, and measurements for the door.

"Now I need to measure my desk, bed, and dresser when I get home."

When they got back, Chad measured his furniture and entered all of the data in his computer. He used drawing software to create a floor plan and move around the desk, bed, and other items to plan his room's layout.

Measurements help us figure out things. We measure lots of things—ingredients for recipes, how far we can jump, or how much we can lift. You might have a special spot in your home where your parents measure your height as you grow.

John the apostle saw a gold measuring stick in heaven. This happened as John had a vision of the future. An angel holding a gold measuring stick was measuring the new Jerusalem that God will send to earth in the future. The measurements show it is huge and demonstrate God's power.

As you track your growth, don't forget to measure yourself against God. You'll never be able to grow to his height, but you should strive to become as close to him as you can.

WEIRD FACTS: MEASUREMENTS

☞ The average human nose is more than two inches long.

☞ Your body has enough iron in it to make an iron nail three inches long.

☞ Your eyes never grow. They remain the same size as the day you were born.

☞ You would measure taller in space because there's no gravity to pull you down.

✝ PRAY

Ask God to help you to always measure yourself against your Savior, because Jesus is the one you want to become like.

Life's Guidebook Says

You must grow in the grace and knowledge of our Lord and Savior Jesus Christ.
2 PETER 3:18

TOO MUCH BREAD

"Hey, Mom, did you mean to get all this bread?" Daniel asked as he helped her put away the groceries.

"Oh, no!" Mom said. "It looks like your dad and I both picked up bread and a few other things, like extra eggs and milk. We should make French toast."

"Sounds good."

A few hours later, Daniel's friend Jeff came over to spend the night.

"Mom," Daniel said, "Jeff is really hungry. Can you make extra French toast and bacon?"

Daniel's mom nodded.

At dinner, Jeff devoured his food as soon as it hit his plate.

"This is great," Jeff said. "I haven't eaten all day."

As they talked more, Daniel's parents discovered that Jeff's dad had lost his job.

The next morning, Daniel snuck downstairs before Jeff woke up and found his mom. "Mom, I think God let us buy extra food for Jeff and his family."

Mom smiled. "I was thinking the same thing. You can pack the bread, eggs, milk, and cereal in a box." Daniel added his favorite snacks and a package of microwave popcorn, too.

When Jeff's mom came to pick him up, she went home with more than just her son.

God wants us to share what we have and to give it cheerfully. When we share, even if it means having a little less, it reflects God's giving nature and how he sacrificed for us. Is there anything you could give up so that your family might have a little extra money to help hungry people? Talk about it, and come up with a plan to help friends—or even people you don't know—get enough to eat.

LIFTOFF LIST

Check off ways you can help the less fortunate in your area (make sure to get your parents' permission first):

___ Check your family's pantry and give away extra food.

___ Use some money you saved to buy rice, soup, or pasta.

___ Have a yard sale and use the money to feed the hungry.

___ Make sandwiches for a homeless shelter.

___ Go through your clothes and toys. Donate stuff in good condition to a homeless shelter.

✝ PRAY

If you know a family in need, pray for ways to help. Ask God to help your unemployed friends and family members find jobs.

Life's Guidebook Says

You must each decide in your heart how much to give. And don't give reluctantly or in response to pressure. "For God loves a person who gives cheerfully."
2 CORINTHIANS 9:7

SWEET MONEY

DARYL SAW THE COST of the science trip and cringed. His dad didn't have a job, and his mother made very little money. He raised his hand and asked, "Could we sell candy to raise money to help pay our way?"

The teacher checked with the school office and organized a fund-raiser. Jordan liked the idea, too, because his family didn't have enough money for the trip. "I'm going to sell more candy than you," he said to Daryl.

That weekend, Daryl checked with the grocery store near his house, and the manager agreed he could sell the candy in front of the store. Daryl stood there every day and sold chocolate bars. At the end of the month, he had earned enough to go on the trip to the space center. A few other kids also earned money for the science trip by selling candy, but Jordan wasn't one of them. He kept talking about selling it but never put in the work.

Sometimes we need to figure out ways to earn money for something we want. The Bible tells us that work brings profit. But being lazy or saying you'll do something and not following through will get you nowhere. It's good to make a plan and earn money to reach your goals.

WEIRD FACTS: MONEY

☞ The US $20 bill is the most counterfeited currency in the world.

☞ Long ago, cows and other animals were used instead of money.

☞ Shells were used as coins for hundreds of years.

☞ People used to shave the edge off coins to skim off a little extra gold or silver. Ridges were added to edges of coins to stop the shaving problem. A quarter has 119 grooves around the edge.

☞ Heads or tails? The head side of a coin weighs more than the side called tails. So when you flip a coin, it actually comes up tails more often.

✝ PRAY

Ask God to give you ideas for ways to earn money for something you want or to raise money to help other people.

Life's Guidebook Says
Work brings profit, but mere talk leads to poverty!   PROVERBS 14:23

BREAD STAND

MASON AND HIS BROTHER looked at the counter piled high with zucchini.

"I don't think I can eat another bite of zucchini," Ben said, "not even zucchini muffins."

"We'd get rich if we could sell it," Mason said.

"That's it! Let's make zucchini bread and have a bread stand."

The boys used money they had saved to buy flour, sugar, eggs, and other ingredients. They made lots of zucchini bread. They sold muffins, slices of bread, and different-sized loaves. They also sold fresh zucchini and copies of their mom's zucchini bread recipe. People lined up for the delicious bread. The boys sold everything they made and picked more zucchini. By the end of summer, they had filled their piggy banks. They talked about what to do with the money and made plans. They spent some of the money to take their family to the movies. They put some in the bank. They used a little to buy computer games. They also put some money in the church offering.

It's good to make money. But it's also good to remember who the money belongs to. Ultimately, all money comes from God and belongs to him. He might give you money through earning an allowance or getting a summer job. But everything belongs to him and should be used for his glory. God wants you to enjoy the fruits—or vegetables—of your labor. He rewards hard work. So enjoy your money after working to earn it, but also think of what you can do to give back to God.

WACKY LAUGHS

Q. Why wasn't there any money in the breadbox?

A. It only held loaf-ers.

Q. Why did the woman take her ducks to the store?

A. Because they had bills.

Q. What did the football coach say when he dropped a coin?

A. Please give me my quarterback.

✞ PRAY

Ask God to help you learn to use money wisely.

Life's Guidebook Says
Tell the godly that all will be well for them. They will enjoy the rich reward they have earned! ISAIAH 3:10

GOING TO THE DOGS

MACK CHECKED HIS CELL PHONE. Mrs. Kay had sent him a text message. She needed him to dog sit. *Yeah!*

The week before, Mack had passed out flyers around his neighborhood. He'd hand-delivered them to all the neighbors he knew, explaining the services he could provide. He made sure to greet people's pets and remember their names. On the first day he advertised, one of the neighbors came over to his house and told his parents, "I have to go out of town for a few days next week. I'd like Mack to take in the mail every day, turn on the lights at night, and water the plants." Mack listened and took notes. When the neighbor left, he thanked his mom for giving him the idea to advertise. She had helped him design the flyer and told him to be polite and to go beyond what people asked.

Now he had his second client. Mack liked dogs, so it wasn't even a *ruff* job! Mrs. Kay was just gone over the weekend. When she returned, Mack went over to her house and said, "Mabel was very good and liked to run to the park. I also noticed your plant in the dining room needed water, so I added a little."

"I like how you notice what needs to get done," Mrs. Kay said. "You're a good worker."

She paid him the price they'd agreed on and then gave him a tip. *Wow!* Mack hadn't expected that. He'd just hoped she'd use him again and tell others he did a good job. It was nice working for her.

Like Mack, you should always do your best at any job you do. When you put extra effort into your chores or your schoolwork, your parents and teachers will notice. God will notice too.

PLEXER
Solve this plexer to learn why people put money in the bank. (If you don't remember what a plexer is, see p. 9.)

M O n e y interest

✝ PRAY
Tell God that whatever you do, you'll work hard and do your best.

Life's Guidebook Says
Lazy people want much but get little, but those who work hard will prosper.
PROVERBS 13:4

Answer: Money grows with interest.

PAYDAY

MICHAEL DUG AND PLANTED. He carried sod and bags of seed all week for a landscaper. At the end of the week, he jumped for joy when he received a check for all his work. Michael immediately walked to the store and bought ice cream. That night he asked his family to join him to celebrate. He took out two gallons of ice cream and said, "Whenever Dad gets a raise, he takes us out to eat. I just got my first paycheck and want to share ice cream with you. I have one gallon in the freezer that's all mine, but this one is for everyone."

His brothers and sisters clapped and grabbed spoons.

Money cannot buy happiness or love, but the way we use money can bring smiles and joy to others. Jesus said where you put your money says a lot about the desires of your heart (see today's verse). If you spend a lot on computer games, entertainment may play a big role in your life. But if your money goes toward fashion, then image may be important to you. In the story, Michael bought ice cream for himself, but he also showed that he had a heart for his family by getting them a treat too. Think about what you have that you can share. Bringing joy to other people is a great way to use your money.

AWESOME ACTIVITY: MOVING COINS
Try these coin tricks:

☞ Stack 10 coins of the same value on top of each other. Take another coin of the same value and flick it to hit the bottom coin. Watch it push the bottom coin out and take its place.

☞ Place several coins of the same value side by side on a flat tabletop, touching one another. The line of coins should be placed vertically (away from you). Then take two coins of the same value and lay them a few inches behind the line of coins. Flick the back coin with your finger, sending the two coins into the end of the line of coins. Watch as two coins fly out from the group. Try it with three or four coins. Whatever number of coins hits the line causes the same number of coins to split away.

✝ PRAY
Ask God to help you have a generous heart.

Life's Guidebook Says
Wherever your treasure is, there the desires of your heart will also be.
MATTHEW 6:21

WANT AD

JEROME SAT BY THE PHONE, waiting for someone to call. He had placed an ad in the newspaper's special section for free ads from kids. He was offering to wash windows for one dollar each.

The first woman who called asked if the size of the window mattered. Jerome said they were all one price. She asked him to come over to do the work. When Jerome and his dad got to the house, Jerome couldn't believe what he saw. She had a glass house with two-story-high windows!

"She's getting a good bargain," Dad said.

"I better be careful what I promise next time," Jerome agreed.

Jerome worked all weekend to finish cleaning the windows. When he finished the work, the woman paid him much more than what he'd quoted. She was happy that he had agreed to keep his word but felt all his hard work deserved more pay. Jerome was thrilled with the surprise.

Sometimes we can make a bad deal or come out on the short end of the stick. Maybe we feel cheated. God doesn't like cheaters, but he also wants us to keep our promises. When Jesus saw money changers in the Temple, he overturned their tables and called them robbers. These merchants exchanged foreign money and sold animals that could be used as sacrifices in the Temple, but they cheated people. They gave out less money than they should have and charged extra for the sacrifices. Jesus also disliked how the business in the Temple court interfered with people worshiping God.

Jesus wants us to treat people fairly, whether it's with our money or our actions.

PUZZLE IT OUT: SWAPPING LETTERS

Swap every third letter with the one before it to decode this message:

Hnoetsy si teh bset hcocie.

_____.

✝ PRAY

Ask God to help you be honest and treat people fairly.

Life's Guidebook Says

[Jesus] said to them, "The Scriptures declare, 'My Temple will be called a house of prayer,' but you have turned it into a den of thieves!" MATTHEW 21:13

Answer: Honesty is the best choice.

PUPPET SHOW OF GOODWILL

Pennies for puppets.
Pennies for puppets.
One, two, three, four. Let's see some more.
Pennies, that's what!

THE PUPPETS DANCED ON STAGE. The puppeteers called out. The crowd dug into its pockets to find loose change. This little song raised a lot of money, but not for the puppet team. James, one of the puppeteers, wanted to give puppets and a stage to an orphanage. The puppet team performed every day for Vacation Bible School. James asked the church if collecting coins could be a mission project for the kids who came that week. Every day the puppets would sing and ask kids to find pennies, dimes, and quarters to help the orphans have puppets. By the end of VBS, they had collected over 7,000 coins that added up to more than $300! The puppeteers pored over catalogs with James and chose several puppets to buy. They also made a video on how to use puppets.

The next month, James led a team in performing a puppet show for the children at the orphanage. They taught the kids to make puppets out of folded paper. Then they gave the orphanage the stage and the puppets. The smiles and clapping children made the puppeteers happy they had spent time doing the project.

God wants us to work together to accomplish a goal. When we work together with God, we can do amazing things . . . even helping orphans in far-off countries.

AWESOME ACTIVITY: FOLDED PAPER PUPPET
Transform a piece of paper into a puppet.

Stuff You Need
- ☞ Paper
- ☞ Markers or crayons

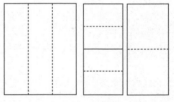

Try It
1. Fold the paper lengthwise into thirds.
2. Fold the paper in half.
3. Take each folded end and fold it halfway between the end and the center fold to form a puppet head. One end has two folds. That's the mouth. The other end has openings for your hand and thumb.
4. Put your thumb into the bottom opening. Put your fingers into the top opening. Move your fingers and thumb to open and close the puppet's mouth.
5. Use markers or crayons to add eyes, nose, and lips. Add a tongue inside the mouth.

✝ PRAY
Pray for a spirit of cooperation, so you will work well with other people.

Life's Guidebook Says
We work together with God.   1 CORINTHIANS 3:9, NIrV

OCTOBER

HIDDEN FOR GOOD

RAY HULSTEIN was just 11 years old when the Germans invaded the Netherlands during World War II. Following the invasion, Ray's parents went to a meeting at church and formed the Committee for Jewish Rescue. Soon his quiet Christian family became active in hiding Jewish people and helping them escape the atrocities of concentration camps. Over the next five years, the Hulsteins housed dozens of families and kept them safe from the German army. Many times Ray and his eight brothers and sisters had to sacrifice their own comfort, giving up food or their beds for their Jewish guests. But they were glad to do it, knowing they were living out Jesus' command to "love your neighbor as yourself" (Mark 12:31).

Ray and his family risked their lives to save others. The Bible tells many stories of people who put themselves in harm's way to help other people. In 1 Kings 18, we learn about Obadiah. When the evil King Ahab and Queen Jezebel were in power, they ordered that all the Lord's prophets be killed. Obadiah hid 100 prophets in caves. Then he brought them food and water.

Just like Ray's family, Obadiah followed the Lord. As a Christ follower, you may be called to sacrifice to help people. Look for opportunities to make a difference in God's Kingdom.

PUZZLE IT OUT: HIDING VERSE

Corrie ten Boom and her family also hid Jewish families during WWII. You can read about her faith and family in her book *The Hiding Place*. Look closely at the words below. One letter is missing from the second word in each pair. Write that letter on the spaces to discover the missing word from Corrie's favorite psalm.

1. read	red
2. pecan	cape
3. glob	lob
4. cape	cap
5. flour	four
6. shot	hot

"He will order his __ __ __ __ __ __ to protect you wherever you go." —Psalm 91:11
              1 2 3 4 5 6

✞ PRAY

Ask God to protect Christians around the world who risk their lives to help others.

Life's Guidebook Says
Jesus replied, "The most important commandment is this . . . 'You must love the LORD your God with all your heart, all your soul, all your mind, and all your strength.' The second is equally important: 'Love your neighbor as yourself.' No other commandment is greater than these." MARK 12:29-31

Answer: angels

LET US PRAY

HAVE YOU EVER BEEN at church or around a dinner table when somebody prayed a long, beautiful prayer? Did it make you feel like your prayers were kind of measly? God doesn't look at it that way.

While some people have a natural knack for speaking to God, God wants to hear from *you*. When you pray, it's good to remember that God is more concerned about the condition of your heart than the content of your words. He wants to hear what's on your mind, even if you don't know exactly what to say. One thing that God doesn't want is for you to make a show with your prayers (see today's verse). Imagine if a student stood up on his chair right before a test and raised his hands in the air:

Jonathan (shouting): "O God, help me to remember everything I studied last night. Bless my teacher. Thank you for giving me such an awesome brain. And, Lord, bring judgment on Rick, who cheated on the last test and wasn't caught. Amen."

That probably wouldn't go over very well. Prayer can be a funny thing. The Bible tells us to "never stop praying" (1 Thessalonians 5:17). But if we walked around with our eyes closed, we'd run into a lot of stuff and get injured. The verse is saying that prayer needs to be a big part of your life. You can say quick prayers to God—keeping your eyes open—as you go through your day. Planning a specific time and place to pray can also help . . . just as long as that place isn't the middle of the lunchroom.

LIFTOFF LIST

Check off everything you pray for.

____ Health for family and friends
____ Blessings for Christians spreading God's truth around the world
____ To do well on a test
____ Thanking God for his goodness
____ Safety for persecuted Christians who are hurt or jailed
____ The food I eat
____ My team to win a game
____ Jobs for people who need work
____ Courage to live for Christ when people make fun of me
____ Thanking God for sending his Son to save me
____ Forgiveness when I break God's commands

✝ PRAY

Tell God you want an active and growing prayer life.

Life's Guidebook Says

[Jesus said,] "When you pray, go away by yourself, shut the door behind you, and pray to your Father in private. Then your Father, who sees everything, will reward you." MATTHEW 6:6

BE READY

"PEOPLE GET READY. Jesus is coming. Soon we'll be going home. People get ready. Jesus is coming to take from the world his own." Around 20 years ago, the song "People Get Ready . . . Jesus Is Coming" lit up Christian radio stations. Crystal Lewis's tune was the song of the year in 1996.

But waiting for Christ's return is nothing new. The Bible promises that Jesus is coming back. The Lord won't be a baby this time; he'll be a conquering King. Christians in the early church looked around and thought Jesus might be coming back any day—and that was nearly 2,000 years ago! More recently, books have been written and movies have been made that predict Christ's return in our lifetime.

While it's great to be excited about Jesus coming back to earth, no one except God knows the timing. Jesus even said that he and the angels didn't know—"only the Father knows" (Mark 13:32). And since we don't know when Christ is coming back, we need to stay alert and be ready.

To prepare yourself for Jesus' return, all you need to do is live for him. You don't need to try and grow a beard or live in the forest. There's no ark to construct. You just need to know your Bible, pray to God, and follow his Word. And since Jesus could come any day, you should tell your friends about him. You don't want them to miss out on the celebration.

PLEXER

See if you can solve this plexer. (If you don't remember what a plexer is, see p. 9.)

```
J
E
S
U
S
earth
```

✟ PRAY

Praise God that Jesus is coming back in glory. Tell him that you'll be ready.

Life's Guidebook Says

No one knows the day or hour when these things will happen, not even the angels in heaven or the Son himself. Only the Father knows. MARK 13:32

Answer: Jesus descending to earth

HEAR THAT?

WHAT'S WRONG with this conversation?

Brad: Hey, Jeff. Can you help me look for my cat? She ran away.
Jeff: You won't believe it. I just beat the MegaAsteroids 4 video game!
Brad: I'm really worried about Buttercup.
Jeff: The last asteroid belt was superhard.
Brad: She's never spent the night outside.
Jeff: I was playing for the last three hours.
Brad: I don't even know if she can catch mice to eat.
Jeff: Look, my thumb's got a blister!
Brad: Maybe I should hang up posters.
Jeff: Maybe I should go buy MegaAsteroids 5 while I'm still in the zone.

You probably figured out the problem pretty quickly. Nobody's listening! Both boys are talking without any concern about what the other person is saying. Brad and Jeff are each stuck in their own world.

Sometimes problems come up or exciting things happen that take all of our attention. But we have to be careful about being so absorbed in our world that we miss what's happening around us. The Bible says we should be quick to listen and slow to speak (see today's verse). That's good advice—because what do you think is going to happen next between Brad and Jeff? They're going to get mad at each other, right? When we don't communicate well with our friends due to poor listening skills, it hurts our relationships. So always remember to open your ears before you open your mouth.

WACKY LAUGHS

Q. Why are goats not good at listening to others?
A. They always butt in.

Q. How do ducks learn if they don't go to school?
A. They swim above a school of fish and listen closely.

Q. What did the rabbit say when it was listening to its friend?
A. "I'm all ears!"

✝ PRAY

Ask God to give you wisdom to know when to speak and when to listen.

Life's Guidebook Says
Understand this, my dear brothers and sisters: You must all be quick to listen, slow to speak, and slow to get angry. JAMES 1:19

WISE WORKERS

ANTS SEEM TO BE EVERYWHERE. According to experts, an estimated one quadrillion ants live on—or under—the earth. That's 1,000,000,000,000,000! Compare that to the number of humans, just over 7,000,000,000, and you can see we're horribly outnumbered. Fortunately, we're much bigger.

Ants may be small, but they can do amazing work. Ants work tirelessly during the summer to store up food for winter. A famous writer noticed this fact and wrote a story about the ant and the grasshopper. The grasshopper jumped around all summer and played. Meanwhile, the ant carried pieces of corn, grass, and leaves into its home.

"Come chat with me," the grasshopper said, "instead of working so hard."

"It's better to work hard now," the ant replied, "so I can survive and rest during the winter."

The grasshopper thought the ant was really missing out. But when winter came, the grasshopper was the one missing out—on food.

That's a sad story. But Aesop, who wrote this fable around 600 years before Jesus lived, wasn't the first person to notice the hardworking ants. The book of Proverbs was written more than 900 years before the birth of Christ. And Proverbs 30:24-25 tells us that ants are small but wise, because they store up food.

It's good to plan ahead, whether that's making sure to have enough food, saving money for Christmas gifts to give your family, or even planning how you'll finish a big homework assignment. So learn from the ants, and be wise.

AWESOME ACTIVITY: ANTS AT THE AMUSEMENT PARK

Log rides at the amusement park can be a lot of fun. This delicious recipe sends ants riding into your stomach.

Stuff You Need
- ☞ Celery
- ☞ Knife
- ☞ Peanut butter or cream cheese
- ☞ Raisins

Try It
1. Make sure the celery is washed, then cut it into sticks.
2. Spread peanut butter or cream cheese in the center of each celery stick.
3. Place raisins, like ants, on top.
4. Send the ants sliding down your throat! *Wheeee!*

✝ PRAY

Ask God to help you be a wise worker and learn from the people around you.

Life's Guidebook Says
There are four things on earth that are small but unusually wise: Ants—they aren't strong, but they store up food all summer. PROVERBS 30:24-25

ALL-KNOWING GOD

HAVE YOU EVER HEARD that God is omniscient? That's just a fancy way of saying that God knows everything. He knows what happened in the past. He knows what's happening right now. He even knows what's going to happen in the future.

Wouldn't it be nice to have that ability? School would certainly be a lot easier. You'd know the answer to every question on every test. You'd even know the questions before they were written.

You: Great test, teacher. You really tried to trick us with number 6.
Teacher: What are you talking about? I haven't written the test yet.
You: Oh, you will.

It's kind of amazing to think that God knows every detail of your life. He knows the number of hairs on your head. He even knows your pet's name. In Psalm 50:11, the Lord says, "I know every bird on the mountains, and all the animals of the field are mine." That's awesome.

At first, when you think about God being omniscient, it can be kind of scary. If he knows everything, then he knows all the bad stuff we do and the mean thoughts we have. But the more you think about it, it's actually comforting to understand that God knows everything. That means you can trust him with any question and give over your dreams to him. He knows everything about you, and he readily forgives you. The all-knowing God of the universe wants you to have an abundant life. That's a fact worth knowing.

LIFTOFF LIST
Trying to understand everything God knows or what it'd be like to be omniscient is impossible. But the Bible makes it clear that God's knowledge is limitless. Check these verses, and write down what you find out in each one.

___ Job 37:16 _____
___ Psalm 147:5 _____
___ Isaiah 55:9 _____
___ Matthew 10:29-30 _____
___ 1 John 3:19-20 _____

✝ PRAY
Praise God that he knows you so intimately and still loves you so much.

Life's Guidebook Says
[God said,] "I know every bird on the mountains, and all the animals of the field are mine." PSALM 50:11

BUGGIN' YOU

Buzz! Have you ever had a gnat or fly buzz around your ears? It can be really irritating. The constant buzzing can drive you batty.

Some people have a medical condition called tinnitus, which causes a ringing or buzzing in their ears. Sometimes it lasts a few minutes. Other people suffer from it for years. Doctors say one out of 10 people may suffer from tinnitus. But when Pharaoh kept God's people captive in Egypt, *everybody* suffered from a buzzing in their ears!

In the book of Exodus, God sent Moses to free his people from slavery in Egypt. But Pharaoh liked having the strong, free workforce and didn't want to let them go. So God brought 10 plagues on the land. In one of them, Aaron touched his staff to the ground and all the dust turned to swarms of gnats (Exodus 8:16). *Yikes!* Gnats infested the land and covered all the people and animals. If that wasn't bad enough, God sent a plague of flies that filled houses and covered the ground (verses 21-24).

God got Pharaoh's attention by sending a buzzing in his ears. At some point in your life, God may want to get your attention. Maybe he'll want you to change a behavior or fix a bad attitude. He probably won't send gnats and flies. But God can grab your attention by something you read in the Bible, something a friend says to you, or something you hear from a pastor or parent. Make sure you always listen to God, instead of doing what Pharaoh did and telling God to buzz off.

PUZZLE IT OUT: PESKY PESTS

Look for these bothersome creatures. Search up, down, across, diagonally, and backward.

W	O	M	R	F	G	N
A	O	O	F	L	Y	A
S	M	T	T	A	N	G
P	P	H	Q	Z	U	E
E	C	I	L	B	O	L
W	I	B	D	L	U	T
I	B	E	M	E	T	E
L	B	E	A	T	R	E
F	W	O	R	M	E	B

Bedbug
Bee
Beetle
Fly
Gnat
Lice
Moth
Spider
Wasp
Worm

✝ PRAY

Promise God that you'll be ready to listen—and change—if he ever needs to get your attention.

Life's Guidebook Says

Pharaoh's magicians tried to do the same thing with their secret arts, but this time they failed. And the gnats covered everyone, people and animals alike. "This is the finger of God!" the magicians exclaimed to Pharaoh. EXODUS 8:18-19

TOY TURNABOUT

WHAT'S YOUR FAVORITE TOY? Maybe it has changed over the years. Is it one of these things?

- ☞ Etch A Sketch
- ☞ Rubik's Cube
- ☞ Transformer robot
- ☞ Super Soaker squirt gun
- ☞ Razor scooter

Probably not. But those toys were the hottest items years ago. Kids in the 1960s couldn't wait to get their hands on an Etch A Sketch to make pictures by drawing grayish lines by turning knobs. Solving a Rubik's Cube was huge in the 70s. Squirt guns took a powerful leap forward in the 1980s. And nearly every kid rode a Razor around the turn of the century. But where are these toys now?

Come to think of it: Where are your favorite toys from past years? Maybe you loved your Furby, but now it's gone. Stuff on this planet doesn't last. Toys break. Video consoles stop working. Moths eat your clothes and money.

Wait, you're probably thinking. *What's that part about moths?*

When Jesus walked the earth, he told his followers not to store up treasures on earth, because moths would eat them (see today's verse). Moth larvae will eat nearly anything. They enjoy flower nectar and tree sap. But they're also attracted to salt, which is why they'll ruin clothes that have sweat in them.

As you play with your favorite toy, have fun with it. But remember that it won't last. You'll have lots of different favorite toys growing up. But there's only one true God—and his Kingdom lasts forever. Focus most of your time and energy on building treasures in heaven, because those will go on and on.

TWISTY TONGUE TWISTERS

Try to say these tongue twisters 10 times without stopping.

Many moths make Mark's mom mad.
Tara's treasure teeter-tottered on top of a tree.
Toy boat about to topple.

✝ PRAY

Thank God for your toys and that you can store treasures in heaven.

Life's Guidebook Says

[Jesus said,] "Don't store up treasures here on earth, where moths eat them and rust destroys them, and where thieves break in and steal." MATTHEW 6:19

WHAT'S COOKING?

HAVE YOU EVER WALKED into a house as freshly baked bread was being pulled from the oven? The smell is heavenly. *Mmm.*

Maybe that's why Jesus compared the Kingdom of Heaven to bread. In Matthew 13:33, Jesus says, "The Kingdom of Heaven is like the yeast a woman used in making bread. Even though she put only a little yeast in . . . it permeated every part of the dough." Yeast is only a small part in making bread; about a tablespoon makes a large loaf. But without it, the recipe wouldn't work.

Yeast is a single-celled fungus. But Jesus wasn't calling Christians fungi (although you probably are one—*ha!*). Yeast reacts with the sugars in the dough to help it rise. Yeast also bonds the dough and makes it stretchy and strong. If you don't have yeast, your bread will be a hard, crumbly rock. *Yuck!* Because yeast grows and affects all parts of the dough, it helps bread turn out perfectly.

Do you see the parallels? Jesus wants us to affect the people around us—strengthening our Christian friends and helping our friends who don't know Christ to rise up. Plus, Jesus knows the Kingdom of Heaven may feel small now, but God grows great things from small beginnings!

EXPERIMENT: DAILY BREAD

Yeast creates a chemical reaction, so baking bread is a delicious experiment.

Stuff You Need

- ¾ cup warm water
- 1 package active dry yeast
- 2 bowls
- 1 teaspoon salt
- 1½ tablespoons sugar
- 1 tablespoon cooking oil
- ½ cup warm milk
- 3 cups flour
- Greased loaf pan

Try It

1. Dissolve yeast in water for 10 minutes.
2. Add salt, sugar, oil, and milk to a separate bowl. Stir in the yeast mixture.
3. Mix in two cups of flour. Knead in more flour with your hands until the dough is soft and not sticky.
4. Cover dough and let rise for one hour.
5. Punch the dough in the middle. Knead it with more flour for a few minutes.
6. Place dough in a greased loaf pan. Cover and let rise another 30 minutes.
7. Preheat oven to 375 degrees.
8. Bake for 45 minutes or until golden brown. Let cool and enjoy!

✝ PRAY

Tell God you want to act like yeast.

Life's Guidebook Says

[Jesus said,] "The Kingdom of Heaven is like the yeast a woman used in making bread. Even though she put only a little yeast in three measures of flour, it permeated every part of the dough." MATTHEW 13:33

THANKS BE TO GOD

DOESN'T IT FEEL as if Thanksgiving is being forgotten? Sure, you get the day off school. But the world seems to be caught in a Christmas craze. In the Philippines, radio stations start playing carols as soon as the month ends in *ber*—as in September!

That might be true, you may be thinking, *but who cares about Thanksgiving now?*

Well, it's never too early to be thankful to God, who provides for all our needs. But different countries celebrate Thanksgiving at different times. In Canada, the second Monday in October marks the Thanksgiving celebration. In South Korea, it's celebrated in August. In the United States, the original Thanksgiving festival began on December 13, 1621, and lasted three days. Today, Thanksgiving barely lasts an afternoon as families often turn to football or shopping immediately after their big dinner.

In our own lives, it's easy for thanksgiving to get pushed out of the way. We believe in our own ability to "make things happen" instead of understanding that God controls everything.

As we enter the holiday season, we need to pause and be thankful. In the book of Revelation, the apostle John describes a scene where all the angels worship God with the words, "Blessing and glory and wisdom and thanksgiving and honor and power and strength belong to our God forever and ever!" (7:12). Focus on the words "thanksgiving and honor . . . belong to our God forever." That's the attitude we should live with.

QUIZ: HAPPY HOLIDAYS

Match these holidays to the correct country.

1. *La Tomatina*	a. United States
2. Boxing Day	b. Canada
3. Bastille Day	c. Spain
4. Independence Day	d. France

✞ PRAY

Tell God you're going to be thankful to him forever and ever and ever.

Life's Guidebook Says

[The angels said,] "Blessing and glory and wisdom and thanksgiving and honor and power and strength belong to our God forever and ever! Amen." REVELATION 7:12

Answers: 1. c (La Tomatina happens the last Wednesday of August, when 20,000 people throw tomatoes at each other in the "World's Biggest Food Fight.") 2. b (Boxing Day occurs the day after Christmas, when people box up gifts to give to the less fortunate.) 3. d (On July 14, the French remember the storming of the Bastille prison and the start of the French Revolution.) 4. a (Independence Day celebrates the signing of the Declaration of Independence on July 4, 1776.)

TOUGH TEST

YOU WALK INTO MATH CLASS and see two dreaded words written on the board: *Pop Quiz!* "Okay, class," your teacher says. "If you pass this quiz, you get an A for the semester. But if you don't do well, you'll receive an F on your report card."

You look at the paper. Only two questions. The first says, "An alley separates two tall buildings. Engineers decide to attach cables to the buildings for strength. The cables go from the base of one building to the roof of the other and crisscross in the middle. One of the cables is 240 feet. The other is 160 feet. If the cables crisscross 40 feet above the ground, how wide is the alley?"

The other question is just an equation: If $\frac{1}{m+q} = \frac{1}{n}$, then q = _____.

That's so unfair, you think. *There's no way I can pass this test.*

Abraham was probably thinking the same thing when God gave him a pop quiz to test his faith. But his test was way harder. In the beginning of Genesis 22, God tells Abraham to sacrifice his beloved son Isaac. Abraham had seen God do amazing things and bless him immeasurably. Now God was asking him to do the unthinkable.

The Bible doesn't tell us if Abraham had to think twice about God's request. It just says Abraham got up, saddled his donkey, chopped some firewood, and headed toward Mount Moriah. You probably know the rest of the story. Just as Abraham was about to strike Isaac down, God provided a different sacrifice. The Bible says Abraham's faith pleased God. God is still pleased when we show faith in him by rising up to a difficult test.

QUIZ: MASTERFUL MATH
Follow the instructions to discover how many days Abraham and Isaac traveled to reach Mount Moriah.

Pick a number between 1 and 10.
Double that number, then add 12.
Divide your total by 4. (Fractions are okay.)
Subtract your original number.
Add 5, and then multiply your total by 2.
Add your original number.
Subtract 13.

The answer is _____.

✝ PRAY
Tell God you're up for any test to prove that you are faithful to him.

Life's Guidebook Says
Some time later, God tested Abraham's faith. "Abraham!" God called. "Yes," he replied. "Here I am." GENESIS 22:1

Answer: Three (Genesis 22:4)

GREATEST GOD

YOU'VE PROBABLY NOTICED that not everybody believes the same things about Jesus that you do. Some kids believe in Jesus Christ as their Lord and Savior. Some don't believe anything. Others believe in a different god.

The situation is nothing new. At some points in history, things were even worse for those who believed in the one true God. About 3,000 years ago, King Ahab and Queen Jezebel tried to wipe out all of God's prophets. They believed in the false god Baal. Baal worshippers did terrible things to themselves and to women, and children. Just when it looked like everyone who followed God would be wiped from the land, Elijah showed up and threw down a challenge. He said he'd face off against 450 prophets of Baal.

"You call on your god, and I'll call on mine," Elijah said. "Whichever God sends down fire is the one true God." It sounded like a good idea to the people, so the battle was on. You can read everything that happened in 1 Kings 18:16-40. But to make a long story short, things didn't go well for those who followed the false god Baal.

That's a good lesson to remember. When you don't follow any god or choose to follow someone other than Jesus Christ, things won't go well for you. God knows everything, controls everything, and can do anything. He may not rain fire down from heaven to prove he's real these days, but his power and grace are evident in so many other ways. Be sure to look for God's power displayed in your everyday life . . . and then point out those things to your friends.

PLEXER

See if you can solve this plexer that describes the God you serve. (If you don't remember what a plexer is, see p. 9.)

Most

✞ PRAY

Pray for more people to know the one true God.

Life's Guidebook Says
[Elijah said,] "Call on the name of your god, and I will call on the name of the LORD. The god who answers by setting fire to the wood is the true God!"
1 KINGS 18:24

Answer: Most High

DESERT TEMPTATION

YOU MIGHT HAVE READ today's title and thought, *Desert temptation—that sounds delicious! I hope it's a double-fudge chocolate sundae with extra caramel.*

That would be a temptation almost too hard to resist. But that's a *dessert* temptation. This is a very different temptation that happened to Jesus in the *desert*. You may know the story. After Jesus was baptized, God led him into the desert, where he didn't eat for 40 days. Jesus was God's Son, but he was also human—which meant after 40 days without food, he felt hungry.

That's when Satan showed up and said, "If you are the Son of God, tell these stones to become loaves of bread" (Matthew 4:3). Bread probably sounded pretty good. And Jesus certainly had the power to turn stones to bread . . . or even a Happy Meal. But Jesus didn't blink. He quoted God's Word back to Satan, explaining that man doesn't live by bread alone but by the Word of God (verse 4). Next, Satan took Jesus to the top of the Temple in Jerusalem. "Jump!" the devil said. "Because the Scriptures say God won't let you get hurt."

"The Scriptures also say, 'You must not test the LORD your God,'" Jesus replied (4:7). After one more test where Satan offered Jesus all the kingdoms of the world if he'd worship him, Jesus sent Satan away, saying, "You must worship the LORD your God and serve only him" (verse 10).

Notice that every time Jesus was tempted, he responded with Scripture. How well do you know God's Word? You're probably getting better and better every day. And the better you get, the better you'll be at resisting temptations.

PUZZLE IT OUT: STRONG RESISTANCE
Solve these math problems and fill in the correct word to discover what James 4:7 says.

"So humble yourselves before God. _____ ____ _____, ____ ___ _____
                                     3x1+0   2+2   21-12   24÷4 3+5 22÷11

_____ _____ ___."
(2x3)-1 16-9 1x1

    1 – you   6 – and
    2 – will   7 – from
    3 – resist   8 – he
    4 – the   9 – devil
    5 – flee

✝ PRAY
Commit to learning God's Word so you'll have the wisdom to resist temptations.

Life's Guidebook Says
"Get out of here, Satan," Jesus told him. "For the Scriptures say, 'You must worship the LORD your God and serve only him.'" MATTHEW 4:10

Answer: "Resist the devil, and he will flee from you."

ON TRIAL

"WHEN THERE WERE JUST TWO cookies left in the package, what did you do?" The lawyer glares at you as he asks the question.

Actually, a lot of people are staring at you. The judge looks down at you from his bench. A jury watches every move you make from its box. You start to sweat.

"I—I took them both," you say.

"How could you commit such a heinous act?!?" the lawyer screams. "Your selfishness left no cookies for your sister. And she would've really enjoyed a cookie."

"Guilty," says the judge.

"I'm so sorry," you say as you're led from court.

Fortunately, we don't have to go on trial for every selfish, prideful, or mean thing we do. If we did, court systems around the world would be clogged, because we're all sinners. Facing a judge can be a very uncomfortable experience. The Bible tells us that in the future every person will stand before God to give an account for himself (Romans 14:12). As followers of Christ, we receive the amazing gift of forgiveness of our sins. But that doesn't mean we can do anything we want and then ask to be forgiven. God wants us to act more like him every day.

King David tried to live like God. He made a ton of bad decisions but continued to have a strong faith. In Psalm 26:2, he asks the Lord to put him on trial and "test my motives and my heart." David didn't want to wait to be judged. He wanted to test his actions every day. That's the way we should live too.

WACKY LAUGHS

Q. Where does a hamburger go when it commits a crime?
A. The food court.

Q. What did the judge say when a skunk walked up to the witness stand?
A. "Odor in the court!"

Q. What do lawyers wear to court?
A. Lawsuits.

✝ PRAY

Ask God to look at your heart and help you make it more like his.

Life's Guidebook Says

Put me on trial, LORD, and cross-examine me. Test my motives and my heart. PSALM 26:2

GIVE IT ALL TO GOD

SOME PEOPLE THINK the Bible is just a big book of rules. If you read your way through the Old Testament, especially Leviticus, you may be thinking, *They're right!*

The Old Testament does have a lot of rules, because God's people needed a lot of direction. Story after story shows how people chose to follow their own path or turn to false gods. In the book of Malachi, the prophet puts out a challenge. For years the Israelites had wandered from God and cheated each other. They even cheated the Lord by not bringing their tithes to the Temple. God commanded that people give a tithe—or 10 percent—back to him (Leviticus 27:30). But the people didn't like to give up their stuff, so they didn't tithe. Malachi brought a message from the Lord: "Bring all the tithes into the storehouse so there will be enough food in my Temple. If you do . . . I will pour out a blessing so great that you won't have enough room to take it in!" (Malachi 3:10). How's that for a challenge? God blesses us with everything, and asks only that we give a fraction back to him. He's basically saying, "You can't outgive me."

That's definitely true. God proves that in the next book after Malachi in the Bible—Matthew. God sends the gift of his Son to take away the sins of the world. Jesus also changed the way his followers looked at Old Testament laws. Jesus came to give us life . . . not a lot of rules.

LIFTOFF LIST

Check off every way that you give back to God.

___ I volunteer at church.
___ I put money in the offering plate.
___ I help older neighbors.
___ I tell others about Jesus.
___ I've organized a canned food drive.

✝ PRAY

Commit to giving back to God, whether it's your money, time, or talent.

Life's Guidebook Says
"Bring all the tithes into the storehouse so there will be enough food in my Temple. If you do," says the LORD of Heaven's Armies, "I will open the windows of heaven for you. I will pour out a blessing so great you won't have enough room to take it in! Try it! Put me to the test!" MALACHI 3:10

AXMEN

CARTER LOOKED OUT THE WINDOW and saw the first flakes of snow start to fall. Winter came early high up in the Rocky Mountains.

"Do you see what I see?" Dad asked, walking into the room.

"Yeah, it's going to start getting cold."

"That means we'll have to stock up on firewood," Dad said. "I think you're old enough to help this year."

"Cool!" Carter said. His family depended on building fires to heat their house in the winter.

The next morning Carter and his dad hiked into the forest. Dad carried a chain saw, while Carter held an ax. Once Dad found some fallen trees and dead timber, he fired up the chain saw. While his dad cut up the trees, Carter's job was to hack off the branches. At first, Carter chopped off the branches with ease. After a couple of hours, it took him longer. He kept swinging harder, but he started falling behind his dad. Just when he felt too tired to continue, Dad powered down the chain saw.

"How's it going?" he asked.

"It's too hard," Carter said. "I can't do it."

Dad walked over and looked at the ax. "I think I know the problem."

He pulled a gray, gritty, hockey puck–like object from his pocket and started rubbing it in a circular motion over the ax blade. He did it to both sides until Carter could see the ax gleam.

"Now try it," Dad said.

Carter took a swing. *Chop!* The blade carved through a small branch like butter.

"A dull blade takes more effort," Dad said. "The Bible says a wise man stops to sharpen his blade."

What's true in cutting trees is also true in life. Instead of working harder, God wants you to work smarter. If a task feels too difficult, stop and think. When you use God's wisdom, it'll help you succeed.

TWISTY TONGUE TWISTERS
Try to say these tongue twisters 10 times without stopping.

How much wood could a woodchopper chop, if a woodchopper would chop wood?
Alex asks for aluminum axes.

✝ PRAY
Ask God to help you be wise and sharpen yourself with his wisdom.

Life's Guidebook Says
Using a dull ax requires great strength, so sharpen the blade. That's the value of wisdom; it helps you succeed. ECCLESIASTES 10:10

NOT AFRAID

THIS TIME OF YEAR it's hard to ignore all the scary stuff on TV, at the movies, and lining store shelves. Researchers say people like feeling scared—as long as there's no real danger. That's why riding roller coasters, skydiving, and other adrenaline-filled sports are so popular (of course, some of those activities can actually be dangerous). But many times frightening images, especially from movies, can get stuck in our brains, causing us to have bad dreams or be afraid.

Instead of getting caught up in the grotesque, scary, or evil stuff this time of year, God wants us to focus on him. (We should be living like this every other time of year too.) He doesn't want us to be afraid. He came to cast out fear. Psalm 118:6 says, "The LORD is for me, so I will have no fear. What can mere people do to me?" Because God lives in us through the Holy Spirit, we have no reason to be afraid. Our eternity is secure with our heavenly Father. We may have moments of fear, but deep down we should know that with God on our side, we have no reason to stay afraid.

In this season of fear, stand out by living fearlessly. Be courageous. Be bold. Be excited about God. If you have friends who struggle with fear, tell them about the peace that comes from knowing the one and only Savior. And have no fear.

AWESOME ACTIVITY: FIGHT FEAR

Fear can sneak up and grab hold of our lives if we're not careful. Try these tips to cast off fear:

- ☞ Memorize Bible verses. If you start to feel afraid, say these verses in your head or out loud—Psalm 56:4; John 14:27; and 2 Timothy 1:7.
- ☞ Hum or sing a Bible song. Hearing your voice praise God can give you strength.
- ☞ Play your favorite Christian music.
- ☞ Talk about your fears with your parents, and pray together.

✞ PRAY

Tell God you're going to stand in his truth during this season and not get sucked into the culture of fear.

Life's Guidebook Says

The LORD is for me, so I will have no fear. What can mere people do to me?
PSALM 118:6

MASTER BUILDER

As you grow into a man, there are some important skills you may have to learn, such as . . .

- ☞ how to talk with girls.
- ☞ how to grill the perfect hamburger.
- ☞ how to act selflessly.
- ☞ how to use power tools.

Okay, it's true you can grow into an awesome man of God without all those skills (except the acting selflessly part), but there's something sort of manly about using power tools. According to a popular website, every man should own four key power tools: the cordless drill, the reciprocating saw, the oscillating multitool, and the circular saw. With just those tools, most fixes around the house can be done in a flash.

Guys love tools, because we love to fix things. Jesus could fix things too. He worked as a carpenter with his earthly father, Joseph. Jesus could probably build a wall, fix a chair, or hang a door. But Jesus didn't come just to "fix" things. He came to build something that lasts—his Kingdom.

The Old Testament talked about a "stone" that would be rejected but ultimately become the chief cornerstone (Psalm 118:22). A cornerstone is the first stone set in a foundation. It's the building's most important stone. Every other stone gets placed based on the cornerstone. In Acts, Peter explains that Jesus is the cornerstone (Acts 4:11). He's the most important piece of the Christian faith. Peter goes on to say, "There is salvation in no one else! God has given no other name under heaven by which we must be saved" (verse 12).

Only Jesus can save. God builds his Kingdom on Christ. As a Christ follower, you're a part of building God's Kingdom . . . and you don't even have to know how to use a power tool.

PLEXER

See if you can solve this plexer that describes Jesus. (If you don't remember what a plexer is, see p. 9.)

✝ PRAY

Ask God to use you to build his Kingdom.

Life's Guidebook Says

Jesus is the one referred to in the Scriptures, where it says, "The stone that you builders rejected has now become the cornerstone." ACTS 4:11

Answer: Cornerstone

HOW ABOUT THEM APPLES?

WHAT'S YOUR FAVORITE THING made from apples?

You might have answered: apple pie, apple turnovers, applesauce, apple fritters, or just plain apples dipped in caramel. Anyway you serve them, apples are awesome.

Apples grow in nearly every state in the United States, even parts of Florida and Hawaii, as long as you count pineapples. (It's good those don't grow on trees, because if one fell on you, it'd really hurt.) Around 2,500 kinds of apples are grown in the United States, and more than 7,500 kinds can be found around the world.

Fall is a perfect time for apples. If you live near an apple orchard, ask your parents to take you over so you can pick ripe ones right from the tree. You can also check out different varieties at the store to discover your favorite one to eat.

Apples taste great, but they also hold a neat surprise inside. Carefully slice open an apple crosswise and you'll see the seeds form a star. God hid that star inside the fruit.

Whenever you eat an apple or a slice of apple pie, remember that God knows you're a star too, although your qualities and talents might still be hidden. You could even say you're the apple of God's eye (see today's verse)! Be ready to let the star inside you show.

AWESOME ACTIVITY: EXTRA SAUCE, PLEASE

Make your own easy and tasty applesauce.

Stuff You Need

- ☞ 2 apples (Rome apples make pink applesauce.)
- ☞ Knife
- ☞ Peeler (optional)
- ☞ Microwave-safe container
- ☞ ½ teaspoon cinnamon
- ☞ 2–3 tablespoons water
- ☞ Spoon
- ☞ Fork or something else to use for mashing apples
- ☞ Sugar or other sweetener

Try It

1. Cut apples into quarters. Remove the core. Peel if desired, or leave on skin of red apples.
2. Put apple pieces into a microwave-safe container. Add water and cinnamon.
3. Cook on high for five minutes. Stir. Cook a few more minutes at a time until the apples are soft and mushy.
4. Mash the apples. While the mixture is hot, add sugar to sweeten it as desired.
5. If you left the skins on, you can eat them or strain them out.
6. Chill and serve.

✝ PRAY

Ask God to bring out the star in you.

Life's Guidebook Says

Keep me as the apple of Your eye.   PSALM 17:8, NKJV

CAPTURED!

You ARMY-CRAWL toward a house with a submachine gun in your hands. Through your night-vision goggles you can see the rest of your SWAT team members getting into position. A dangerous drug dealer lives in this house. He's been selling to kids and hurting people who get in his way.

What a lowlife, you think as you scramble behind a bush and take careful aim. An informant walks toward the door, trying to draw the drug dealer outside and away from his weapons. As the drug dealer steps onto the porch, the SWAT team springs from its positions.

"Freeze—police!" you shout.

Hands fly into the air. You run toward the pair and quickly subdue the drug dealer. A fellow SWAT team member takes the informant into custody, so nobody will know he supplied the information. At the end of the night, it's one bad guy off the street, no shots fired, and a safer neighborhood.

As exciting as that sounds, a similar battle goes on every day in people's minds. But instead of capturing bad guys, it's a fight to capture rebellious thoughts. The apostle Paul says we need to knock down strongholds of human reasoning and destroy false arguments (2 Corinthians 10:4). Learn what's in God's Word so you can build a strong SWAT team in your brain. Then you can destroy rebellious thoughts in your life and in the lives of people around you.

AWESOME ACTIVITY: SWAT TACTICS
Special Weapons and Tactics (SWAT) teams are the elite in law enforcement. They train in many ways:

- ☞ Physical: Muscle and endurance strength is important. Jog around your neighborhood, and increase the number of push-ups you can do.
- ☞ Mental: You must be able to think clearly, follow orders, and stay calm under pressure. Do problem-solving puzzles, like Sudoku. Also, develop a never-give-up attitude. Not everybody who tries out for the SWAT team makes it right away. You can't give up.
- ☞ Tactics: SWAT team members study various tactics to be safe in different situations. Play strategy games like chess, The Settlers of Canaan, and Battleship.

✝ PRAY
Pray for wisdom to capture rebellious thoughts and fully obey Christ.

Life's Guidebook Says
We destroy every proud obstacle that keeps people from knowing God. We capture their rebellious thoughts and teach them to obey Christ.
2 CORINTHIANS 10:5

WARNING, WARNING!

SOME PRODUCTS come with funny warning labels.

☞ A hairdryer warns, "Do not use while sleeping."

☞ A carton of eggs says, "Product may contain eggs."

☞ A washing machine points out, "Do not put any person in this washer."

☞ A cereal bowl comes with a sticker: "Always use this product with adult supervision."

While it's nice to eat as a family, consuming Frosted Flakes probably doesn't need adult supervision. And who dries his hair while he's sleeping? That's just ridiculous.

In the book of Romans, Paul gives a much more helpful warning. He says, "I give each of you this warning: Don't think you are better than you really are" (12:3). Paul knew that pride was a problem. He battled with it himself. In his letter to the church in Philippi, Paul said he had plenty of reasons to boast. He was a pure-blooded citizen of Israel and a Pharisee who followed the law. But those things were worthless compared to the righteousness he found in Jesus (Philippians 3:5-7). Paul could've had a big head, yet he didn't because he understood that everything good in him came from God.

Take Paul's warning to heart. Don't think too highly of yourself. Be honest about what you're good at and where you have weaknesses.

And while you're following warnings, don't forget about this actual label on a Superman costume: "This costume does not enable flight or super strength."

EXPERIMENT: POP PRIDE

You're probably pretty awesome. Remember that God is more awesome. This experiment will help you pop pride before you get a big head.

Stuff You Need

☞ Long strips of paper

☞ Pencil

☞ Bible

☞ Large, round balloon

Try It

1. Write Bible verses about pride on pieces of paper. These are some good ones: Proverbs 11:2; Proverbs 16:5; Proverbs 27:2; and Romans 12:16.
2. Roll up the thin strips of paper as tightly as you can and push them into the balloon.
3. Blow up the balloon.
4. Play with the balloon for a while, but then pop it and read the verses.

✞ PRAY

Thank God for his warnings. Ask him to help you stay humble.

Life's Guidebook Says

Because of the privilege and authority God has given me, I give each of you this warning: Don't think you are better than you really are. Be honest in your evaluation of yourselves. ROMANS 12:3

HIDE-AND-SEEK GONE WRONG

HAVE YOU EVER PLAYED hide-and-seek? What's the best hiding place you've ever found? Don't write it down—you may want to use that spot again.

A girl in Utah discovered the worst place to hide when she climbed into her family's washing machine during a game in January 2014. (She must *not* have read the warning label.) The 11-year-old did a good job staying out of sight, but then she realized she was stuck. She screamed for help, and her family came running. They tried pouring water on her and smearing her with peanut butter to get her out. Nothing worked. So they called 911. Firemen came to her rescue and had to dismantle the machine to set her free. At first, her legs didn't work because of severe cramping, but she eventually started walking fine and didn't have to go to the hospital.

Hide-and-seek can be fun as long as you don't hide in a dangerous place . . . or play with God. That's what Adam and Eve learned in Genesis 3. After they sinned, the couple sewed fig leaves together as clothes and hid when the Lord walked through the Garden of Eden. God easily found them and called them out on their sin.

When you break one of God's laws, don't hide from him—run toward him! Confess your sin to God and ask for forgiveness. Hiding will do you no good, especially if you sneak inside a washing machine.

WACKY LAUGHS

Q. What did Eve's license plate say in the Garden of Eden?
A. ADAM 8 1 2

Sunday school teacher: When were Adam and Eve in the Garden of Eden?
Child: In the summer.
Sunday school teacher: How do you know?
Child: Well, we know it was before the Fall.

Q. Why did Adam and Eve wear fig leaves in the Garden?
A. Because the poison ivy was too itchy.

✞ PRAY

Ask God to expose any hidden sin you have in your life. Pray for forgiveness, and promise not to hide from God.

> *Life's Guidebook Says*
> *The LORD God asked[,] "Have you eaten from the tree whose fruit I commanded you not to eat?"* GENESIS 3:11

BE YOURSELF

WHAT WOULD YOU HAVE to do to dress up like one of the men in your family? Would you need to grow a beard to be like your dad? Maybe you could lift weights to build muscles like your cousin. Perhaps you'd have to throw on sweatpants and a flannel shirt to look like your uncle. But would you strap a bunny to your arm to pretend to be your brother?

That's what Jacob did . . . well, sort of. Genesis 27 tells the story of Jacob stealing Esau's blessing. Jacob was probably a little jealous that his twin brother would get a special blessing as the older son. He wanted the blessing, even if it meant putting on a costume. *Besides,* he may have thought, *I'm only a few minutes younger than my hairy older brother.*

Jacob's mom helped with the plan. She killed some young goats to make a delicious meal and strapped the goatskins to Jacob's smooth arms. Jacob also put on some of Esau's clothes. Jacob's dad, Isaac, couldn't see well, so he asked to feel his son's arm.

"The voice is Jacob's, but the hands are Esau's," Isaac said (Genesis 27:22). Isaac asked his son to come even closer, so he could make sure he was blessing the correct son. When he smelled Esau's clothes, he said, "Ah! The smell of my son is like the smell of the outdoors" (verse 27). Then he gave Jacob the blessing that was meant for Esau.

You can learn a few things from this story.

First, Esau must not have washed his clothes very often.

Second, and more important, pretending to be somebody you're not is never a good idea.

Third, jealousy always ends badly. Esau vowed to kill Jacob, and Jacob had to flee the country—which broke up their family.

WEIRD FACTS: GOT YOUR GOAT?
☞ Goats have great balance and can jump five feet high.
☞ People tamed goats 9,000 years ago to get their fur, milk, and meat.
☞ Some families have pet goats that they teach to be housebroken, like a dog.
☞ Goats have no top front teeth.

✝ PRAY
Thank God for creating you exactly how he wanted you to be. Ask him to help you not be jealous of others.

Life's Guidebook Says
You must not covet your neighbor's house. You must not covet your neighbor's wife, male or female servant, ox or donkey, or anything else that belongs to your neighbor. EXODUS 20:17

SERIOUS BED HEAD

BEN WOKE UP with serious bed head. He had rolled around on his pillow all night, and now his hair was a mess. Tufts of hair shot in all directions. Ben grabbed a comb and tried to tame his unruly mane. But his comb got stuck in a lollipop. It took him some time to pull out the sticky candy. Then Ben kept combing and found a quarter, and a nickel . . . and a dime.

One more quarter and I could buy a candy bar, he thought.

Ben pulled the comb through his hair one more time. *Meow!* He reached back and brought out his cat. "There you are, Fluffy," Ben said.

All right, nobody could have bed head that bad. But the Bible says one morning David's head looked like a goat. Actually, it *was* a goat—a goat-hair cushion, that is. Before David ruled Israel, King Saul wanted to kill him. David's wife, Michal, told him to escape before Saul's soldiers could capture him. Michal helped David climb out a window and then created a dummy David in bed (1 Samuel 19:12-13). She put a statue under the covers and added a goat-hair cushion for a head. Then she told the soldiers that David was sick and couldn't come with them. When the soldiers came back to drag David out of bed and take him away, they realized they'd been tricked.

A goat-hair cushion may have fooled Saul's soldiers, but it wouldn't fool God. The Bible says God knows every hair on your head. He watches over you with his protective power. God can keep you safe when dangers arise. The Lord doesn't want you to be afraid of earthly threats. He desires that you fear and follow him . . . even on bad hair days.

TWISTY TONGUE TWISTERS

Try to say these tongue twisters 10 times without stopping.

Gray goats give great gifts.
Hairy Harry hollers at heavy hares.
Shaky soldiers shook shattered shields.

✟ PRAY

Praise God that he knows you and that you're valuable to him.

Life's Guidebook Says

The very hairs on your head are all numbered. So don't be afraid; you are more valuable to God than a whole flock of sparrows. LUKE 12:7

WORST MISTAKE EVER

WHAT'S THE BIGGEST FLUB you've ever made? Perhaps you've tripped while playing soccer or accidentally called your teacher "Mom." Aren't you glad millions of people weren't watching during your most embarrassing moment?

Bill Buckner wasn't so fortunate. Millions of people *did* see his biggest mistake. Buckner's Boston Red Sox were on the verge of winning the World Series. Boston led the New York Mets three games to two. One more victory and they'd win the Series. On this day in 1986, they were ahead of the Mets 5–3 with two outs in the 10th inning. New York clawed back with three straight hits to tie the game 5–5. Then the Mets' Mookie Wilson hit a slow grounder to Buckner at first base. Buckner, who had battled ankle injuries all season, hobbled toward the ball, bent down, and watched it go between his legs! The Mets won the game on the error and went on to win the World Series.

Buckner's mistake has been called the most epic failure in sports history. It's been shown thousands of times on TV. For years Buckner was scorned, but eventually emotions calmed. A Boston-based band even made an album called *Forgiving Buckner*.

Did Buckner make a terrible mistake? Yes. Did he deserve forgiveness? Double yes! Forgiveness helps us move on and heal from past mistakes. Jesus talked a lot about forgiveness. He said we need to forgive each other as well as ask forgiveness from our heavenly Father.

WEIRD FACTS: WORST MISTAKES IN SPORTS

- ☞ During a 2005 game, Carolina Hurricanes defenseman Niclas Wallin passed the puck back to his goalie to avoid pressure. Just one problem—his team had pulled the goalie and the puck went in his own net!
- ☞ Legendary Minnesota Vikings defensive end Jim Marshall gathered in a fumble and raced into the end zone—the wrong end zone—during a game against San Francisco in 1964. The play resulted in the 49ers scoring two points on a safety.

✝ PRAY

Tell God you're going to be quick to forgive.

Life's Guidebook Says

If you forgive those who sin against you, your heavenly Father will forgive you. But if you refuse to forgive others, your Father will not forgive your sins.
MATTHEW 6:14-15

COMMON MISTAKE

COLTER LOVED to tie a bath towel around his neck and fly around the house like a superhero. Other times he'd tape a piece of construction paper together, cut some zigzags, and put it on his head as a crown.

If you've ever pretended to be someone else, it's probably been a knight, superhero, or prince. Kids often dress up as something they aspire to be. But in the Bible, a powerful king did the exact opposite. He dressed up as a common soldier, and the results were devastating.

After King Josiah had God's Temple restored and returned the holy Ark during a huge party, the king of Egypt decided to go to war at Carchemish. That meant the Egyptians had to walk across Josiah's land. Josiah wanted to stop them, but King Neco of Egypt sent a message saying God had told him to go to war, so Josiah shouldn't interfere with God or him (2 Chronicles 35:21). Josiah didn't listen. He disguised himself as a common soldier and led his army into battle. Egyptian archers shot their arrows into the approaching army. Some of the arrows hit Josiah. His men took him from the battle, but he died a short time later.

Josiah had been a great servant of God. He turned his country back toward the Lord. But then he made a terrible mistake by not listening to a message from the Lord. God wants us to always listen to him. Sometimes he tells us what to do through the Bible. Other times God uses our parents or other family members to guide us. Always make sure you pay close attention to what God is saying to you.

PLEXER

Solve this plexer to discover one of the greatest things Josiah did as king. (If you don't remember what a plexer is, see p. 9.)

✝ PRAY
Commit to God that you won't ignore his commands.

Life's Guidebook Says
Josiah refused to listen to Neco, to whom God had indeed spoken, and he would not turn back. Instead, he disguised himself and led his army into battle on the plain of Megiddo. 2 CHRONICLES 35:22

Answer: Smashed idols

SWEET TOOTH

WILLY LOVED CANDY. His room was piled with mounds of Mounds wrappers. He learned to do math by subtracting M&M'S from their package until they were all gone. Whenever he took a break from doing schoolwork, he'd eat a KIT KAT bar. Willy even consumed so many Bit-O-Honeys that his sweat tasted sweet.

"Willy, you've got a problem," his best friend, Charlie, said. "Mix in a carrot once in a while. Plus, a lot of fruits are sweet. Maybe you could skip the SNICKERS and pick up an orange."

"Nah," Willy said. "When I want some fruit, I just eat Skittles."

Do you have a sweet tooth like Willy's? Hopefully not. Being addicted to candy is not a healthy habit. Doctors say that eating too much sugar can lead to a ton of medical problems, including diabetes and heart disease.

Actually, any addiction is bad for you, whether it's eating sweets, playing video games, taking risks, or stealing. Overcoming a bad habit isn't easy. You should always start with a prayer for God to help change your desires. In his letter to the Galatians, Paul wrote that when you let the Holy Spirit guide your life, then you won't do what the sinful nature craves (see today's verse). Taking small steps always helps. Instead of giving up sugar or video games altogether, slowly cut back. Eat just one candy bar a day, instead of three, and turn off the console after an hour. As you slowly step away from what you're addicted to, your cravings will go away.

And if you're addicted to sugar, try chewing some sugar-free gum. It tastes sweet and can be good for your teeth.

PUZZLE IT OUT: CHOCOLATE CHUNKS

M	S	N	I	C	K	E	R	S
M	M	H	E	R	S	J	O	N
K	I	O	M	I	L	K	H	R
I	L	L	R	E	E	S	E	S
T	K	O	K	A	Q	X	R	T
K	D	R	B	Y	C	T	S	W
A	U	K	L	E	W	R	H	E
T	D	B	H	I	Y	A	E	N
T	S	W	X	I	A	Y	Y	P

Hershey
Kit Kat
Milk Duds
Milky Way
Reese's
Rolo
Snickers
Twix

✝ PRAY

Ask God to help you overcome any addiction you might have.

Life's Guidebook Says

I say, let the Holy Spirit guide your lives. Then you won't be doing what your sinful nature craves. GALATIANS 5:16

EVIL IN DISGUISE

SNAKES DON'T SEEM VERY SMART. They just slither along the ground. You don't see them studying to be aeronautical engineers or finding a cure for cancer. Yet the Bible encourages us to be "wise as serpents" (Matthew 10:16, NKJV) in the way we live our lives.

Recently, scientists discovered that snakes have a greater capacity for learning than we thought. Snakes can figure out how to get themselves through a maze or even open a door. It turns out snakes are pretty good at problem solving. And, of course, snakes have always been great at hiding in safe places and sensing danger.

Maybe that's why Jesus encouraged us to be wise as serpents. We need to be able to sense danger and figure out a way to avoid it. Sometimes those dangers are obvious. Other times danger comes in attractive packages. Satan can disguise himself as an angel of light (2 Corinthians 11:14). That's why we need to dig below surface appearances. A disguise is only skin deep. At his core, Satan is always evil. We can unmask his ploys when we're wise.

So be like a snake. Be wise. Be cautious. Stick out your tongue and taste your surroundings before you take a step. (Okay, that may be going too far.) But do be wary as you encounter new people and new experiences to test and make sure they're godly.

Thinking about Satan in this way may seem a little scary, but don't worry. In the end, God will punish Satan and his servants for all their wickedness.

WACKY LAUGHS
Q. What did the mommy snake give her son when she tucked him into bed?
A. A goodnight hiss!

Q. What is a snake's least favorite exercise?
A. Push-ups.

Q. What is a snake's favorite Christmas carol?
A. "Sssssssilent Night."

✝ PRAY
Ask God to help you be wise as a serpent when it comes to spotting Satan's ploys.

Life's Guidebook Says
It is no wonder that his servants also disguise themselves as servants of righteousness. In the end they will get the punishment their wicked deeds deserve. 2 CORINTHIANS 11:15

MYSTERIOUS MAN

ZOOM! JACKSON LIKED RIDING his new bike. His family went on bike rides all the time. Jackson always rode in the front. Today, he was ahead by a long way. As he rounded a curve, Jackson started going down a long, steep hill. On one side, trees guarded a deep ravine. In front of him, a wooden fence blocked riders from veering off the path.

I'm going too fast, Jackson thought.

He began to panic. His bike was so new and he felt so scared that he couldn't remember how to work the brakes. He thought about turning into a tree, but that looked like it would hurt. Jackson kept going faster and faster. Just when Jackson decided to try and turn his bike into a skid, a man appeared from out of the trees. He stood in front of Jackson and grabbed the handlebars to stop him.

"Thanks!" Jackson said.

"God bless you," the man replied with a smile as he walked away.

Less than a minute later, Jackson's family rode up. When he told his parents what had happened, they wanted to thank the man. They looked everywhere but couldn't see him. He seemed to have disappeared! Jackson's mom thought the man might have been an angel. Whoever it was, Jackson was grateful that God provided help exactly when he needed it.

Do you think the man could've been an angel? It's a possibility. Jackson's story is based on real events. God's Word says guardian angels are near. And in the book of Hebrews, it says we should show kindness to strangers because we might entertain an angel without realizing it (see today's verse)! We may not always be able to recognize angels. But they always know who—and where—we are.

TWISTY TONGUE TWISTERS

Try to say these tongue twisters 10 times without stopping.

Angels always act accurately.
Billy blew by a bluebird on his big black-and-blue bike.

✝ PRAY

Thank God for his amazing angels.

Life's Guidebook Says

Don't forget to show hospitality to strangers, for some who have done this have entertained angels without realizing it! HEBREWS 13:2

OUT OF BOUNDS

KYLE LIKED PLAYING BASKETBALL with Shane. Shane was the best player at school, but he wasn't a ball hog. Sure, he scored the most points, because he had a great jump shot and could drive to the basket. But Shane also liked to get his teammates involved by passing the ball. Just one thing bothered Kyle about playing with Shane: whenever Shane missed a shot, he would mutter a cuss word under his breath. And if a game got really competitive, Shane would start using more and more bad language. Pretty soon, when Kyle missed a shot, a bad word would pop into his brain. He didn't say the word out loud, but he didn't like it rattling around in his head.

Have you ever known somebody who seemed really nice but used a lot of bad language? Some kids don't think cussing is a big deal. Others say crass words because they think they sound cool. The Bible says what comes out of our mouths *is* a big deal. In Psalm 19:14, David writes, "May the words of my mouth and the meditation of my heart be pleasing to you, O LORD."

Do you think cuss words please God? No way! He wants our words to be packed with kindness, wisdom, and truth. But when you hang out with kids who cuss, it can rub off on you. If you find yourself in a situation like Kyle's, try these ideas:

1. Set an example with how you talk. Don't follow the crowd.
2. Politely ask your friend to stop using foul language around you.

When your friends see that cussing is out of bounds for you, they may try harder to watch their words.

PUZZLE IT OUT: FOULED OUT

Follow the directions and read the leftover words to discover what Ephesians 4:29 says about the way you should talk.

1. Cross out all five-letter words.
2. Cross out all words that rhyme with *dog*.
3. Cross out all words related to fall.

DON'T	HOGS	BRING	GIFTS
USE	FOUL	OR	FOG
AUTUMN	ABUSIVE	LEAVES	CLOG
LIGHT	LANGUAGE	JOGS	QUICK

✝ PRAY

Commit to keeping your language and thoughts clean.

Life's Guidebook Says
May the words of my mouth and the meditation of my heart be pleasing to you, O LORD, my rock and my redeemer. PSALM 19:14

Answer: Don't use foul or abusive language.

GOING, GOING, GOURD

How FAR COULD you chuck a pumpkin? Could you throw it a mile? That's nearly how far people chunk pumpkins at the annual World Championship Punkin Chunkin competition that happens every year in Delaware. What started as a simple competition around 30 years ago has turned into a high-tech contest where air cannons and catapults launch pumpkins thousands of feet through the air.

The rules don't allow explosives to be used, and the pumpkin has to stay intact until it hits the ground. In 2013, American Chunker, Inc., developed an air cannon that launched a pumpkin 4,694.68 feet—more than 15 football fields!

That's pretty far, but it's nowhere near the height of God's love for you. King David wrote, "His unfailing love toward those who fear him is as great as the height of the heavens above the earth" (Psalm 103:11). In other words, it's immeasurable! God's love never fails, and it's far more powerful than the mightiest punkin shooter on the planet.

EXPERIMENT: AIR WE GO!
Make this mini air shooter, but be careful not to aim it at anyone.

Stuff You Need
- ☞ Pen
- ☞ Round chopstick
- ☞ Scissors or knife
- ☞ Ruler
- ☞ Tape
- ☞ Pieces of toilet paper
- ☞ Water

Try It
1. Remove the top and bottom of the pen. You just need the tube.
2. Cut off the tip of the chopstick, so it's just a couple of inches longer than the tube. You may need a parent's help.
3. Wrap tape around one end of the chopstick, so it's thicker around than the tube. This is your stopper. When the chopstick is inserted into the tube, the stopper should keep the chopstick about one-fourth inch from the end of the tube.
4. Wet toilet paper with water. Roll into a small piece. Use the chopstick to push it to the far end of the tube. Roll another piece and insert it into the open end of the tube. Push it with your chopstick, and the other piece of toilet paper will shoot out!

✞ PRAY
Thank God for the powerful love that he has for you.

Life's Guidebook Says
His unfailing love toward those who fear him is as great as the height of the heavens above the earth. PSALM 103:11

NOVEMBER

ENLIGHTENING WORDS

OUCH! It's easy to bump into things in the dark. Without any light, you might stumble on toys and shoes in your path. Having enough light isn't a big problem like it was before the late 1800s. That's when the world became brighter as Thomas Edison developed the electric light bulb. Before that time, homes were lit with candles, lanterns, or oil lamps.

People just a hundred years ago would be amazed at the different kinds of lights we have today, like a popular app that turns smartphones into flashlights. But that's nothing compared to the world's brightest light beam. The Luxor hotel in Las Vegas uses 39 xenon lamps to produce a beam of light that's as bright as 40 billion candles (don't try to re-create this at home). The light is so bright that airplane passengers can see it from more than 250 miles away!

Nothing travels faster than light. And nothing illuminates the world like God's Word. The Bible brings light into our hearts. Proverbs 4:18-19 tells us that the path of believers is like the light of day, while the way of the wicked is like total darkness. God's Word lights our path. By reading the Bible, we gain insight into how God wants us to act. The more we know about God, the better we'll understand life as the Word enlightens our minds.

Jesus wants us to be light to the world (Matthew 5:14). That means we need to reflect God's light to people walking in the darkness. When we walk the way that Jesus commands, we can be even brighter than 39 xenon lamps!

AWESOME ACTIVITY: PASS THE LIGHT
See how well you can reflect light with at least two friends.

Stuff You Need
- ☞ Mirrors
- ☞ Flashlights

Try It
1. Have a few friends hold mirrors.
2. Shine the light at a mirror. That person needs to hold the mirror to let the light bounce off and hit the mirror of the next person.
3. Try bouncing the light with more friends to see how far you can reflect it.

✝ PRAY
Ask God to help you understand what you read in the Bible and to make the choices Jesus would make.

Life's Guidebook Says
Once you were full of darkness, but now you have light from the Lord. So live as people of light! EPHESIANS 5:8

FIRED UP

IT'S TOUGH to contain a wildfire. Just ask people who live in Colorado Springs, Colorado. During the summers of 2012 and 2013, wildfires burned down more than 750 homes and consumed thousands of acres of forest. Firefighters did everything they could to save lives and houses. But high winds, dry vegetation, and hot conditions made the fires burn out of control.

While wildfires can be devastating in neighborhoods, they're all part of God's plan for his creation. Forestry experts say wildfires are actually good for forests. Fire reenergizes a forest as important nutrients go back into the soil. Then new plants pop up to bring life to the landscape. Eventually, new, healthier trees grow as the forest returns stronger than ever.

Firefighters may know the power of wildfires, but the prophet Jeremiah understood the uncontainable awesomeness of God. The prophet said that he tried not to think or speak about God. But then a fire burned inside his bones until the message exploded out of him (see today's verse). Have you ever felt like Jeremiah—like you had to tell somebody about Jesus? People who are filled with God's love often say they are "on fire for God."

God's truth can act like a fire inside you. It's great to feel on fire for God. Then you can spread your warmth to other people. God wants his truth to spread around the world like a wildfire. Let God's Word fire you up today.

WACKY LAUGHS

Q. How did the soldier defeat the enemy with just his mouth?
A. He fired words at them.

Q. What happened to the bread when it got too close to the flame?
A. It was toast.

Q. What book of the Bible do firefighters like?
A. Hose-a.

Q. What do firefighters put in their soup?
A. Fire-crackers.

✝ PRAY

Ask God to help you get fired up about sharing his Word.

Life's Guidebook Says

Sometimes I think, "I won't talk about him anymore. I'll never speak in his name again." But then your message burns in my heart. It's like a fire inside my very bones. I'm tired of holding it in. In fact, I can't. JEREMIAH 20:9, NIrV

PRAYER FOR THE PERSECUTED

WHAT'S THE WORST THING that could happen to you if you told your friends about Jesus?

a. You'd be teased.
b. You'd be ignored.
c. You'd be beaten up.
d. You'd be thrown in jail.

In most countries, the answer is *a* or *b*. But in parts of the world, Christians experience a lot of *c* and *d*. Some organizations estimate that more than 100 million Christians around the world suffer for their faith. In North Korea, families may be sent to prison for owning a Bible. In Laos, Christian children aren't allowed to attend public school. In other countries, Christians could even be killed for believing in Jesus or talking about him.

Today's Christians aren't the first to face persecution. Jesus told his followers, "Since they persecuted me, naturally they will persecute you" (John 15:20). Nearly all of Jesus' original 12 disciples were killed for their faith. Acts tells the story of Stephen being stoned to death (Acts 6–7). Try not to be frightened by these facts. Use the examples of great Christians—the amazing men, women, and children of faith who came before you—to make you strong. And don't forget that God promises to be with you and give you the courage you need in any situation.

At the beginning of every November, Christians around the world pause to pray for their brothers and sisters in Christ who suffer harm because of their beliefs. The International Day of Prayer for the Persecuted Church was created to remind God's people that when part of the Christian body suffers, it affects the whole body. Find out what day the world is praying for Christians this year, then encourage your friends and family to stop and take part in this important day.

LIFTOFF LIST

What can you do to help people persecuted for their faith?

___ Pray.
___ Talk to my youth pastor about having an event at my church.
___ Learn more about the problem at kidsofcourage.com.
___ Write letters to encourage those who are being persecuted.
___ Send a care package to a persecuted family through a Christian organization.

✞ PRAY

Thank God that you can worship him freely. Tell him you want to remember to pray for persecuted Christians more often.

Life's Guidebook Says
Everyone who wants to live a godly life in Christ Jesus will suffer persecution.
2 TIMOTHY 3:12

CUDDLY LIZARD

AN ONLINE VIDEO shows a bearded dragon lizard cuddling with a cat. Another features a cat playing with a lizard (and not because it's about to eat it—they're actually friends). Animals surprise us when they get along with another animal that is usually an enemy.

People can teach dogs and cats to live together in peace, especially if they start when the animals are babies. It also helps to make sure pets are well fed and cared for before trying to let them meet a different type of animal. An animal that is hungry or hurt is more likely to try to hurt animals or people.

Isaiah 11:6-9 talks about animals that will one day rest together instead of preying on each other. Lions will lie down with cows, and wolves with sheep. Even snakes and people will get along!

People can learn to live in peace with one another too. Even if you have different opinions and interests, you can learn to listen and care for other people around you. You might have to work at it. And it's best when both people want to live in peace. Think of ways to make peace with someone you sometimes fight with, like a brother, sister, or classmate. Write down a couple of ideas here:

_____

_____

TWISTY TONGUE TWISTERS

Try to say these tongue twisters 10 times without stopping.

Lizards, lions, and llamas lie lazily on lawns.
Bobtail lizards bobbing bright blue tongues.

✝ PRAY

Ask for God's help to live in peace, especially with anyone who has hurt or bullied you. Pray for God to help you forgive people who hurt you.

Life's Guidebook Says

The baby will play safely near the hole of a cobra. Yes, a little child will put its hand in a nest of deadly snakes without harm. Nothing will hurt or destroy in all my holy mountain, for as the waters fill the sea, so the earth will be filled with people who know the LORD. ISAIAH 11:8-9

LOGOS

IF YOU GO to the refrigerator or look in your closet, you'll probably find a lot of logos. The Coca-Cola white script on a red can is one of the best-known logos in the world. Companies spend millions of dollars to create their logos and build their brands. If you see the golden arches (another popular logo), you probably know exactly what you're going to eat.

In the beginning of John's Gospel, he uses the word *logos*, but it has a very different meaning. *Logos* in Greek means "a divine reason or plan." It's a creative, logical force. When John writes, "In the beginning the Word already existed. The Word was with God, and the Word was God" (John 1:1), the word that's translated into English as "Word" is *logos*. The *logos* that John writes about is the force of God. It's a creative, divine force that changes the world and energizes lives. The Word (Jesus) and his Word (the Bible) give you power, energy, wisdom, creativity, and courage. Isn't that amazing to think about?

Go way back to the beginning of the Bible and read how God made everything by speaking. He said, "Let there be light," and there was light (Genesis 1:3). That's the power of the Word. That's the power of Jesus. Read and memorize as much of God's Word as you can, so that it can empower you.

AWESOME ACTIVITY: VERSE CONCENTRATION
Use a game to help you remember Scriptures.

Stuff You Need
☞ Index cards
☞ Pen

Try It
1. Write each verse you want to memorize on two index cards (or print out verses and glue them on the cards). Make a stack of the pairs of verses.
2. Turn the cards facedown and lay them out.
3. Get a friend or a parent and play a game of concentration. Take turns flipping over cards and reading the verses to find a match.
4. Make it more challenging by writing half a verse on one card and the other half on another card. In this game, you must match up the two halves.

✝ PRAY
Thank God for the power of the Word. Ask him to help you remember it, one verse at a time.

Life's Guidebook Says
In the beginning the Word already existed. The Word was with God, and the Word was God. JOHN 1:1

BREATHE!

CAN YOU SOLVE THIS RIDDLE?

It is a part of us and then replaced.
It escapes our bodies and goes into space.
Without it in us, we would die.
It fills balloons that touch the sky.
What is it?

The answer is *air*. Your body breathes in air about 20 times a minute. You never had to learn how to do it. God created your body to automatically breathe on its own to supply all the oxygen you need. When you exercise hard, you breathe harder, because you need more oxygen. Sometimes a few deep breaths will help you "catch your breath" (which is a funny saying, because you can't catch air—except on a skateboard or bike).

Breathing shows life. Paramedics always check to see if a sick or injured person is breathing and has a pulse. Breath is also powerful. When people do CPR, they blow into someone's mouth to bring that person back to life. God even used his breath to give life to Adam in the Garden of Eden (Genesis 2:7).

The Bible says that God's Word is God breathed. He put life and power into the Word so that it is alive. That makes the Bible different from any other book—it comes directly from God. Every time you read the Bible, you can learn something new. So take a deep breath and dive into God's Word.

WEIRD FACTS: BREATHE IT IN
- ☞ If your lungs were laid flat, they would cover a tennis court.
- ☞ Hyperventilating is breathing too fast and not getting enough oxygen. Breathing like you're blowing out a candle or into a paper bag can help you calm down.
- ☞ The brain uses more oxygen than any other part of your body.
- ☞ Your nose has a four-stage filter system. Your mouth has only one. So breathing through your nose cleans the air better.

✝ PRAY
Thank God for his Word, and ask him to use it to train and correct you.

Life's Guidebook Says
All Scripture is inspired by God and is useful to teach us what is true and to make us realize what is wrong in our lives. It corrects us when we are wrong and teaches us to do what is right. 2 TIMOTHY 3:16

THE HARDWORKING WORD

THE WORLD'S LARGEST CHURCH is in South Korea. At its height, one million people called this church home. That's amazing, especially when you consider the church started in the 1950s with just five people. Sixty years ago, only about 50,000 people believed in Jesus Christ in Korea. Now that number is over 10 million!

The Christian faith has grown in South Korea because people prayed and preached God's Word. But before the church could expand like it has, missionaries had to travel to Korea and translate the Bible into Korean. In the late 1800s, the Bible was translated and printed in Korean. That might sound like a long time ago. But the first English New Testament was published in 1526—more than 350 years earlier! When you think about that, Christianity in South Korea has grown really quickly.

The Bible says that the Word will prosper and do what God wants it to do (see today's verse). It will accomplish his work. God's Word even has power in hard times. During World Wars I and II, American volunteers worked long hours to translate the Bible into the languages of every country involved in the wars. They raised money and sent copies of the Bible around the world. They also organized 5 million people to pray. Many soldiers read Scriptures and came to know Christ because of those efforts. Natives in the Pacific Islands helped many American soldiers because they had received Bibles and believed in Jesus.

Never be afraid to give someone a Bible or share a verse you learned. In Korean, *Yaesu nu sa dang da* means "Jesus loves you." Try saying it. Then live it out!

PLEXER
Solve this plexer to find out where believers will live forever. (If you don't remember what a plexer is, see p. 9.)

Dice Dice

✝ **PRAY**
Ask God to help you share his Word and trust it will do its work.

Life's Guidebook Says
It is the same with my word. I send it out, and it always produces fruit. It will accomplish all I want it to, and it will prosper everywhere I send it.
ISAIAH 55:11

Answer: Paradise

A SAFE TREE

WHAT WOULD BE THE WORST part of sleeping in a tree?

You could fall. That's true. But imagine waking up with a huge snake wrapped around your body. *Yikes!*

Bob discovered just how dangerous tree sleeping could be when he went to a conference of Christian leaders. Some of the leaders had built huge ministries that broadcast God's message around the world. Others had started churches that attracted thousands every week to hear God's Word. Everybody had gathered to talk about ways to share God's Good News with more and more people.

As Bob scanned the room, he found one man that seemed out of place. His clothes weren't fancy. He often looked down, instead of looking other people in the eyes. Bob didn't know his name or where he'd come from.

One by one, people began to tell about their ministries and share prayer requests. One man asked for additional funds to be raised so he could buy more airtime on the radio to get his program to more people. Another needed money and workers to print and deliver Bibles. When it came time for the quiet man to speak, he said he was a pastor in a small Asian country. He traveled from village to village to preach about God. He also trained other pastors to spread the gospel. His prayer was for a safe tree.

What does that mean? Bob wondered.

The young pastor explained that he often slept in trees as he walked through the jungle. Once he woke up and discovered that a gigantic snake had wrapped itself around his body. Poisonous spiders and other dangers also lived in trees.

God wants to hear all our prayers. Prayers for the big things we need and smaller prayers . . . even for a safe tree.

PUZZLE IT OUT: RIGHT DIRECTIONS

Cross out every *b, f, j, q, u, v, x,* and *z.* Then write the remaining letters in order below to discover how to walk with God.

```
b  i  j  n  a    q  l  u  l  z  t  f  h  u  y  b  w  z  a  f  y  s
a  j  c  k  f  j  n  o  x  f  w  b  l  e  q  f  d  g  u  f  b  e
h  j  f  i  b  m  a  q  u  n  b  d  v  f  z  j  h  u  e  b  b
z  z  s  f  b  h  a  x  q  l  l  b  f  d  q  i  x  r  e  b  c  t
t  b  f  h  x  z  y  p  f  b  q  a  t  z  h  f  s  b  b  f  q  z
```

"___ ____ ___ _____ ____,
____ ___ _____ _____ ___ _____."

✝ PRAY

Thank God that he hears and cares about all our prayers.

Life's Guidebook Says

I tell you, you can pray for anything, and if you believe that you've received it, it will be yours. MARK 11:24

Answer: "In all thy ways acknowledge him, and he shall direct thy paths." (Proverbs 3:6, KJV)

BIG CHOICES

MICHAEL SPENT MONTHS raising money to spend the summer on a mission trip to Honduras. Just as all the funds came in, he found out his team had made it to the finals of the space design competition, giving them the opportunity to attend space camp. Both events took place at the same time.

Now Michael had a choice to make: Should he go to space camp or the mission trip? As part of the space competition, he'd meet astronauts and spend a week at the space center. His brother was also on the space team, so they'd be together. Michael had dreams of working with the space program. But he'd already made a commitment to the mission trip and really wanted to serve God over the summer. Michael prayed and prayed. He finally chose to go on the mission trip. He wanted to follow Jesus and build a school for orphans. That would make a lasting difference.

On the trip, he enjoyed playing with the orphans, as well as the hard construction work. His space team picked an alternate, went to the competition, and won! Michael's brother had a great time at space camp and told him all about it.

Sometimes it's hard to choose between two really great opportunities. Like Michael did, it's best to pray about it. God loves to have men who ask him to guide their decisions. That's part of being a hero for God. God knew his plans for Michael would include more great opportunities. He became a rocket scientist and works at the space center—the same one he missed going to as a teen.

LIFTOFF LIST

When you have a decision to make, what do you do?

___ Pray.
___ Talk to my parents.
___ Ask God to give me peace about the right decision.
___ Listen to what God puts in my heart and mind.
___ Read the Bible and see what God shows me.
___ Ask other people to pray too.
___ Make a list of reasons for each choice, both the good and the bad.
___ Ask myself what Jesus would choose.

✝ PRAY

Ask God to help you make the best choice when you have a decision to make.

Life's Guidebook Says

Take delight in the LORD, and he will give you your heart's desires.
PSALM 37:4

A MOMENT TO HEROISM

WILLIAM (BILL) TUREK enjoyed his work for the Coast Guard. He liked helping to protect American shores from threats, keeping drugs out of the country, and rescuing distressed people at sea. As a marine inspector, he made sure that ships were running correctly to keep their crews safe.

During a routine inspection of the *Cape Diamond*, Bill noticed a big problem. While testing the ship's carbon dioxide (CO_2) system, he realized a dangerous level of the gas had been released into the engine room. The crew was in danger! Humans breathe out CO_2 all the time. But when there's too much CO_2, it replaces the oxygen in a room and can suffocate people.

Without hesitating, Bill raced to the engine room and gave orders to get out. He ran inside to push the other men to safety. He saved lives that day, but he died doing it. In the time it takes to blink, Bill chose to put the lives of others before his own. He didn't look for an opportunity to become a hero; he simply responded to danger because he cared about people. Love guided his choice. Following his death, he was awarded the Coast Guard Medal. His name was also put on the Wall of Fame at the Coast Guard Academy in 2012.

Each day, we may have split-second decisions to make. Choose to love other people and do what you can to help them.

TWISTY TONGUE TWISTER

Some days we do harder things than other days. The *Guinness Book of World Records* states that this is the hardest tongue twister to say:

The sixth sick sheik's sixth sheep's sick.

Try a few more tongue twisters:

Six swift ships swiftly shift.
The black-spotted haddock helped heal an eel.

✝ PRAY

Ask God to help you love others and choose actions that show your love.

Life's Guidebook Says

There is no fear in love; but perfect love casts out fear. 1 JOHN 4:18, NASB

DAY OF HONOR

AT THE 11TH HOUR, on the 11th day, during the 11th month of 1918, fighting ended in the Great War. More than 16 million people died during that war—which was later renamed World War I. Over 100,000 American soldiers gave their lives fighting for the Allies and for freedom.

Weeks later, soldiers still on the battlefield and those returning home received a special surprise at Christmas. Volunteers started secretly preparing the celebration in July and kept the news quiet for months. They planned a huge merry Christmas for US soldiers everywhere. During the Christmas season, 1,500 YMCA huts in Europe displayed decorated trees and held dances. They passed out care packages to two million soldiers. Every wounded American soldier woke up to find a red stocking at the foot of his bed filled with candy, a pocketknife, and other gifts. Soldiers in New York received tickets to attend shows and free dinners at restaurants.

Right away, President Woodrow Wilson proclaimed November 11 as Armistice Day. This holiday was renamed years later—in 1954, Congress changed the official name to Veteran's Day, to honor all American soldiers who have served in a war. These brave men and women were willing to lay down their lives for their country. Jesus said there is no greater love than to lay down your life for your friends (see today's verse).

This week is a perfect time to send care packages to soldiers so they will get them in time for Christmas. They can be filled with candies, puzzle books, and little surprises as well as notes and Christmas cards. When you see someone in the military, remember to say, "Thanks for serving, and may God bless you."

PLEXER

Solve this plexer to discover the name of a great American soldier. (If you don't remember what a plexer is, see p. 9.)

(If you don't remember what a plexer is, see p. 9.)

2000washPOUNDS

✞ PRAY

Ask God to keep women and men serving in the military safe.

Life's Guidebook Says
There is no greater love than to lay down one's life for one's friends.
JOHN 15:13

Answer: Washington

FAITHFUL HEROES

WHAT DO YOU THINK you need to do to be a hero for God? List a few ideas:

1. _____
2. _____
3. _____

You probably didn't list lying, murder, or deceiving others, but that's what some men did before they became heroes. Isaac lied by calling his wife his sister. David had another woman's husband killed to cover up his sin. Jacob deceived his father and brother to get a better inheritance. But they all changed and started following God more closely.

God called these men—and many others throughout history—to follow him. Newspapers and Craigslist weren't around, but God's want ad may have looked like this:

Wanted: *Men of faith willing to be teased, beaten, possibly sawed in half, poor; may need to sleep in caves or holes in the ground, be imprisoned, and wear goatskins.*

That sounds pretty tough . . . and gross (especially being sawed in half). But that was the fate of many of God's faithful followers. Hebrews 11 lists God's Hall of Faith—men and women who lived their faith and said yes when God called them. They suffered through many of the situations listed in the want ad.

The verses also tell us that mighty things happened when these heroes believed: they shut mouths of lions, conquered kingdoms, escaped death, became mighty, and obtained promises. Being a hero means having faith in God and saying yes to him. That one word can make an ordinary young man extraordinary.

QUIZ: HALL OF FAITH MATCH
See if you can recall what each man listed in the Hall of Faith did.

1. Gideon   A. Conquered Jericho (Joshua 6)
2. Moses   B. Saved people and animals in an ark (Genesis 6:13-22)
3. Noah   C. Pleased God, taken to heaven (Genesis 5:23-24)
4. Jacob   D. Led people out of Egypt and across the Red Sea (Exodus)
5. Enoch   E. Saved people from starving (Genesis 41:49-54)
6. Joshua   F. Had 12 sons who became the nation of Israel (Genesis 49)
7. Joseph   G. Conquered the Midianites with only 300 men (Judges 6–9)

✝ PRAY
Ask God for the courage to follow him and say yes when he calls.

Life's Guidebook Says
Faith is the confidence that what we hope for will actually happen; it gives us assurance about things we cannot see. HEBREWS 11:1

Answers: 1. G; 2. D; 3. B; 4. F; 5. C; 6. A; 7. E

FAITH UNDER FIRE

WHIZZ! Bang! Bullets whipped past Bill Tolar's head. Bill had spotted six wounded soldiers who were being pinned down by enemy fire. The marine had a choice: try to rescue his fallen friends or save himself. For Bill, it was no choice at all—he was going to save his friends.

He and another soldier crawled through a rice paddy and worked their way to the men as the enemy continued to target them. They grabbed an abandoned jeep and started loading the wounded soldiers. *Bang! Bang!* The enemy kept shooting. But not one bullet touched them! Later, Bill would say that God was sitting beside him in the jeep. Then a US plane dove toward the enemy and dropped bombs to scare them off.

Five of the six men that Bill rescued survived their injuries. For his heroics during the Korean War, Bill was awarded the Silver Star—one of the highest medals of valor. When Bill returned to his hometown after the war, he continued to show love and help others when he saw a need.

People said, "Bill was the genuine article; he loved you and made no bones about it. You could never doubt his sincerity. When there was a need, Bill was there." Bill never planned to be a hero. But he became one when he showed genuine care for the wounded men. He put the needs of others before his own. God asks us to love one another. Love can give you the courage to be brave and the strength to help others. When you sacrifice to help others, you reflect God to the world around you.

EXPERIMENT: STRONG PAPER
Paper is easy to cut and rip, yet it can surprise you with its strength.

Stuff You Need
- ☞ Paper
- ☞ Sharp knife
- ☞ Potato

Try It
Fold the paper in half around the sharp side of the knife. Slice a potato by holding the handle of the knife but not touching the paper. *Surprise!* The knife cuts the potato but not the paper, because the potato is softer than the paper fiber.

✝ PRAY
Ask God to show you ways you can help people.

Life's Guidebook Says
Your love for one another will prove to the world that you are my disciples.
JOHN 13:35

HONEST ABE

WOULD YOU LIKE TO BE known for being honest? What about having an "honest" nickname? Try it out. Say, "I'm Honest (fill in your name)."

President Abraham Lincoln is considered one of the greatest presidents in US history. He earned the nickname Honest Abe early in life when he worked at a store. One day Abe discovered he had a few pennies too many in the cash drawer and walked many miles to return the money he owed to a customer to whom he had not given the correct change. He took care to be honest in little actions and in his words. Abe cared deeply for poor people and slaves and wanted to help them.

Once when a friend teased him as he read the Bible, Abe replied, "Take all that you can of this book upon reason, and the balance on faith, and you will live and die a happier man." President Lincoln understood the value of the Bible and the need for guidance through life.

Joshua was also a man who stood up for God and his truth. In the Old Testament, Joshua told the people that he would continue to serve the Lord above the other gods in their culture (see today's verse).

Each day you have a choice. You can go along with what other people are doing. Or you can choose to be honest, read the Bible, and follow Jesus.

WACKY LAUGHS

Check out these jokes and clever sayings by President Lincoln.

- ☞ "If I were two-faced, would I be wearing this one?"
- ☞ "Things may come to those who wait, but only the things left by those who hustle."
- ☞ "We can complain because rose bushes have thorns, or rejoice because thorn bushes have roses."
- ☞ Once when Lincoln was asked why he walked so crookedly, he reportedly replied, "Oh, my nose, you see, is crooked, and I have to follow it!"

✞ PRAY

Ask God to help you be honest and to live in a way that would cause others to follow you.

Life's Guidebook Says

[Joshua said,] "Choose today whom you will serve. Would you prefer the gods your ancestors served beyond the Euphrates? Or will it be the gods of the Amorites in whose land you now live? But as for me and my family, we will serve the LORD."
JOSHUA 24:15

TRUTH SEEKERS

BILLY GRAHAM has been called "America's pastor." But it may be more accurate to call him "the world's pastor." He has preached the Good News about Jesus to 215 million people in over 185 countries. His radio and TV broadcasts have been heard by 2.2 billion more. His organization says more than 3.2 million people accepted Christ as their Savior at his crusades.

When Billy spoke, he had a simple message: "Look to the Cross." Billy shared the truth of God's love and forgiveness in straightforward terms. We're sinners in need of a Savior. Only Jesus can save us. While talking about Jesus can make some people an outcast, it did the opposite for Billy. He appeared on the list of most admired people in America over 55 times—more than any other person! He has met, prayed for, and advised every US president since WWII. His consistency in reaching out with God's love has made him respected around the globe.

Billy didn't preach only to adults; he especially loved preaching to students, because they often saw and understood God's truth more quickly. They wanted to learn about Jesus and understand more about becoming like him. Simply put: they became truth seekers.

Choose to be a truth seeker. Read your Bible. Wake up every day ready to proclaim the good news that Jesus saves. Be willing to talk with God and ask him each day to guide your life.

WEIRD FACTS: SAVING GRACES

Studies show that people 14 years old and younger are much more open to accepting Christ as their Savior. So try these tips and remember these facts:

- ☞ It's very important to tell friends about Jesus now.
- ☞ People alive today have more opportunity to hear about Jesus than at any other time in history.
- ☞ More than three out of every four adults are searching for a more meaningful life. That means they are more open to finding out about Jesus.
- ☞ People start attending church for the relationships, but stay for the teaching.

✝ PRAY

Ask God to lead you each day and open opportunities for you to tell others about him.

Life's Guidebook Says
Sing to the LORD; praise his name. Each day proclaim the good news that he saves. PSALM 96:2

MOON PRINTS

IF YOU TRACK MUD or snow across the kitchen floor, your mom probably makes you clean it up.

When astronaut Jim Irwin saw his footprints in the dust on the moon, he knew they would possibly remain forever. No air or wind exists on the moon to blow the prints away. They stay unless more dust covers them or a meteorite crashes on top of them. Jim was one of just 12 people to ever walk on the lunar surface. But he almost didn't make it back to earth.

Jim and David Scott landed the lunar module on the edge of a crater, which caused the module to tilt. The control center in Houston realized the module had a water leak and told the astronauts to investigate. When they fixed the leak, they realized the tilt of the craft had kept the water from hitting electrical circuits and short-circuiting the wires. Burnt wires could have prevented the lunar module from lifting off and left them stranded on the moon.

Long before Jim's moon walk, he understood that God controlled everything. Jim never expected to be an astronaut. He applied a month before he reached the age limit of 36. But God let him soar into space, walk on the moon, and then come back to earth to tell others about him. God placed you on the earth and gave you responsibilities as well. One of those is helping care for the earth . . . and anywhere else you might walk in the universe.

EXPERIMENT: METEORITE FUN

Meteorites form craters when they hit the moon. They usually burn up when they enter the earth's atmosphere but leave tiny particles in the air. Catch some meteorite dust when it rains.

Stuff You Need
☞ Container
☞ Coffee filter or fine fabric
☞ Strong magnet

Try It
1. When it rains, place the container under a drain spout and collect water.
2. Pour the water through the filter. Remove leaves, bugs, and other debris. Look for fine black particles. Let the particles dry.
3. Test the black particles with a magnet. If they are magnetic, they could be tiny particles from meteorites that contain a lot of iron.

✝ PRAY

Ask God to help you be responsible and trust him to give you great opportunities in life.

Life's Guidebook Says
You gave them charge of everything you made, putting all things under their authority. PSALM 8:6

SPLENDOR IN THE SKY

WHAT'S THE MOST FAMOUS star in the Bible?

Jesus is the "star" of God's Word. But the star the wise men followed to find baby Jesus may be the most famous physical star. And that's not the only time stars are mentioned. First Corinthians 15:41 says, "The sun has one kind of glory, while the moon and stars each have another kind. And even the stars differ from each other in their glory." For more than 1,000 years, nobody fully understood that verse. Then modern science started classifying stars with letters—O, B, A, F, G, K, and M. (You can remember that by thinking, *Oh, be a funny guy, kick me!*) O stars are the hottest. M-class stars are the coolest. Our sun is a middle G star.

Another verse reminds us that God names every star (Psalm 147:4). He put the stars in the sky as signs to mark seasons and sacred times. Scientists have gained knowledge from studying stars. Some people worship the stars or think stars can tell the future. But the wise men had it right. They followed the star but worshiped Jesus. God wants us to enjoy the heavenly sights he created. But we should worship only him—not the stars he made.

PUZZLE IT OUT: STAR CROSSED

Men have connected stars like dots to see pictures in the sky that help them find their location at night. Use the numbers to trace the lines in the square to form letters. So, 1793 is U and 71254 is P.

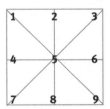

"___ ___ ___ ___ ___ ___ ___ ___ ___
317965 13971 28745 28 314697 71539 13971 7125459 2145478

___ ___ ___ ___ ___ ___ ___ ___ ___ ___ ___ ___
317965 178 13971 7125459 28 13971 1793 314697 1328 174639 713964 7193

___ ___ ___ ___ ___ ___ ___."
1328 174639 2145478 71539 13971 13971 7193

✝ PRAY

Thank God for making stars, especially the sun that gives us light.

Life's Guidebook Says

[The wise men said,] "Where is the newborn king of the Jews? We saw his star as it rose, and we have come to worship him." MATTHEW 2:2

Answer: God is more glorious than the moon (from Job 25:5).

HEAVEN AND HELL

WHAT DO YOU THINK of when you picture heaven? Cartoons often make heaven appear like a bunch of people sitting on clouds playing harps. The Bible gives us little glimpses of a very different heaven. Maybe you've read enough to have ideas of what's really there.

Scripture describes God's throne with a rainbow around it. Heaven doesn't need the sun or electric lights, because the light of God shines everywhere. Heaven is beautiful, joyful, and filled with people and amazing beings. God lives there. It's a place with no tears, sadness, fear, or sickness.

Long ago, Jesus told us about heaven so we would know it's real (John 14:3; Matthew 5:3-12). Jesus also talked about hell, so we can trust that is a real place of torment and eternal fire where we don't want to go (Matthew 25:41; Mark 9:43-48; Revelation 20:10). God created hell for Satan and those who reject God's love and mercy. He created heaven as his home and a place where his followers will enjoy living forever.

Years ago, Randy Alcorn dug into the Bible to find answers to the most common questions kids ask about heaven. He wrote a great book called *Heaven for Kids*. You can find lots more details about your heavenly home in that book.

But there's one detail you don't want to overlook. Only those who believe in Jesus will be allowed in heaven. John 3:16 is probably the most well-known and memorized verse in the Bible. In it, Jesus tells us that everyone who believes in him will go to heaven. If you haven't memorized that verse before, do it today.

LIFTOFF LIST

If you believe in heaven, ask God to give you the courage to tell others about heaven. Check off everything that's true for you.

___ I believe in heaven.
___ I believe Jesus died for me.
___ I want the people I love to go to heaven too.
___ It's important to tell friends—and everyone else—about Jesus and heaven.

✝ PRAY

Thank God for creating heaven. Praise God that he wants you to live there forever.

Life's Guidebook Says

This is how God loved the world: He gave his one and only Son, so that everyone who believes in him will not perish but have eternal life. JOHN 3:16

SOUNDS FROM HEAVEN

"YOU ARE MY DEARLY loved Son, and you bring me great joy." How would you like your mom or dad to say those words about you? It'd be pretty cool, huh?

In the Bible, we read those exact words as God the Father says them from heaven at the baptism of Jesus (Mark 1:11). And those aren't the only sounds from heaven that are described in the Bible.

Harpists play sounds like the roar of a mighty ocean (Revelation 14:2). Many voices join together to shout, "Praise the LORD!" (Revelation 19:1). Angel wings make crashing sounds like waves splashing on the shore (Ezekiel 1:24). These are all happy noises. But the most joyful sound comes from the four creatures that the apostle John described in Revelation 4:7-8. One looked like a lion, another like an ox, the third had a human face, and the fourth appeared like an eagle. Day and night the four creatures stood in front of God's throne and praised him, saying, "Holy, holy, holy is the Lord God, the Almighty."

Why do you think they say, "Holy, holy, holy"? It could be because God is three persons in one. The Trinity includes God the Father, Jesus the Son, and the Holy Spirit.

There are a lot of sounds in heaven, but none of them drown out your prayers. God hears all your prayers as soon as you speak them. To God, prayers are sweet-smelling incense that fills golden bowls (Revelation 5:8). Whether you pray silently in your heart, shout loudly, or use a soft voice, God listens to you. When you talk to your heavenly Father, it brings him great joy.

WACKY LAUGHS

Q. What kind of bugs can you find on the moon?

A. Lunarticks.

Q. What free trip in the heavens do you get every year?

A. A trip around the sun.

Q. How do you know there's not much money on the moon?

A. Because at least once a month it gets down to its last quarter.

✟ PRAY

Talk to God. Praise him. Let him know what you're thinking and what you need.

Life's Guidebook Says

God did listen! He paid attention to my prayer. PSALM 66:19

WHERE'D HE GO?

SWIFTY: SWIFTY HERE, the top reporter with *Pharisee Nightly News*. It seems like weird stuff always surrounds Jesus and his disciples. It's been rumored that someone went up into the clouds and disappeared. I'm here with one of the disciples now. John, what can you tell us?

John: I saw Jesus rise into the heavens.

Swifty: He died, and you've been tricking us into thinking he's alive. Is this another trick?

John: He rose after he died. Hundreds of people have seen him. Now he's gone up into the clouds.

Swifty: Maybe someone used a rope and lifted him into a tree.

John: No strings attached.

Swifty: Sounds like Jesus is a tricky guy. I never saw him after he died.

John: I saw him several times. You should have stuck with me.

Swifty: What happened after he went up in a puff of cloud?

John: Two men in white clothes showed up and asked why we were still looking into the sky.

Swifty: Wait a minute. Where'd they come from?

John: I was busy watching the clouds, so I can't really say.

Swifty: Did they say anything else?

John: Yes, they explained, "Jesus has been taken from you into heaven, but someday he will return from heaven in the same way you saw him go!" [Acts 1:11].

Swifty: Does that mean you'll keep watching the clouds?

John: No. We have to pray and wait. He's sending us his Holy Spirit.

Swifty: What's that?

John: The Spirit of God, who will give us power, teach us, and help us.

Swifty: It sounds like there are more strange happenings to come. I'll keep my camera on you and your friends for a while.

PLEXER

See if you can solve this plexer. (If you don't remember what a plexer is, see p. 9.)

CLOUDS
U
S
E
J

✝ PRAY

Ask God to fill you with his Holy Spirit and teach you and give you power to witness.

Life's Guidebook Says

"You will receive power when the Holy Spirit comes upon you. And you will be my witnesses, telling people about me everywhere. . . ." After saying this, [Jesus] was taken up into a cloud while they were watching. ACTS 1:8-9

Answer: Jesus went up into the clouds.

HEAVENLY TREASURE

CARL SWEPT HIS METAL DETECTOR back and forth along the beach. Suddenly, he heard a high-pitched noise and started digging. He'd learned that the sound told him what the detector had found. Hums, warbles, and different tones and pitches helped him know if it was just aluminum foil and old batteries, or actual treasure of gold or silver. Carl liked to use his detector to help other people. He had returned several school rings to owners and helped a woman find her lost wedding ring. When he looked for treasure, he usually found a few coins each day. *Zap!* Once he'd found an 1859 half-dollar.

Treasure hunting and collecting can be fun. God collects treasure too. We're his treasure. In the book of Exodus, God's people were freed from Pharaoh and went into the desert to find the Promised Land. "Now if you will obey me and keep my covenant," the Lord told his people, "you will be my own special treasure from among all the peoples on earth" (19:5). God rules the earth. Everything belongs to him. But when he looks at the people who follow him, he sees treasure.

Have you ever found a dollar in your pocket or a quarter on the ground? It's a great feeling. When God sees you obeying his commands and living for him, he gets that same feeling—times a million! Live like you're a great treasure.

WEIRD FACTS: AMAZING TREASURES

☞ The Rosetta Stone is considered a priceless treasure. It's a stone tablet with writing that provided the key to decoding Egyptian hieroglyphics.

☞ The Hope diamond is the largest deep-blue diamond ever discovered. No one gets to wear it. It's in the Smithsonian Institution for all to see its beauty.

☞ A man in Nevada died alone in 2012 and no one noticed for a month. They discovered he had hoarded a treasure of gold coins worth $7.5 million.

☞ Jesus praised a widow for giving a few pennies to God. It was all she had and thus a great treasure.

✝ PRAY

Ask God to fill your heart with the knowledge that you're worth so much to him.

Life's Guidebook Says

[God said,] "Now if you will obey me and keep my covenant, you will be my own special treasure from among all the peoples on earth; for all the earth belongs to me." EXODUS 19:5

PARADE FOR JESUS

MORE THAN THREE MILLION people line the streets of New York City every year to watch the famous Thanksgiving Day parade. It's one of the most popular parades in the world and symbolizes the start of the Christmas season. Since its beginning in 1924, this parade has become known for its gigantic balloons.

Dozens of people hold strong ropes to keep the balloons gently gliding above the streets of New York. Over the years numerous famous characters have flown through the sky, including Spider-Man, Snoopy, Shrek, and SpongeBob SquarePants. Felix the Cat was the first big balloon to join the parade in 1927. Then, in 1934, Mickey Mouse floated into the celebration.

Nearly 1,900 years before the first Thanksgiving Day parade in New York, people lined the roads of Jerusalem for an unplanned parade that honored Jesus. News of his miracles had spread, and his presence excited people. Jesus sat on a baby donkey that had never been ridden. People spread their garments and palm branches in the dirty street. They cheered *Hosanna*, which means "save us."

This parade did not make everyone happy. The noise angered religious leaders. They didn't like people paying attention to Jesus. They worried he might take away their power. The leaders told Jesus, "Rebuke your followers" (Luke 19:39). Jesus didn't stop the noise. He said if the people became quiet, then the stones would yell out.

Floating balloons are cool. But screaming rocks? Now that's awesome. Be a screaming rock for Jesus.

PLEXER

Solve this plexer to see what God wants you to do. (If you don't remember what a plexer is, see p. 9.)

JEbelieveSUS

✝ PRAY

Praise Jesus and shout *Hosanna*—because he really saves us!

Life's Guidebook Says

[Jesus] replied, "If they kept quiet, the stones along the road would burst into cheers!" LUKE 19:40

Answer: Believe in Jesus.

DON'T FORGET

You may have heard the story of Jesus healing 10 lepers. Only one remembered to thank him. The other nine begged for his help but never said a word of thanks once they were healed. Write down a few times that you've been thankful this month.

1. _____

2. _____

3. _____

Did any of those include thanking God for the day or for answered prayers? The little word *thanks* does more than make your mom feel good because you remembered to use your manners. Studies show gratitude can actually help you be healthier.

A study of teens showed that kids who showed more thankfulness were happier and more hopeful, kept a more positive attitude, had better social lives, and behaved better in school. Another study showed that people who spent 15 minutes before bed writing or journaling reasons to be thankful fell asleep faster and slept better than people who did not fall asleep with a spirit of thankfulness.

Gratefulness is also linked with healthier immune systems and decreased stress. Grateful people bounce back from problems easier because they have more hope for the future. Make gratitude part of your daily life. What are you thankful for today?

PUZZLE IT OUT: THANKSGIVING ACROSTIC

Fill in the blanks with things you can be thankful for all year. Thank God for them, and think of other blessings for which you can be thankful.

1. T __ __ __   Items to play with
2. H __ __ __   Where you live
3. __ A __ __ __ __   The people who live with you
4. __ __ __ N __ __ __ Your homeland
5. __ __ __ K __   You read these
6. S __ __ __ __ __   Where students learn
7. G __ __   He made you
8. __ __ I __ __ __ __ Pals
9. __ __ V __   Parents give you this from their heart.
10. __ __ I __ __   You believe, so you have this
11. __ __ __ __ __ N   Where believers live forever
12. G __ __ __ __   You play these

✝ PRAY

Thank God today and ask him to show you who else you should thank.

Life's Guidebook Says

Be thankful in all circumstances, for this is God's will for you who belong to Christ Jesus. 1 THESSALONIANS 5:18

Answers: 1. Toys; 2. Home; 3. Family; 4. Country; 5. Books; 6. School; 7. God; 8. Friends; 9. Love; 10. Faith; 11. Heaven; 12. Games

GIVING THANKS

How do you praise God and show him thanks? Do you . . .

a. dance like David? (1 Chronicles 15:25-29)
b. stack stones like the Israelites? (Joshua 4:8-9)
c. write a prayer of thanksgiving like Paul? (for example, Ephesians 1:3-8)
d. start a chant of "God Rules!" at school?

All of those ideas are good ones. (But if you do the last one, make sure to make a video of it and upload it to the Internet—with your parents' permission, of course.) You may just sing to God or say thank you at the end of a prayer. David and the other writers of the Psalms spent a lot of time thanking God. As their words flowed, it was almost like they were counting their blessings and the blessings given to their parents, grandparents, and other ancestors. They mentioned each blessing and thanked God for it. They thanked him after successes. They thanked him in the middle of troubles. And they thanked him on special feast days. The Psalms reminded people to enter God's presence with thanksgiving (Psalm 100:4).

When you pray, be sure to also thank God. Even when bad things were happening in their lives, the psalmists still thanked him. When he had many great losses in one day, Job said that if we accept good from God, then we should also accept troubles (Job 2:10). It's a heart attitude to choose to be thankful even when we face problems. God has done so much for you that it's important to remember each night before you sleep to thank God for the day and the blessings he sent.

PUZZLE IT OUT: GOING AND GOING

Psalm 136 and several other verses in the Bible use a phrase for why we should thank God. Solve the math problems and write in the correct letter to find the phrase.

H = 1	F = 7	S = 2	R = 8	O = 3	U = 9
I = 10	V = 5	E = 11	N = 6	D = 12	L = 4

"
___ ___ ___ ___ ___ ___ ___ ___ ___ ___ ___ ___ ___
9-8 2x5 8÷4 6-2 9÷3 2+3 6+5 8+3 2x3 3x4 3x3 16÷2 7+4 6÷3

___ ___ ___ ___ ___ ___ ___."
3+4 6÷2 5+3 4+7 1+4 2+9 4x2

✝ PRAY

Read a psalm as a prayer (especially Psalms 107, 118, and 136).

Life's Guidebook Says
Give thanks to the LORD, for he is good. His love endures forever.
PSALM 136:1, NIV

Answer: "His love endures forever."

JUST IN TIME

POLICE INVESTIGATION—around 2060 BC

Detective: Abraham, I understand you had a close encounter today.

Abraham: Yes, but my son is fine, as you can see.

Detective: I meant you saw a UFA, an unidentified flying angel.

Abraham: Well, an angel from heaven spoke to me.

Detective: What did the angel look like?

Abraham: I only heard the angel speak.

Detective: What did the angel say?

Abraham: "Don't lay a hand on the boy!"

Detective: Were you about to harm your son?

Abraham: God told me to offer Isaac as a burnt sacrifice.

Detective: He would've been toast, and I would've had to arrest you.

Abraham: I trusted God would bring Isaac back from the dead.

Detective: Still, God demanded quite a sacrifice.

Abraham: God wanted to make sure he's number one in my life.

Detective: *Hmm.* So is God mad at the angel now?

Abraham: No, he commanded the angel to come. He plans to bless me.

Detective: Isaac, you must be upset with your dad for trying to hurt you.

Isaac: No, he's the best dad around. I heard the angel too. God will also bless me.

Detective: This case isn't closed. I want you two to report to me any other UFA sightings you have.

Abraham: We will, Detective. But this one was out of sight!

WACKY LAUGHS

Q. What baseball team do people in heaven cheer for?

A. The Los Angeles Angels of Anaheim.

Q. How do angels greet one another?

A. They wave *halo*.

Q. What do angels do if they forget the words to a song?

A. They wing it.

✝ PRAY

Thank God for using angels as his messengers.

> ### Life's Guidebook Says
> *"Don't lay a hand on the boy!" the angel said. "Do not hurt him in any way, for now I know that you truly fear God. You have not withheld from me even your son, your only son."* GENESIS 22:12

BETTER LATE THAN NEVER

IF YOUR PARENTS WANTED to send you a message, how long would you have to wait to receive it?

With modern technology, we can send messages with our smartphones in an instant. But in the 1940s, messages took a long time to get from place to place. During World War II, Ray Sasser recorded a message to his family, but it took 65 years to reach his daughter.

During the war, the United Service Organizations set up machines for soldiers to make records. Ray recorded a message but died five months before the birth of his daughter, Joyce. Years later, the record was discovered. The old vinyl grooves still worked. Relatives found Joyce, and a recording studio helped her hear her dad's voice as he expressed his love.

Sometimes messages are worth the wait. Daniel trusted God and saw him answer numerous prayers. But one time God sent him a vision without explaining its meaning. Daniel prayed for understanding. God didn't answer. Daniel became sad. He waited a few days. Then he stopped eating for three weeks as he waited.

Finally, an angel appeared. The angel started by saying what angels usually say, "Don't be afraid." God loved Daniel and had sent the angel on the first day Daniel prayed, but demons had delayed him. God sent another angel to help him fight off the demons. The messenger explained that Daniel's vision showed future events.

God doesn't always send messages in such amazing ways, but it's good to know his angels are always around to deliver what he wants to tell us.

AWESOME ACTIVITY: WHIP UP AN ANGEL

Stuff You Need
- Whip cream
- Spoon
- Plastic knife

Try It
1. Squirt or scoop a bunch of whip cream onto a plate.
2. Gently press a spoon into the whip cream to form an angel head and body.
3. Move a plastic knife back and forth in a quarter circle on both sides of the body for wings. Draw a line above the head to form the halo.

✝ PRAY
If you have an unanswered prayer, don't give up. Keep praying and trust God's timing.

Life's Guidebook Says
[The angel] said, "Don't be afraid, Daniel. Since the first day you began to pray for understanding and to humble yourself before your God, your request has been heard in heaven. I have come in answer to your prayer." DANIEL 10:12

TRUTH OR CONSEQUENCE

HAVE YOU PLAYED the "telephone game," where a secret message is whispered by each person around a circle? At the end, the message seldom sounds like the original.

Urban legends start in similar ways. They begin with a grain of truth but are retold and changed until they hardly sound like the original story. People pass them on through e-mail or talking to each other until it's hard to figure out what the truth is. So, no, a hunter in Texas did not shoot Bigfoot, and baby carrots are not deformed carrots soaked in chlorine. Myths and false stories can make it hard for people to know the truth.

Zechariah had heard about angels speaking to men, but it had been hundreds of years since any man had heard from a heavenly being. One day, as Zech served in the Temple, an angel appeared and gave him a wonderful message: he and his wife would have a special son who would turn the hearts of people back to God.

"How can I be sure this will happen?" Zech said. "I'm an old man now, and my wife is also well along in years" (Luke 1:18).

Oops! Wrong thing to say to one of God's angels. The angel Gabriel told old Zech he'd be unable to speak until his son was born. For nearly a year, Zech couldn't talk. But once the baby was born and Zech wrote, "His name is John!" (Just as the angel had told him to do), his voice returned and he praised God.

When you don't believe God's Word or follow false myths, there are consequences. Make sure you're getting your information from the right sources. You can always trust God and the angels he sends.

WEIRD FACTS: GOD SPEAKING

God spoke to people in the Bible in various ways:

- ☞ Through putting a plan in a heart or mind (Nehemiah 2:12; 7:5)
- ☞ Through angels (Revelation 1:1)
- ☞ In a small voice (1 Kings 19:12-13)
- ☞ In an audible voice (Acts 10:19)
- ☞ Through dreams and visions (Acts 10:9-16)

✝ PRAY

Ask God for wisdom to know when he or an angel is speaking to you.

Life's Guidebook Says

[The angel said,] *"Since you didn't believe what I said, you will be silent and unable to speak until the child is born. For my words will certainly be fulfilled at the proper time."* LUKE 1:20

IF I HAD A HAMMER . . .

WHACK! BANG! CRACK! Franco kept hammering the dull-looking rock that his family had found while walking through the Utah desert. Finally, the rock cracked open. Franco knew this wasn't an ordinary rock—it was a geode. These plain stones hide sparkling minerals inside. As Franco carefully chipped the rock in two, he could see beautiful purple amethyst crystals inside.

"That will go great with your collection," Dad said.

"I'll put it next to my yellow citrine quartz," Franco said.

Franco knew a lot about rocks, but geodes were his favorite. Not many rocks can be split by a hammer to reveal a treasure inside.

The Bible calls God's Word a hammer that shatters a rock (see today's verse). The hearts of wicked people are compared to rocks because they are filled with anger and evil. It takes a lot to change rock-hard hearts. God's Word acts like a hammer to whack away the hardness of pride, stubbornness, and selfishness. It crumbles anger and meanness. God wants to hammer off the hardness of evil. Then his love can grow inside the heart like beautiful amethyst.

A hammer not only breaks things apart, it can also be used to build. Once God smashes away the hardness of hearts, he builds something new and better. A heart changed by God's love is filled with peace and joy. Let God work on any hard spots in your heart to make it more like his.

LIFTOFF LIST

Do you have character traits that need to be hammered away? Check off areas God is working on in you with the hammer of his Word.

____ Pride

____ Unkindness

____ Selfishness

____ Stubbornness

____ Timidity about sharing the Word

____ Anger

____ Meanness

____ Adding joy and love

✝ PRAY

Ask God to soften your heart to his Word and build you into a strong believer.

Life's Guidebook Says

"Does not my word burn like fire?" says the LORD. "Is it not like a mighty hammer that smashes a rock to pieces?" JEREMIAH 23:29

LADDER TO HEAVEN

NOBODY LIKES CLIMBING STAIRS, right? That's why escalators were invented. Yet people can end up climbing a lot of stairs. Every year competitors gather in New York City to race up the Empire State Building. Runners sprint up 1,576 stairs in around 10 minutes. Climbing to the top of Mount Niesen in the Swiss Alps requires even more steps. It has 11,674 steps, making it one of the longest stairways in the world.

Think of the longest staircase you've ever climbed. It probably had nowhere near 12,000 steps. In the Old Testament, Jacob had a dream where he saw the longest ladder in the universe. Angels climbed up and down it to heaven. As he looked up the unending ladder, God told him he would have an unending family. His family would be like the dust of the earth and live in all directions from where Jacob slept. Jacob stood up a stone to remind himself of God's amazing vision. Like all of God's promises, it came true.

No one else has seen what Jacob saw, but the Bible tells us we will see a heavenly staircase one day (see today's verse). Heaven will open and Jesus will be the stairs between heaven and earth that the angels go back and forth on.

Next time you climb a staircase, pause to think about your heavenly home. One day you'll live with God forever . . . and you won't have to take the stairs to get there.

WACKY LAUGHS

Q. What's the difference between a person going upstairs and a person looking upstairs?

A. One steps upstairs, and the other stares up steps.

Q. What goes up and down but never moves?

A. The stairs.

Q. Why did the boy take a ladder to class?

A. He wanted to go to high school.

✝ PRAY

Thank God for the heavenly visions he gives us in the Bible and the promise of living with him in the future.

Life's Guidebook Says

[Jesus] said, "I tell you the truth, you will all see heaven open and the angels of God going up and down on the Son of Man, the one who is the stairway between heaven and earth." JOHN 1:51

SECRET SERVICE PROTECTION

BEING PART OF THE SECRET SERVICE looks cool. Secret Service agents wear dark sunglasses and suits, drive bullet-proof cars, talk in special code names, and protect the president. In 1981, Secret Service agent Tim McCarthy became a hero by throwing himself in front of a bullet intended for President Ronald Reagan. Both McCarthy and Reagan were hit, but both men survived. As a Secret Service agent, you're trained to go toward danger instead of duck away from it.

Secret Service agents have always been known for paying attention and noticing everything going on around them. But when the Secret Service was founded in 1865, its main job was tracking down counterfeit money. After the assassination of President William McKinley in 1901, the Secret Service was given the job of protecting the president.

In the New Testament, Jesus says that boys and girls have a special Secret Service to care for them—angels! But angels do more than watch children. They fly into the presence of God. Jesus warned people not to harm a child, because each child's angel sees God (see today's verse). You may be small—or not so small—but you have mighty protectors. Remember always how much God cares for you.

AWESOME ACTIVITY: UPDRAFTS

As you watch steam cause paper to swirl and rise, think of angels rising to heaven and dancing in praise.

Stuff You Need
- ☞ White tissue paper
- ☞ Scissors
- ☞ Thread 4 inches long
- ☞ Tape
- ☞ Straw
- ☞ Steaming cup of water or cocoa

Try It
1. Cut the white tissue paper into a 3-inch circle. Starting at the outside, cut a spiral.
2. Tape the inner circle to the thread.
3. Tape the other end of the thread to the short end of a flex straw.
4. Hold the tissue above the hot water and watch it twirl. Be sure to keep the free end of the spiral above the cup.

✝ PRAY

Ask God to send angels to protect you.

Life's Guidebook Says

[Jesus said,] "Beware that you don't look down on any of these little ones. For I tell you that in heaven their angels are always in the presence of my heavenly Father." MATTHEW 18:10

DECEMBER

THE HEART SPEAKS

STAND UP RIGHT NOW and do 20 jumping jacks. Sit back down and put your hand on the center of your chest. *Lub-dub. Lub-dub.* Do you feel the beating of your heart? Can you *rat-a-tat-tat* the beat your heart makes with your fingers on the table? When you make sounds on a table or drum, you're doing more than making noise. You're creating vibrations.

Every time you open your mouth to speak, you also create vibrations. Words start as vibrations in your vocal cords (voice box). A muscle near your stomach called the diaphragm pushes air from your lungs through your voice box. The motion of the cords creates vibrations that you learn to control and turn into words.

Before you make a sound, something even more important happens. Your words spring from what's in your heart and mind. Grumpy words, whining, and complaining show that you're not happy. You might be worried, angry, or hurt. Laughter, compliments, and pleasant words usually reflect a happier heart.

Remember this acrostic to help your heart stay in good condition so you can speak better words:

Hold onto happy thoughts and God's love.
Erase hurt by forgiving others.
Appreciate the words of others and understand that their hearts may not be happy.
Remove jealousy and anger by confessing your negative emotions.
Trust God to take care of your worries and problems.

Speak up with pleasant words from a joyful heart!

LIFTOFF LIST
How do you keep your heart happy?

___ Jokes and laughter
___ Forgiving others
___ Singing
___ Doing acts of kindness for others
___ Memorizing Scripture
___ Telling family members that I love them
___ Treating friends nicely

✝ PRAY
Ask God to help you keep your heart healthy and help you control the words you say.

Life's Guidebook Says
Whatever is in your heart determines what you say.   MATTHEW 12:34

THE WHOLE TRUTH

"HEY, DID YOU HEAR that Johnny was afraid to go home because someone wearing a mask was blocking his path?"

"No, what happened? Did he call the police?"

"No, he just waited for the next batter to hit the ball and then ran home."

Get it? Johnny was playing baseball and had stopped at third base because the catcher had the ball. The truth can turn into a mixed-up story when facts get left out.

Have you ever left out some facts when telling a story? Maybe you wanted to make yourself look better or were trying to stay out of trouble. Leaving out important facts is just like lying because it leads other people to believe something that's not true.

If you're talking to your parents about visiting a friend, doing homework, or going to other activities, make sure to give all the facts. Try not to deceive your friends and family with the stories you tell. Being open and honest helps people trust you. As a follower of Jesus Christ, you should always be truthful. Sometimes it's fun to tell a tricky story as a joke. But in areas that really matter, you should include the facts of *who* was with you, *what* you did, *where* you were, *when* you did it, and *why* you were doing what you were doing.

When you think through the facts and commit to always telling the truth, it'll help you make wise decisions in your life.

AWESOME ACTIVITY: SECRET SANDWICH

Test your communication skills to see if you can give clear instructions to a friend.

Stuff You Need
- ☞ Blindfold
- ☞ Bread
- ☞ Peanut butter
- ☞ Jelly
- ☞ Knife

Try It
1. Let your friend look at the items on a counter. Blindfold your friend.
2. Use only words to direct your friend in making a sandwich. See how well he does.
3. Let your friend blindfold you, and see how well you listen to directions.

✝ PRAY

Commit to God to always give the facts clearly.

Life's Guidebook Says
Each of you must get rid of your lying. Speak the truth to your neighbor.
EPHESIANS 4:25, NIrV

T2U

YOU MIGHT USE T2U ("talk to you") in communicating with your friends. Texting codes save time and space in typing a message. Do you know what these codes mean?

a. PAW
b. PIR
c. KPC
d. I<3KFC

The answers are: "parents are watching," "parents in room," "keep parents clueless," and "I love Kentucky Fried Chicken." Many guys use the last one the most. But if you type the others a lot, you're trying to hide things—and you may want to ask yourself why.

You may also want to ask yourself why if you find yourself texting all the time. Using cell phones to send coded messages can keep you from real conversations with the people around you. Plus, text-speak can creep into how you talk and write. Teachers say they're seeing the language of text messages slip into some kids' assignments for school.

Texting is an easy way to send quick messages. Quick communication is nice. But people often shoot off texts without thinking. These messages can be mean, rude, or thoughtless. TB4T ("thinking before texting") is important.

Peter got in trouble when he gave answers without thinking. When some Pharisees asked if Jesus paid taxes, Peter answered yes without thinking (Matthew 17:24-25). Then when Jesus talked about his future suffering, Peter started to scold Jesus, saying it would never happen (Matthew 16:22-23). Each time Peter spoke too soon, Jesus corrected him.

TBH ("to be honest"), God knows what you are texting. Even in these short messages, he wants you to be faithful with your words. So remember to be polite, truthful, and kind with what, where, and when you text.

PUZZLE IT OUT: SECRET CODES
See if you can figure out these text codes about God.

1. GBY&YF
2. F8th
3. WWJTXT?
4. Dad&hvn
5. jsus
6. GDLU

✝ PRAY
Ask God to give you wisdom and help you remain open when communicating with others.

Life's Guidebook Says
Never let loyalty and kindness leave you! Tie them around your neck as a reminder. Write them deep within your heart. PROVERBS 3:3

Answers: 1. God bless you and your family; 2. Faith; 3. What would Jesus text?;
4. Our Father who art in heaven; 5. Jesus; 6. God loves you.

DEM BONES

Dusty: Ace reporter Dusty coming to you from the *Desert Daily News*. I'm checking in on a strange occurrence with some old bones.

Man: Thanks, Dusty, but I'm not a bunch of old bones.

Dusty: No, you're not. I thought you were dead.

Man: I was. Then I was thrown onto the prophet Elisha's bones and came back to life.

Dusty: Wait, how did you end up in Elisha's grave?

Man: A prowling band of Moabites charged toward the men digging my final resting place. They got scared and just tossed me into Elisha's grave.

Dusty: That must have hurt.

Man: I was dead, so I didn't feel a thing. But once I banged against Elisha's bones, I came back to life and looked around. *Yikes!* That's when I got scared.

Dusty: Scared? I would have thought you'd be excited.

Man: I was surrounded by bones. You would've been scared too.

Dusty: Good point. What did you do next?

Man: What any live person in a grave would do. I stood up and got out of there.

Dusty: I imagine the Moabites thought they saw a ghost when you ran out.

Man: I didn't stop to notice.

Dusty: We'll be keeping an eye on Elisha's grave to see if anything else happens with those strange bones. I guess God's power never stops working. He can do miracles through his people . . . even when they're just a bunch of bones.

WACKY LAUGHS

Knock, knock.
Who's there?
Bone.
Bone who?
Bone *appétit*!

Q. What kinds of animals are always afraid?
A. Invertebrates—they have no backbone!

Q. Why do skeletons have messy homes?
A. They're a bunch of lazy bones.

Q. What does a dog like with its paycheck?
A. A bone-us.

✝ PRAY

Praise God that he has power over life and death.

Life's Guidebook Says

Once when some Israelites were burying a man, they spied a band of these [Moabite] raiders. So they hastily threw the corpse into the tomb of Elisha and fled. But as soon as the body touched Elisha's bones, the dead man revived and jumped to his feet! 2 KINGS 13:21

BODY TALK

HAVE YOU EVER LOOKED at a friend and known how he felt before he said a word? You're not a mind reader, but you may have picked up on your friend's body talk. People talk with words, but most of what we're saying is communicated with our body language.

When Jesus saw a crippled man at the pool of Bethesda, the Lord knew exactly what he was thinking. (It didn't hurt that he was God and knew everything.) This was a special pool, because every now and then an angel would give the water a whirl and God would heal the first person to splash into the pool. This man lay too far away to plunge in first. He had been waiting there for 38 years and had probably given up.

"Do you want to be healed?" Jesus asked the man.

His body appeared to say, "It's hopeless. God won't heal me."

Then the man's mouth dribbled off one complaint after another. "No one will help me." "I'll never be first in."

Jesus listened, and then he healed the man. Nothing—and nobody—is hopeless with God. (You can read the whole story in John 5.)

Follow Jesus' example by tuning in to people and reading their body talk. Then be ready to signal positive messages with your own body language.

WEIRD FACTS: BODY LANGUAGE BASICS

There are four main signals that show your emotions:

- ☞ Closed: Arms folded across the chest, looking at your feet, closing hands into fists. It says, "Don't bother me."
- ☞ Open: Arms open, looking at another person, legs uncrossed. That's body talk for, "Hey, I'm all ears."
- ☞ Forward: Leaning forward means you agree. Pointing fingers (forward) shows a desire for control.
- ☞ Backward: Backing off shows disagreement or desire to escape.
- ☞ Faces talk too! Downcast eyes and closed lips show sadness. A grin reveals happiness. Anger is seen in a hard-set chin, tight mouth, and squinted eyes. A shy face looks down and then cautiously up.

Caution: Don't try to decode every signal. People may fold their arms because they're cold.

✝ PRAY

Ask God to help you use your body to show openness and to have wisdom in understanding others.

Life's Guidebook Says

When Jesus noticed him lying there [helpless], knowing that he had already been a long time in that condition, He said to him, "Do you want to become well?" JOHN 5:6, AMP

FRESH-BAKED HELP

BRENT COULDN'T IGNORE the homeless. As he drove with his parents through downtown Kansas City, he saw men on several street corners holding signs that asked for help. They looked tired, cold, and hungry.

But what can a 12-year-old do to help? Brent thought.

He started to cook up an idea—a delicious one. He couldn't guarantee these men would have a warm bed at night. But he could make sure they had a warm treat in their stomachs. He called some friends, asked his mom to take him to the store, and started baking. Yes, baking. He and his friends made around 500 fresh, hot cookies. Then Brent and his mom delivered the cookies to the City Union Mission. Brent saw men sleeping on floors and crammed into old bunk beds. The kitchen staff thanked him for the cookies, which were quickly devoured.

A little while later, the mission called and asked for more cookies. Brent and his friends mixed up another batch of God's love. Soon Brent and his buddies became the unofficial baking crew.

The Bible talks a lot about God's people helping the needy. The Lord wants us to give generously to the poor. Your cookies may taste like hockey pucks, but maybe there's something else you can do to help the homeless in your community. Food banks and homeless shelters often need extra help during the holidays. Maybe you can call your local mission and ask what it needs, or you can come up with an idea of your own. God loves it when you step out to make a difference.

PUZZLE IT OUT: BE GENEROUS

Look closely at the words below. One letter is missing from the second word in each pair. Write that letter in the spaces to discover the missing word from Deuteronomy 15:11.

1. sold	old	
2. shear	ears	
3. year	rye	
4. heart	heat	
5. cakes	sack	

"There will always be some in the land who are poor. That is why I am commanding you to _ _ _ _ _ freely with the poor."

  1 2 3 4 5

✝ PRAY

Pray for people in need. Ask God to give you ideas on how you can help.

Life's Guidebook Says

Give generously to the poor, not grudgingly, for the LORD your God will bless you in everything you do. DEUTERONOMY 15:10

Answer: share

WORDS THAT BUILD

How DO YOU REACT to these words?

"I'm proud of you."

"Can't you do anything right?"

"Thanks for doing a good job."

"You didn't make the team."

Words are powerful. They can build you up or tear you down. As you go through life, you're sure to encounter your share of unkind words. Kids may tease you. Friends will say something mean. Teachers will scold you.

You can't put words into the mouths of other people or make them be nicer. But you can stop replaying the hurtful words in your mind, forgive the person who said them, and choose to use kind words. Experts say you need to hear 10 good things to balance out every one negative comment that comes your way. So try to hang out with positive people, and make sure to tell your mom or dad how much it means when they encourage you.

God wants your words to be good and helpful (see today's verse). Is that how you'd describe your speech? If not, work on it. And if you're not getting enough kind words coming your way in everyday life, turn to God. He has plenty of great things to say about you!

AWESOME ACTIVITY: GOD'S PEP TALK

When you need to hear a kind word, listen to God:

☞ When you are criticized, God praises: "You are wonderfully made" (Psalm 139:14).

☞ When you feel discouraged, God encourages you to keep going (Galatians 6:9).

☞ When you feel useless, God says you can do things for him by helping others (Matthew 25:40).

☞ When you are unfairly judged, God tells you, "Your faith has saved you" (John 3:17-18).

☞ When you are ridiculed, God accepts you (Luke 10:20).

☞ When you are lonely, God is with you (Matthew 28:20).

☞ When you are afraid, God says, "Trust in me" (Matthew 10:31).

✝ PRAY

Ask God to make you wise in the words you listen to and say.

Life's Guidebook Says

Let everything you say be good and helpful, so that your words will be an encouragement to those who hear them. EPHESIANS 4:29

WRITTEN WORDS

WHAT BOOKS HAVE YOU READ that you really enjoyed? Write down your favorite titles:

1. _____
2. _____
3. _____

Books can take you to other places—even other worlds—in your mind. Some books make you laugh and some can make you sad. Books and words can even change someone's thinking. That can be good or bad. Knowing the truth can help you make the right decisions. But clever talk can trick people and make them do foolish things.

God used the apostle Paul to explain many great truths about following and knowing God. Paul tried to use plain words in his messages. He didn't want to use clever or tricky speeches (see today's verse). He knew God's Spirit, not Paul's clever twists of phrase, would change lives.

It's important to learn to write well and use words correctly, even when you send an e-mail or write a note. Reading good books, including the Bible, can help with that. Words are the tools that connect us to people and help us share thoughts.

The Holy Spirit gave Paul the right words to share God's love and help people believe in Jesus. You don't have to be great with words to share your faith. Trust the Holy Spirit to help you tell your friends about Jesus.

EXPERIMENT: WRITING AND FOCUS

It's not easy to do two things at once. Try these experiments to see how distractions cause writing problems.

Stuff You Need
- ☞ Pencil
- ☞ Paper

Try It
1. Sit at a table or desk and start to write.
2. As you move one foot in a counterclockwise circular motion, try to continue writing. What happens?
3. Sing or hum your favorite song as you write. What do you notice?
4. Turn on the TV and keep writing. Does it change anything? God created you to be most effective when you focus on doing one thing at a time.

✝ PRAY

Ask God to help you know what to say or write when you want to tell someone about Jesus.

Life's Guidebook Says
My message and my preaching were very plain. Rather than using clever and persuasive speeches, I relied only on the power of the Holy Spirit.
1 CORINTHIANS 2:4

SENSE-SATIONAL FEELING

HAS SOMEONE EVER SNUCK UP to tap your shoulder or put their hands over your eyes? *Guess who?* You may have jumped from surprise. Your skin is your body's largest organ. It protects your body, helps keep you the right temperature, and allows you to have the sense of touch. Touch is one of your five senses and a way for you to communicate, like when you express love by hugging someone.

After Jesus began his ministry of healing people and teaching about God, crowds followed him everywhere. One time when people surrounded Jesus, he felt somebody touch his clothes. The disciples said it was just the crowd, but Jesus knew power went out of him (Luke 8:43-48).

The touch of Jesus heals and changes people. On that day, a woman silently pressed forward to touch his cloak. She believed that one touch would heal her, when years of seeing doctors had not helped. When Jesus asked, "Who touched me?" the woman fell at his feet and trembled. She explained what she had done. Jesus called her "Daughter," and said her faith had made her well. Her sorrow was replaced by acceptance. Her pain left in the presence of God's love. Jesus' touch changes lives.

As the hands and feet of Jesus today, you can pass out high fives to your friends. Then pray that God will give them peace.

WEIRD FACTS: ISN'T THAT TOUCHING?

☞ Touching someone lowers blood pressure and stress. So give a friend a high five, or pat him on the back. You could also hug your mom.

☞ The middle of your back is the least touch-sensitive part of your body.

☞ You have more pain nerve endings in your body than any other type of nerve endings.

☞ Your most sensitive areas of touch include your fingertips, soles of your feet, lips, tongue, face, and back of the neck.

✝ PRAY

Thank God for the sense of touch and for the ability to hug people you love.

Life's Guidebook Says

Jesus said, "Someone deliberately touched me, for I felt healing power go out from me." LUKE 8:46

THE REAL BUZZ

JOHNNY TOSSED TWO EGG-SHAPED MAGNETS high in the air. They twirled and buzzed as they came together in a magnetic type of dance.

You may have seen this type of trick magnet. Many are made from hematite with magnetic poles in the tips. As the poles try to find each other, they vibrate and create a sound. If you spin one of these magnets on a table and place another nearby, the twirling one pulls at the other magnet and causes it to spin too. Finally, the two magnets will collide and buzz.

With magnets, opposites attract, while identical poles push each other away. You may find the reverse is true for you. You're probably drawn to people like you, while you stay away from people who don't share your interests.

Jesus draws people to himself like a magnet. Before we know Jesus, we're the polar opposite of him. He's perfect and holy. We're sinful and dirty. But when we come in contact with Jesus, he changes us.

During Jesus' time on earth, people were drawn to him for healing. Once they encountered God's Son, they created quite a buzz as they told others about his miracles.

☞ "Hey, look—I'm healed!"
☞ "One touch and he cures everyone, no matter what the illness."

We can create that same buzz today. As believers in Christ, we become more like Jesus when we stay near to him. By walking with Jesus, he'll "magnetize" you. So if you've ever wanted to be "attractive," stick close to Jesus and attract other people to him.

EXPERIMENT: MAGNETIC POWER TRANSFER
Transform an ordinary metal object into a temporary magnet.

Stuff You Need
☞ Metal object (nail, needle, or scissors)
☞ Paper clips
☞ Strong magnet

Try It
1. See if the metal object can pick up a paper clip.
2. Rub the magnet in one direction over the metal object about 50 times.
3. Try picking up the paper clip again, and see how it has pulled magnetic powers from the actual magnet.

✞ PRAY
Thank God for drawing you to him. Ask Jesus to help you draw people to him too.

Life's Guidebook Says
My old self has been crucified with Christ. It is no longer I who live, but Christ lives in me. GALATIANS 2:20

GRUMBLING MUMBLES

"IT'S MY TURN!"

"Why do I have to take out the garbage?"

"Can't you buy me that new video game? Everyone else has it."

It's easy to complain and argue. But it doesn't make life very peaceful. When you constantly grumble, you can cause yourself—or the people around you—to become angry. Anger comes from a Greek word that means "to lose control." God doesn't want you to be out of control. He desires for us to show self-control as much as we can when it comes to our emotions.

In the Old Testament, the Israelites grumbled a lot. It usually showed they didn't believe God would take care of them—but he always did. They grumbled when they were thirsty or hungry, and God provided food and water. God had plans to care for his people when he freed them from slavery in Egypt. He just wanted them to trust him. Often they didn't.

We can't always see God's plans for us, but we should trust him to have our best interests in mind, because he does. The Bible tells us to "do everything without complaining and arguing" (Philippians 2:14). When you grumble in discontent, it shows that you don't trust God. God may not give you everything at the exact time that you want it, but just like your parents, he will supply what you need. So enjoy what you already own. Praise God for your blessings, and strive to be happy and content. And if anybody hears a grumble coming from you, it should just be from your hungry stomach.

WACKY LAUGHS

Q. What do you call a complaining lawn?

A. Crab grass.

Q. What was the taxi driver's problem?

A. He was always driving away his customers.

Q. What lives in a hive and always complains?

A. Grumble bees.

Q. Which animal complains the most?

A. The whine-oceros.

✞ PRAY

Ask God to help you be content with what you have and not complain or argue.

Life's Guidebook Says

Do everything without complaining and arguing.   PHILIPPIANS 2:14

IN THE SHADOW OF GREATNESS

WHAT IS AS BIG as an elephant but as light as a feather?

An elephant-sized feather. *Just kidding.* The answer is an elephant's shadow. When it's sunny outside, shadows follow you everywhere. Do you think you can make an elephant-looking shadow? Use a flashlight or bright lamp in a dark room to experiment holding your fingers different ways to create animal shadows. Here are a few you can try:

- ☞ Make a rabbit by sticking up two fingers for ears and overlapping the rest for the body.
- ☞ Use your arm to create a camel. Relax your hand. Your thumb goes up, fingers down, and your little finger is spread apart.
- ☞ Form a bird by putting your thumbs together pointing up. Spread and flap your hands with your fingers together for wings.

The shadows you make can create smiles and laughter. But the apostle Peter's shadow healed people. When his shadow crossed over the sick, they were cured. As word got out, people started bringing their friends to where Peter was walking, so his shadow could touch them and make them well (see today's verse).

Your shadow probably doesn't have healing powers. But make sure when people are near you, they're touched by your kindness, compassion, and fun personality.

AWESOME ACTIVITY: SHADOW FUN

Have fun with shadows:

- ☞ Track shadows by using chalk. Draw a line where a tree, house, or other object casts a shadow on the sidewalk. Write the time. Come back an hour later and check the shadow. Use a different color to draw a line this time. Trace shadows throughout the day to see how they change.
- ☞ Use a flashlight to create shadows. Notice how the shadows change as you move the angle of the light.
- ☞ Go outside with a friend and see if you can combine your shadows to look like a supertall person. Become a giant with four arms. Pretend you're boxing, or do a silly dance.

✝ PRAY

Thank the Lord that his power can be seen in everything, even shadows and light.

Life's Guidebook Says

As a result of the apostles' work, sick people were brought out into the streets on beds and mats so that Peter's shadow might fall across some of them as he went by. ACTS 5:15

WRESTLING AN ANGEL

WOULD YOU EVER WRESTLE with an angel? Not if you were smart. It'd be sort of like grappling against all the strongest, biggest professional wrestlers in the world . . . at the same time. There's just no way you could win. But one man in the Old Testament wrestled an angel and won—sort of.

One night Jacob prayed for God's help. Later that night, a man came and wrestled with Jacob. They struggled all night. At daybreak the man could tell Jacob wasn't giving up. The man touched Jacob's hip, causing it to dislocate. Still, Jacob clung to the man and asked for a blessing, because Jacob knew the man was really an angel. The angel blessed him and changed his name to Israel. He said that Jacob had fought with God and with men and won (Genesis 32:28). *Hooray!* God blessed him. But the angel's touch changed Jacob, and he limped from that day on.

Israel means "God fights" or "He struggles with God." The name Israel reminded Jacob of his struggle for the rest of his life. Sometimes living the Christian life feels like a struggle. When we prayed to accept Christ, Jesus didn't promise an easy life. In fact, he said the opposite. The Lord said the world may hate us. We'll have to overcome obstacles. But God also promised that he'd be with us every step of the way and that he'd help us overcome (see John 16:33).

When you pray for God to answer a prayer, don't give up if you can't see an answer right away. It's okay to struggle and wrestle with God. He wants you to be persistent. Keep believing, and keep asking for his blessing.

PLEXER

Solve this plexer to see what your friends would give you if you wrestled an angel and won. (If you don't remember what a plexer is, see p. 9.)

```
┌───────────┐
│           │
│   FIVE    │
│           │
│           │
└───────────┘
```

✝ PRAY

Pray again for a prayer that hasn't been answered yet. Be persistent.

Life's Guidebook Says
Jacob struggled with the Angel and prevailed.   HOSEA 12:4, HCSB

Answer: A high five

WISE WINNER

DAVID WISE LOVES TO FLY. He has since he was a boy. After watching the movie *Mary Poppins*, he and his older sisters thought it'd be a good idea to jump off the roof of their house holding an umbrella. David went first. He was old enough to know that an umbrella couldn't make him fly, but he thought it might act as a parachute and slow him down a little.

It didn't.

Fortunately, the roof was low enough, the ground was soft enough, and David was flexible enough that he didn't get hurt.

These days David is known for a different kind of flying. With two skis, nobody flies higher or does cooler tricks than David. He zooms up icy half-pipes and launches himself 20 feet above the rim—over 40 feet above the ground. Then he unleashes a dizzying array of stunts.

From 2012 to 2014, David won three straight X Games championships. Then at the 2014 Winter Olympics, David took home the gold medal.

While David's tricks are sky high, his ego is not. He stays grounded leading worship for his church youth group and hanging out with his family.

"When I am having the most fun is when I feel the most connected to God," David told Christian sportswriter Jeremy Jones. "When I'm out there skiing, I'm using what He's given me and doing the best I absolutely can with it and enjoying every moment. It's a form of worship."

You can worship God with whatever you do. From schoolwork to playing an instrument to basketball to skiing, work with all your might at everything you put your hand to.

PUZZLE IT OUT: OLYMPIC-SIZED SEARCH

Find these Winter Olympic sports by searching up, down, across, diagonally, and backward.

S	L	O	V	L	U	G	E
D	K	X	C	A	N	P	H
E	Y	I	L	I	J	L	O
L	G	N	I	L	R	U	C
S	B	K	B	N	S	H	K
B	S	K	A	T	N	I	E
O	W	R	Z	V	O	M	Y
B	S	K	A	T	I	N	G

Bobsled
Curling
Hockey
Luge
Skating
Skiing

✝ PRAY

Tell God you're going to work hard at everything you do to honor him.

Life's Guidebook Says
Work willingly at whatever you do, as though you were working for the Lord rather than for people. COLOSSIANS 3:23

DREAM COME TRUE

HAVE YOU EVER SEEN a dog whine or bark in its sleep? Or maybe you've had a dog whose legs move when it's sleeping. If it looks like your dog is dreaming, that's because it is.

Scientists say the sleeping brain-wave activity of humans and dogs is very similar. Scientists also believe dogs most frequently dream of chasing squirrels or eating a big steak. *Just kidding.* Researchers have no idea what dogs dream.

While dogs have dreams like we do, it's probably safe to say that an angel has never appeared to a napping canine. But that's what happened to Joseph at the beginning of the New Testament. He was engaged to be married to a young woman named Mary—yes, *that* Mary. One night an angel of the Lord appeared to him in a dream and told Joseph to take Mary as his wife, because her child was God's Son, who would save his people from their sins (see today's verse). When Joseph woke up, he knew exactly what to do. He'd do what God's angel said (that's always good advice).

You may never be visited by an angel in a dream, but you can still learn from Joseph. He obeyed God. He celebrated the birth of Jesus. And he trusted everything the angel said. Jesus did come to save us from our sins! He's a dream come true.

WEIRD FACTS: YOU DREAMIN'?

☞ Over the course of your life, you'll spend over 6 years dreaming—compared to 25 years sleeping.

☞ You have five or six dreams every night but often can't remember any of them in the morning.

☞ Research at the Massachusetts Institute of Technology has shown that rats dream of mazes they've previously run.

✞ PRAY

Thank God for sending his Son.

Life's Guidebook Says

"Joseph, son of David," the angel said, "do not be afraid to take Mary as your wife. For the child within her was conceived by the Holy Spirit. And she will have a son, and you are to name him Jesus, for he will save his people from their sins." MATTHEW 1:20-21

HIGHER CALLING

WHAT HAVE YOU been called to?

a. A life that honors God
b. Treating others with kindness
c. Passing along the good news about Jesus
d. Dinner
e. All of the above

The answer is *e*. Following your calling is sometimes difficult (unless it's being called to dinner. That's easy. All you need is a fork). God doesn't call us to an easy life. But when we follow him, he promises to bless us.

That was certainly the case for Abram. Genesis 12 couldn't have started out much better for him. God tells him: "I will make you into a great nation. I will bless you and make you famous, and you will be a blessing to others" (verse 2). That's certainly a great calling. Who wouldn't want to be famous and bless others? But God says something *before* that awesome message. In verse 1, he tells Abram to leave his country and family and move to a different land.

Any move is difficult, but this one proved to be especially hard. Abram and Sarai experienced a bunch of bumps in the road. They didn't always do a perfect job of following God's plan. But they always came back to the Lord and trusted him to fulfill his promise. And for your information, Abram *did* become a great nation, *is* still very famous, and *was* a blessing to others.

LIFTOFF LIST

Abram heard directly from God about his calling. Check off all the ways God may use to call you:

__ Talents and passions
__ Encouragement from family members
__ A verse in the Bible
__ A list of positives and negatives
__ A leading through prayer
__ An unexpected opportunity
__ A favorite subject in school

✝ PRAY

Ask God to help you find his calling. Then pray for the courage to follow it.

Life's Guidebook Says

"I will make you into a great nation. I will bless you and make you famous, and you will be a blessing to others." GENESIS 12:2

A FLIGHT TO REMEMBER

WILBUR AND ORVILLE WRIGHT spent a lot of time watching birds in flight. If you want to learn to fly, you might as well learn from an animal that God created with that specific talent. The Wright brothers noticed how birds soared into the wind, allowing the curves of their wings to create lift. The bicycle-shop–owning brothers from Ohio decided to test their ideas of flight near the ocean in North Carolina because of the hilly and windy conditions. After experimenting with gliders for three years, the Wright brothers made a historic flight on this day in 1903 when their plane took off and flew 120 feet in 12 seconds.

Airplanes have come a long way since then. Now they can fly faster than the speed of sound and carry hundreds of people around the world.

And to think it all started with bird watching. King David probably did some bird watching of his own. In Psalm 55:6, he says that if "I had wings like a dove; then I would fly away and rest." If you could fly, what would you do?

Resting is important. You've probably just worked really hard during the fall semester of school. If you're not on Christmas break yet, you soon will be. Take some time to rest. Maybe you'll want to slip away from your family to read a book for fun or just find a quiet place to pray. Rest your brain and find the peace that only God can provide. Sometimes it's in our rest that our biggest dreams are born . . . like dreams of flying.

WACKY LAUGHS

Q. Who made the first plane that couldn't fly?

A. The Wrong Brothers!

Q. What do you call a flying cheeseburger?

A. Fast food.

Q. Who was the only man in the Bible who could fly?

A. Pontius Pilate.

Q. Why are people scared when they fly?

A. Because they're near the *at-most-fear*.

✝ PRAY

Ask God to help you rest and have peace during the Christmas season.

Life's Guidebook Says
Oh, that I had wings like a dove; then I would fly away and rest! PSALM 55:6

ALL ABOUT RESPECT

ARE YOU GOOD AT SPELLING? The English language has so many rules, such as, "Use *i* before *e*, except after *c* or when it sounds like *a*, such as in *weigh*." That's almost more confusing than just trying to memorize how everything is spelled. But one three-letter word that's easy to spell is the name of the Creator of the universe—*G-d*.

Wait! you're probably thinking. *Where's the o? It's spelled* G-o-d.

That's true . . . but not always. In the Jewish culture, God's name is so highly honored that it can never be erased or destroyed. So some Jews don't spell out God's name, because it would be disrespectful to erase it. That's why they write *G-d*. In Judaism, God is so highly revered that the Hebrew name for God isn't spoken out loud.

Do you respect God that much? In the Old Testament, some of God's priests didn't show much respect at all. Eli's sons, Hophni and Phinehas, were greedy and selfish. They used their positions as priests to do evil things (1 Samuel 2:12-17). God warned Eli that he would honor those who honored him but despise those who thought little of him. Hophni and Phinehas didn't change their ways and met a horrible fate.

As you try to grow closer to God, remember to show him the respect he deserves. You don't necessarily have to change the way you spell *God*, but honor him any way you can.

WEIRD FACTS: SPELLING BEES

- ☞ The National Spelling Bee began in 1925. Scripps Howard took it over in 1941.
- ☞ The winning words in recent years include *knaidel* (2013), *stromuhr* (2010), *appoggiatura* (2005), and *succedaneum* (2001). If you know what any of those words mean, give yourself a star.
- ☞ National Spelling Bee champions receive over $30,000 in cash, scholarships, and prizes.
- ☞ The bee is so popular that the finals have been broadcast on TV every year since 1994.

✞ PRAY

Tell God you want to show him the honor and respect he deserves.

Life's Guidebook Says

[God said,] "I will honor those who honor me, and I will despise those who think lightly of me." 1 SAMUEL 2:30

BUMPY FLIGHT, BIG REVELATION

HAVE YOU EVER BEEN on a really turbulent plane ride? A lot of families fly to be with their loved ones during Christmas. Shane Everett from the Christian music duo Shane & Shane can remember an especially bumpy trip. He boarded a plane in Dallas to go to a concert in Florida. It was storming outside, and things got even worse when the plane took off.

Bump! Rattle! Shake! The airplane quaked and groaned as it flew through the storm. Shane couldn't see a thing through the clouds. The plane felt like it might break apart. Shane prayed. An instant later, the aircraft broke through the clouds. . . . It was beautiful! The sun shone brightly. Everything looked peaceful and perfect.

"In that moment," Shane says, "it reminded me of the fact that, even when I cannot see God, he's still shining."

Maybe you've had times in your life when you couldn't feel or see God. Joshua certainly experienced that in the Old Testament. When he led God's people into the Promised Land, they didn't win every battle. Difficult times came when it would've been easy to doubt God's love. But Joshua held on to the Lord's words: "Be strong and courageous! Do not be afraid or discouraged. For the LORD your God is with you wherever you go" (Joshua 1:9).

Wherever you go, God goes there too. In tough times, it's hard to feel his presence, but that's when it's especially important to remember that God's love never stops shining. Keep going and you're sure to break through to sunnier times.

AWESOME ACTIVITY: PLANE GAME
Try to make the perfect paper airplane.

Stuff You Need
- ☞ Paper
- ☞ Paper clip (optional)

Try It
1. Fold your paper into an airplane. Throw it and see how far it goes.
2. Try a different design. Experiment with various shapes and sizes for the wings. Add a paper clip in front for extra weight. Ask a parent if you can go online to find different ideas.
3. Keep experimenting until you discover the perfect plane. You can also try to make a stunt flyer.

✝ PRAY
Thank God that he's always with you, even if you can't feel that he's there.

Life's Guidebook Says
[God said,] "This is my command—be strong and courageous! Do not be afraid or discouraged. For the LORD your God is with you wherever you go."
JOSHUA 1:9

COLORS OF THE SEASON

WHEN YOU LOOK AROUND this time of year, what colors do you see the most? If you live where it snows a lot, you might say white. But the most popular colors at Christmas are probably red and green. In addition to being festive, these two colors have special meaning.

Red: Red holly berries represent life in the face of death, which is exactly what Jesus gives us. Holly berries have been used in Christmas decorations for hundreds of years. Red apples also used to be a big part of Christmas celebrations. On Christmas Eve in many parts of Europe during the Middle Ages, "Paradise plays" were performed to explain the Bible story. Red apples were tied to green evergreen trees to represent the fruit that Adam and Eve ate that brought sin into the world.

Green: Evergreens have served as Christmas trees since the tradition started hundreds of years ago. Evergreen trees are a symbol of our life with Jesus—it's *ever*green. We will live forever and ever with Christ. Mistletoe and ivy, two other green plants, are often used as decorations as well.

Of course, there are other colors you can see at Christmas. Another popular choice is purple. That's very appropriate, because in the Bible, purple symbolizes royalty. When Jesus was brought before Pontius Pilate, the soldiers put him in a purple robe (see today's verse). The Romans meant to mock Jesus, but they didn't realize how fitting the color was, because he's the King of kings.

As we celebrate Christmas and enjoy the colors and celebrations, don't forget the meaning of the season. The baby in the manger changed the world as the coming King.

PLEXER
Solve this plexer to discover a popular Christmas carol. (If you don't remember what a plexer is, see p. 9.)

MAawNGEayR

✝ PRAY
Praise Jesus that he is the King of kings.

Life's Guidebook Says
Jesus came out wearing the crown of thorns and the purple robe. And Pilate said, "Look, here is the man!" JOHN 19:5

Answer: Away in a Manger

NO LYIN', HE'S A LION

JESUS IS A LION. No kidding. Revelation 5:5 calls Jesus the Lion of Judah. It's kind of cool to think about your Savior being a powerful lion. In the Chronicles of Narnia, C. S. Lewis used the lion Aslan to symbolize Christ. But even before Jesus was born, people were talking about the Messiah being a lion.

More than 2,500 years ago, Jacob called his sons around him to pass down some last words. He called his son Judah a young lion and added, "The scepter will not depart from Judah, nor the ruler's staff from his descendants, until the coming of the one to whom it belongs, the one whom all nations will honor" (Genesis 49:10). Who do you think is "the one whom all nations will honor"? If you said "Jesus," you're right.

Fast-forward to Jesus' birth and you'll see that Jacob's words came true. Jesus came from Judah's family (Matthew 1:1-3). And soon Judah's other prophecy will come true—every nation will worship the one true Lord.

AWESOME ACTIVITY: ICE LIGHTS

Stuff You Need
☞ Round balloons
☞ Water
☞ Bowl
☞ Electric flameless tea lights
☞ Aluminum foil

Try It
1. Fill a balloon halfway with water.
2. Blow a little air into the balloon and tie it shut.
3. Place the balloon in the bowl, and put it in the freezer.
4. Check the balloon in four or five hours to see if the water makes a sloshing sound.
5. Water freezes from the outside to the inside, so once the outside is frozen, pop the balloon.
6. Dump out the water so there's an ice bowl in the center.
7. Put the ice bowl back in the freezer to harden. Make more ice luminaria by following the same steps.
8. When it's dark, wrap the base of the flameless tea lights in aluminum foil. Turn on the tea light and place it inside the ice bowl. Use the ice luminaria to line your porch or driveway. Remember the light that Jesus brings to the world chases away darkness—just like a lion chases away any danger to his pride.

✝ PRAY
Praise God that he's a powerful lion that all nations will one day worship.

Life's Guidebook Says
This is a record of the ancestors of Jesus the Messiah, a descendant of David and of Abraham: . . . Jacob was the father of Judah and his brothers. Judah was the father of Perez and Zerah. MATTHEW 1:1-3

SING IT OUT

Do YOU HAVE A FAVORITE Christmas carol? This time of year you hear them on the radio and sing them at church. One of the cool things about Christmas carols is that they've been sung for hundreds of years.

Do you know what was given on the seventh day in the "Twelve Days of Christmas"? Kids before the Civil War could've told you. That song began to be sung in 1842. "Silent Night" was first sung in a church in 1818. Do you want to bring more "Joy to the World"? That song was written in 1719—more than 50 years before the United States became a nation! And when it comes to "We Wish You a Merry Christmas," that song's been around since 1640. Even the Pilgrims may have sung it. But when it comes to *really* old Christmas carols, you can't beat "Angels We Have Heard on High." The words to that song were basically taken from the angels who appeared to the shepherds when Jesus was born: "Glory to God in the highest, and on earth peace, goodwill toward men!" (Luke 2:14, NKJV).

Not many songs have been around for more than 2,000 years. The words *Gloria, in excelsis Deo!* are Latin for "Glory to God in the highest." Isn't that cool? So as you sing Christmas carols this year, remember to sing with a heart filled with praise. Because when you raise your voice to sing, you're joining millions of Christians over the years—and more than a few angels—who have sung those exact words.

WACKY LAUGHS

Q. What did Tarzan sing to the monkeys during Christmas?
A. "Jungle Bells."

Q. What is a snake's favorite Christmas carol?
A. "Sssssssilent Night."

Knock, knock.
Who's there?
Owl.
Owl who?
Owl be home for Christmas.

Q. What do shoppers sing at Christmas?
A. "Deck the Malls."

✝ PRAY

Tell God you're going to praise him as you sing Christmas carols.

Life's Guidebook Says
Suddenly there was with the angel a multitude of the heavenly host praising God and saying: "Glory to God in the highest, And on earth peace, goodwill toward men!" LUKE 2:13-14, NKJV

SPECIAL DELIVERY

THIS TIME OF YEAR you might receive an overnight special delivery package as family members try to get gifts to you before Christmas. Special deliveries take extra effort and cost more money. Special deliveries also tend to bring joy as someone arrives with an unexpected gift.

At the beginning of the New Testament, the angel Gabriel made a special delivery about a *very* special delivery. The angel came to a young lady named Mary with a great and wonderful message. "Greetings, favored woman!" he said as he appeared (Luke 1:28). God had chosen her to have his Son, the Son of the Most High.

Mary didn't question the reality of the angel or his message, but she did ask how it could happen. The angel explained that her baby would be a miracle of the Holy Spirit. This baby boy she would give birth to would deliver the world from sin. That's a really special delivery!

Mary may not have understood everything the angel was asking of her, but she was willing to serve God. She told the angel, "I am the Lord's servant. May everything you have said about me come true." Later, Mary praised God and his great deeds (Luke 1:34-56).

God wants you to follow in the faith that Mary showed. When we have willing hearts, we'll boldly follow him—even when we don't totally understand what's going to happen next.

PUZZLE IT OUT: ANGELIC WORDS

Samuel Morse developed a code to send messages across telegraph wires using short and longer tones called "dots" and "dashes." The first message, sent in 1844, said, "What hath God wrought?" Use the code to decipher what an angel said about the birth of Jesus.

A •—	B —•••	C —•—•	D —••	E •	F ••—•	G ——•
H ••••	I ••	J •———	K —•—	L •—••	M ——	N —•
O ———	P •——•	Q ——•—	R •—•	S •••	T —	U ••——
V •••—	W •——	X —••—	Y —•——	Z ——••		

The __ __ ____ __ ____ ___ — _____ __ __, __ __ __
    ••• •— ••• — •• ——— •—• —•— • ••• — •••• •

____ __ ___ ___ •• •— •••• — •••• • •—•• ——— •—• —••
—— • ••• ••• •• •— •••• — •••• • •—•• ——— •—• —••

____ __ ___ ___ • • __ __ ___ __ __ __ __ ___ __ __."
•••• •— ••• —••• • • —• —••• ——— •—• —• — ——— —•• •— —•—

✟ PRAY

Thank God that Mary said yes and tell him you are also willing to follow his call.

Life's Guidebook Says
[Elizabeth said to Mary,] "You are blessed because you believed that the Lord would do what he said." LUKE 1:45

Answer: "The Savior—yes, the Messiah, the Lord—has been born today."

376

SUGARY CANE

Look at your Christmas tree. Are any candy canes hanging from it? Nearly two billion candy canes are sold every year, which means a lot of trees are decorated with these sweet treats. If you lined up all two billion candy canes end-to-end, they'd stretch around the world about four and a half times! (But why would you want to line up your candy canes, when it's so much better to eat them?)

As you've eaten a candy cane, you've probably noticed how much it looks like a shepherd's staff. Jesus is called the "Good Shepherd" (see today's verse). Speaking of Jesus, candy canes also look like the letter *J*. Some people believe candy canes were designed this way on purpose. The colors of a candy cane can also have special meaning. The white represents Jesus' purity, while the red reminds us that he bled and died for our sins.

Those are some pretty powerful messages from such a tiny candy. But as you're about to celebrate Christmas, it's important to turn your focus toward Jesus. For many kids, Christmas is all about what they get. For those who believe in God, tomorrow's celebration is all about what Jesus gave. Jesus came to earth to die for your sins so you could have a relationship with your Creator. Remember that truth every time you see a candy cane.

AWESOME ACTIVITY: CHRISTMAS "CROOKIE"

Stuff You Need
- ☞ Package of sugar cookie dough
- ☞ Red food coloring
- ☞ 1/2 teaspoon of peppermint extract
- ☞ Lightly floured surface
- ☞ Ungreased cookie sheet

Try It
1. Allow the dough to thaw, then split it in half.
2. Mix four drops of food coloring and the peppermint extract into half the dough.
3. Put the dough back in the refrigerator until stiff.
4. On a lightly floured surface, roll about one tablespoon of plain dough into a six-inch rope for each cookie.
5. Create a red rope in the same way.
6. Twist the ropes together and pinch the ends.
7. Place the twisted rope on an ungreased cookie sheet and form into a candy cane shape.
8. Bake the candy cane cookies at 350° F for 8 to 10 minutes.

✝ PRAY
Thank Jesus for coming to earth and sacrificing himself for you.

Life's Guidebook Says
[Jesus said,] "I am the good shepherd. The good shepherd sacrifices his life for the sheep." JOHN 10:11

BIG THINGS FROM LITTLE PLACES

WHERE WERE YOU BORN? If someone had asked your great-great-great-great-great-great-great-great-great-great grandpa, would he have known where you'd be born? Probably not. You don't have a lot of control over where you're born. That's pretty much decided by your parents.

But around 700 years before Jesus came to earth, everybody knew where he'd be born. The prophet Micah wrote, "But you, O Bethlehem Ephrathah, are only a small village among all the people of Judah. Yet a ruler of Israel, whose origins are in the distant past, will come from you" (Micah 5:2). To be a good prophet, the prophecies you make have to come true. And Micah was a very good prophet.

Jesus couldn't control where his mom would give birth, but God orchestrated everything. Mary and Joseph lived in Nazareth, not Bethlehem. But right before Jesus was born, Caesar Augustus called for a census, which made every family return to the town where their ancestors had come from. Although Mary was very pregnant, she and Joseph made the 70-mile trip to register. While she was in Bethlehem, Mary gave birth to her baby—and the prophecy came true.

Jesus' life fulfilled hundreds of prophecies. Many he had no control over, such as where he was born. According to mathematician Peter Stoner, the probability of one man fulfilling just eight prophecies is one in one octillion (which is seven times larger than a billion)! In other words, it can't happen. But with Jesus, it did happen. He's the promised Messiah. He fulfills the prophecies. And he was born in Bethlehem.

WEIRD FACTS: "O LITTLE TOWN . . ."
Journey through these facts about Bethlehem.

☞ It's located about five miles southwest of Jerusalem.
☞ In Hebrew, *Bethlehem* means "house of bread." In John 6:33, Jesus says, "The true bread of God is the one who comes down from heaven and gives life to the world."
☞ Bethlehem is also called the "City of David," because King David was born there. In Luke 18:38, Jesus is called the "Son of David." David was one of Jesus' distant ancestors, which fulfilled another prophecy.

✝ **PRAY**
Praise Jesus for fulfilling so many prophecies that prove he's the Son of God.

Life's Guidebook Says
The Scriptures clearly state that the Messiah will be born of the royal line of David, in Bethlehem, the village where King David was born. JOHN 7:42

BOX IT UP

WHAT'S THE PURPOSE of the holiday known as Boxing Day?

a. To allow two guys to strap on gloves and punch each other.
b. To tape together as many cardboard boxes as possible in 24 hours.
c. To give to people in need.
d. All of the above.

If you answered "All of the above," you've got some weird ideas for a holiday. The answer is *c* (but you already knew that if you read the devo on October 10). Boxing Day is big in Australia, Great Britain, New Zealand, and Canada. Nobody knows exactly how the holiday started or where it got its name. It's believed that centuries ago, merchants in Britain gave boxes of food to people who worked for them as a tip for all their hard work. Others say churches used to set out boxes so people could give money and gifts to the poor. Eventually, the name Boxing Day stuck. No matter how the holiday came about, it's a great reminder to care for others.

Giving to the needy is a big theme in the Bible. Throughout God's Word, his followers are encouraged to help the poor. When John the Baptist was preparing the way for Jesus, he said, "If you have two shirts, give one to the poor. If you have food, share it with those who are hungry" (Luke 3:11). Find a way today to follow John's encouragement and Jesus' example of helping those in need.

LIFTOFF LIST

Check off ways you can celebrate Boxing Day:

___ Use some of your Christmas money to buy shoes for needy children.
___ Box up your old clothes to give to a homeless shelter.
___ Use a leftover Christmas box to wrap a special gift for someone you know didn't receive much for Christmas.
___ Plan to pack a shoebox for Operation Christmas Child next year.
___ Put on some winter gloves and sneak up behind your little brother.
___ Give some money to church to help the needy in your congregation.

✝ PRAY

Tell Jesus you're going to think of ways to help people—just like he did.

Life's Guidebook Says
John replied, "If you have two shirts, give one to the poor. If you have food, share it with those who are hungry." LUKE 3:11

THE NOSE KNOWS

IF YOU WALKED INTO YOUR HOUSE, how quickly would you know if your mom was cooking bacon? Immediately, right? But could you smell bacon cooking from a mile away? Probably not.

A polar bear could, and so could an albatross. Researchers say an albatross can smell fish as it flies through the air. The huge bird will change direction in midair to head toward a school of fish that there's no way it could see. As an albatross soars above the ocean, it can detect fish a mile away. Polar bears may be even more impressive. They can smell a seal that's buried under three feet of snow from over a half mile away! Food is scarce in the Arctic, so God gave polar bears the ability to find seals from a long way off.

Can people smell you from a great distance? God can. The apostle Paul said that Christians are the "aroma of Christ to God" (2 Corinthians 2:15, ESV). We smell great to the Lord and fellow believers, but those who don't know God may be turned off by our scent. So it's good to be smelly!

Make sure your aroma is a pleasing one to God. That doesn't mean putting on deodorant or cologne (which aren't bad ideas either—though neither one replaces taking a shower); it means spreading God's Good News and love with your words and actions.

WEIRD FACTS: SMELLY TRUTHS

☞ Five percent of the human brain is devoted to smell, but 35 percent of a dog's brain is involved with that sense. That's one reason dogs have a much better sense of smell than humans.

☞ Smells can often trigger memories because of the olfactory bulb in your brain.

☞ If you have *hyperosmia*, you have a strong sense of smell. People with *anosmia* don't have the ability to smell.

☞ Moths smell with their antennae, not noses. They can detect scents more than a mile away.

✝ PRAY

Ask God to help you give off a good aroma to him.

Life's Guidebook Says
We are the aroma of Christ to God among those who are being saved and among those who are perishing. 2 CORINTHIANS 2:15, ESV

YOUR STUFF

WHAT CHEESE ISN'T YOURS?

Nacho cheese. *Ha!* Maybe you've heard that joke before. But have you heard this? All your Christmas presents, toys, clothes, money, and furniture are *not yours* either. Everything is God's. That's exactly what King David said in 1 Chronicles 29:11: "Everything in heaven and earth is yours" (NIV). It all belongs to God. But the cool thing is he lets you take care of and use all of his neat stuff. That's the way it's worked since the beginning.

When God created the heavens and the earth, he placed Adam in the Garden of Eden and told him to watch over it (Genesis 2:15). The Garden wasn't Adam's. He just took care of it. The same thing is true with your stuff—it's not yours; you just get to take care of it.

Everything is God's, so it's all God's stuff. Your job is to act as a "steward," or caretaker, of God's stuff. Right now, you're a steward of clothes, toys, video games, and other possessions. As a steward, you need to do your best to take care of them, make sure you don't lose anything, and help things last as long as possible. When you're older, God may give you a job and lots of money. Guess what? That's his too. Make sure to use God's stuff wisely and give back to him what he deserves.

PLEXER

Solve this plexer to find a phrase that describes God. (If you don't remember what a plexer is, see p. 9.)

Ruler
all

✞ PRAY

Thank God for allowing you to care for his stuff. Let him know you're going to try to do a good job.

Life's Guidebook Says

Yours, LORD, is the greatness and the power and the glory and the majesty and the splendor, for everything in heaven and earth is yours.
1 CHRONICLES 29:11, NIV

Answer: Ruler over all

MYSTERIOUS CAMP BUFFET

POLICE INVESTIGATION—around 850 BC in Samaria

Detective: Gentlemen, you'll have to excuse me if I don't come too close. You're lepers, you know.

Leper One: We know. That's why we hang out together.

Detective: So the four of you chased away the great Aramean army?

Leper Two: Not exactly. We were sitting next to the city gate starving, so we figured we'd go out and surrender.

Detective: You guys were giving up?

Leper Three: What else could we do? The city had been surrounded for so long by the Arameans that nobody had food. A cup of bird poop cost five pieces of silver [2 Kings 6:25].

Detective: Gross! Well, there's plenty of food now. What happened?

Leper One: When we got to the Aramean camp, nobody was there! The Lord had made them hear a great army approaching, so they ran off.

Detective: What'd you do next?

Leper Four: We feasted! I couldn't believe how much food they had.

Detective: Some gold and silver was reported stolen.

Leper Two: Okay, we took a little. But then we went to tell the people at the palace what had happened.

Detective: What did they do?

Leper Three: Nothing at first. The king thought it was a trick. But then he remembered what the prophet Elisha had told him the day before: "By this time tomorrow in the markets of Samaria, six quarts of choice flour will cost only one piece of silver" [2 Kings 7:1].

Leper One: The king didn't think it was possible to go from famine to feast so quickly. But God had made it happen!

Detective: So where's the Aramean army now?

Leper Four: Probably still running for their lives.

WACKY LAUGHS

Q. What is a camera's favorite food?

A. Cheese.

Q. What is the loudest food?

A. Talk-os.

Q. What kind of food do dentists avoid?

A. Tartar sauce.

✝ PRAY

Praise God that he knows the future and provides for his people.

Life's Guidebook Says

Everything happened exactly as the man of God had predicted when the king came to his house. 2 KINGS 7:17

OOPS, THAT'S GOOD

FRANK EPPERSON was 11 years old when he mixed some flavored soda powder into a cup of water with a wooden stick. Then he got distracted and accidently left the cup outside. On that night in Oakland, California, temperatures dipped below freezing. When Frank found the cup the next morning, it was frozen solid. Frank freed the fruit-flavored treat from the cup using the stick and licked it. *Amazing!*

Eighteen years later, in 1923, Frank applied for a patent for "frozen ice on a stick," which he called an *Epsicle*. By that time, Frank's children had started calling their dad's treats "Pop's sicles." The kids' name stuck. Two years later, Frank sold the idea for Popsicles for a hefty profit. Since that time, millions of Popsicles have been made and eaten.

Have you ever made a mistake that turned into something good? It happens all the time, especially for people who follow Christ. Jesus is an expert at turning bad things into something good.

Don't get discouraged by your mistakes. You may have one plan, but God could have another. Guess which plan wins? That's right, God's (see today's verse). So if something isn't going your way and you feel frozen, be on the lookout for God to give you a sweet ending.

WEIRD FACTS: MISTAKES THAT WORKED

Check out these other mishaps that turned out really well:

- ☞ Naval engineer Richard James was trying to create a meter to read power levels on ships. When he dropped a tension spring that he was working on, it bounced around in a fun way . . . and the Slinky was born.
- ☞ Chef Katie Speck Wicks was frying donuts and peeling potatoes at the same time. A little slice of potato fell in the hot oil. Katie pulled it out and tasted it. *Pow!* The first potato chip was created.
- ☞ Noah and Joseph McVicker created a doughy material that could be used to rub soot and dust off of wallpaper. In the early 1950s, their sister started using the material in her classroom instead of clay. Kids loved it . . . and they still do. It's Play-Doh.

✝ PRAY

Thank God that his purposes always win and that he can turn mistakes into something good.

Life's Guidebook Says

You can make many plans, but the LORD's purpose will prevail.
PROVERBS 19:21

ALL ARE WELCOME

FOR MONTHS you've been crowded into a steamship crossing the Atlantic Ocean. Finally, on this night in 1891, you stand on the deck and look out at the Statue of Liberty. The city of New York stands in the distance. Near Lady Liberty sits Ellis Island. The next day, you and your family will get off the boat, walk onto Ellis Island, and be welcomed to the United States!

From 1892 to 1954, millions of immigrants passed through Ellis Island before entering America. Experts believe that 4 out of every 10 people living in the United States today can trace back their ancestry to at least one family member who came through Ellis Island.

Tomorrow is the start of a new year. For more than 700 immigrants who waited on boats on this date in 1891, "tomorrow" symbolized the start of a new life. Ellis Island welcomed people from across the world. Jesus does the same thing. In Paul's second letter to the church in Corinth, he wrote that Christ "died for everyone so that those who receive his new life will no longer live for themselves" (2 Corinthians 5:15). Once you believe and receive Jesus as your Savior, you begin a new life. You no longer live for yourself. You're a new creation who lives for Christ. Even your citizenship changes, just like it did for many people on those boats. As a Christian, you're a heavenly citizen. You're now part of a much better place. So celebrate . . . and welcome in the start of a new year and a new life.

PUZZLE IT OUT: PERFECT START

Tomorrow starts a new year, so go forward one letter each time to complete this verse from Romans 5:18.

"Christ's one act of righteousness brings a right relationship _____ _____ _____

vhsg   Fnc   zmc

_____ _____ for everyone."

mdv   khed

✝ PRAY

Praise God that he gives you new beginnings and a new life.

Life's Guidebook Says
He died for everyone so that those who receive his new life will no longer live for themselves. Instead, they will live for Christ, who died and was raised for them.
2 CORINTHIANS 5:15

Answer: with God and new life